YOU WERE SAYING, ANDY CAPP

by

Smythe

FAWCETT GOLD MEDAL   •   NEW YORK

2-26

GET IT Y'SELF, PET – I'M JUST GOIN' OFF TO THE DOCTOR'S

NOT AGAIN?!

I FEEL OUT OF SORTS – JUST LOOK AT MY TONGUE

2-28

SAVE YOUR LEGS, KID – OFFHAND, I'D SAY IT JUST NEEDS A REST

'E SAYS A MAN IS AS YOUNG AS 'E FEELS—

I WISH 'E'D STOP TRYIN' TO PROVE IT!

3-1

WHERE ARE YOU OFF TO?

3-8

ER..... JUST POPPIN' DOWN TO THE PUB TO DISCUSS THE TEAM FOR NEXT WEEK'S DARTS MATCH

—THAT WASN'T 'IS DARTS FACE!

3-15

OH-OHH!
MY
GIRL FRIEND–!

PRETEND
YOU'RE
MY WIFE

3-22

4-1

4-7

TCH! THE TIME! BETTER OPEN UP, I SUPPOSE. ANY OF YOU LOT WHO FANCY RUNNIN' A JOLLY LITTLE PUB SHOULD THINK TWICE....

4-14

YOU'RE RULED BY THE CLOCK IN THIS JOB — THAT'S JUST ONE OF THE DRAWBACKS...

THIS IS ANOTHER

BAR

4-23

Smythe

HEY! NOT SO FAST! — WHO'S T' BLAME FOR THAT LIPSTICK ON YOUR SCARF?

YOU! IF I DIDN'T ALWAYS 'AVE TO RUSH 'OME I'D 'AVE TIME TO RINSE IT OUT IN THE CANAL!

4·28

JUST WHEN YOU THINK YOU'VE HEARD 'EM ALL—

≷SIGH≷

4-29

GUESS WHO I SAW YOUR GIRL FRIEND WITH LAS'NIGHT—

I DON'T GO FOR THAT SORT OF CONVERSATION!

IT DOESN'T LEAVE MUCH— IF I TALK ABOUT OTHERS I'M A GOSSIP, AN' IF I TALK ABOUT MESELF I'M A BORE

4-30

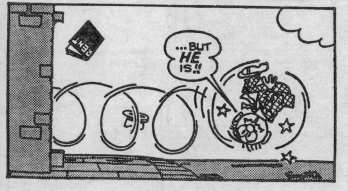

5-9

5-12

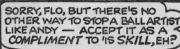

SORRY, FLO, BUT THERE'S NO OTHER WAY TO STOP A BALL ARTIST LIKE ANDY — ACCEPT IT AS A *COMPLIMENT* TO 'IS *SKILL*, EH?

NATURALLY—

5-13

ALLOW ME TO *RETURN* THE COMPLIMENT

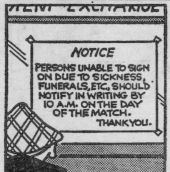

5-21

THAT'S THEIR IDEA OF COURTESY UP 'ERE — THEY POINT TO AN EMPTY SEAT AN' RACE YOU FOR IT

6-2

I'M BEGINNIN' TO WONDER WHAT'S MORE IMPORTANT TO YOU — ME OR MY PURSE!

MONEY CAN'T BUY 'APPINESS, Y'KNOW!

6-15

TRUE, PET, TRUE

— BUT IT 'ELPS YOU TO LOOK FOR IT IN A LOT MORE PLACES

CLUB

CABARET

THERE MUST BE *SOME* REASONS TO ACCOUNT FOR THE WAY THAT LITTLE 'OOLIGAN PLAYS —

— APART FROM THOSE PUT FORWARD BY 'IMSELF AN' 'IS MISSUS, I MEAN

YOU SEEMED A LONG TIME AT THE DOLE OFFICE, PET

YOU CAN SAY THAT AGAIN — BLIMEY, THINGS REALLY *ARE* BAD —

YOU SHOULD 'AVE SEEN THE *QUEUE* —

I'M NOT KIDDIN' — I 'AVEN'T SEEN ANYTHIN' LIKE IT SINCE THE 'SOUND OF MUSIC'!

6-20

6-28

7-5

PENGUIN BOOKS

THE ARCHITECT'S APPRENTICE

Elif Shafak is an award-winning, bestselling novelist; a champion of women's rights and freedom of expression; and the most widely read female novelist in Turkey. Her books have been translated into more than forty languages. Her novels include *The Flea Palace, The Saint of Incipient Insanities, The Bastard of Istanbul, The Forty Rules of Love,* and *Honor,* and she is also the author of a memoir, *Black Milk: On the Conflicting Demands of Writing, Creativity, and Motherhood.* An active political commentator, columnist, and public speaker, she lives in London and Istanbul with her family. Her Web site is www.elifshafak.com.

★ ★ ★

Praise from America and England for *The Architect's Apprentice*

"An impressive achievement, a novel populated by swashbuckling soldiers, mysterious Gypsies, and more than a few guileless courtesans. It's also a love poem to the cosmopolitan beauty of Istanbul. . . . As she traces these characters' colorful stories, Shafak unfurls what may be her most accomplished novel—and is certainly her most expansive."
—*The New York Times Book Review*

"Architecture is a powerful motif in Elif Shafak's intricate, multilayered new novel, which excels both in its resplendent details and grand design. . . . This edifying, emotionally forceful novel shows how hate and envy destroy, and how love might build the world anew."
—*The Observer* (London)

"Narrated with impeccable prose and a distinct magical undertone that compels readers to become lost in the text. The enchanting magical realism, explicit search for morality, and philosophical discoveries that Shafak unveils in *The Architect's Apprentice* assemble a novel of wisdom and innocence, equality and transcendence. . . . A story of discovery, power, balance, and humanity, *The Architect's Apprentice* offers a narrative that is both thought-provoking and suspenseful."
—*World Literature Today*

"The exuberant offspring of a rich body of Turkish folk literature. At once epic and comic, fantastical and realistic, it is firmly rooted in oral storytelling traditions and permeated by diverse cultural influences from across Asia and Europe . . . Like the astonishing mosques Sinan built, Shafak's novel is a carefully crafted work of imagination that both reveals and conceals its skill. It will confirm Shafak's reputation as a writer of impressive range, who quietly resists categorization and is not afraid to ask the big questions."

—*Financial Times*

"Shafak's novel is a vigorous evocation of the Ottoman empire at the height of its power. Jahan's experiences lie at the heart of a fascinating work in which building a fulfilling life can be as difficult as creating one of Sinan's masterpieces."

—*The Sunday Times* (London)

"This is Shafak's most ambitious novel yet, and it is her best—told with a generous humanity that will surely realign attitudes both to the imaginative possibilities of fiction and to the constructed reality of the world around us."

—*The Independent* (London)

"A gripping page-turner that blends mystery with Ottoman history and Turkish folklore . . . An exquisitely realized historical yarn of the sixteenth-century Ottoman empire."

—*The Pittsburgh Post-Gazette*

"[A story] of freedom, art, love, devotion, and humanity . . . Jahan is well drawn and the scenes depicting his relationships with the elephant, Sinan, and the Princess Mihrimah are among the most satisfying in the novel."

—*Milwaukee Journal Sentinel*

"An adventure story complete with battles, kings, sea voyages, prisons, disguises, artists, a curse, betrayal, and a Romany king."

—*The Christian Science Monitor*

"Rewardingly intelligent and touching . . . *The Architect's Apprentice* is a defiantly opulent thing, a leisurely splendor of a thousand glittering details, and in this it resembles the gorgeous buildings of its titular architect, the great sixteenth-century builder Sinan."

—*Open Letters Monthly*

"A powerful, dazzling novel, rooted in history but also in a sense of eternal human considerations . . . Shafak's prose delivers such a clear sense of place and time that you feel immersed in this lush segment of history in a warm and intriguing way. There's a sense of magic to the way her words move from page to page."

—*BookPage*

The Architect's Apprentice

ELIF SHAFAK

PENGUIN BOOKS

PENGUIN BOOKS
An imprint of Penguin Random House LLC
375 Hudson Street
New York, New York 10014
penguin.com

First published in Great Britain by Viking, an imprint of Penguin Books Ltd, 2014
First published in the United States of America by Viking Penguin,
a member of Penguin Group (USA) LLC, 2015
Published in Penguin Books 2016

THE LIBRARY OF CONGRESS HAS CATALOGED THE HARDCOVER EDITION AS FOLLOWS:
Shafak, Elif, 1971–
The architect's apprentice : a novel / Elif Shafak.
pages ; cm
ISBN 9780525427971 (hc.)
ISBN 9780143108306 (pbk.)
1. Sinan, Mimar, 1489 or 1490–1588—Fiction. 2. Architects—Turkey—16th century—Fiction.
3. Mihrimah Sultan, 1522–1578—Fiction. 4. Turkey—Social life and customs—16th century—
Fiction. 5. Turkey—History—Süleyman I, 1520–1566—Fiction. 6. Turkey—History—Ottoman
Empire, 1288–1918—Fiction. I. Title.
PS3619.H328A89 2015
813'.6—dc23
2014038539

Printed in the United States of America
7   9   10   8   6

Set in Bembo Book MT Std

This is a work of fiction. Names, characters, places, and incidents either are the product
of the author's imagination or are used fictitiously, and any resemblance to actual persons,
living or dead, business establishments, events, or locales is entirely coincidental.

*For apprentices everywhere — no one told us that love
was the hardest craft to master*

At one glance I loved you with a thousand hearts
. . . Let the zealots think loving is sinful
Never mind,
Let me burn in the hellfire of that sin.

> – Mihri Hatun, sixteenth-century Ottoman poetess

I have searched the world and found nothing worthy of love,
hence I am a stranger amid my kinfolk
and an exile from their company.

> – Mirabai, sixteenth-century Hindu poetess

Of all the people God created and Sheitan led astray, only a few have discovered the Centre of the Universe — where there is no good and no evil, no past and no future, no 'I' and no 'thou', no war and no reason for war, just an endless sea of calm. What they found there was so beautiful that they lost their ability to speak.

The angels, taking pity on them, offered two choices. If they wished to regain their voices, they would have to forget everything they had seen, albeit a feeling of absence would remain deep in their hearts. If they preferred to remember the beauty, however, their minds would become so befuddled that they would not be able to distinguish the truth from the mirage. So the handful who stumbled upon that secret location, unmarked on any map, returned either with a sense of longing for something, they knew not what, or with myriads of questions to ask. Those who yearned for completeness would be called 'the lovers', and those who aspired to knowledge 'the learners'.

That is what Master Sinan used to tell the four of us, his apprentices. He would regard us closely, his head cocked to one side, as if trying to see through our souls. I knew I was being vain, and vanity was unfit for a simple boy such as I, but every time my master would relate this story I believed he intended his words for me rather than for the others. His stare would linger for a moment too long on my face, as if there were something he expected from me. I would avert my gaze, afraid of disappointing him, afraid of the thing I could not give him — though what that was I never figured out. I wonder what he saw in my eyes. Had he predicted that I would be second to none with respect to learning, but that I, in my clumsiness, would fail miserably in love?

I wish I could look back and say that I have learned to love as much as I loved to learn. But if I lie, there could be a cauldron boiling for me in hell tomorrow, and who can assure me tomorrow is not already on my doorstep, now that I am as old as an oak tree, and still not consigned to the grave?

There were six of us: the master, the apprentices and the white elephant. We built everything together. Mosques, bridges, madrasas, caravanserais, alms houses, aqueducts . . . It was so long ago that my mind softens even the sharpest features, melting memories into liquid pain. The shapes that float into my head whenever I hark back to those days could well have been drawn later on, to ease the guilt of having forgotten their faces. Yet I remember the promises we made, and then failed to keep, every single one of them. It's odd how faces, solid and visible as they are, evaporate, while words, made of breath, stay.

They have slipped away. One by one. Why it is that they perished and I survived to this feeble age only God and God alone knows. I think about Istanbul every day. People must be walking now across the courtyards of the mosques, not knowing, not seeing. They would rather assume that the buildings around them had been there since the time of Noah. They were not. We raised them: Muslims and Christians, craftsmen and galley slaves, humans and animals, day upon day. But Istanbul is a city of easy forgettings. Things are written in water over there, except the works of my master, which are written in stone.

Beneath one stone, I buried a secret. Much time has gone by, but it must still be there, waiting to be discovered. I wonder if anyone will ever find it. If they do, will they understand? This nobody knows, but at the bottom of one of the hundreds of buildings that my master built rests hidden the centre of the universe.

Agra, India, 1632

Istanbul, 22 December 1574

It was past midnight when he heard a fierce growl from the depths of the dark. He recognized it immediately: it came from the largest cat in the Sultan's palace, a Caspian tiger with amber eyes and golden fur. His heart missed a beat as he wondered what – or who – could have disturbed the beast. They should all be sound asleep at so late an hour – the humans, the animals, the *djinn*. In the city of seven hills, other than the watchmen on the streets making their rounds, only two kinds of people would be awake now: those who were praying and those who were sinning.

Jahan, too, was up and about – working.

'Working is prayer for the likes of us,' his master often said. 'It's the way we commune with God.'

'Then how does He respond to us?' Jahan had once asked, way back when he was younger.

'By giving us more work, of course.'

If that were to be believed, he must be forging a rather close relationship with the Almighty, Jahan had thought to himself, since he toiled twice as hard to ply two trades, instead of one. He was a mahout and a draughtsman. Dual crafts he pursued, yet he had a single teacher whom he respected, admired and secretly wished to surpass. His master was Sinan, the Chief Royal Architect.

Sinan had hundreds of students, thousands of labourers and many more adherents and acolytes. For all that, he had only four apprentices. Jahan was proud to be among them, proud but, inwardly, also confused. The master had chosen him – a simple servant, a lowly elephant-tamer – when he had plenty of gifted novices at the palace school. The knowledge of this, instead of swelling his self-esteem, filled him with apprehension. It preyed on his mind, almost despite himself, that he might disappoint the only person in life who believed in him.

His latest assignment was to design a *hamam*. The master's specifications were clear: a raised marble basin, which would be heated from below; ducts inside the walls to allow the smoke to exit; a dome resting

3

on squinches; two doors opening on to two opposite streets so as to prevent men and women from seeing one another. On that ominous night, this was what Jahan was working on, seated at a rough-hewn table in his shed in the Sultan's menagerie.

Leaning back, frowning, he inspected his design. He found it coarse, devoid of grace and harmony. As usual, drawing the ground plan had been easier than drawing the dome. Though he was past forty – the age when Mohammed had become Prophet – and skilled in his craft, he still would rather dig foundations with his bare hands than have to deal with vaults and ceilings. He wished there could be a way to avoid them altogether – if only humans could live exposed to the skies, open and unafraid, watching the stars and being watched by them, with nothing to hide.

Frustrated, he was about to start a new sketch – having pilfered paper from the palace scribes – when he again heard the tiger. His back stiffened, his chin rose as he stood transfixed, listening. It was a sound of warning, bold and bloodcurdling, to an enemy not to draw any closer.

Quietly, Jahan opened the door and stared into the surrounding gloom. Another snarl rose, not as loud as the first but just as menacing. All at once, the animals broke into a clamour: the parrot screeched in the dark; the rhinoceros bellowed; the bear grunted in angry response. Nearby the lion let out a roar, which was met with a hiss from the leopard. Somewhere in the background was the constant, frantic thumping that the rabbits made with their hind legs whenever they were terrified. Though only five in number, the monkeys raised the racket of a battalion – screaming, bawling. The horses, too, began to whinny and shuffle about in their stables. Amid the frenzy Jahan recognized the elephant's rumble, brief and listless, reluctant to join the tumult. Something was frightening the creatures. Throwing a cloak on to his shoulders, Jahan grabbed the oil lamp and slipped into the courtyard.

The air was crisp, tinged with a heady perfume of winter flowers and wild herbs. No sooner had he taken a couple of steps than he noticed some of the tamers huddled together under a tree, whispering. When they saw him coming, they glanced up expectantly. But Jahan did not have information, only questions.

'What is happening?'

'The beasts are nervous,' said Dara the giraffe-tamer, sounding nervous himself.

4

'It might be a wolf,' Jahan suggested.

It had happened before. Two years ago. One bitter winter eve, wolves had descended on the city, prowling the neighbourhoods of Jews, Muslims and Christians alike. A few had crept in through the gates, God knew how, and attacked the Sultan's ducks, swans and peacocks, creating mayhem. For days on end they had had to clear bloody feathers from under the bushes and brambles. Yet now the city was neither covered in snow nor was it exceptionally cold. Whatever it was that was agitating the animals, it came from inside the palace.

'Check every corner,' said Olev the lion-tamer – a hulk of a man with flaming hair and a curling moustache in the same shade. Not a single decision was taken around here without his knowledge. Mettlesome and muscular, he was held in high regard by all the servants. A mortal who could command a lion was someone even the Sultan could admire a little.

Scattering hither and thither, they inspected the barns, stables, pens, pounds, coops and cages to make sure no animal had escaped. Every resident of the royal menagerie seemed to be in its place. Lions, monkeys, hyenas, flat-horned stags, foxes, ermines, lynxes, wild goats, wildcats, gazelles, giant turtles, roe deer, ostriches, geese, porcupines, lizards, rabbits, snakes, crocodiles, civets, the leopard, the zebra, the giraffe, the tiger and the elephant.

When he went to see Chota – a thirty-five-year-old, six cubits tall and unusually white Asian male elephant – Jahan found him high-strung, unsettled, holding out his ears like sails to the wind. He smiled at the creature whose habits he knew so well.

'What is it? You smell danger?' Patting the elephant's side, Jahan offered him a handful of sweet almonds, which he always carried ready in his sash.

Never refusing a treat, Chota popped the nuts into his mouth with a swing of his trunk as he kept his gaze on the gate. Leaning forward, his massive weight on his front legs, his sensitive feet pasted to the ground, he froze, straining to catch a sound in the distance.

'Calm down, it's fine,' intoned Jahan, though he did not believe in what he said and nor did the elephant.

On the way back, he saw that Olev was talking to the tamers, urging them to disperse. 'We searched everywhere! There's nothing!'

'But the beasts –' someone protested.

Olev interjected, pointing at Jahan. 'The Indian is right. Must have been a wolf. Or a jackal, I'd say. Anyway, it's gone. Get back to sleep.'

No one protested this time. Nodding, murmuring, they trudged to their pallets, which, though coarse and prickly and full of lice, were the one safe and warm place they knew. Only Jahan lingered behind.

'You're not coming, mahout?' called Kato the crocodile-tamer.

'In a moment,' Jahan replied, glancing in the direction of the inner courtyard, where he had just heard a curious muffled sound.

Instead of turning left, towards his shed of lumber and stone, he turned right, towards the high walls separating the two yards. He walked warily, as if waiting for an excuse to change his mind and go back to his drawing. Upon reaching the lilac tree at the furthest end, he noticed a shadow. Dusky and unearthly, it so resembled an apparition that he would have dashed away had it not just then turned aside and showed its face – Taras the Siberian. Surviving every disease and disaster, he had been here longer than anyone else. He had seen sultans come, sultans go. He had seen the mighty humbled and the heads that used to carry the loftiest turbans rolled in mud. *Only two things are solid*, the servants taunted: *Taras the Siberian and the misery of love. Everything else perishes* . . .

'Is that you, Indian?' Taras asked. 'The animals woke you up, eh?'

'Yeah,' Jahan said. 'Did you just hear a noise?'

The old man gave a grunt that could have been a yes or a no.

'It came from over there,' Jahan insisted, craning his neck. He stared at the wall stretching before him, a shapeless mass the colour of onyx, blending seamlessly into the dark. In that moment he had the impression that the midnight haze was full of spirits, moaning and mourning. The thought made him shudder.

A hollow crash reverberated across the yard, followed by a cascade of footsteps, as if a throng of people was scampering about. Deep from the bowels of the palace, a woman's scream rose, too wild to be human, and almost at once was stifled into a sob. From a different corner another scream ripped through the night. Perhaps it was a lost echo of the first one. Then, as abruptly as it had started, everything fell into stillness. On impulse, Jahan made a motion towards the wall in front of him.

'Where are you going?' whispered Taras, his eyes glittering with fright. 'It's forbidden.'

'I want to find out what's going on,' said Jahan.

'Keep away,' said the old man.

Jahan hesitated – albeit momentarily. 'I'll take a look and come back right away.'

'I wish you wouldn't do that, but you won't listen,' said Taras with a sigh. 'Just make sure you don't go further. Stay in the garden, your back close to the wall. D'you hear me?'

'Don't worry, I shall be quick – and careful.'

'I'll wait for you. Won't sleep till you return.'

Jahan gave an impish smile. 'I wish you wouldn't do that, but you won't listen.'

Recently Jahan had worked with his master in the repair of the royal kitchens. Together they had also expanded parts of the harem – a necessity, since its population had grown considerably over the last years. So as not to have to use the main gate, the labourers had made a shortcut, carving out an opening in the walls. When a consignment of tiles had been delayed, they had sealed it with unbaked bricks and clay.

A lamp in one hand, a stick in the other, Jahan tapped on the walls as he ambled along. For a while he heard only the same dull thud, over and over again. Then an empty thump. He stopped. On his knees he pushed the bricks at the bottom with all his might. They resisted at first, but eventually gave way. Leaving his lamp behind, intending to pick it up on the way back, he crawled through the hole and into the next courtyard.

The moonlight cast an eerie glow over the rose garden, now a rose cemetery. The bushes, adorned with the brightest red and pink and yellow throughout spring, looked withered, burnished, spreading out like a sea of silver water. His heart was pounding so fast and so loud he was afraid someone might hear it. A shiver ran through him as he recalled stories of poisoned eunuchs, strangled concubines, beheaded viziers and sacks thrown into the waters of the Bosphorus, their contents still wriggling with life. In this city some graveyards were on the hills, others a hundred fathoms under the sea.

Ahead of him was an evergreen with hundreds of scarves, ribbons, pendants and laces dangling from its limbs – the Wish Tree. Whenever a concubine or odalisque in the harem had a secret that she could share with no one but God, she would persuade a eunuch to come here with a trinket that belonged to her. This would be tied to a branch, next to someone else's curio. Since the aspirations of one woman often went against those of another, the tree bristled with clashing pleas and warring prayers. Even so, right now, as a light breeze ruffled its leaves, mixing the wishes, it appeared peaceful. So peaceful, in fact, that Jahan could not help walking towards it, although he had assured Taras he would not venture this far.

There were no more than thirty paces to the stone building in the background. Half hiding behind the bole of the Wish Tree, Jahan peered around very slowly, only to pull himself back at once. It took him a moment to dare to look again.

About a dozen deaf-mutes were scuttling left and right, going from one entrance through to another. Several were carrying what seemed to be sacks. The torches in their hands traced streaks of umber in the air, and each time two torches crossed paths, the shadows on the walls grew taller.

Unsure what to make of the sight, Jahan sprinted towards the rear of the building, smelling the rich earth, his strides as imperceptible as the air he inhaled. He made a half-circle, which brought him to the door at the far end. It was oddly unguarded. Unthinking, he went in. If he started to reflect on what he was doing, he would be crippled by fear, he knew.

Inside it was damp and chilly. Groping in the semi-dark, he went on, even though the skin on the back of his neck prickled and the hairs stood up. It was too late for regret. There was no going back; he could only move forward. He crept into a faintly lit chamber, sidling along the walls, his breath coming fast. He looked around: mother-of-pearl tables with glass bowls on each; sofas topped with cushions; carved and gilded mirror frames, tapestries hanging from the ceilings, and, on the floor, those puffed sacks.

Glancing over his shoulder to make sure no one was coming, he inched ahead until he caught sight of something that froze his blood – a hand. Pale and slack, it rested on the cold marble, under a mound of fabric, like a fallen bird. As if guided by an external force, Jahan loosened the burlap sacks, one after the other, and opened them halfway. He blinked in confusion, his eyes refusing to admit what his heart had already grasped. The hand was attached to an arm, the arm to a small midriff. Not sacks, not sacks at all. They were dead bodies. Of children.

There were four of them, all boys, laid side by side, from the tallest to the shortest. The oldest was an adolescent, the youngest still a suckling infant. Their royal robes had been carefully arranged to ensure they retained in death the dignity of princes. Jahan's gaze fell on the closest corpse, a light-skinned boy with ruddy cheeks. He stared at the lines on his palm. Curved, sloping lines that blurred into one another, like markings in the sand. Which fortune-teller in this city, Jahan wondered, would have foreseen deaths so sudden and so sad for princes of such gentle birth?

They seemed at rest. Their skin glowed, as if lit from within. Jahan could not help but think that they had not died, not really. They had stopped moving, stopped talking, and turned into something beyond his comprehension, of which only they were aware, hence the expression on their faces that could have been a smile.

Legs trembling, hands quivering, Jahan stood there, unable to stir. Only the sound of approaching footfalls yanked him out of the fog of his bewilderment. Barely mustering the strength but finding time to cover the dead, he made a dart towards a corner and hid behind a ceiling-to-floor tapestry. In a moment the deaf-mutes entered the room, bringing another body. They put it down beside the others, gingerly.

Just then one of them noticed that the cloth on the corpse furthest away from him had slid off. He drew closer and looked around. Unsure whether it was they who had left it like that or someone else had sneaked in after they had left, he signalled to his companions. They, too, stopped. Together they started to inspect the room.

Alone in the corner, a flimsy fabric separating him from the murderers, Jahan was breathless with fright. So this was it, he reflected; his entire life had come to naught. So many lies and deceits had carried him this far. Oddly, and not without sadness, he recalled the lamp he had left by the garden wall, flickering in the wind. His eyes watered as he thought of his elephant and his master: both must have been innocently asleep by now. Then his mind wandered to the woman he loved. While she and others were safely dreaming in their beds, he would be killed for being where he was not supposed to be and seeing what he was not supposed to see. And all because of his curiosity – this shameless, unbridled inquisitiveness that all his life had brought him only trouble. Silently, he cursed himself. They should write it on his gravestone, in neat letters:

Here lieth a man too nosy for his own good,
Animal-tamer and architect's apprentice.
Offer a prayer for his ignorant soul.

Pity, there was no one to relay this last wish for him.

9

The same evening, in a mansion at the other end of Istanbul, the *kahya**
was awake, a rosary dangling from her hand, thumbing the beads. Her
cheeks wrinkled as dry raisins, her thin frame hunchbacked, she had
gone blind with age. Still, as long as she was within the confines of the
master's abode she had excellent sight. Every nook and cranny, every
loose hinge, every creaky stair . . . There was no one under this roof
who knew the house as well as she did, and no one as devoted to its lord
and master. Of this, she was certain.

It was quiet all around, save for the snoring that rose from the lodgings
of the servants. Every now and then she caught a soft breathing, so faint
as to be scarcely perceptible, from behind the closed library door. Sinan
was sleeping there, having worked till late, again. He would ordinarily
spend the evenings with his family, retreating before supper to the *haremlik*, where his wife and daughters lived and where no apprentice ever ventured. But tonight, as on many nights, after breaking his fast, he had gone
back to his drawings and fallen asleep amid his books and scrolls, in the
room that welcomed the sun before the rest of the large, generous house.
The *kahya* had prepared a bed for him, spreading a mat on the carpet.

He worked too much, despite being eighty-five years old. At his age
a man ought to rest, eat well and make his devotions, surrounded by
his children and grandchildren. Whatever strength was left in his limbs
he should use to go on a pilgrimage to Mecca, and if he perished on the
way there, all the better for his soul. Why was the master not getting
ready for the hereafter? And if he was getting ready for it, what on
earth was he doing on construction sites, his elegant kaftans covered in
dust and mud? While the *kahya* was cross at the master for not taking
better care of himself, she was also cross at the Sultan and at every
passing vizier for working the man so hard; and she was furious at Sinan's apprentices for not removing the extra load from their Lord's
shoulders. Lazy lads! Not that they were lads any more. She had known
the four of them since they were clueless novices. Nikola, the most

---

* The chief servant of a house.

talented and the most timid; Davud, eager and earnest but impatient; Yusuf, mute and full of secrets, like a dense, impenetrable forest; and that Indian, Jahan, who was always asking questions, *Why is this so, How does that work*, though he scarcely listened to the answers.

Pondering and praying, the *kahya* stared for a while into the abyss inside her eyes. Her thumb, forefinger and third finger, which had been pushing the amber beads, one by one, slowed down. So did her muttering, '*Alhamdulillah, Alhamdulillah.*'* Her head began to droop, and her mouth opened, releasing a gasp.

A moment or an hour later, she couldn't tell, she woke up to a noise in the distance. The clatter of hooves and wheels on cobblestones. A carriage was travelling at full tilt, and, by the sound of it, heading in their direction. Sinan's house was the only residence on a deadend street. Should the carriage round the corner, it could be coming only for them. A shudder ran through her, as if a sudden chill had passed down her spine.

Murmuring a prayer against unholy spirits, she stood up briskly, despite her years. With short, swinging strides she went down the stairs, along the corridors and out on to the patio. Divided into raised terraces, adorned with a pool and redolent of the sweetest fragrances, the garden filled the heart of every visitor with joy. The master had made it by himself, conveying water to the house with a special permit from the Sultan – thus arousing the jealousy and resentment of his enemies. Now the water-wheel turned serenely, its steady gurgle assuring her with a predictability that life itself always lacked.

Above her, the moon, a sickle of silver, hid behind a cloud, and for a fleeting instant, in slate-grey, the sky and the earth were welded together. Down the path to her right there was a steep-sided grove, and, far below, a *bostan* where they grew herbs and vegetables. She took the other path, wending her way up towards the courtyard. On one side stood a well, its water icy cold, winter and summer. Clustered in the opposite corner were the privies. She avoided them, as she always did. The *djinn* held their weddings there, and whoever disturbed them in the pitch of night would be left crippled until doomsday, the curse so strong it would take seven generations to wipe it out. Since she hated

---

* Praise to Allah.

using a chamber pot even more than visiting the privies in the dark, every day after dusk the old *kahya* would stop eating and drinking, so as not to be at the mercy of her body.

Distraught, she reached the gate that opened on to the street. Of three things in this life she expected no good: a man who had sold his soul to Sheitan; a woman proud of her beauty; and the news that could not wait till the morning to be delivered.

Shortly the carriage came to a halt on the other side of the high fence. The horse gave a snort; heavy footsteps were heard. The *kahya* smelled sweat in the air, whether of the beast or of the messenger, she couldn't tell. Whoever this intruder was, the old woman was in no hurry to find out. First she needed to recite Surah al-Falaq seven times. *I seek refuge with the Lord of the Dawn, from the evil of everything He has created and from the evil of the dark and from the evil of the women who blow on the knots . . .*

In the meantime, the messenger was tapping on the door. Polite but persistent. The kind of knocking that would escalate into pounding if left unanswered for a bit too long – and indeed, very soon, did so. The servants, only just waking up, scurried to the garden one by one, carrying lamps, pulling their shawls over their gowns. Unable to postpone the moment any longer, the *kahya* uttered *Bismillah al-Rahman al-Rahim** and drew back the bolt.

A stranger appeared as the moon slid from behind the clouds. Short, stocky and, by the shape of his eyes, a Tatar. A leather flask across his shoulder, a swagger in his pose, he frowned, not hiding his annoyance at finding so many people watching him.

'I come from the palace,' he announced, in an unnecessarily loud voice.

The silence that ensued was anything but welcoming.

'Need to talk to your master,' the messenger said.

Straightening his shoulders, the man was about to walk in when the *kahya* raised her hand, stopping him. 'Are you entering right foot first?'

'What?'

'If you are crossing this threshold, you ought to come in with your right foot first.'

He peered down at his feet, as if he feared they might run away;

---

*In the name of Allah the Beneficent, the Merciful.

then the messenger took a careful step. Once inside, he proclaimed he was sent by no other than the Sultan himself on a matter of urgency, though he didn't need to say any of this: they had all understood as much.

'I've been ordered to collect the Chief Royal Architect,' he added.

The *kahya* trembled, her cheeks drained of colour. She cleared her throat, the words she could not utter piling up inside her mouth. She would rather inform this man that she could not disturb the master, who had already slept so little. But, of course, she said no such thing. Instead she muttered, 'You wait here.'

She turned her head to one side, her eyes flittering into empty space. 'Come with me, Hasan,' she said to one of the pages, who was there, she knew, because he smelled distinctively of grease and of clove candy, which he popped into his mouth on the sly.

They set off, she leading the way, the boy following with a lamp. The floorboards creaked under their feet. The *kahya* smiled to herself. The master erected magnificent buildings near and far but forgot to repair the floors in his own house.

Upon entering the library, they were surrounded by a balmy smell – the scents of books, ink, leather, beeswax, cedar rosaries and walnut shelves.

'*Effendi*, wake up,' the *kahya* whispered, her voice soft as silk. She stood still, listening to the rise and fall of her master's breathing. She called again, louder this time. Not a stir.

The boy, meanwhile, having never been this close to the master, was scrutinizing him: the long, arched nose, the wide forehead with deep lines, the thick, hoary beard that he restlessly tugged at when lost in thought, the scar on his left eyebrow – a reminder of the day when, as a youngster working in his father's carpentry workshop, Sinan had fallen on a wedge. The boy's gaze slid to the master's hands. With strong, bony fingers and rough, callused palms, they were the hands of a man accustomed to outdoor work.

The third time the *kahya* called his name, Sinan opened his eyes and sat up in bed. A shadow fell on his features as he saw the two figures by his side. He knew they would never have dared to awaken him at this hour unless a calamity had occurred or the city had burned to the ground.

'A messenger arrived,' the *kahya* explained. 'You are expected in the palace.'

Slowly, Sinan heaved himself out of bed. 'May it be good news, *insha'Allah*.'

Holding out a bowl, pouring water from a pitcher and feeling rather important, the boy helped his master to wash his face and get dressed. A pale shirt, a kaftan, not one of the new ones but an old, brown one, thick and trimmed with fur. Together the three of them clambered downstairs.

The messenger bowed his head upon seeing them coming. 'I beg your pardon for disturbing you, *effendi*, but I have commands to take you to the palace.'

'One must do one's duty,' Sinan said.

The *kahya* interjected, 'Can the boy accompany the master?'

The messenger raised an eyebrow, staring directly at Sinan. 'I've been instructed to bring you and no one else.'

Anger, like bile, rose in the *kahya*'s mouth. She might have snapped had Sinan not placed a calming hand on her shoulder and said, 'It'll be fine.'

The architect and the messenger walked outside into the night. There wasn't a creature in sight, not even a stray dog, of which there were so many in this city. Once Sinan was settled in the carriage, the messenger closed the door and hopped up on to the seat next to the driver, who had not spoken a single word. The horses lurched, and soon they were speeding through the drab streets, bobbing up and down.

To hide his unease Sinan moved aside the tightly drawn curtains and stared outside. As they galloped through crooked streets and under boughs that bent with sorrow, he mused on the people sleeping in their homes, the rich in their *konaks*, the poor in their shacks. They passed by the Jewish quarter, the Armenian quarter and the neighbourhoods of Greeks and Levantines. He observed the churches, none of which were permitted to have bells, the synagogues with square courtyards, the mosques roofed with lead, and the mud-brick and wooden houses that leaned against each other as if for solace. Even the gentry had their houses built of poorly baked bricks. He wondered, for the thousandth time, how a city so rich in beauty could be crammed with houses so poorly built.

14

Finally, they reached the palace. At the end of the first courtyard the carriage drew to a halt. The palace runners came around for help, their movements deft and practised. Sinan and the messenger made their way across the Middle Gate, which no one save the Sultan could pass through on horseback. They strode past a marble fountain that glowed in the dark, like a being from another world. The pavilions by the seaside, which loomed up in the distance, resembled sulky giants. Having recently expanded parts of the harem and renewed the imperial kitchens, Sinan was quite familiar with his surroundings. Suddenly he stopped, seeing a pair of eyes looking at him from the depths of the dark. It was a gazelle. Big, shiny, liquid eyes. There were other animals around – peacocks, turtles, ostriches, antelopes. All of them were, for a reason he could not comprehend, awake and alarmed.

The air was chilly and crisp, tinged with myrtle, hellebore and rosemary. It had rained earlier in the evening, and the grass yielded beneath their feet. The guards moved aside to let them pass. They reached the massive stone building, the colour of storm clouds, and passed through a hall illuminated with tallow candles trembling in the draught. After crossing two chambers they halted in the third. No sooner had they reached this room than the messenger excused himself and vanished. Sinan squinted to accustom his eyes to the vastness of the place. Every pitcher, every cushion, every ornament cast eerie shadows that squirmed and writhed on the walls as though they craved to tell him something.

In the opposite corner the light was softer. Sinan winced when he noticed the sacks on the floor. Through an opening he could see the face of a corpse. His shoulders sank, his eyes watered, as he observed how young the boy had been. He understood. There were rumours this would happen, though he had refused to believe them. Dazed, aghast, he staggered against the wall. His prayer, when he could find the words, was slow, interrupted by a gasp each time he fought for breath.

He had not yet said *amin*, not yet wiped his face with both hands, when a creak came from behind him. Finishing his prayer, he glared at the tapestry hanging on the wall. He was sure that was where the sound had come from. His mouth dry as chalk, he shuffled towards it and pulled the fabric aside – only to find a familiar figure, shivering and sallow with fear.

'Jahan?'

'Master!'

'What are you doing here?'

Jahan leaped out, thanking his lucky stars – the stars that had sent not the deaf-mute to throttle him but the one person in the entire world who could come to his rescue. On his knees, he kissed the old man's hand and put it to his forehead.

'You are a saint, master. I always suspected. Now I know. If I get out of here alive, I shall tell everyone.'

'Sssh, don't speak nonsense and don't shout. How did you get in?'

There was no time to explain. Footfalls pounded down the corridor, echoing off the high ceilings and ornamented walls. Standing up, Jahan inched towards his master, hoping to become invisible. The next moment Murad III entered the room, his entourage following. Not tall, rather portly, he had an aquiline nose, a large beard close to blond and bold brown eyes under arching brows. He paused, deciding which tone to employ: his soft one, his harsh one or his harshest one.

Sinan quickly composed himself, kissing the hem of the sovereign's kaftan. His apprentice bowed low and went rigid, unable to look up at the Shadow of God on earth. Jahan was puzzled not so much by the Sultan as by finding himself in his imperial presence. For a sultan Murad had now become. His father, Selim the Sot, had tripped on wet marble in the *hamam*, falling to his death, three sheets to the wind, so they gossiped, even though he had repented of his ways and sworn never to touch wine again. Just before dusk, amid much adulation and praise, and a cascade of fireworks, drums and trumpets, Murad had been girded with the sword of his ancestor Osman and proclaimed the new padishah.

Outside, far off, the sea soughed and sighed. Not daring to budge, Jahan waited quiet as a tomb, sweat breaking out on his forehead. He listened to the silence weighing down his shoulders, bringing his lips so close to the floor he could have kissed it like a cold lover.

'Why are the dead here?' asked the Sultan as soon as he glanced at the sacks on the floor. 'Have you no shame?'

One of his attendants replied immediately: 'We beg your pardon, my Lord. We thought you might wish to see them one more time. We will take them to the mortuary and make sure they are respected as they should be.'

The Sultan said nothing. He then turned towards the figures kneeling down before him. 'Architect, is this one of your apprentices?'

Sinan replied, 'He is, your Highness. One of the four.'

'I had asked for you to come alone. Did the messenger disobey my orders?'

'It's my fault,' Sinan said. 'Forgive me. At my age, I need help.'

The Sultan considered this for a moment. 'What is his name?'

'Jahan, my felicitous Lord. You might remember him as the palace mahout. He looks after the white elephant.'

'An animal-tamer and an architect,' the Sultan scoffed. 'How did that happen?'

'He served your glorious grandfather, Sultan Suleiman, upon whom be Allah's peace. Seeing his talent in building bridges, we took him into our care and have trained him since he was a youngster.'

Unheeding, the Sultan murmured, as though to himself, 'My grandfather was a great sovereign.'

'He was praiseworthy like the prophet he was named after, my Lord.'

Suleiman the Magnificent, the Law Giver, Commander of the Faithful and Protector of the Holy Cities – the man who had ruled for forty-six winters and spent more time on his horse than on his throne; and, even though buried deep down, his shroud decomposed, he could be recalled only in a hushed tone.

'May the mercy of Allah be upon him. I thought about him tonight. What would he have done in my position, I asked myself,' Sultan Murad said, his voice cracking for the first time. 'My grandfather would have done the same. There was no other choice.'

Panic gripped Jahan as it dawned upon him that he was talking about the dead.

'My brothers are with the Sustainer of the Universe,' said the Sultan.

'May heaven be their abode,' said Sinan quietly.

Silence reigned until the Sultan spoke again. 'Architect, you were ordered by my venerable father Sultan Selim to build a tomb for him. Weren't you?'

'Indeed, your Highness. He wanted to be buried by the Hagia Sophia.'

'Build it, then. Start the work without delay. You have my permission to do what is necessary.'

'Understood, my Lord.'

'It is my wish to bury my brothers next to my father. Make the *turbeh* so grand that even centuries on people can come and pray for their innocent souls.' He paused and added in an afterthought, 'But . . . don't make it too spectacular. It should be just the right size.'

From the corner of his eye Jahan saw his master's face go white. He picked out a smell in the air, or rather a mixture of smells, perhaps juniper and birch twigs, with a sharp undertone, possibly burned elms. Whether it was coming from the sovereign or from Sinan, he did not have a chance to find out. Panicking, he bowed again, his forehead touching the floor. He heard the Sultan heave a sigh, as if searching for something else to say. But he said nothing. Instead he came closer, closer, his frame blocking the candlelight. Jahan shivered under the sovereign's gaze. His heart skipped a beat. Had the Sultan suspected that he had trespassed into the inner courtyard tonight? Jahan felt his royal eyes running over him for another moment, no more, after which he strode off, his viziers and guards at his heels.

And this is how, in the month of December, an early day in Ramadan, in the year 1574, Sinan, in his capacity as Chief Royal Architect, and his apprentice Jahan, who had no place at this meeting and yet was present, were given the task of constructing inside the gardens of the Hagia Sophia a monument that was large and impressive enough to befit five princes, the brothers of Sultan Murad, but neither so large nor so impressive as to remind anyone of how they had been strangled, on his orders, on the night he ascended the throne.

What none of those present could foresee was that years later, when Sultan Murad died, on another night like this, as the wind moaned and the animals in the menagerie cried, his own sons – all nineteen of them – would be strangled with a silken bowstring, so as not to spill their noble blood, and, by a twist of fate, buried in the same place that was built by the architect and the apprentice.

Before the Master

The Prophet Jacob had twelve sons, the Prophet Jesus twelve apostles. Prophet Joseph, whose story is told in the 12th surah of the Qur'an, was his father's favourite child. Twelve loaves of bread the Jews placed at their tables. Twelve golden lions guarded the throne of Solomon. There were six steps up to the throne, and, since every climb had a descent, that meant six steps down, twelve in total. Twelve cardinal beliefs wafted through the land of Hindustan. Twelve imams succeeded the Prophet Mohammed in the Shia creed. Twelve stars ornamented Mary's crown. And a boy named Jahan had barely completed twelve years of his life when he saw Istanbul for the very first time.

Skinny, sunburned and restless as a fish in midstream, he was rather short for his age. As if to make up for his height, a thatch of black hair grew upwards and perched on his head like a creature with a life of its own. His hair was the first thing people saw when they looked at him. Next came his ears, each the size of a thug's fist. But his mother said that some day girls would be charmed by his dazzling smile and by the single dimple in his left cheek, a cook's fingerprint on soft dough. This she had said; this he believed.

Lips red as a rosebud, hair lustrous as silk, waist thinner than a willow branch. Nimble as a gazelle, strong as an ox, blessed with the voice of a nightingale – which she would use to sing lullabies to her babies, not for idle chatter, and never to defy her husband. Such was the bride his mother would have wanted for him had she been alive. But she was gone – the vapours, the physician had said, though Jahan knew it was the beating she received every day from his brute of a stepfather, who also happened to be his uncle. The man had cried his heart out at the funeral, as if it was someone else who had caused her early death. Jahan had hated him with all his being ever since. When he had boarded this vessel, he regretted leaving home without having taken his revenge. Yet he knew if he had stayed either he would have killed his uncle or his uncle would have killed him. Since he was still too young, and not strong enough, it would have probably been the latter. When the right time arrived, Jahan would return for retribution. And he would find his beloved. They would marry in a ceremony of forty days and forty nights, stuffing themselves with sweetmeats and laughter. Their first daughter he would name after his mother. It was a dream he told no one.

As the caravel approached the port, the boy began to see birds in greater numbers. And a greater variety: seagulls, sandpipers, curlews, sparrows, jays and magpies – one of them carrying a shiny gaud in its beak. A few – the brave or the foolish – alighted on the sails, too close to the humans. The air carried a new odour underneath, foreign and foul.

After weeks of sailing in the open sea, catching sight of the city had a strange effect on Jahan's imagination – especially on a misty day such as this. He peered ahead at the line where the water lapped against the shore, a strip of grey, and could not make out whether he was sailing towards Istanbul or away from it. The longer he stared the more the land seemed like an extension of the sea, a molten town perched on the tip of the waves, swaying, dizzying, ever changing. This, more or less, was his earliest impression of Istanbul, and unbeknown to him, it would not change even after a lifetime.

Slowly, the boy walked across the deck. The sailors were too busy to mind him being under their feet. He reached the end of the bow, where he had never been before. Ignoring the wind on his face, he squinted into the heart of Istanbul, which he couldn't quite see, not yet. Then, little by little, the mist dissolved, as though someone had pulled back a curtain. The city, now clearly defined, opened up before him, burning bright. Light and shadows, crests and slopes. Up and down through hill after hill, covered here and there with groves of cypress, she seemed like a wen of opposites. Denying herself at every step, changing disposition in each quarter, caring and callous at once, Istanbul gave generously and, with the same breath, recalled her gift. A city so vast she expanded left and right, and up towards the firmament, striving to ascend, desiring more, never satisfied. Yet enchanting she was. Though he was a stranger to her ways, the boy sensed how one could fall under her spell.

Jahan hurried to the hold. The elephant was in a crate, turgid and listless.

'You've made it. Look, you are here!' This last word he uttered with a slight quaver, since he didn't know what kind of a place 'here' was. It didn't matter. Whatever awaited the animal in this new kingdom couldn't be worse than the voyage he had just endured.

Chota was sitting on his haunches, looking so still that for a moment the boy feared his heart had stopped beating. Detecting the animal's soft, ragged breathing upon approaching him, Jahan felt a small relief. The glimmer, however, had gone from the beast's eyes, the lustre from his skin. The day before he had not eaten, not slept. There was a scary lump behind his jaws and his trunk was visibly swollen. The boy splashed water on his head, uneasy about yet again using seawater, which left salty marks all over his skin that must have prickled.

'When we get to the palace, I'll wash you with sweet waters,' Jahan promised.

Gently, carefully, he applied turmeric to the elephant's swellings. The animal had lost weight. The last stages of the journey had been particularly tough for him.

'You'll see. The Sultana will dote on you. You'll be the darling of concubines,' Jahan said. Then, as another possibility came to mind, he added, 'If it turns out they're not kind, you can run away. I'll come with you too.'

He would have gone on longer in this vein but he heard footsteps on the stairs. A sailor dashed in, bellowed, 'Oi, the Captain wants to see you. Now!'

A moment later the boy was in front of the Captain's door, listening to the sound of hacking and spitting coming from inside. He was scared of the man, though he tried not to show it. Captain Gareth was known to all and sundry as Gavur* Garret or Delibash Reis – Captain Crazyhead. One moment he could be joking and laughing with some sailor, and the next pulling out his sword to butcher him into a thousand pieces. Jahan had seen it happen.

Born in a coastal town in England, this seadog, who loved nothing more than a slab of slow-roasted pork belly and a draught of ale, had, for a reason no one quite understood, betrayed his countrymen and joined the Ottoman naval force with precious secrets under his hat. His fearlessness had made him dear to the palace and earned him a fleet

*Infidel.

of his own. It had amused Sultan Suleiman no end that he attacked and plundered Christian ships with a ferocity no Ottoman seafarer had ever displayed. The Sultan granted him protection but did not trust him. He knew that a man who stabbed his own companions in the back would never be a true friend to anyone else. The creature who arrived at your door, having bitten the hand that fed him all along, would not hesitate to sink his teeth into your flesh once he was inside.

When the boy entered the room, he found the Captain sitting at his desk, looking less scraggly than usual. His beard – washed, combed and anointed – was not the dark chestnut that it had been for weeks on end, but a lighter brown, almost tawny. A scar ran from his left ear to the corner of his lips, making his mouth seem like a continuation of the wound. Having cast off his everyday umber shirt, he was clad in a loose, pale shirt and a camel *shalwar*; a string of turquoise beads against the evil eye was around his neck. On the table beside him were a candle burned to a stub and a ledger where he noted down the booty captured along the way. The boy noticed him covering the page, although there was no need. Jahan could not read. Letters were not his friends but shapes and pictures were. Mud, clay, goatskin, calfskin, on whatever surface he could he drew. Throughout the voyage he had made endless sketches of the sailors and the ship.

'See, I'm a man of my word. I brought you here in one piece,' Captain Gareth said and spat with force.

'The elephant is sick,' the boy said, eyeing the bowl where the phlegm had landed. 'You didn't allow me to take him out of his crate.'

'When he tramples solid ground he'll mend in no time.' The Captain's tone grew condescending. 'What is it to you anyway? It's not your beast.'

'Nay, it's the Sultan's.'

'That's right, lad. If you do as I say we'll all benefit from it.'

Jahan lowered his gaze. The man had mentioned this matter before, but Jahan had hoped he would forget about it. Apparently, he hadn't.

'The palace is full of gold and gems. A thief's paradise,' said Captain Gareth. 'When you get there you're goin' to steal for me. Don't try to ransack the place – the Turks will chop your hands off. You'll do it slowly, bit by bit.'

'But there are guards everywhere, I cannot –'

Swift as a thought the Captain pounced on the boy. 'Are you sayin' you won't do it? You forgotten what happened to that miserable mahout, eh?'

'I have not,' said Jahan, his face ashen.

'Remember, you could have met the same end! If it wasn't for me, lad like you would never have survived.'

'I'm obliged,' said the boy quietly.

'Show your gratitude with jewels, not empty words.' He coughed, spittle dribbling from his lip. He pulled the boy closer. 'The mates would've chopped up the elephant and fed him to the sharks. And you . . . They'd have mounted you, all of 'em. When they tired of your pretty arse, they'd have sold you to a bawdy house. You owe me, little scamp. You're goin' to the palace straight away. You'll pretend you're the beast's tamer.'

'What if they notice I don't know anything about elephants?' said Jahan.

'Then that means you've failed!' said the Captain, his breath sour. 'But you won't. A canny lad like you. I'll wait till you find your feet. I'll come and find you. If you go against me, I swear to God I'll have you gutted alive! I'll tell everyone you are an impostor. You know how they punish a man who lies to the Sultan? They lift him to the gibbet . . . higher and higher . . . and then . . . drop him down . . . on an iron hook. It takes three days to die. Imagine, three bloody days! You'd beg for someone to kill you.'

Jahan wriggled out of the man's grip. He bolted out of the cabin, sprinted across the deck and ran down into the hold, where he crawled in beside the elephant, who, though silent and sick, had become his only friend. There, he wept like the child that he was.

Once the ship docked they waited for the freight to be unloaded. The boy listened to the flurry upstairs, and, although he longed for fresh air and was starving, he dared not move. He wondered where the rats had gone. Did rodents, like genteel passengers, disembark in file when a boat was in the quay? In his mind's eye he saw dozens of red-black tails scurrying in all directions, disappearing into the warren of streets and alleys that was Istanbul.

Unable to wait any longer, he climbed to the deck, which, to his relief, was empty. As his eyes scoured the dock ahead he saw the

Captain talking to a man with an elegant robe and a high turban. A senior official, no doubt. When they noticed him the Captain made a gesture for him to approach. Jahan crossed the rickety wooden plank, jumped down and walked towards them.

'The Captain tells me you are the mahout,' said the official.

Jahan hesitated for the briefest moment – that passing doubt one feels before uttering a lie. 'Yes, *effendi*. I came from Hindustan with the elephant.'

'You did?' A shadow of suspicion flickered across the man's face. 'How is it that you speak our language?'

Jahan was expecting this question. 'They taught me in the Shah's palace. I learned more on board. The Captain helped me.'

'Very well. We'll get the elephant out tomorrow afternoon,' said the official. 'First we need to unload the freight.'

Aghast, Jahan threw himself on the ground. 'If you would be so good, *effendi*. The beast is sick. He'll die should he stay in that hold another night.'

There was a surprised silence until the official said, 'You care for the animal.'

'He's a good boy,' the Captain said, his eyes cold despite his smile.

Five sailors were assigned the task of getting the elephant out. Eyeing the animal with disdain, swearing a blue streak, they tied ropes around him and pulled with all their might. Chota didn't budge. The boy watched the men toil, his anxiety growing with each passing moment. After much deliberation, it was decided not to force the elephant out but to winch the crate up with him inside it. A brigade of haulers unlatched the covers of the hold, leaving it wide open, and tied hawsers to four sides of the crate, which they coiled around aged oak trees. When ready, the men towed in unison, their arms jerking in tandem, their cheeks puffed with exertion. With one last tug, a large plank came off, falling down with a crash, miraculously not hurting anyone. Bit by bit, the crate levitated, then stopped. Down below, people gaped in astonishment at the elephant, which they could see through the gaps in the crate; he was dangling in the air like some half-bird, half-bull creature, *dabbat al-ard*, the beast of the earth that the imams said would appear on the Day of Judgement. Other men ran to help, the crowd of spectators thickened, and soon every person in the port was either watching or pulling. Jahan scampered back and forth, trying to lend a hand but not knowing quite how.

When the crate landed it did so with a loud, sickening thud. The elephant's head hit the roof-slats. The haulers did not want to bring him out for fear the beast would attack them. It took the boy a lot of pleading to assure them that Chota would not.

Once out, Chota's legs gave way. He collapsed like a puppet without strings. Limp with exhaustion, he refused to move, shutting his eyes as if he wanted this place and these people to disappear. They pushed and yanked and hoisted and flogged him, ultimately managing to thrust him on to a mammoth cart pulled by a dozen horses. Just as Jahan was about to hop on, an arm clutched at his elbow.

It was Captain Gareth. 'Farewell, son,' he said loud enough for everyone to hear. Then, dropping his voice to a whisper, he added, 'Go now, my little thief. Bring me diamonds and rubies. Remember, if you do me wrong, I'll cut off your balls.'

'Trust me,' Jahan mumbled – words carried away by the wind as soon as they left his lips – and climbed on to the cart.

In every street through which they passed, people moved aside in fright and delight. Women drew their babies close; mendicants hid their begging bowls; old men grabbed their canes as though in defence. Christians made the cross; Muslims recited surahs to chase Sheitan away; Jews prayed benedictions; Europeans looked half amused, half awed. A big, brawny Kazakh went pale, as if he had just seen a spectre. There was something so infantile in the man's fright that Jahan could not help but chuckle. Children, only they, stared up with sparkling eyes, pointing at the white beast.

Jahan glimpsed partly hidden female faces behind latticed windows, ornamented birdhouses on the walls, domes that caught the last rays of sun and lots of trees – chestnut, linden, quince. Wherever he turned he saw seagulls and cats, the two animals that were given free rein. Perky and pert, the seagulls soared in circles, diving to peck at the bait in a fisherman's bucket, or the fried liver on a street vendor's tray, or the pie left to cool on a windowsill. Nobody seemed to mind.

Even when they chased away the birds, they did so reluctantly, making a show of it.

Jahan learned that the city had twenty-four gates and was composed of three towns: Istanbul, Galata and Scutari. He observed that people were attired in different colours, though according to what rule, he could not fathom. There were water-carriers with dainty china cups and pedlars hawking everything from musk to dried mackerel. Here and there he spotted a tiny wooden shack where they sold drinks in earthenware cups. 'Sherbet,' said the official, smacking his lips, but Jahan had no clue what it tasted like.

As they drove along, the official pointed things out: *This cove is Georgian, that one Armenian. The scrawny figure over there is a dervish, the one beside him a dragoman. This man, a wearer of green, is an imam, for only they can put on the colour favoured by the Prophet. See the baker around the corner, he is Greek. They make the best bread, those infidels, but don't you dare eat any, they draw the sign of the cross on every loaf. One bite and you'll turn into one of them. This shop-owner is Jewish. He sells chickens but can't kill the birds himself and pays a rabbi to do that. That fella with sheepskin over his shoulders and rings in his pierced ears is a Torlak – a holy soul, some say, a sluggard if you ask me. Look at those Janissaries over there! They are not allowed to grow beards, only moustaches.*

The Muslims wore turbans; Jews had red hats; and Christians, black hats. Arabs, Kurds, Nestorians, Circassians, Kazakhs, Tatars, Albanians, Bulgarians, Greeks, Abkhazs, Pomaks . . . they walked separate paths while their shadows met and mingled in knots.

'There are seventy-two and a half tribes,' the official said; 'each has its place. As long as everyone knows their limits we live in peace.'

'Who are the half?' Jahan asked.

'Oh, the Gypsies. No one trusts them. They are forbidden to ride horses, only donkeys. They are not allowed to breed but they multiply anyhow, they got no shame. Stay away from the whole cursed bunch of these stinking heathens!'

Nodding, Jahan decided to steer clear of anyone who looked like a Gypsy. Gradually, the houses became sparse, the trees grew taller, and the din subsided.

'I ought to make the elephant ready before we present him to the Sultan,' Jahan said eagerly. 'A gift from the Indian Shah must look handsome.'

The man raised an eyebrow. 'Don't you know, lad? Your padishah is gone.'

'What do you mean, *effendi*?'

'Al-Sultan al-Azam Humayun . . . While you were on that ship, he lost his throne. All he has left is a wife and a couple of servants, we heard. He's not a ruler any more.'

Jahan pursed his lips. What would happen to the elephant now that the king who had sent him was king no more? He had no doubt that should Sultan Suleiman ship the animal back he would die on board. Perturbed, he said, 'Chota won't survive another voyage.'

'Don't fret. They won't return him,' said the official. 'We've all sorts of beasts in the palace, but never had a white elephant before.'

'Do you think they'll like him?'

'The Sultan won't be bothered. He's got important tasks. But the Sultana . . .'

The official lapsed into silence. A haunting look came over his face as he stared hard and long at something in the distance. When Jahan followed his gaze, he saw, looming high atop a promontory, the outline of a huge building, its torches twinkling in the dark and its gates closed like lips guarding secrets.

'Is this the palace?' Jahan whispered.

'This is it,' said the man proudly, as if the place belonged to his father. 'You are now in the abode of the Lord of East and West.'

Jahan's face lit up with expectation. Every chamber under its roof must abound with silks and brocades, he thought. Every hall must echo with joyous laughter. The Sultana's diamonds must be so large that each has a name prettier than that of a concubine.

They reached the Imperial Gate, under the stern gaze of the guards, who showed no interest in Chota, as though they were used to seeing a white elephant every day. When the party arrived at the Middle Gate, which had conical towers on each side with flaming torches, they got down from the carriage. The wind shifted just then, carrying a putrid smell. It was in that instant that Jahan, on impulse, glanced up towards the shadows in the background. He froze as he caught sight of the gibbets. There were three of them. One short, two tall. Mounted on each was a severed head, silently rotting away; swollen, empurpled, the mouth stuffed with hay. The boy caught an almost imperceptible movement, the insatiable greed of maggots crawling inside human flesh.

'Traitors . . .' said the official under his breath and spat with force.

'But what have they done wrong?' asked Jahan, his voice frail.

'Treachery, as likely as not. Either that or theft, I'd say. They had it coming, for sure. This is what happens to those who play false.'

Dazed, whey-faced, dwarfed by the columns ahead of him and suddenly bereft of words, Jahan trudged through the massive gate. Though he was gripped by an urgent desire to run away, he could not bring himself to leave the elephant. Like a convict trudging to the gallows, surrendering to a fate he could neither avoid nor accept, he followed the official and entered Sultan Suleiman's palace.

All the boy glimpsed that night, as on the ensuing nights, were massive walls, a mammoth door with iron studs, a courtyard so vast it could have swallowed the world, and more walls. It occurred to him that you could live in a palace all your life but never see much of it.

They were taken to a barn with an earthen floor, thatched roof and lofty ceiling – Chota's new home. Inside was a sullen, sinewy fellow of indeterminable age. He had magical fingers that healed animals, though they were of no use when it came to human diseases. His name was Taras the Siberian. Although there were no horses in sight, they could hear them shuffling about and neighing nearby, made nervous by their presence. Since time immemorial horses had disliked elephants, Taras said. It must have been an ill-founded equine fear, he added, since he had never heard of an elephant laying into a horse.

Taras examined Chota's mouth, eyes, trunk, excrement. He glared at Jahan, clearly blaming him for the animal's condition. The boy felt small, ashamed. They had been on the same ship, but Chota was on the brink of collapse while he was healthy as the crescent above.

Deftly, gingerly, the healer applied some foul-smelling ointment to Chota's lumps, and wrapped his trunk with burlap full of crushed leaves and a fragrant resin that Jahan later on learned was called myrrh. Not knowing how to help, the boy brought a bucket of fresh water, which he placed next to the piles of shrubs, apples, cabbages and hay – a banquet after the awful grub in the ship. But Chota didn't even look at them.

Jealousy gnawed at the boy's heart. He was torn between wishing, with all his being, for this man to make the elephant better, and dreading that once back on his feet the animal would love the healer more than he loved him. Sultan Suleiman's gift Chota might be, yet deep down Jahan saw him as his own.

Laden with such shabby thoughts, he was ushered outside. There, another man welcomed Jahan with a wide smile. An Indian by the name of Sangram, he was ecstatic to meet someone who spoke his mother tongue, and moved towards the boy the way a cat inches towards a stove, in need of warmth.

'*Khush Amdeed, yeh ab aapka rahaaish gah hai.*'[*]

Jahan stared at him deadpan.

'What's the matter? Can't understand what I'm saying?' asked Sangram, now in Turkish.

'Our words are different,' said Jahan quickly. He told him about the village he came from, so high in the mountains that they slept above the clouds, lodged between the earth and the firmament. He talked about his sisters and his late mother. His voice trembled slightly.

Sangram regarded him with a puzzled stare. He seemed about to say something grave. But then, brushing aside whatever had crossed his mind, he sighed and smiled again. 'All right, let me take you to the shed. Meet the others.'

As Sangram explained the ways of the Ottomans, they strode down a path that snaked between the garden pavilions and towards a large pond where all kinds of fish splashed around. The boy had a slew of questions regarding life inside the palace, but each time he got a curt whisper by way of an answer. Still, he was able to pick up a few things. Though he had yet either to see or to hear them, he learned that there were lions, panthers, leopards, monkeys, giraffes, hyenas, flat-horned stags, foxes, ermines, lynxes, civets, dogs and wildcats, all within reach. Beneath the acacia trees to their right stood the cages of wild animals – the animals it was their responsibility to feed, clean, pacify and keep safe day and night. Recently a rhinoceros had arrived from Habesh but had not survived. When not in demand the beasts were sent to other menageries across the city, and their tamers along with them. The larger animals sojourned in the old Palace of the Porphyrogenitus. The imperial residence that once hosted the Byzantium nobility and those born to the purple was now home to the animals of the Sultan. Other creatures were kept in an ancient church near the Hagia Sophia. Chota would have probably been sent to the church, but, because he was still an infant and exceptionally white, it was decided to keep him at the seraglio for now.

Some of the caretakers originated from the four corners of the empire, others from unmapped islands. Those responsible for the birds and fowl dwelled in another lodging, south of the aviary. From dawn to dusk, gazelles, peacocks, roe deer and ostriches roamed in and out of the pavilions.

[*] 'Welcome, this is now your home.'

The Sultan's menagerie was a world unto itself. And, while full of ferocious creatures, it was, all in all, really no wilder than the city outside.

The wildlife in the palace came in two sorts: the feral and the ornamental. The former were here because of their savage nature; the latter because of their winsomeness. Just as leopards did not mix with nightingales, so their keepers did not rub elbows. The trainers of the fiercest animals were a separate bunch. Among the hundreds of slaves amid these walls, they were neither the highest paid nor the best fed, though they remained the most respected.

Jahan's accommodation was to be a lean-to made of lumber and baked bricks. There were nine men inside. A hulk of a red-haired, red-moustached fellow who was in charge of the lions and was called Olev; a cross-eyed Egyptian giraffe-trainer by the nickname of Dara; an African crocodile-tamer who had scars all over his body and answered to the name of Kato; Chinese twins who took care of monkeys and apes and, as Jahan would soon find out, were addicted to hashish; a bear-trainer known as Mirka, who, with his broad shoulders and heavy legs, resembled a bit of a bear himself; two Circassian ostlers who attended to the thoroughbred horses; and the healer he had met earlier, Taras the Siberian. They greeted him with an irritated silence, surprised by his youth, exchanging glances, as if they understood something about him that he couldn't grasp.

Sangram brought him a bowl of *sutlach*.* 'Have some, it tastes of home,' he said and added in a conspiratorial whisper, 'Their food is not as good as ours. Better get used to it.'

Jahan wolfed down his dish while they all watched him with mute curiosity. His hunger was not sated but nothing else was offered and he didn't ask. He changed into the garments they handed him. A pale shirt with wide sleeves, a fleece vest, a *shalwar* and, for his feet, soft leather boots. Afterwards he and Sangram took a stroll. The manservant popped a round, waxy substance into his mouth. Little did the boy know that it was a paste made of spices and opium. In a little while Sangram's face softened, his tongue loosened. He told Jahan about Sultan Suleiman's silence code. Although it did not apply as strictly in the first and second courtyards as in the third and fourth, everyone

---

* Rice cooked in sweet milk.

everywhere was expected to be quiet. Talking loudly, laughing or bellowing were forbidden.

'What about singing? Chota likes to listen to lullabies before he goes
to sleep.'

'Singing . . .' Sangram repeated, as if he were explaining something
he himself did not quite comprehend. 'Singing is allowed if done in
silence.'

Having thus approached the garden walls, they stopped. There they
found copses of tall firs, like soldiers standing guard, their branches
forming a canopy.

'Don't go beyond this wall,' said Sangram, his voice tight.

'Why?'

'Don't question. Obey your elders.'

Jahan felt a lurch in his belly. His discomfort must have been apparent, for Sangram said, 'Your face is all wrong.'

'What?'

'You're pleased, it shows. You're scared, there it is.' He shook his head.
'Women can't hide their feelings because they're weak. Lucky for them,
they hide behind veils. But a man has to learn to mask his emotions.'

'What should I do?' asked Jahan.

'Hide your face, seal your heart,' said Sangram. 'Otherwise it won't
be long before they make a hash of both.'

About an hour later, on his first night in Istanbul, Jahan lay stiff on a
coarse pallet, listening to the sounds of the evening. An owl hooted
nearby, dogs barked somewhere in the distance. Inside the shed it was
no less noisy, his companions snoring, tossing, talking, farting, grinding their teeth in their sleep. One of them, though he couldn't make
out which, spoke in a language he had never heard before, if it was a
language at all. His stomach joined the ruckus, rumbling. He reflected
on food, particularly spicy meat pasties, but this always brought his
mother to his mind, so he stopped. He rolled towards the window,
stared up at a chink of sky. It was so unlike the blue yonder he had
seen, day in and day out, on the ship. He thought he would never be
able to sleep, but his weariness defeated him.

He woke up with a start, surfacing from dark, disturbed dreams. Somebody was breathing down his neck, rubbing himself against his haunches. A hand covered his mouth as another hand yanked at his *shalwar*. Jahan squirmed out of his grasp, but the man, being stronger, pushed him down and pressed him hard. The boy choked, unable to breathe. Only then did the man, realizing he was almost suffocating Jahan, move his hand aside. It was in that moment that Jahan sank his teeth, with all his might, into his assaulter's thumb. A gasp of pain was heard. Sudden, galled. The boy jumped to his feet, shaking. In the powdery light from a candle stood the bear-tamer.

'Come here,' Mirka hissed.

Jahan understood from his tone that he didn't want to be discovered. So he shouted, at the top of his voice, against every silence code, not giving a damn as to what would happen if the guards heard him. 'You touch me again and my elephant will trample you! We'll kill you!'

Mirka stood up, pulling his *shalwar*. Without so much as a glance at the other tamers, who were now awake, he strode to his pallet, muttering, 'Your elephant is a baby.'

'He'll grow,' howled Jahan.

The boy noticed that Olev was observing him with a mixture of affection and approval. The lion-tamer interjected from his corner: 'Mirka, you sod! If you touch the Indian again, I'll nail your balls to the wall, hear me?'

'Curse you,' said Mirka.

His heart hammering, the boy crawled into his bed, this time turning his back to the window, so as to keep an eye on the room. He understood that inside the palace he had to be vigilant at all times, even in sleep. He couldn't stay here long. He had to find out fast which chamber the Sultan's riches were kept in, fill his bags and leave. He would have to abandon the white elephant, he realized sadly. Chota was a royal creature; Jahan was not.

Little did he know that down in his barn Chota was also awake, listening, worrying. Somewhere in the heart of the inky night, so dense that it subjugated every other colour, he had picked up the scent of the only animal that filled him with fear – the tiger.

No one could tell for sure how many souls resided within the palace walls. Taras the Siberian, who had been around longer than anyone could remember, said it was as many as the stars in the heavens, the hairs in a pilgrim's beard, the secrets wafting in the *lodos*.* Others believed it was at least 4,000. At times Jahan caught himself staring at the gigantic gates separating them from the inner courtyards, wondering what kind of people lived on the other side.

He wasn't the only one who burned with curiosity. Every animal-tamer that he knew prattled on in muted tones about the various residents of the palace – the head of halvah-makers, the master of ceremonies, the tasters who savoured each dish before it arrived at the sovereign's table. Eager to find out more about them, the tamers gossiped in earnest, relishing every scrap of tittle-tattle, sweet as boiled sugar in their mouths. Above all, they were fascinated by the concubines and the odalisques. That they were invisible to all men, save the Sultan and the eunuchs, allowed the tamers to imagine them in any way they wished. In their minds they could paint freely the women's faces, blank and promising like empty scrolls. One could never prattle on about the favourites of the Sultan, not even in whispers, unless it was the Sultana, whom everybody seemed to hate and felt justified in slandering.

They had heard plenty of tales about the harem, some real, most fanciful. Its gates were guarded by black eunuchs who had been castrated so badly that they could pass water only with the help of a tube they carried in their sashes. Since Islam forbade castration of any kind, Christian and Jewish dealers employed slave merchants to do the job elsewhere. Boys were captured from the deepest recesses of Africa and unmanned. Those who survived were bought by the palace and shipped to Istanbul. Of these many died during the voyage, their corpses dumped into the sea. If they were lucky and talented, they made their way up. Thus a sin for which no one took the blame, yet to which everyone contributed, lived on. Sangram said it wasn't just their

* Strong wind that blows from the sea.

balls that had been removed but also, much too often, their hearts. The mercy that they had been denied in the past they now denied to all. If a concubine attempted to escape, it would be these eunuchs who would be the first to find her.

The harem flowed through life in the palace, hidden but forceful. They named it the *darussaade* – 'House of Happiness'. Every single one of its rooms and halls was said to be connected to the bedchamber of the Valide, the mother of the Sultan. For years, she and she alone had scrutinized what hundreds of women ate, drank, wore and did every day. Not a cup of coffee was brewed, not a song was chanted, and not a concubine caught the eye of the Sultan without her blessing. The Chief Black Eunuch had been her ears and her eyes. But now she was dead. And all her power, and much more besides, had passed into the hands of the Sultana.

Hurrem was her name, yet many called her witch, *zhadi*. Of admirers and foes, she had plenty. They said she had put a spell on the Sultan, poisoning his sour-cherry sherbet, sprinkling potions under his pillow, tying his clothes into knots on nights of full moon. Breaking a 300-year-old tradition, the Sultan had married her in a ceremony so lavish it was still the talk in every tavern, brothel and opium den in town. Not that the boy knew anything about taverns, brothels and opium dens, but Sangram did and he loved scattering bits of gossip. Most of Jahan's knowledge about what was happening inside and outside the palace came from him.

Witch or not, the Sultana had a soft spot for curiosities and went to great lengths to collect them. The tiniest female dwarf in the empire or a musical box with secret compartments; a peasant girl with skin like a lizard's or a bejewelled dollhouse – she took possession of each one with the same delight. Being fond of birds, she frequently visited the aviary. One parrot there was her favourite – a green-bellied, crimson-winged macaw – and she taught it about a dozen words, which the animal squawked at the top of its ugly voice whenever Sultan Suleiman came close, making him smile. Hurrem enjoyed feeding the gazelles and foals, but she rarely, if ever, spent time with the wild animals. All the better, Jahan thought, for he feared her. How could he not fear a woman who read minds and stole souls?

The first weeks in the *payitaht*, the 'Seat of the Throne', passed by eventlessly. Chota recovered slowly, regaining his weight and good humour. He was given two saddlecloths: one for everyday, yards of blue velvet embroidered with silver thread; and one for festivities, a golden mantle made of heavy brocade. Jahan loved the feel of the needlework on the tips of his fingers. He no longer lamented the precious cloths that Shah Humayun had sent with the elephant, but that Captain Gareth's sailors had shamelessly plundered on that ominous ship.

At night, as soon as he closed his eyes, his stepfather's face appeared from out of the gloom. A part of him yearned to return to his village – and kill him. The way he had taken the life of his mother. Kicking her in her belly, even though he knew, for how could he not, that she was pregnant. Another part, a wiser part, whispered he should return but not immediately. After stealing the Sultan's gems, what harm could there be in saving a few for himself? Captain Gareth would never know. Then he could go home, rich and mighty. His sisters would greet him. Forlorn as they must have been that he had left on a whim, the immensity of their joy upon seeing him again would wipe away their sorrow. Kissing their hands, Jahan would unload the riches at their feet: diamonds, emeralds, jade.

Then, one day, he would come upon a young maiden, pretty as the full moon. Her teeth like pearls, her breasts like ripe quinces, she would walk away from him, but not before honouring him with a furtive smile. He would save her from a terrible danger (drowning or a gang of robbers or a ferocious animal – this part of his dreams always changed). Her lips, when she kissed him, would taste like raindrops, her embrace would be sweeter than honeyed figs. They would fall in love, her caresses washing over him like fragrant waters. So immaculate would be their bliss that, even years after they died of old age in each other's arms, people would remember them as the happiest couple under God's sky.

His early days in the menagerie would have been harder were it not for Olev the lion-tamer, who took him under his wing. A man unrivalled in bravery and recklessness but oddly besotted with his moustache, which he combed, waxed and perfumed five times a day. Like Jahan, he had a family waiting for him somewhere – a life he had lost when, at the age of ten, he had been taken by slave traders. His reddish hair, robust build and, especially, his dauntlessness had determined his destiny. Snatched from his family, he was brought to the Ottoman palace, which he was never to leave.

Each morning at dawn the tamers washed their faces in a marble fountain that ran so cold their hands turned raw red. Before noon they shared wheat soup and bread; in the evenings they tucked into rice dripping with sheep's-tail fat. When darkness fell, they rested their heads on coarse sacks that housed a horde of creeping lice. The nits were everywhere. And fleas. They leaped from animals to humans, from humans to animals. When they bit, which they did often, they left angry marks that swelled into bumps if scratched. Time and again, the tamers examined their animals, the large and the small, scrubbing them with crushed camphor, cardamom and lemongrass. However thoroughly they searched, one flea would always survive. And one flea was all it took.

Twice a week the Chief White Eunuch, who was known to all and sundry as Carnation Kamil Agha, dropped in for an inspection. He never scolded. Never raised his voice. Yet he was one of the most feared men in the palace, his scowl sharper than steel. His skin was so pale that one could see the fine tracery of veins underneath. He had dark circles under his eyes and was said to spend the nights walking the corridors because he could no more sleep than an owl on the hunt. Knowing that the slightest grime was enough to make his hackles rise, the tamers cleaned to no end. They wiped urine off the basins, picked up the faeces, rinsed the feeding cups. Jahan was not sure the animals thought much of this frenzy. Deprived of natural odours – theirs and their mates' – they got confused about their territories. None of the tamers had the heart to reveal this to the eunuch. Still, they took good care of their animals. Their lives depended on their well-being. When they thrived, so did they; when they fell from favour, so did they.

One day in mid-April a strange thing happened. Jahan was taking Chota back to the barn when he heard a rustle from behind a row of bushes – faint but so close as to give him a start. Pretending not to have noticed anything, he remained alert. Before long, an embroidered silk slipper poked out from under the shrub like a baby snake, unaware of being in the open.

Now that Jahan knew it was a girl hiding there, he racked his brains as to who she could be. There were no females among the tamers. The concubines could not get this far, and certainly not unchaperoned. As he did not wish to scare her, he kept his distance, assuming all she wanted was to see the white elephant up close. So he went on with his work and let her spy on them. She kept coming back – he could hear the crack of twigs beneath her feet, the swish of her robe, always on the sly. By the end of the month Jahan had got used to the mysterious snooper. Such was his acceptance and such her stealth that they would never have spoken to one another had it not been for, of all things, a wasp.

That morning Jahan was cleaning a lump of soil stuck on Chota's tail when a shriek pierced the air. A girl darted out from behind the hedge, her hair fluttering every which way. Waving her hands, screaming an incomprehensible stream of words, she whisked past them, dashed into the barn and closed the door so harshly it bounced back open.

'Shoo.' Jahan grabbed a large leaf and flapped it at the wasp that was chasing her.

Buzzing frantically, the insect circled a few times in frustration and, having tired itself out, steered for the closest rosebush.

'It's gone,' Jahan said.

'I am coming out. Lower your head, servant.'

She emerged, tall, lithe and reedy. Scrunching up her nose she declared, 'May Allah forgive me for saying so, but I don't understand why He would create wasps.'

She walked towards the elephant, curious to see the animal this close. Jahan glanced furtively in her direction, noticing the tiny freckles on her cheeks, the colour of marigold. Her robe of palest green appeared almost white against the sunlight, and her wavy hair peeked from beneath her scarf, which she wore loosely.

'Has my venerable father, his Majesty, seen the beast?' she asked.

Jahan swallowed, only now realizing with whom he was speaking. He bowed as low as he could. 'Your Highness Mihrimah.'

The Princess nodded nonchalantly, as if her title were of no interest to her. Her eyes of dark amber slid back to Chota.

'Would your Excellency like to pat the elephant?'

'Would it bite?'

Jahan smiled. 'I can assure your Highness there is only kindness in Chota.'

With a wary look she approached the beast and touched its crinkled skin. In that moment Jahan had another chance to inspect her. He saw a precious necklace with seven milky-white pearls, each larger than a sparrow's egg. His gaze strayed to her hands. Such delicate hands she had, now raised to her bosom, now nervously clasped. It was this last gesture that got to him: he sensed that, beneath the surface of colours and contrasts, she carried a fretful soul, like his. Otherwise he would never have dared to say what he said next. 'Humans are frightened of animals but we are cruel, not they. A crocodile or a lion . . . None of them are as wild as we are.'

'What a ridiculous thing to say! These are fierce beasts. That's why we keep them in cages. They would gobble us up.'

'Your Serene Highness, ever since I came here I have not heard of an animal attacking anyone unless we starved it to death. If we don't disturb them, they won't disturb us. But humans are not like that. Whether hungry or not, man is prone to evil. Where would you sleep more peacefully? Next to a stranger with a full belly or next to a well-fed lion?'

She regarded him for a moment. 'You are a strange boy. How old are you?'

'Twelve.'

'I'm older than you,' she said. 'I know better.'

Still bowing, Jahan could not help but smile. She had not said the obvious: that she was noble-born and he, a no one. She had said she was older, as though they were, or could some day become, equals. As she turned back on her heel, she demanded, 'What's your name?'

He blushed. Somehow saying his name felt awkward, almost intimate. 'The elephant's name is Chota, your Highness. Mine is Jahan. But my mother –'

'What about her?'

This he had not told anyone and didn't know why he was doing so now, but he said, 'She named me Hyacinth.'

Mihrimah laughed. 'What a funny name for a boy!' Realizing he was offended, she added, more quietly, 'Why?'

'When I was born, my eyes were a strange purple. Mother said it was because she had eaten hyacinths while she was heavy with me.'

'Hyacinth eyes . . .' she muttered. 'And where is your mother now?'

'No longer in this mortal world, your Highness.'

'So you are an orphan,' she said. 'I feel the same way sometimes.'

'Your noble parents are alive, may God grant them long life.'

Just then a woman's voice was heard from behind. 'I have been looking for you everywhere, Excellency. You really shouldn't have come here on your own.'

A stocky woman appeared. She had a florid complexion, a penetrating gaze and thin lips pursed in disapproval. Her jawline was strong and sharp, giving the impression of clenched teeth. Without so much as a glance at either the elephant or at the mahout, she marched by as if there were nothing in this vast garden of flowers and animals to rest her gaze upon, even for an instant – save the Princess.

Mihrimah turned to Jahan with an impish delight. 'My nursemaid,' she said. '*Dada* is always worried about me.'

'How can I not worry when my beloved is full of light and the world is so dark?' the woman said.

Mihrimah laughed. 'My *dada* doesn't like animals, unfortunately. Only one of them. She is fond of her cat, Cardamom.'

A glance was exchanged between them: subtle, elusive and impenetrable. Suddenly Mihrimah seemed troubled. 'Has My Lady Mother inquired about me?'

'Indeed, she has. I told her you were in the *hamam*, taking a bath, your Highness.'

'Aren't you my saviour?' said Mihrimah, smiling. 'What would I do without you?' She raised her hand, as if to wave an imaginary handkerchief. 'Farewell, Chota. Perhaps I'll come again to see you.'

Thus expressing her good wishes to the elephant, but without a word to the mahout, the Princess, with the nursemaid hard on her heels, strode down the garden path. Jahan was left behind. He stood there for a moment, forgetting where he was and what he was doing. Unasked questions in his mind, a perfume in his nostrils and a jolt in his chest he had never known before.

Jahan thought she would never come again. She did. Along with her smile she brought treats for the elephant – not pears and apples but royal delicacies: figs with clotted cream and violet sherbet, marzipan topped with rose-petal jam or honeyed chestnuts, the last of which, Jahan knew, cost at least four aspers an okka. Whenever the ways of the seraglio displeased or daunted her, she came to see the white beast. She watched Chota in amazement, as if wondering how a creature this mighty could be so docile. The elephant was the Sultan of the menagerie, yet so unlike her own father.

There was no pattern to her visits. At times she wouldn't be seen for weeks on end and Jahan was left wondering what she was doing in that treasure chest of secrets that was the harem. Then she would appear almost every afternoon. Always, her *dada*, Hesna Khatun, waited by her side. Always, the nursemaid looked perturbed that the Princess showed such interest in an animal. Though the woman clearly disapproved of Mihrimah's affection for the elephant, she was also careful to keep it a secret.

A full year passed. Then came a sweltering summer. Jahan was hoarding what little he had pilfered: a silver rosary (from the Chief Gardener), a silk handkerchief with golden embroidery (from a new eunuch), jars of almonds and pistachios (from the royal pantry), a golden ring (from a foreign envoy who had visited the menagerie). He knew they were only knick-knacks, not enough to satisfy Captain Gareth. He had still not been able to learn where they kept the Sultan's gems, and the truth was, as time went by and he got used to life in the menagerie, he thought less and less about it. He had not heard from Captain Gareth since that day, though the man still appeared in his dreams, a menace who jumped from out of the shadows. Why he had not shown up, Jahan could not fathom. For all he knew he might have gone on a voyage and met a wretched end.

Almost all the words that the Princess and the mahout exchanged were about Chota, who was thriving, expanding in height and weight. Hence Jahan was taken aback when one day, out of the blue, Mihrimah asked him about his life back in Hindustan and how he had ended up here. And this is the story that he told her the next day – she seated under a lilac tree, he on his knees; she observing him, he not daring to glance up; she so close he could smell the scent in her hair, he unable to forget there were worlds between them.

The story the mahout told the Princess

In the great and rich land of Hindustan there lived a poor boy named Jahan. His home was a shack, a stone's throw away from the road that the soldiers trampled en route to and from Shah Humayun's palace. He slept under the same roof as his five sisters, his mother and his stepfather, who also was his eldest uncle. Jahan was a curious boy, who loved putting together things with his hands. Mud, wood, stone, dung or twigs, all would be made use of by the boy. Once he built a large furnace in the backyard that pleased his mother immensely, because, unlike anything she had possessed before, it did not emit dark, dizzying smoke.

When Jahan was not yet six his father – for he had once had a father – vanished into thin air. Each time he asked his mother his whereabouts, she gave the same answer: 'He's gone by water.' On board a ship, destined for a city of lights and shadows, far away – where they had another shah or sultan, and treasures beyond imagining.

Another boy would have seen through her fib. Not Jahan. It would take him years to make sense of the fine and flimsy lies his mother had woven around him, like wispy spider webs, there and not there. Even when his mother was married off to his uncle – a man who constantly sneered at her – the boy refused to accept that his father was not coming back. In helpless anger he watched his uncle sit in his father's chair, sleep in his father's bed, chew his father's betel leaves and not utter a word of gratitude. Nothing his mother did satisfied the man. The fire she lit was not warm enough, the milk she touched curdled, the *puris* she fried tasted no better than soil, and the body she gave to him every night served no purpose since she still had not gifted him with a son.

When he wasn't grousing or swearing, his stepfather raised war elephants. He taught these peaceful animals how to charge and to kill.

Jahan's sisters helped him, though never Jahan. Such was the boy's hatred of his stepfather that he steered clear of the man and his beasts. Except for one – Pakeeza.

A thousand days into her pregnancy, Pakeeza had yet to give birth. Three autumns and three winters had gone by, and it was spring again. The amaltas tree down the road had blossomed gold; the slopes were swathed in wildflowers; snakes had awakened from their darkest sleep – but the baby had not been born. Pakeeza had gained so much weight that she could hardly move. Every day she would mope, her eyelids as heavy as her heart.

Every morning Jahan would bring Pakeeza fresh water and a bucketful of fodder. Laying a hand on her crinkled skin, he would murmur, 'Maybe today is the big day, huh?'

Pakeeza would lift her head, a slow, reluctant gesture, yet enough of one to show she had heard him and that, despite her weariness, shared his hope. Then the sun would inch its way across the sky, paint the horizon in streaks of crimson, and another day would be over. It was the last few weeks before the wet season, the air muggy, the moisture unbearable. Secretly Jahan suspected something might have happened to the calf in the womb. It even occurred to him that Pakeeza was suffering from a bloated tummy, and that behind her swollen flesh there was nothing but emptiness. Yet, whenever he placed his ear on her huge, sagging belly, so low it almost touched the ground, he heard a heartbeat, timid but steady. The little one was there but, for reasons obscure to everyone, he was biding his time, waiting, hiding.

Meanwhile, Pakeeza had developed an appetite for the strangest things. With gusto she licked muddy puddles; smacked her lips at the sight of dried clay; gobbled down cow-dung bricks. Whenever she had a chance she chomped the flakes off the barn's lime-washed walls, inciting Jahan's uncle to whip her.

Pakeeza's family dropped by every other day to see how she was faring. Leaving behind the forest, they ambled past in single file, their eyes fixed on the dusty path, their steps beating to a rhythm only they could hear. Upon reaching the place, the males fell silent while the females drew closer, calling out in their ancient tongue. Inside the yard Pakeeza pricked up her ears. Occasionally she answered them. With what little strength she had, she told them not to worry for her. Mostly she stayed still – whether numbed by dread or soothed by love, Jahan could not tell.

People came from far and wide to see the miracle. Hindus and Muslims and Sikhs and Christians swarmed around their shack. They brought garlands of flowers. They lit candles, burned incense and sang airs. The baby must be blessed, they said, his umbilical cord stuck in an unseen world. They tied scraps of cloth on the banyan tree, hoping their prayers would be heard by the skies. Before they left, the visitors made sure to touch Pakeeza, promising not to wash their hands until their wishes had been granted. The most impudent tried to pluck a hair or two from her tail; for them, Jahan kept a lookout.

Every so often a healer appeared at their gate, either out of a desire to help or sheer curiosity. One of them was Sri Zeeshan. A gaunt man with flaring eyebrows and a habit of embracing trees, rocks and boulders to feel the life within them. The year before he had lost his balance and toppled down a cliff while trying to enfold the sunset in his arms. He had remained in bed for forty days, unspeaking and unmoving, except for a nervous twitch behind his eyelids, as if in sleep he was still falling. His wife had already begun to mourn him when, on the afternoon of the forty-first day, he scrambled to his feet, wobbly but otherwise fine. Since then his mind moved back and forth, like a saw at work. Opinion was divided as to the result of the accident. Some believed it had propelled him to a higher realm no other sage had ever reached. Others said that, having lost his wits, he could no longer be entrusted with the sacred.

Either way, here he was. He put his ear on Pakeeza's belly, his eyes closed. He spoke in a low, husky voice that sounded as though it came from the bottom of that precipice he had tumbled into, saying, 'Baby's listening.'

Jahan held his breath, awed and thrilled. 'You mean, he can hear us?'

'Sure. If you shout and cuss, he'll never come out.'

Jahan flinched as he recalled the many times there had been cursing and chiding in the house. Clearly, his brute of an uncle had scared the young one out of his wits.

The healer waved a gnarled finger. 'Hear me out, son. This is no ordinary calf.'

'What do you mean?'

'This elephant is too . . . sentimental. He does not want to be born. Comfort him. Tell him it'll be all right; this world is not such a bad place. He'll come out like an arrow from a bow. Love him and he'll never leave you.' With that he gave Jahan a wink, as though they now shared an important secret.

That afternoon, as Jahan watched the sky grow dark, he racked his brains. How could he persuade the baby this world was worth being born into? Rumbling, bellowing, roaring, elephants conversed all the time. Even so, it was a task beyond his powers. Not only because he didn't speak their tongue, but also because he didn't have anything to say. What did he know about life beyond these walls, beyond his egg-shell heart?

Lightning in the distance. Jahan waited for a thunder that didn't come. It was in that lacuna, as he was expecting something to happen, that an idea rushed through his head. He didn't know much about the world, true, but he knew how it felt to be afraid of it. When he was a toddler and got scared he would hide under Mother's hair, which was so long it reached down to her knees.

Jahan ran into the house, to find Mother washing her husband in a wooden tub, scrubbing his back. His uncle loathed bath times and would never agree to them were it not for the fleas. He would emerge from the water, the colour of his skin having changed, but not his character. Now he was lying in the tub, eyes closed, while the camphor oil worked its wonders. Jahan gestured at Mother, begging her to follow him into the yard. Next he whisked his sisters – all of whom had inherited Mother's hair, though not quite her pretty looks – out of the house. In a tone he hadn't known he was capable of, he asked them to stand beside Pakeeza. To his relief they did, holding hands, unsmiling, as if there were nothing queer in any of this. They inched closer, as he instructed them, their copious hair billowing in every direction. With their backs to the wind, and their heads bent forward, their hair caressed Pakeeza's enormous belly. Together they made a mantle that hung halfway in mid-air, like a magic carpet. Jahan could hear his uncle bellowing from inside the house. No doubt Mother heard him too. Even so, they didn't budge, not one of them. There was something beautiful in the air, and if he had had the word for it back then he might have called it a benison. In that passing moment the boy whispered to the calf in the womb, 'See, it's not bad out here. You might as well come now.'

Afterwards his uncle beat his mother for her disobedience. When Jahan tried to interfere, he received his share of the blows. He slept in the barn that night. In the morning he woke up to an uncanny stillness. 'Mother!' he yelled. Not a sound.

He was standing beside Pakeeza, who looked the same as she did on any other day, when he saw her midriff convulse, once, then twice. Noticing that her rear was swollen, he called out to Mother again, and to his sisters, though by now he had understood there was no one in the house. Pakeeza began to trumpet as her pouch twitched and quivered, expanding horribly. Jahan had seen animals give birth before, horses and goats, but never an elephant. He reminded himself that this was her sixth calf, and she knew what to do; however, a voice inside his head, a wiser voice, warned that he should not trust nature to take its course and that he should lend a helping hand – whether now or later, the voice didn't say.

A sac emerged, wet and slimy as a river stone. It fell on the ground, sending forth a gush of fluid. Astonishingly fast the calf was out, bespattered with blood and a sludgy substance so pale as to be translucent. A boy! Dazed and frail, he looked worn out as if he had come a great distance. Pakeeza sniffed the baby, nudging him gently with the tip of her trunk. She chewed the glassy sac. Meanwhile, the calf clambered to his feet, blind as a bat. There were ivory wisps of hair all over his body. It was his size and his colour that perplexed Jahan. In front of him was the tiniest elephant in the empire. And he was as white as boiled rice.

Pakeeza's son was almost half the size of other newborns. Like them, his trunk being too short, he needed to use his mouth to drink his first milk; but, unlike them, his head did not even reach his mother's knees. In the next hour Jahan watched the mother elephant prod the baby, at first mildly, soon with growing impatience, pleading with him to come closer, to no avail.

Convinced that he had to do something, the boy sprinted towards the back of the barn, where they kept all kinds of oddments. In one corner stood a rough-hewn barrel, half filled with the fodder they fed the animals in winter. A rat scurried past when he moved it aside. His feet now dredged with a layer of ancient dust, he emptied the barrel and rolled the clumsy thing to where the mother and baby stood. Then he ran to the house to fetch a stewpot. Lastly, he shoved the barrel as close to Pakeeza as he could and climbed up on it.

He was taken aback by the sight of her swollen teats. Cautiously, he wrapped his thumb and forefinger around one of them and squeezed, hoping to milk her like a goat. Not a drop. He tried using more fingers and more force. Pakeeza flinched, almost knocking him down. Doing his best not to inhale, Jahan placed his lips around one of her nipples and sucked. As soon as the first drops reached his mouth he retched. It was the smell that got to him. He never knew milk could smell so foul. His second and third attempts were no more successful than the first, and before he knew it he was outside in the yard, throwing up. Elephant's milk was like nothing he had tasted before. Sweet and tart at once, thick and fatty. The nape of his neck was slick with sweat and his head felt dizzy. Covering his nose with a handkerchief helped. After that he was able to make headway. He sucked and spat the liquid into the pot, sucked and spat. When the pot was one third full, he stepped down and proudly carried his gift to the calf.

Throughout the afternoon he repeated this. The milk that he had so painfully extracted was always consumed by the baby in one happy slurp. After a dozen trips the boy awarded himself a break. While he rested, rubbing his sore jaw, he glanced at the calf, whose mouth had twisted into what he could only describe as an impish smile. Jahan smiled back, realizing they had become milk brothers.

'I shall call you Chota,'* he said. 'But you'll grow big and strong.'

The calf made a funny sound in agreement. Although there would be many who would want to rename him according to their hearts' wishes, at no stage of his life, neither then nor later, would the animal respond to any name other than the one Jahan had given him. Chota he was and Chota he remained. In three weeks he had grown tall enough to reach his mother's teats. Soon he was stomping around the yard, chasing chickens, frightening the birds, fully plunged into the discovery of the world. Loved and pampered by all the females in the herd, he frolicked. A brave elephant he was, scared of neither the thunder nor the whip. Only one

* Small.

49

thing seemed to fill him with fear. A sound that every now and then rose from the depths of the wilderness, gushing through the valley, like a dark, rowdy river. The sound of a tiger.

When Jahan finished, still on his knees and having talked for the last hour at a tuft of grass, he dared neither to sit up nor to stare at her. If he had taken so much as a glance, he would have seen a smile etch on her lips, delicate as the morning mist.

'Tell me what happened next?' Mihrimah said.

Yet, before Jahan could open his mouth, the nursemaid broke in, 'It's getting late, your Highness. Your mother might return at any moment.'

Mihrimah sighed. 'Fine, *dada*. We can go now.'

Smoothing her long kaftan, the Princess rose to her feet and, with a swinging stride, trod down the garden path. Hesna Khatun watched her quietly for a while. Then, as soon as Mihrimah was out of earshot, she spoke, in a tone so soft and so caring that Jahan did not grasp the chiding underneath until the nursemaid, too, was gone.

'Hyacinth eyes. Milk brother to an elephant. You are a strange one, Indian. Or else a gifted liar. If that's right, if you are deceiving my good and gracious Excellency, I swear I'll find it out and make you regret it.'

The next time they came to see the elephant the nursemaid was seven steps behind and silent as a corpse. As for the Princess, Jahan thought that, in the receding light of the late afternoon, she looked more beautiful than ever before. On her finger shone a diamond, the size of a walnut and the colour of pigeon's blood. Jahan was aware that if he could only get his hands on it, he would be a rich man all his life. And yet, somehow, he also knew he could never steal from her. After feeding Chota dried prunes, she sat under the lilac tree. A faint odour, of flowers and wild herbs, wafted from her hair.

'I'd like to hear what happened afterwards.'

Jahan felt a shiver run down his entire body, but he managed to say, calmly, 'As you wish, your Highness.'

The story the mahout told the Princess

About a year after Chota was born, Shah Humayun received an unusual visitor in his magnificent palace – an Ottoman admiral who had lost half of his crew and all of his fleet in a terrible storm. After listening to his ordeals the Shah promised the man a new caravel so that he could return home.

'I set sail to fight the heathen,' said the Ottoman. 'But a gale brought me to this land. I now understand why. Allah wished me to witness the Shah's generosity and to convey this to my Sultan.'

Pleased to hear this, Humayun rewarded the admiral with robes and jewels. Afterwards he retired to his private chambers, and it was there, in a bathtub full of rose petals, that an idea occurred to him. His troubles were endless; his enemies aplenty, including his own flesh and blood. His late father had given him some hard advice: *do not harm your brothers even though they may well deserve it.* How could he fight them without harming them, Humayun wondered. And if he did not defeat them, how could he remain in power? There he was, as naked as the hour in which he was born, drained by the steam, contemplating this quandary, when a rose petal caught his eye. Swimming gracefully, it slid towards him as if guided by an invisible hand and fastened itself to his chest.

Gentle by birth, mystical by disposition, Humayun gasped. Surely this was an omen. The rose petal had shown him his weakest side: his heart. He ought not to be enfeebled by his feelings. The more he thought about it, the more it seemed that the shipwrecked captain had been brought to him just like this petal. God was telling him to wage war on his enemies and, if necessary, to get support from the Ottomans. He left the bath, delighted and dripping.

Between the two Muslim sultanates there were sporadic exchanges – merchants, emissaries, mystics, spies, artisans and pilgrims travelled to and fro. Also, gifts. The last came in all sizes: silks, jewels, carpets, spices, mother-of-pearl cabinets, musical instruments, lions, cheetahs, cobras, concubines and eunuchs. From one ruler to the other, messages were carried along with tokens of largesse, and the answer, whether affirmative or not, would arrive with reciprocal flamboyance.

Humayun, *Giver of Peace and the Shadow of God upon Earth*, was curious about Suleiman, *Swayer of Sea and Land and the Shadow of God upon Earth*. He had heard from his spies that every night before he went to sleep the Sultan wore the Seal of Solomon, the signet ring that had given his namesake command over animals, humans and *djinn*. Suleiman's strengths were apparent. But what were the foibles and the fears that festered under those precious kaftans, each of which he was rumoured to wear but once?

Humayun had also heard about Hurrem – the queen of Suleiman's harem. Recently she had ordered a thousand pairs of turtledoves from Egypt that had been trained as carriers, tiny papers wrapped around their claws. The birds had been sent to Istanbul over seas and rivers, and when they were released, the sky above turned as black as pitch and the people ran to the mosques, fearing the Day of Judgement.

Humayun decided to impress the Ottoman Sultana with a matchless present. His offering would honour the Sultan but at the same time remind him of the lands beyond his reach and, thus, of his limits. Swathed in a cape, the Shah called for his ewer-bearer, Jauhar, in whose wisdom he trusted.

'Tell me. What would be the right gift to send to a man who has everything?'

Jauhar replied, 'Not silks or gems. Nor gold or silver. I'd say, an animal. Because animals have personalities and each is different.'

'Which animal would best convey to him the greatness of our empire?'

'An elephant, my Lord. The biggest animal on land.'

Shah Humayun gave this some thought. 'What if I'd like to imply that my kingdom, though splendid enough to have such an elephant, is in need of his help?'

'In that case, my Lord, send him a baby elephant. It'll be our way of saying that we cannot do battle just yet. We need a helping hand. But we shall grow and fight, and when we fight, we shall triumph, God willing.'

The morning Jauhar arrived with a regiment of soldiers, Jahan was feeding Chota, now weighing almost eight kantars and still the colour of ivory.

Jahan's uncle, delighted to have such a respectable guest in his court-yard, bowed and scraped. 'Our noble Shah's noble servant, how can I be of help?'

'I heard you had a white elephant,' Jauhar said. 'You must give it to us. The Shah wishes to send it to the Ottomans.'

'Of course, what an honour.'

'You're not giving Chota away, are you?' came a voice from behind. Everyone turned to look at Jahan.

His uncle threw himself on the ground. 'Forgive him, venerable master. His mother passed away last month. Awful disease. She was fine one day, gone the next. She was with child, poor thing. The boy doesn't know what he's saying. Grief got into his head.'

'Mother died because of your cruelty. You beat her every day —' Slapped by his stepfather, Jahan tumbled down, unable to finish his words.

'Don't hit your son!' said Jauhar.

'I am not his son,' yelled Jahan from where he had fallen.

Jauhar smiled. 'You are a brave boy, aren't you? Come closer. Let me look at you.'

Under the burning gaze of his uncle, Jahan did as he was told.

'Why don't you wish to let go of the animal?' asked Jauhar.

'Chota is like no other elephant: he's different. He can't go anywhere.'

'You love the beast, that's good,' said Jauhar. 'But he'll be fine. In the Ottoman palace he'll be treated like a prince. And your family will be rewarded.' The Shah's ewer-bearer then gestured to a servant who, out of his robe, produced a pouch.

Jahan's uncle's eyes glinted when he saw the coins. He said, 'Don't mind the lad, my Lord. What does he know? The calf is yours. Do with him as you wish.'

Once Chota's fate was sealed, Jahan took it upon himself to make the elephant ready for his long journey. He fed him remedial herbs that would ease digestion; washed and oiled and perfumed his skin; trimmed the pads under his feet; clipped his nails – all the while knowing that it wasn't he who would be accompanying Chota when the time came to climb aboard. A mahout, five years older and supposedly experienced, had been appointed for the task. A stumpy youth with a protruding chin and close-set eyes. He was called Gurab – a name the boy would never forget. One did not forget the name of one's enemy.

A massive cage was sent from the palace, its corners welded in gold and silver, its bars adorned with flowers and tassels. Upon seeing it, Jahan's eyes brimmed over. Chota, frisky and of good cheer since the day he was born, would be kept in chains and put under lock and key like some common criminal. Try as he might to accept that this was the only way the animal could go by water, he could not bear the thought. Withdrawing into misery, he ate and spoke little. His sisters were worried; even his uncle left him alone.

Gurab dropped round every now and then to see how things were coming along and, as he put it, *to make familiar with the beast*. Jahan watched him like a hawk; and his heart warmed when the elephant paid his new mahout no heed.

'Hold this!' Gurab would shout, lifting the cane in his hand.

Chota would stay put, not even glancing at him.

'Come, grab this stick!' Jahan would yell from another corner and the elephant would veer towards him, ever so obedient.

A few times the two youngsters had come close to exchanging blows. Even so, since Chota listened to no one save Jahan, to make things easy it was agreed that the boy would travel with them to the port of Goa. There, the elephant would be loaded on to the vessel that would take him to Istanbul, and Jahan would return to Agra.

The morning they set off, Jahan's eldest sister pulled him aside. Inhaling ever so slowly, she held her breath deep down in her lungs, not yet ready to let go either of her breath or of her brother.

'You are leaving,' she said, as if it needed to be announced.

'I'll help Chota and come back with uncle,' said Jahan, putting into his sack the bread she had baked. 'Just for a few days.'

'The road can be short or long, who knows. This morning I asked myself, if Mother were here, what would she counsel you? I prayed to God that He would let me know so that I could tell you, but nothing came.'

Jahan kept his head down. He, too, wanted to know what his mother would have told him had she been alive. When he looked outside, he saw the elephant, glowing. The peasants had painted his trunk in swirling colours and embellished his mantle with sequins. As he watched him, these words spilled from Jahan's mouth: 'Be kind to the beast, and to the weak, she might have said.'

His sister's eyes, which had been dark and doleful, now lit up. 'That's right. Whatever you do, she would have said, don't hurt anyone and don't let anyone hurt you. Be neither a heartbreaker nor heartbroken.'

The clouds above the Port of Goa rolled away across the pewter sky, bringing them the favourable wind they had been awaiting for days. The anchors were raised, the sails were hoisted, a pair of old and torn breeches was thrown into the water to expel bad luck. Gurab was rigged out in an embroidered jacket the colour of dead leaves. Next to the tatters Jahan wore, his clothes shone like a maharaja's. Scowling at the boy, Gurab said, 'You better take yourself off. We don't need you any more.'

'Not going anywhere until the ship leaves.'

'You brat,' Gurab said.

Jahan pushed him. Caught unawares, Gurab tumbled down, soiling his jacket. He stood up and hissed, 'I'll kill you.'

Jahan dodged the blows with ease, savvy about how to protect himself – thanks to the training of his uncle, who was watching the brawl from one side, amused. Being taller and older, Gurab could have roughed him up, but he didn't. He had seen the madness in the boy's eyes, that brittle savagery. For him, Chota was but one elephant among many. For Jahan, he was like no other – his best friend, his milk brother.

'Plague upon thee,' Gurab said, but he had already stopped fighting.

Still shaking, Jahan went to Chota. Just standing beside him deepened the sadness creeping into his heart. He said, 'Fare you well, my brother.'

The elephant, now shackled, swung his trunk.

'You're going to be fine. The Sultan will welcome you and the Sultana will adore you, by my troth.'

And with those words the boy strode away, wiping his tears, though he could not go far. On impulse he hid behind a wall to spy. After a while, Gurab returned, having cleaned his jacket. Confident that he had got rid of his rival, he scoffed, 'Ay, big beast. From now on it's you and me. If you don't obey me, I'll starve you to death.'

Getting the elephant on to the vessel would be no mean feat. Chota had not even glanced at his cage. When the moment came, Gurab instructed the elephant to move – a command that went ignored. He smacked the elephant with his cane. Chota didn't budge. Gurab hit him again. Jahan's mind began churning. If he entrusted his milk brother to this ogre, the elephant might not make it alive to the Ottoman lands.

By now, the *khalasi* had finished loading the freight into the ship. Chota and his cage were among the last items on the dock. Upon Gurab's call, four men appeared and tied ropes around Chota's torso. Not liking this at all, the elephant trumpeted and rumbled. Though not yet a year old he was strong. The four men became ten, half pushing half pulling in unison. As soon as the elephant was shoved into the cage, the iron door was shut and bolted. Chota turned back, slowly, a painful look in his eyes, only now understanding that he was trapped. The cage was fastened with chains from above and hoisted with the help of a tackle. Chota, already in mid-air, stared about, not at anyone in particular but towards the distant lush forests and the misty valleys where elephants plodded along, free and reckless.

It was then that something caught Jahan's eye. Ahead of him a crate lay on the ground; some of its planks had peeled off, leaving an opening through which he could see its contents: parcels wrapped in cloth. They would carry this to the ship at the end. He glanced at the elephant; he glanced at the crate. Making sure no one was watching, Jahan sneaked into the half-filled crate. His lips curved into a smile at the thought of his uncle searching everywhere for him. He waited, still as a stone. After an eternity, he felt a jolt, a bounce that jarred every bone in his body. The porters were carrying him, and not as gently as he had hoped. As the crate was thrust aside with a thump, he knocked his head against the timber. He was on board.

The carrack in which he found himself was named *The Glowing Sun*. She had four masts, and large castles fore and aft. On the main mast, where some sunburned sailor sat inside the crow's nest, were bonnets that could be added depending on the wind's whim. There were seventy-eight seamen. In addition there were a small number of missionaries, pilgrims, emissaries, merchants and gadabouts.

Jahan was careful not to go out in broad daylight. As soon as the rays of light on the floorboards receded, he crept out and searched for the elephant. It didn't take him long to find him: he was on the other side of the hold, which was horribly dark and damp. The mahout was nowhere to be seen. When he noticed the boy, Chota made a sweet, chirping noise. Jahan sat next to the animal, telling him he would make sure he arrived in Istanbul safe and sound, and that only then would he return to his sisters.

The next morning, his stomach empty as a dry well, Jahan was up on the deck. From a sailor who had no idea who he was and didn't much care, he managed to get some water and bread. On the way back he visited Chota. He was alone, again. Gurab, apparently, had no intention of spending time inside the hold. Emboldened, Jahan began to visit Chota more often – until he was caught.

'You!' a familiar voice roared.

Jahan turned around to find Gurab by the entrance, his eyebrows arched into the middle of his forehead. 'Damn you! Why're you here?'

'Why are you not here? Every time I come Chota is alone.'

'Hang thee! What is it to you? It's the Sultan's damn beast. Not yours.'

They kept shouting at each other, though neither seemed willing to come to blows. The sailors came running at the commotion and took them to the Captain – a swarthy man with a penchant for opium and high-heeled leather boots, which clattered as he paced about.

'One elephant, two tamers,' the Captain said. 'One of you is too many.'

'I was chosen for this task,' Gurab said. 'He's only a boy.'

'I care for the animal. He doesn't!' Jahan inveighed.

'Quiet!' the Captain said. 'I'll decide who goes, who stays.'

He never did. Day after day, Gurab and Jahan waited in suspense, avoiding each other, watching over the elephant in shifts. They were treated well, surviving on contributions of salted meat, biscuits, hard-tack and beans. Chota, however, unhappy with his diet and with the atmosphere in the hold, lost weight day by day.

The sailors were a superstitious lot. There were words you should never utter, for they invited bad luck. 'Sink', for instance, or 'rocks' or 'disaster'. You should not say 'storm', even if you found yourself in the midst of one. If you heard the chant of mermaids, you ought to throw a pinch of salt behind your left shoulder, because it was the devil calling. The crew had incantations, which they repeated often; they whistled, though never at night; and whenever they heard something they disliked, they spat and stomped their feet. Certain things they regarded as harbingers of doom – upside-down buckets, tangled ropes, bent nails and pregnant women on board.

Jahan was surprised to learn they were fond of rats. Since the rodents were known to abandon a ship bound to go down, their presence was a warm assurance that everything was fine. Yet when a crow landed on one of the masts, it was cursed and chased away. One of the sailors explained to the boy that he had gone to a sorcerer before they raised anchor and had bought three auspicious winds for the journey. He would have liked to purchase more, he said, but this was all he could get for his silver coin.

Nonetheless one afternoon the rats disappeared. The sky, a blameless blue, turned black. Shortly afterwards came that which should never be said out loud. Rain pelted down in buckets; cloudbursts hit them full in the face; and the waves, getting higher every passing minute, began to spill on to the deck. The storm-sails could not be raised. The rudder, broken down, was swept away. It is the end, Jahan thought. Little did he know that it was, though only for him and the elephant.

On the third day of the storm a group of sailors descended the stairs to the hold. One glance at their grim faces and Jahan felt his blood chill.

'Ay, the beast must go,' said one man through half-closed lips.

'We should never have had him on board,' butted in his chum. 'White elephant! Dark omen. It's all his doing.'

'You think we brought on the storm? Are you out of your minds?' Jahan said, but his words were muffled by the sailors' grumbling. No one was listening to him. Helpless, the boy turned to Gurab. 'Why don't you do something?'

'What can I do?' Gurab answered with a shrug. 'Go talk to the Captain.'

Out and up dashed Jahan. It was hell on the deck. Seething, swelling, the sea slapped them from all directions. Drenched and dizzy, holding on to the rails so as not to be swept away, Jahan found the Captain barking orders. Grabbing him by the arm, he begged him to come downstairs and appease his men before they harmed the elephant.

'The boys're rattled,' the Captain said. 'They don't want a white elephant on board. Don't blame 'em.'

'So you're going to throw us into the water?'

The Captain gawked at the boy as though the possibility had never occurred to him. 'You can stay,' he said. 'The creature goes.'

'I can't let Chota drown.'

'He can swim.'

'In this weather?' Jahan shouted on the verge of crying. A new thought came to him, a glimmer of hope. 'What do you think Sultan Suleiman will say when he learns what you've done to his gift?'

'Better the wrath of the Sultan than the sea's.'

'You say it's bad luck to have a white elephant on board. What will happen if you kill it? That's bigger bad luck!'

Chewing his moustache, the Captain said, 'I'll give you a boat. There's an island not far off. You'll be fine.'

A rowboat was lowered. Gurab and Jahan stared at it wide-eyed.

'Jump in,' said the Captain.

'Hey, I got nothing to do with the elephant,' said Gurab. 'It's not mine.'

'Well . . .' The Captain turned to Jahan. 'How about you?'

The boy did not feel he was making a decision so much as accepting a decision that had already been made for him. Without a word he stepped into the rowboat, scared witless.

'It's like the story of the Prophet Solomon,' said the Captain before another wave smashed on to the deck. 'Two women claim to be mother to the same baby. The fake one says, split him into two. But the true mother won't agree to that. See, now we know who is the real mahout, and who is the impostor.'

Chota was brought up to the deck; wild with fear, his feet kept slipping on the wet boards. After a few attempts they gave up trying to move him into the boat and shoved him into the sea. He fell down with an ear-splitting squeal. The water, dark and furious, opened its mouth and swallowed the animal as if he were a mere empty shell.

When Jahan stopped talking, he saw that Princess Mihrimah was staring at him in horror. She asked, 'How did you survive?'

'We were washed ashore on an island. From there we were saved by another ship,' he replied. '*Behemoth*, was the name.'

She gave a smile of relief. 'Were they nice to the elephant?'

'No, your Highness. They were horrible. The sailors got sick midway. Scurvy, the worst kind. Someone said elephant flesh was the cure. They almost killed Chota. Captain Gareth saved us. We owe our lives to him. The rest, you already know. We arrived in Istanbul and were brought here.'

'Pity, your tale has ended,' said Mihrimah with a sigh. 'If you had kept talking for another thousand days, I would have listened without cease. I was fond of daydreaming about your feats.'

Jahan felt awful when he realized how stupid he had been to finish the story. He could have made it much longer. What if the Princess left now and never came back? He began to panic. Just as he was cudgelling his brains for another way to continue with the tale, he heard a sudden wheezing and hacking. Hesna Khatun was bending down, her face suffused with red, her breath coming out in ragged gasps. She was having an asthma attack. The Princess and the mahout, each giving her an arm, walked her to the tree and helped her to sit down. Deftly, Mihrimah pulled out a pouch tucked in the nursemaid's sash, opened it and brought it to the woman's nose. A sharp odour pervaded the air. So this was it, Jahan thought. The smell he had picked up on the Princess, time and again, was from the wild herbs the nursemaid carried with her everywhere. Meanwhile, the woman was inhaling deeply. Bit by bit, her breathing calmed.

'Let's go, *dada*,' Mihrimah said. 'We shouldn't tire you.'

'Yes, Serene Highness,' the woman responded, as she arranged her headscarf and rose.

Mihrimah turned to the elephant and said, in a tone of tenderness, 'So long, Chota. You've gone through so much, poor thing. Next time I shall bring you the best treats in the palace.'

She added with a swift sideways glance, 'I am glad you did not leave the elephant alone, hyacinth boy. That was so kind of you.'

'Your Majesty –' Jahan said, but could not continue.

Just then she did something he could never have imagined her doing, not in a hundred years. She touched him. Placing a hand on his face, she pressed lightly on his cheek, as if searching for the single dimple that was now hiding behind a blush of embarrassment. 'You have a good heart, mahout. I wish we could spend more afternoons together.'

Dazed and smitten by her affection, Jahan could not move, could not breathe, let alone utter a word of gratitude. There was no time to rejoice or to invent new stories. Once again all he could do was to watch her leave him and wonder if she would ever come back.

'Hey, mahout, where the hell are you?'

Jahan went to see who was yelling outside his shed. It was the Chief White Eunuch, arms akimbo. 'Where were you?'

'I was cleaning –'

'Go get ready. The Grand Mufti needs the beast.'

'Wh . . . what for?'

Carnation Kamil Agha took a step forward and slapped him on the face. 'What are you asking? Do as I say.'

With the help of the tamers, Jahan fastened the howdah on the elephant's back. When Chota was ready, the eunuch gave them a look that bordered on contempt. 'Off you go. Sangram will show you the way. A heretic is on trial!'

'Yes, *effendi*,' said Jahan, though he didn't have a clue what that meant.

It was a drizzling, bustling Friday morning. Jahan and Sangram, sitting inside the howdah, plodded along through the hilly streets. What the Chief White Eunuch refused to reveal, Jahan was able to extract from Sangram. Their task was to collect the Grand Mufti and carry him to a square where he would question a Sufi preacher famed for his impious views. That a royal elephant had been assigned to the service of the Chief Religious Officer was the Sultan's way of showing his support for the *ulema*.* The Sultan himself was not attending the court case – and had turned down the Grand Mufti's invitation – an indication that he wished to give a wide berth to theological debates.

As they were passing by the ancient graveyard that overlooked the Golden Horn, the elephant stopped abruptly. Jahan prodded him with his cane, but the animal stood transfixed.

'I heard a strange thing about these beasts,' said Sangram. 'They say they choose where they'd like to die. This one seems like he has found his place.'

---

* Muslim scholars who specialized in law and theology.

'What are you saying? Chota is an infant,' Jahan objected, disturbed by the words he had heard.

Sangram shrugged. Thankfully, Chota began to walk again, and the subject was dropped as quickly as it had started.

Before noon they arrived at the Grand Mufti's house, a mansion with a dovecote carved in limestone, a pergola topped with a baldachin and cantilevered bay windows overseeing the Bosphorus. Jahan inspected the place with interest. He noticed that the windows mostly faced north and a few had stained glass, which he thought was a pity, since they did not capture the changing light. It occurred to him that if he could filch paper from somewhere, he could draw this place in the way he was imagining it.

Meanwhile the Grand Mufti appeared. Jahan saluted him under the eyes of his wives and children, who, having never seen an elephant before, were peeking from behind curtains and doors. With the help of a ladder and a dozen servants the old man took his seat inside the howdah. Jahan, as usual, sat on Chota's neck. Sangram would walk.

'Has anyone ever toppled down from up here?' the Grand Mufti yelled when they set off.

'*Chelebi*, I can assure you that has never happened.'

'*Insha'Allah*, I won't be the first.'

To Jahan's surprise the aged man handled the ride well enough. They trudged along the wider streets, avoiding any alleyways too narrow for the elephant. Besides, Jahan had the impression that the Grand Mufti wanted to be seen by as many people as possible. One didn't get a chance to mount Sultan Suleiman's elephant every day.

They entered the square, where a crowd awaited them. Waving and hailing, people greeted them, although who was more heartily welcomed – Chota or the Grand Mufti – was hard to say. There was excitement in the wind. An anticipation for a remarkable spectacle. After being carried down, the Grand Mufti proceeded to lead the Friday prayer, followed by the *ulema* and hundreds of townsmen. Jahan and Sangram waited by the elephant's side, whispering. Every now and then they glanced furtively at the spot where four husky soldiers stood guard. Among them, praying on his own, now getting on his knees, now standing up, was a stranger – a tall, lithe figure with a delicate face and a few days of stubble.

Sangram said his name was Leyli, yet everyone called him Majnun Shaykh. He was the youngest of Sufi scholars, the youngest of Friday preachers. He had eyes the pale grey of autumn rain, freckles like dots of paint, hair fluffy and fair. He was a man of mesmerizing contrasts: a child's curiosity in the inner workings of the world and a sage's unruffled wisdom; brave to the point of recklessness but diffident; full of vigour yet surrounded by an air of melancholy. Good with words, proficient in *ma'rifa*,* his sermons were popular, attended by both believers and doubters from all over the empire. His voice, soft and soothing, gained a lisping lilt whenever he became particularly emotional. His teachings dazed, dismayed and disturbed the *ulema*. The dislike was mutual. Not a day passed without Majnun Shaykh needling or ridiculing religious officialdom. 'When one reaches a higher awareness,' he said, 'one need not pay attention to *haram* and *halal*† as much as to the inner core of faith.' The Sufis, having attained an upper level of understanding, were not bound by the decrees of the *ulema*. Those were invented for the masses, for those who did not want to think and who expected others to think for them.

Majnun Shaykh spoke about love – of God and of fellow human beings, of the universe in its entirety and of the tiniest particle. Prayer should be a declaration of love, and love should be stripped of all fear and expectation, he said. One ought not fear boiling in cauldrons or wish for virgin *houris*, since both hell and heaven, suffering and joy, were right here and right now. How long were you going to shrink from God, he asked, when you could, instead, start to love Him? His followers – a motley collection of artisans, peasants and soldiers – listened to his oration spellbound. His ideas appealed to the impoverished, his manners to the rich. Even women, they said, even ignorant odalisques and resentful eunuchs, set great store by him; even Jews, Christians and the Zoroastrians, who had a book no one had yet seen.

The Friday prayer came to an end, the scholars settled down. Majnun Shaykh pressed on his eyes, like a kid rubbing the sleep out of them, and studied, one by one, his interrogators.

'Do you know what you are being accused of?' asked the Grand Mufti.

'What you call heresy,' he answered. 'But the charge is unfounded.'

* Mystical, intuitive knowledge.
† Sin and vice.

'We'll see about that. Is it true you've declared you are God and everyone is God?'

'What I said was the Creator is present in each person. Whether a farrier or a pasha, we share the same lifeblood as of yore.'

'How is that possible?'

'We are made not only in His divine image but also with His divine essence.'

'Is it true that you said you have no fear of God?'

'Why should I fear my Beloved? Do you fear your loved ones?'

A murmur rose from the crowd. Someone shouted, 'Silence!'

'So you accept that you have claimed to resemble God.'

'You think God is similar to you. Angry, rigid, eager for revenge . . . Whereas I say: instead of believing that the worst in humans can be found in God, believe that the best in God can be found in humans.'

One scholar, Ebussuud Efendi, asked permission to break in. 'Are you aware that what just passed your lips is pure blasphemy?'

'Was it?' Majnun Shaykh paused, as if briefly considering the likelihood.

A shadow crossed Ebussuud's face. 'Instead of feeling remorse, you seem to be scoffing at the high court. Your mind is warped, clearly.'

'I was not mocking. Besides we are not that different, you and I. Whatever you hate in me, does it not also exist in you?'

'Certainly not! We couldn't be more different,' Ebussuud said. 'And *your* God is surely not the same as mine.'

'Oh, but are you not committing *shirk*, talking of my God and your God as if there could be more than one God?'

The crowd rippled with whispers.

Coughing, the Grand Mufti broke in, 'Tell us more about God, then.'

Majnun Shaykh's response to this was that Allah was not a king or rajah or padishah sitting on his celestial throne, watching from above, writing down every sin so that He could punish when the day arrived. 'God is not a merchant – why should He calculate? God is not a clerk – why should He scribble?'

Not liking this answer, the court went on interrogating him from all sides. Each time they got similar responses. Finally they heard these words from the accused: 'Where you draw a line and tell me to stop:

that is only the beginning for me. What you call *haram* is to me pure *halal*. You say I have to shut my mouth, but how can I keep silent when God speaks through me?'

Dusk fell; the sky turned into a crimson mantle above the hills. Far in the distance the lantern of a passing boat shone dimly. Seagulls screeched, fighting over a piece of rotten meat. People got bored, as the excitement of the previous hours began to wear thin. They had tasks to complete, bellies to fill, wives to please. Gradually, the audience melted away. Only the adherents of the heretic remained, their devotion visible in their expressions.

'We give you a last chance,' said the Grand Mufti. 'If you admit you have been speaking sacrilegiously about God and swear to never say such obscenities again, you might be forgiven. Now tell me, once and forever, do you repent?'

'What for?' said Majnun Shaykh, his shoulders straightening as he seemed to make a decision. 'I love the Beloved as the Beloved loves me. Why feel remorse for love? Surely there are other things to rue. Avarice. Ruthlessness. Deception. But love . . . ought not to be regretted.'

In his anxiety Jahan did not notice that he was pulling Chota's reins too tightly. The elephant made a sound of discomfort, which drew everyone's attention.

'This creature . . .' said Majnun Shaykh, regarding Chota with something akin to admiration. 'Is that not testimony to the beauty and variety of the universe? See how it reflects all existence, even though some may say it's no more than a beast. When we die our soul passes from one body to another. There's no death, therefore. No heaven to await, no hell to dread. I do not need to pray five times a day or fast the entire Ramadan. For those who have ascended high enough, the rules of the common people are of little account.'

Silence fell and lengthened into an awkward wait. Into this the Grand Mufti declared, 'Let it be known that the accused was given a chance to see the error of his ways. He has decided his own end. He shall be put to death three sunsets hence. All his followers will be arrested. Those who repent of their sins will be spared. The rest will meet the same fate.'

Jahan lowered his gaze, unable to watch any more. He was startled when he heard the elephant being mentioned again.

'Should the Grand Mufti allow me, I have an idea,' said Ebussuud

Efendi. 'As you know, the people of Istanbul love our Sultan's white elephant. Why not have the renegade die under the beast's feet? No one would forget this.'

The Grand Mufti looked puzzled. 'That has never been done before.'

'My Lords, they exercise this punishment in the lands of Hindustan. Thieves, murderers, rapists are often trodden on by elephants. It has proved effective. Let the elephant trample on him and make of him an example for those who hold similar views.'

The Grand Mufti was pensive for a moment. He said, 'I don't see why not.'

With that, all heads turned towards Jahan and Chota. The mahout opened his mouth but could not speak for panic, at first. His heart thudding, he then managed to say, 'I beg you, esteemed scholars. Chota has never done a thing like that. He wouldn't know what to do.'

'Don't you come from the land of Hindustan?' asked Ebussuud Efendi suspiciously.

Jahan paled. 'Yes, I do, *effendi*.'

The Grand Mufti said the final word. 'Well, then, teach him. You have three days.'

Three days after the trial, shaking like a leaf in a gust of wind, Jahan was sitting atop the elephant, staring down at the sea of spectators. His eyes flicked between them and the man lying supine on the ground, only an arm's length away. Majnun Shaykh's hands and feet were tied, as were his eyes. He was praying in soft tones that were swallowed by the clamour of the crowd.

'Go, Chota!' Jahan yelled, his command devoid of strength.

The elephant didn't budge.

'Move, you beast!'

Jahan prodded the elephant with a stick, then a wooden cudgel. He uttered threats and curses, offered nuts and apples. None of it worked. When Chota did finally care to move, instead of stamping on the convict, he took a step back and waited, flicking his ears nervously.

The jurists, seeing that the public was getting bored, changed the verdict at the last moment. The heretic and his followers were to be killed in the traditional way.

In the end, Majnun Shaykh and his nine disciples were executed by hanging. Their bodies were dumped into the Bosphorus. The last disciple, the one who had escaped because he had been travelling at the time of the trial, waited at the bay where the land jutted into the sea. He knew the tides of the Bosphorus would bring him the bodies. One by one, he fetched them, cleaned them, kissed them, buried them. Unlike all other Islamic graves in Istanbul, theirs would be without headstones.

From the moment he arrived in the menagerie, Jahan expected Sultan Suleiman to inquire about the elephant. But weeks, then months passed without any sign of the sovereign. He was either on a battlefield or on his way to one. On those rare occasions when he stayed in the palace, he was wrapped up in affairs of the state, if not in the entanglements of the harem. Jahan kept waiting for the Sultan to come. Instead it was the Sultana who turned up one afternoon.

Quick as the wind and quiet as a cat after a pigeon, she caught him unawares. One minute the garden was empty and the next she was there, her entourage waiting demurely seven steps behind her. She wore a scarlet petticoat trimmed with ermine, a headdress with tassels that accentuated her sharp chin and an emerald larger than the egg of some queer fowl on her middle finger.

There, behind the erect figure of her mother, apart from everyone and everything, was Princess Mihrimah, gauzy scarves dangling from her headdress. Ruddy and radiant, sparkles of sunlight dancing in her hair. Her eyes, glossy like pebbles at the bottom of a creek, lit up as they caught his admiring gaze. Her lips twisted in a smile, revealing the gap between her two front teeth, which gave her face a mirthful, impish appearance.

Jahan opened and closed his mouth as if unbeknown to him his tongue wished to speak to her. He was almost going to take a step in her direction when a eunuch slapped him on his neck. 'Kneel down! How dare you!'

Startled, Jahan bowed so low and so fast that his knees knocked against the stones. A giggle ran through those present that made him blush up to his ears.

Ignoring the scene, Hurrem walked past, her skirts brushing Jahan's forehead. 'Who looks after this beast?' she asked.

'I do, my Sultana,' Jahan said.

'What's the beast's name?'

'Chota, your Highness.'

'What can he do?'

Jahan found the question so bizarre it took him a moment to answer. 'He's . . . he's a noble animal.'

He wished to tell her, if he only could, elephants were huge not only in size but also in heart. Unlike other animals, they comprehended death; they had rituals to celebrate the birth of a calf or to mourn the loss of a relative. Lions were fierce, tigers were regal, monkeys were smart, peacocks impressive – yet only an elephant could be all of those things at once.

Oblivious to his thoughts, Hurrem said, 'Show us a few tricks!'

'Tricks?' Jahan asked. 'We don't know any tricks.'

He could not see the expression on her face, as he could not look up. Instead he watched her feet – long and shapely, clad in silk slippers – glide a few steps; she came to a halt in front of the elephant and ordered her concubines to fetch a twig. Instantly one was provided. Jahan feared she was going to hit Chota, but she waved it in the air, asking, 'Can the beast catch this?'

Before the boy could answer she flung the twig up towards the elephant. It made a crescent in the air, landing near Chota's hind feet. The animal wagged its trunk as if to ward off an invisible fly, and remained still, unruffled.

The Sultana made a sneering sound. In that instant Jahan saw Chota through her eyes – a massive creature that ate too much, drank too much and, in return, offered nothing.

'Are you telling me there's nothing this creature can do?' Hurrem said – less a question than a statement.

'Your Majesty, this is a war elephant. So were his grandfathers. He might be young, but he has already proved his bravery on the battlefield.'

She turned towards him, this boy who was clearly unfamiliar with the ways of the palace. 'A warrior, you said?'

'Yes . . . your Highness, Chota is a warrior.' Even as the words left his mouth, Jahan felt uneasy, already regretting his lie.

The Sultana took a quiet breath. 'Then you are blessed with luck. The war is soon!' Hurrem half turned to the Chief White Eunuch. 'Make sure the beast joins our valiant soldiers.'

She flounced away, her chambermaids and concubines obediently trotting after her. Carnation Kamil Agha, after giving the elephant and the mahout each a cold stare, followed them. Not everybody had left, though. Two figures had stayed behind and were now watching the boy – the Princess and her nursemaid.

'You've upset My Lady Mother,' Mihrimah said. 'Nobody upsets my mother.'

'I did not intend to,' Jahan mumbled on the verge of tears.

'Tell me, why are you so upset?'

'The elephant does not know how to fight, your Highness.'

'So you lied to my mother?' she asked, less appalled than amused. 'Look at me, mahout.'

No sooner had Jahan glanced at her than he lowered his gaze in shame. In that fleeting instant he had seen her eyes – set wide in her oval face, inherited from her mother – glow with mischief. She said, 'You are more of a fool than I thought. Tell me, have you ever been in a war?'

He shook his head. From a nearby tree came the squawk of a crow. A loud, harsh cry of warning.

'Well, I haven't either. But I have travelled more than My Lady Mother. Even more than my noble brothers! My venerable father loved me so much he asked me to accompany him to many lands. Just the two of us.' A tinge of sorrow crept into her voice. 'But he doesn't take me anywhere any more. You are no longer a child, he says. I must be kept away from the eyes of strangers. My brothers are as free as migratory birds. How I wish I had been born a boy.'

Mystified by this statement, Jahan duly kept his head down. Yet his compliance seemed to annoy her. 'Look at you and look at me! You are a boy, but you are frightened of the battlefield. I am a girl, but I am dying to go to war with my father. I wish we could exchange places, just for a while.'

That evening, mustering his courage, Jahan went to see the Chief White Eunuch. He explained to him Chota was still young and not ready to fight. He blathered on, repeating himself, not because he thought the man hadn't understood but because if he stopped speaking he might begin to cry.

'What does he need to be ready for? Isn't he a war elephant?' the Chief White Eunuch asked. 'Or did the Shah deceive us?'

'Oh, he is. But he has not been trained. There are things he's scared of.'

'Like what?'

The boy swallowed hard. 'Tigers. I've noticed every time the tiger growls the elephant cowers. I don't know why but –'

'In that case, don't fret,' Carnation Kamil Agha scoffed. 'There are no tigers in Black Bogdania.'

'Black Bogdania?' Jahan echoed.

'That's where our army is heading. Now get out of my sight and don't come back to me again with such nonsense!'

It was Olev the lion-tamer who came to his aid. He explained to Jahan that an order, once pronounced, must be followed. In whatever time was left they had to train the elephant.

If the beast was afraid of tigers, they would have to teach him to overcome his fear. With this purpose, Olev found a tiger skin, God knew from where. Then he asked Sangram to bring a sheep. An innocent animal with blank, brown eyes. They let it graze during the day and kept it in the stable at night. Meanwhile, Olev handed a firkin to one of the kitchen boys, instructing him to fill it with blood the next time a chicken was slaughtered.

The following morning, when Chota was out in the yard, Olev asked the same boy to put on the tiger's skin: it was draped round the lad's shoulders, its edges tied around his neck. Olev then instructed him to crawl on all fours around the elephant, growling and snarling.

'Knock down the bucket!'

While the boy did as told, the elephant watched this peculiar creature out of the corner of his eye. That day they did not give him food and there was no water. They sharpened his tusks and kept him chained. The second day Olev stuffed the tiger skin with spuds and placed it near Chota's cage. Again there was no food, no treats, just a tad of water. He did not allow him to go out for a walk either. Upset and irked, the elephant kept glancing at the tiger skin, holding it responsible for his misery.

The third day Olev brought over the sheep and wrapped the tiger skin on its back. The poor animal tried to shake the thing off, but Olev had smeared the insides with a sticky pine resin. He dragged the sheep in this state into Chota's barn. An hour later the elephant was allowed in. By this time Chota was fraught with hunger and thirst, the sheep crazy with fear. Olev took out the filled firkin. He poured the blood over the sheep: its tiger skin and wool got soaked in red. The smell of blood was sharp, sickening. Olev covered the sheep's head with a cloth. No longer able to see anything the animal went wild. Its tension infected Chota, who began to stamp his feet. In its daze the sheep ran left and right, eventually ramming into the elephant. Chota swung his trunk, hitting the sheep with tremendous force. The animal toppled over, then recovered, unleashing awful sounds that would haunt Jahan for weeks to come.

Trembling, Jahan closed the gate on them. He waited, his ear to the door, holding the handle so hard his fingers ached. He heard the sheep's endless bleating – a bloodcurdling wail as if from the bottom of hell. Little by little, all sounds withered away. Gently, they opened the door. It reeked of blood, urine and excrement. There lay the sheep, lifeless, half mutilated.

That night in the menagerie, Jahan sat with the other tamers around a fire scented with cedar wood. They talked in hushed tones, the smoke from their waterpipes swirling in the air. The Chinese twins, wrapped in a hashish daze, kept chuckling at things unseen.

The moon hovered large and low over Istanbul. The sky resembled a sieve of countless holes through which starlight seeped on to the sleeping city. Where there had once been excitement, there was now weariness in Jahan's soul. What was he doing in this garden amid wild animals, apart from his kith and kin? His sisters must be married by now, perhaps had babies each. The thought of them sitting around another fire – one that was so far away it could not warm him – filled his heart with despair. He should be going back home. Instead he was going to war.

Friday afternoon, following the prayer, the Sultan gave the command for the sounding of the war drum, a giant circular instrument moulded from bronze that was struck seven times before every campaign. The spine-tingling noise rumbled through the marble halls, the rose gardens and the animals' cages, vibrated through the neighbourhoods of rich and poor alike.

In front of Jahan's eyes the entire city made ready to do battle. Every mother's son was a soldier of sorts. The Janissaries came out of their barracks. The pashas saddled up their horses. The artisans and the shopkeepers took up arms, as did the gardeners, bakers, cooks, tailors, farriers, furriers, cobblers, potters, weavers, riggers, tanners, chandlers, glaziers, sawyers, stonemasons, coppersmiths, carpenters, tinkers, rope-makers, rat-catchers, caulkers, fletchers, oarsmen, fishmongers, poulterers and even the soothsayers. In each guild there was a flurry of activity, including in that of the prostitutes.

Even so, everyone waited for the Chief Royal Astronomer to announce an auspicious day to launch the war. There was a right time for everything – celebrations, weddings, circumcisions, warfare. Finally, after nights of watching the stars, the date was fixed. At the end of twenty sunsets the troops would be on their way.

Since war meant finding your enemy, unless the enemy found you first, they had to traverse the distance between the Golden Horn and the River Pruth. The elephant and the boy were ordered to march in the front lines. This perturbed Jahan greatly. He did not wish to be that close to the *delibashlar* – the crazyheads. Clad in furs, tattooed from head to toe, ears pierced, scalps shaved, they were erratic, rough and savage. Among them were vicious criminals. Playing trumpets, blowing horns, banging drums of all sizes and hollering as if to wake the dead, they made a terrible racket certain to chill the enemy's blood – and put an elephant into a frenzy.

Jahan mulled over how best to reveal his concerns, but as it turned out there was no need. The morning they set off for Black Bogdania, the mad clamour sent Chota into a rage so fierce that he nearly trampled a soldier. Before dusk the two of them were moved towards the back rows alongside the cavalry. This time, however, it was the horses that got skittish. In the end they had to be relocated again, next to the corps of footmen.

After that things went smoothly. Chota broke into a springy trot, enjoying the open air and the steady march after months of being confined to the palace gardens. From where he sat up on his neck, Jahan could see below and behind, astonished to find himself staring at a sea of bodies with no end in sight. He saw the camels carrying provisions and the oxen pulling cannons and catapults; the Halberdiers of the Tresses, with their hair dangling from their caps; the dervishes chanting invocations; the agha of the Janissaries proudly sitting atop his stallion; the Sultan riding an Arab steed, encircled by guards on both sides – the left-handed archers to his left, the right-handed to his right. In front of him rode a standard-bearer carrying his flag of seven black horsetails.

Propping up their banners and horsetails-on-poles; hoisting lances, scimitars, hatchets, arquebuses, axes, javelins, bucklers, bows and arrows, thousands of mortals were forging ahead. Jahan had never seen so many together. The army was less a horde of men than one lump of giant. The beat of feet and hooves in tandem was hair-raising and stupefying at once. They proceeded uphill against the wind, slicing through the landscape like knife into flesh.

Every now and then Jahan jumped off the elephant, deciding to walk for a while. This is how he met a foot-soldier, lively as a grig-hen, his waterskin slung across his back.

'When you finish off an enemy, it settles in your gait,' the soldier said. 'For every dastard's head you get a mansion in heaven.'

Not knowing much about Paradise or why he would need houses there, Jahan remained quiet. The foot-soldier had fought in the Battle of Mohacs. Droves of infidels had died – falling to the earth like a slew of felled birds. The ground had been strewn with corpses still holding on to their swords.

'It was raining all the time . . . but I saw a golden light,' he said, dropping his voice to a whisper.

'What d'you mean?' asked Jahan.

'I swear. It was so bright. It shone upon the field. Allah was on our side.'

All at once, his words were pierced by a sharp cry of pain. Soldiers ran left and right, barking orders. Murmurs rippled from row to row. Where once was solid ground there was now a large hollow, like an empty eye socket turned towards the skies. The earth had opened up its mouth and swallowed a party of cavalrymen. They had tumbled into a pit with sharpened stakes deep inside – a well-concealed trap left by the enemy. They had died instantly. Only a sable horse was still breathing, gored in the neck, when an archer shot it to end its suffering.

A debate ensued as to whether to take the dead out and bury them or leave them where they were. The light was already receding from the horizon. Time being precious, they were laid to rest together, horses and soldiers sharing the same grave. How unfair, Jahan thought, that only the humans would go to heaven, having attained martyrdom, while the animals that accompanied them and died for them were turned away from the gates of Paradise. It was a thought he didn't know what to do with and kept to himself.

In the days ahead, the army ploughed through pearly valleys and rugged hills, making headway with the sun, camping with the dark. In this manner, after six dawns and five dusks, they reached the banks of the River Pruth. A curtain of fog rolled over the water. There was nothing to convey them to the other shore: no boats, no bridge. They were ordered to set up their tents and get a good rest while a solution was sought.

Bolting towards a bend in the river that had silted up with sludge, Chota threw himself into the pool, wallowing, squelching, trumpeting. Such was his delight that entire regiments stopped to watch him.

'What is he doing?' said the foot-soldier.

'Covering himself with dirt.'

'Why would he do that?'

'They can't sweat like us,' said Jahan. 'Water keeps them cool. The mud protects them from the sun. Taras taught me.'

'Who is Taras?'

'Uhm . . . This old tamer in the palace,' said Jahan nonchalantly. 'He knows everything about every animal.'

The foot-soldier studied him with a glint in his eyes. 'So you learned about the elephant's ways from this Taras. Why didn't you know about your own beast?'

Jahan evaded his gaze, suddenly uneasy. He had said too much. Every time he allowed someone, anyone, to prise open the shell of his soul he repented of it instantly.

Soon it became obvious that Chota was the only one benefiting from the hiatus. Endlessly waiting by the river didn't go down well with the Janissaries, who longed for victory and loot. The wind that had lashed at their faces during the march had abated, but now there were swarms of mosquitoes everywhere. They stung with a vengeance, as if they had been trained by the enemy. The soldiers were tense, the horses fidgety. The foragers were tired of raking through the same villages for food and the soup tasted blander by the day.

In the meantime, a corps of workers had begun building a bridge. They seemed to be doing a fine job, when, unexpectedly shoved by Sheitan, first one then the rest of the piers collapsed. Before the week was over, the foundations of a second bridge had been laid; though thicker and sturdier than the first, its abutment crumbled even faster, wounding half a dozen soldiers and killing one. The third bridge was only a weak attempt. The soil was too boggy, the river's current relentless. Disheartened and bone-weary, they fell into a torpor that sucked them down like the marsh beneath their feet. Jahan didn't even need to ask the foot-soldier what he thought about their predicament: he knew he would say that the Almighty, who had brought them all the way into this bleak landscape, had suddenly forgotten them. If things went on like this, before the war had even started, the Ottoman Army would be defeated by its own impatience.

The Master

By the River Pruth they waited. The water ran wild and deep between the Ottoman Army and the enemy. The Janissaries itched to be on the other shore, athirst for victory.

One morning, Jahan saw the zemberekcibasi* hurrying as fast as his legs would carry him, coming in his direction. Eager to learn what was going on, he was late in moving out of the man's way.

'How is the beast doing, mahout?' asked the zemberekcibasi, quickly righting himself after their minor collision.

'He is very well, *effendi*, ready to fight.'

'Soon, *insha'Allah*. First we need to cross this cursed river.'

And with those words the man disappeared into a hefty tent that had two soldiers outside standing sentinel. Jahan should have stopped there, but he didn't. Not pausing to think whose tent this could be, he walked with such steadiness that the guards took him to be the attendant of the zemberekcibasi and let him pass.

Inside, it was so crowded nobody paid the boy any attention. Quiet as a mouse, Jahan tiptoed to a corner opposite the door, squeezing in between two pages. Cloth walls, brocade cushions, carpets of dazzling colours; salvers piled high with delicacies; braziers, lanterns, incenses with sweet fragrances. He wondered if he could filch a few things for Captain Gareth but even the thought of that was terrifying.

The Grand Vizier was there, a heron's plume attached to his turban. The Sultan was at the far end, clad in an amber kaftan, dignified as a sculpture. He sat on a bejewelled throne set upon risers, a position that allowed him to study. The Shayh al-Islam, the Janissary agha and the other viziers had lined up on either side of him, offering comments. They were discussing whether or not to alter their route, in order to find a bend in the river where the ground would be hard enough to build a bridge. This not only meant losing weeks, perhaps as much as a month, but also the favourable weather.

* Commander of the Janissary unit in charge of catapults.

'My gracious Lord,' Lutfi Pasha said. 'There's someone who can build us a strong bridge.'

When the Sultan demanded who that might be, Lutfi Pasha said, 'One of your elite guards. Sinan is his name, your Haseki* slave.'

Before long a man was ushered in. He kneeled down, merely steps away from where Jahan stood. He had a wide forehead, chiselled nose and dark, sombre eyes that exuded calmness. Asked to come forward, he proceeded slowly, lowering his head, as if against a gusty wind. After listening to why he had been summoned, Sinan said, 'My felicitous Sultan, we shall have a bridge, Allah willing.'

'How many days, by your reckoning, would be needed to complete it?' asked Sultan Suleiman.

Sinan paused, though not for long. 'Ten, my Lord.'

'What makes you think you will succeed when others have failed?'

'My Lord, the others, with pure intentions no doubt, began the construction straight away. I shall build the bridge in my mind. Only after that will I have it set in stone.'

Strange though the answer was, it seemed to please the Sultan. Sinan was given the task. He went back the way he had come, unhurried. As he passed Jahan, he took a look at the boy's face and then did something Jahan had not seen any man of his rank do before. He smiled.

It was then that a thought occurred to the boy. If he worked with this man, he could get close to Sultan Suleiman's riches. Everyone said the sovereign had brought chests full of coins and jewels to distribute to those who demonstrated great courage on the battlefield.

'*Effendi*, wait,' Jahan yelled once he had sneaked out, catching up with the architect. 'I am the elephant's tamer.'

'I know who you are,' said Sinan. 'I have seen you take care of the beast.'

'Chota is stronger than forty soldiers. He could be of great help to you.'

'Well, do you know anything about construction?'

'We . . . we worked with a master mason in Hindustan.'

Holding the boy's eyes in his stare, Sinan gave this some thought. 'What were you doing in the Grand Vizier's tent?'

---

* Sultan's elite Janissary guard, who accompanied him to mosque, out hunting, etc.

'I slipped in on the sly,' said Jahan, this time telling the truth.

The lines around Sinan's eyes softened. 'An elephant could prove useful. A bright, inquisitive boy like yourself might help, too.'

Jahan felt his cheeks burn. In all his time in the world he could not recall anyone having called him bright. And, just like that, the elephant and the mahout joined the army of stonemasons and began working with this stranger called Sinan.

Keen as the labourers were to put their backs into the work, the first day went by without anyone moving a finger. So did the second. Sinan seemed to be dawdling: walking back and forth along the river, staring into the distance, poking canes into the water, taking measurements, carrying scrolls of paper, scribbling numbers, drawing shapes no less obscure than those on an oracle's charts. The soldiers were starting to get nervous, asking what on earth they were waiting for. At nights in the tents and around the fires, rumour had it that Sinan was clearly not the right man for the task.

On the third day Sinan announced they would start construction. To everyone's surprise he had chosen a site two *donum** up the shore-line, where the river was wider. When asked why he was taking them that far, he said a bridge could be short or long, that didn't matter, but its foundations had to be as strong as granite.

Chota carried wooden frames and planks; he moved rocks into place so as to protect the structure from the force of the current. That he could plod in the river easily proved to be opportune. In the fast-flowing water that reached up to their chins he was a great asset. They used massive, watertight barrels, each of which had been sealed inside with clay mortar and lowered into a newly dug hole. Covered in mud, sweat and dirt, Jahan toiled alongside the labourers. Strange men they were. Tough and taciturn, but yet caring towards one of their own. They would put their right hand on their heart whenever they heard some-one mention the prophets Seth and Abraham, the Patron Saints of Stonemasons and Architects. Among them, Jahan felt more at ease than he ever had anywhere. Like them, he found a secret joy in raising stone upon stone. Ten days after Sinan had been entrusted with the job, they finished the bridge.

Seated on his horse, the Sultan was the first to cross, holding the reins tightly in one hand. The Grand Vizier followed, then the others, including Lutfi Pasha, who congratulated himself on having found the

* Amount of land that can be ploughed in a day.

architect. Once the royal entourage reached the opposite bank, every-one rejoiced. The whole army began to traverse the bridge, six men at a time. Here and there prayers were heard – men unafraid of bloodshed but terrified of water. When it was their turn, Jahan and Chota made a move, but they were stopped by the Subashi.

'The beast ought to wait. He's too heavy.'

It was Sinan who came to their rescue. '*Effendi*, this bridge can carry fifty elephants if need be.'

The Subashi grunted his approval. 'If you say so . . .'

Turning to Jahan, Sinan said, 'Come, I'll walk with you.'

Thus they crossed the bridge together, the elephant lumbering be-hind them.

Once on the other shore, Sinan was called urgently. He quickened his steps. Having not been told to stay behind, Jahan followed, and so did Chota.

Ahead of them the notables were having a debate over what would happen to the bridge after the army left. From their expressions Jahan saw that things had become tense. Lutfi Pasha wanted to construct a watchtower and detail a regiment to guard the bridge; the Grand Vizier and the Governor-General of Rumelia, Sofu Mehmet Pasha, dis-agreed. Unable to reach an agreement, they had decided to consult the architect.

'My Lords, if we build a tower, the enemy will capture both the tower and the bridge,' said Sinan. 'They can ambush us from behind.'

'What do you suggest?' the Grand Vizier asked.

'We made it with our hands; we can destroy it with our hands,' Sinan replied. 'Then we can build a new bridge on our return.'

Lutfi Pasha, who, because he had recommended Sinan to the *diwan*, expected obedience from him, became furious. 'Coward! You are scared you'll be left behind to guard the tower.'

Sinan paled but when he spoke he sounded placid. 'My Lords, I'm a Janissary. If the Sultan orders me to raise a tower and to guard it, I shall do as he says. But you have asked my honest opinion, and this I gave.'

Into the ensuing silence the Governor-General said, 'Well, the Arabs have been burning their ships.'

'This is not a ship and we are not Bedouins!' Lutfi Pasha snapped, throwing a cold glance in Sinan's direction.

The meeting came to an end without a solution being reached. Later in the afternoon, the Sultan, who had been informed of the argument, announced his decision. Apparently, he had favoured Sinan's suggestion over Lutfi Pasha's. The bridge was to be demolished.

Destroying a bridge was easier than building it, Jahan soon found out. Yet it pained him to see the stones they had toiled so hard to gather and carefully position now come tumbling down. He disagreed with Sinan more than anyone. How could the man recommend wrecking the bridge, as if the sweat of their brows meant nothing to him?

When he found his chance to talk to Sinan, Jahan began by floundering. '*Effendi*, forgive me. I don't understand why we are doing this. We worked so hard.'

'We shall work harder the next time.'

'Yes, but . . . how could you so easily say, "Let's knock it down"? Doesn't it make you sad?'

Sinan regarded the boy as if they had already known one another in a different time. He said, 'My first master was my father. He was the best carpenter in the region and he was the one who trained me from boyhood. Every Zatik* he'd fast for forty days. Meanwhile he would ask me to carve a lamb out of wood. Then he'd tell me it was not good enough and take it from me. "I have destroyed it," he'd later say; "go make another one." I resented this but my lambs got better.'

Jahan's back tightened as he thought about his stepfather. He recalled how once the man had scoffed at the furnace he had built in the backyard for his mother. Now, years later, he was not surprised to see that the anger he had felt back then was still entrenched deep in his heart.

Oblivious to his thoughts, Sinan continued, 'When my father passed away, we found a chest in his shed. Inside were all the lambs that I had carved as a boy. Father had kept every one of them.'

'I understand he made you a better craftsman, but he wounded you.'

'Sometimes, for the soul to thrive, the heart needs to be broken, son.'

* Armenian Easter.

86

'I don't understand, *effendi*. I wouldn't want anyone to waste my work.'

'In order to gain mastery, you need to dismantle as much as you put together.'

'Then there'd be no buildings left in the world,' Jahan ventured. 'Everything would be razed to the ground.'

'We are not destroying the buildings, son. We are destroying our desire to possess them. Only God is the owner. Of the stone and of the skill.'

'I don't understand,' said Jahan again, albeit this time not as loudly.

Thus, on the bank of the River Pruth, they left behind them their sweat, their faith and their work, lying in ruins that gave no clue as to what an exquisite bridge had once stood in that place.

It was the night before the battle, not the nights afterwards, that would stay etched on Jahan's soul — when he was still complete, still unbroken, and would have remained so had this been a different world. Jahan had been lying on his pallet thinking of Mihrimah. He couldn't help it. His eyes acted on their own, seeing her combing her hair, or strolling through the rose gardens, her smile everywhere. His ears heard her voice. He was powerless as his senses conjured her out of the air.

After sunset the mood in the camp began to shift, and restlessness settled in. By the time darkness had completely descended there was a kind of anticipation in the wind, so intense as to be tangible. All the soldiers in the camp, no matter how high or low in the echelons, knew deep in their hearts that the star-filled sky they looked at could be their last. Tomorrow, when the sun was up and the enemy was within sniffing distance, none of them would hesitate in doing what they had to do. But now they found themselves dangling in a limbo between faith and doubt, bravery and cowardice, loyalty and betrayal.

A feeling of foreboding tore at their nerves. It wasn't this bleak, doomed valley where they wished to die, their bodies picked apart by vultures, their bones left without a headstone and their ghosts wandering till eternity. They would rather be buried in a tranquil graveyard, dotted with cypress trees and roses in bloom, where the soil was familiar, where people knew their names and would say a prayer or two for their souls. The promise of victory and loot was sweet, yet life was sweeter. Many secretly pondered saddling up a horse and breaking loose, as if, being unable to return home, they could now go anywhere.

Despite the sounding of the night drum, the soldiers found it hard to fall asleep. Murmurs percolated inside tents as stories were shared, secrets revealed, promises made, prayers uttered. Walking past a marquee that belonged to the Bombardiers, Jahan came across a grenade-thrower singing in a strange language. The Janissaries were from myriad backgrounds, sons of the Balkans and Anatolia among them. Memories of their previous lives had been locked inside caskets, the keys thrown away. Still, at times like these, when they stood face to face with death, the caskets opened of their own accord and released fragments of their childhood, like a dream they had once had but couldn't piece together.

On the pretext of fetching food for the elephant, Jahan rambled around the camp with a bucket in his hand. He came across dervishes whirling in circles within circles, their right hands open towards the sky, their left hands turned towards the earth, receiving and giving, dead to everyone and yet perhaps more alive than many. He watched pious Muslims praying on tiny rugs, a faint mark on their foreheads from all their kneeling. He met an armourer who kept a scorpion in a box in his sash, which, he said, would sting him should he fall captive to the idolaters. He overheard Janissaries cursing under their breath, a row between mates that would be forgotten tomorrow morning. He saw prostitutes who, even though they had been forbidden to work the day before the battle, prowled among the tents. Tonight of all nights was the most lucrative, since many a man would need their comfort.

Ahead of him were three whores, their faces half hidden under their capes. Curious, as always, Jahan began to follow them. One woman – young, slender and dressed as a Jewess – stopped and glanced back.

'Brave soldier,' she said silkily, 'you couldn't sleep?'

'I'm not a soldier,' said Jahan.

'But you are brave, I am sure.'

Jahan shrugged, not knowing how to respond.

Her smile grew broader. 'Let me look at you.'

At her touch Jahan flinched. She put her arm through his, clutching his hand with so tight a grip that he could not pull away. Her fingers were soft; her body smelled of wood-smoke and damp grass. Trying to hide the shudder that had seized him, Jahan pulled himself free.

'Don't go,' she pleaded like a heartbroken lover.

The request was so unexpected and so innocent, he was nonplussed. When he began to walk, she trotted behind him, the swish of her skirts reminding him of the sound of pigeons ruffling their feathers under the eaves. Staring ahead, as if the night held a riddle he had to solve, Jahan continued onwards. It was getting late, and moving around the camp with a whore on his heels was dangerous. Reluctantly, he headed to his tent.

There were three stable-grooms inside. 'Hey, Indian lad, what did you bring us?' one of them asked. 'A gazelle, eh?'

'She came on her own,' Jahan said scathingly.

For a moment they were silent, considering what to do. The eldest groom, who had a fine pair of boots with which to trade, took the whore to his bed.

Jahan, feigning indifference, retreated to a corner and unrolled his pallet. Sleep would not come. His face set into a grimace as he listened to the grunts, the panting. When he thought it was finally over, he propped up on one elbow and glanced around. By a candle's weak glow he saw them, he rocking on top of her, she lying limp and listless, her eyes wide open and fixed on the shadow of something that wasn't there. She turned to one side. Their gazes locked. In her eyes he glimpsed her universe; in her loneliness he recognized his own. He felt ill, dizzy, the ground tilting beneath his weight. At that moment Jahan discovered – against his better judgement – a wild power smouldering in his heart. There was a dark side to his nature, a secret cellar under the house of his soul that he had not yet visited but always sensed existed.

He jumped to his feet, stomping towards the groom, who didn't notice him until it was too late. He shoved him off her and hit him hard, a punch that sent the man tumbling to the floor, though in truth it hurt Jahan's hand more than the man's chin. The groom, less furious than perplexed, blinked back up at the boy. His lips twisted in disdainful recognition of what had happened until he emitted a chuckle. The other grooms joined in. Jahan looked at the whore and saw that she, too, was laughing at him.

Trembling, he slipped outside the tent, in need of seeing Chota, who was always sweet-tempered and tender-hearted, and, unlike human beings, knew no arrogance or malice.

As usual the elephant was dozing on his feet. Every day he slept no more than a few hours. While Jahan changed his water and checked his food, his mind was awash with images of the whore – her touching him, her following him, her sprawled on a dirty mattress, half naked. Yet, when he lay down on a pile of straw and closed his eyes, it was Mihrimah who appeared, once again, leaning towards him in a kiss. He opened his eyes in panic, embarrassed for daring to think of her in that way – a woman of noble birth, not like that ruined harlot from nowhere. Still, try as he might, he could neither banish the harlot nor stop dreaming of the Princess.

Next morning at dawn he woke with the sound of prayer. The grooms were up and ready. Jahan searched them for a trace of guilt or a sign of fatigue. Nothing. It was as if the night before had never happened.

Slow and tedious the prelude to war had been; the battle itself was swift – or so it felt to Jahan. He heard a rumbling echo, first far off, then too close. The enemy was no longer an obscure shadow: it had a face – a thousand faces, in fact, peering from under their helmets. Atop his elephant Jahan raked his gaze across the battlefield. In the distance, where the two armies were colliding, the colours melted into a cascade of grey. Sparks of light flashed and died, flashed and died, as blades struck against each other. Everywhere he turned he saw metal and flesh: spears, swords and knives; bodies hurling across the plain, staggering, falling.

The sound was deafening. The clatter of iron-shod hooves, the clash of steel, the *thwack* of catapults; the yelling, the choking, the constant repetition of *Allah, Allah*. They fought for the Sultan. They fought for the Almighty. But also for every wrong they had suffered since they were boys, the whips and sticks and blows they had endured. Blood soaked into blood on patches of earth that turned so dark as to be black. Their cheeks puffing, their mouths foaming, the horses galloped, their riders standing in the saddles. Clouds of smoke billowed far and wide. Though it was mid-afternoon, the light was already receding, the sky a mantle of smoke.

Bewildered, flustered, Chota clumped left and right, uneasy under the huge plate armour, which he had still not got used to. His tusks had been honed into sharp blades. Jahan tried talking to him but his words were swallowed up by the clamour. In the periphery of his vision he caught a movement. A hefty Frank, crossbow over his shoulder, lurched forward upon a Janissary, who, having tripped over and dropped his javelin, lay on the ground, momentarily confused. The Janissary ducked the first lunge of the sword, but the next one pierced his shoulder. In an instant Jahan steered Chota in their direction. The elephant barged into the Frank and lifted him up in the air, with his tusk jammed into his abdomen.

'That's enough, Chota,' Jahan yelled. 'Let go!'

The elephant obeyed, for a fleeting moment, dropping the screaming soldier. But instantly he hauled him up again, thrusting his tusk into his chest. Blood spurted from the man's mouth, a look of disbelief in his eyes at meeting his end at the hands of an animal. Jahan watched terrified, only now realizing he had not been commanding Chota; Chota had been commanding him.

After that, Jahan felt more and more like a spectator. Chota propelled himself towards enemy lines, picking, hoisting and dropping off soldiers; he crushed two Franks under his weight. With one soldier he took longer, like a cat with a mouse, as if he wished him to suffer longer. He attacked a Janissary, too, not making any distinction between friend and foe. It was sheer luck that saved the man from being trampled.

Yes, the battle happened quickly, though afterwards Jahan would relive it in his head a thousand times. The deaths he had witnessed but did not see, the cries he had caught but did not hear, would rush back to him. Even decades later, as an old man, Jahan would find himself remembering that afternoon: a blood-stained shield in the mud, a burning arrow with lumps of flesh attached, a horse split open, and, somewhere, behind the veil of time, always, always, the face of the prostitute, laughing at him.

Further off, amid the sea of flames, he saw a soldier tottering, his face a carved mask, his midriff gored with a spear. Jahan recognized the foot-soldier whom he had befriended on the way.

'Halt, Chota!' he shouted. 'Put me down.'

Both orders the elephant disobeyed. Without thinking Jahan threw himself off the animal's back, dropping heavily on his side. He reached the foot-soldier, who, by now, had fallen down on to his knees. His fingers were entwined, as if grabbing an invisible rope. Blood gurgled out from his nose, a few drops spilling on the talisman around his neck. Jahan took off his mahout jacket and pressed it on the wound, from which the head of the spear poked out. He sat beside him, holding his hand between his palms, the man's pulse a fading drum.

The foot-soldier broke into a smile: it was impossible to say whether this was because he was relieved to see a familiar face or because he thought Jahan was someone else. His teeth chattering, he stammered something incomprehensible. Bending over, Jahan listened, his breath warm against the man's cheek.

'The light . . . did you . . . see?'

Jahan gave a tight nod. 'I have. It's beautiful.'

A shadow of solace flitted across the foot-soldier's face. His body grew heavy, his mouth sagged, his eyes remained open as though fixed on a cloud that had already passed.

Later on, when everything was over and the Ottoman Army had triumphed, Jahan could not bring himself to join the revelry. Trudging wearily, he drifted away from the camp into the heart of the battleground. It was a reckless thing to do. He had no weapon on him other than a dagger he wasn't sure he could use. Still, he lumbered across the valley shrouded in mist, pushing on through the field strewn with bodies that only a few hours before had been sons, husbands or brothers. He had the feeling that this place with its shadows and smoke was the end of the known earth, and that if he kept walking he would fall off the edge. He knew Chota would be starving, waiting for him to bring food and water. But the last thing he wanted was to see the elephant.

A few times he stepped on a soft mound here and there, and found out, to his horror, that it was a dead man's thigh or a severed hand. The stench was fierce. The lingering sounds were eerie: the crackle of burning wood, the hoofbeats of riderless horses and, from corners he could not make out, the moans of soldiers still alive.

The pain, when it finally caught him, was like nothing he had experienced before. He checked himself over, unable to find anything. It was in his head, in his limbs. He couldn't tell where it ached, for the pain travelled, now eating at his bones, now clenching his insides. Hunched up, he vomited.

Drawn by a mad instinct, he picked his way through the field, his feet sore, his legs heavy like timber, his forehead beaded with sweat, until he found an old gnarled tree to sit by. A troop of Ottoman miners was excavating a huge pit in the distance. When they were done, they would separate out the dead, and bury their own. What would happen to the corpses of the Franks, he didn't know. So engrossed was he in his thoughts that he did not hear anyone approaching.

'Indian lad,' came a voice from behind. 'What are you doing here?'

Gasping, Jahan turned around. 'Master Sinan!'

'You should not be here, son.'

It didn't occur to the boy that neither should Sinan. He said, apologetically, 'Don't want to go back.'

The man inspected the boy's swollen eyes, his marred face. Slowly, he sat down next to him. The sun was setting, a crimson tinge on the horizon. A flock of storks flew over, heading towards warmer lands. Jahan started to cry.

Taking a blade out of his sash, Sinan chipped a chunk from a log nearby. As he carved, he began talking about Ağırnas, the village where he had been born – the hedged crop fields, the Greek and Armenian churches with no bells, and the icy winds that hummed like sad songs; the yoghurt soup his mother made and served cold in the summer, hot in the winter; the carpentry his father had taught him, where even the tiniest piece of wood was breathing and alive. Becoming a Janissary and converting to Islam when he was twenty-one, he had joined the Hearth of Haci Bektash, named for the dervish patron of the Janissary corps, and taken part in war after war: Rhodes, Belgrade, Iran, Corfu, Baghdad and, the bloodiest of them all, Mohacs. He had seen the bravest turn tail, the timid bloom into lionhearts.

'My elephant . . .' said Jahan when he could find his voice. 'Olev and I taught him how to kill. Now he has killed. Many.'

Sinan stopped carving. 'Don't be upset at the animal. Don't blame yourself.'

The boy shivered, suddenly cold. 'When we made that bridge, I felt useful, *effendi* . . . I wish we had stayed there.'

'When you do things from your soul, you feel a river moving in you, a joy.'

'Who said this?'

'A poet, a wise man.' Sinan placed his hand on the boy's forehead. It was hot. 'Tell me, would you like to build more?'

'Yes, I'd like that very much,' Jahan replied.

When darkness descended, they headed back to the camp. Halfway there they came across a saddled horse trotting around on its own, its rider gone. Sinan made Jahan sit on the horse, and led it by the reins back to camp. He took Jahan to his tent and told the grooms to take care of the elephant while the boy got some rest.

Burning with fever, Jahan fell into a painful slumber as soon as he lay down. Sinan stayed beside him, putting vinegar-soaked cloths on his face and arms, and continuing with his carving. At dawn, when Jahan's temperature dropped, Sinan opened the boy's clenched fist, placed a gift upon his palm and left. The next morning, when the boy woke up, drenched in sweat but otherwise fine, he found himself holding a wooden elephant. On its face, instead of sharp, lethal tusks, it had two flowers.

The city was awaiting its army. Since sunrise people had been pouring out, filling the streets and squares like thick, gooey *shurub*.* Climbing up on trees, perching on roofs, squeezing into every smidgen of space alongside the road from Adrianople Gate to the palace, thousands were eager to welcome the victors. Istanbul, with its serpentine alleys, underground passages and closed bazaars, had donned her best gown and was, for once, all smiles.

'The soldiers're comin'!' exclaimed an urchin who had planted himself above a fountain. His words, ripples on the surface of a pond, spread out, reaching the shores of the crowd and from there pushing back towards the centre – altered along the way. By the time the same child heard the echo of his exclamation, it sounded rather different: 'The Sultan's givin' out coins!'

Townsmen with joy and pride in their hearts, merchants with pouches sewn into their hems, liver vendors with strips of meat hanging from poles and stray cats on their heels, Sufis with the ninety-nine names of God on their tongues, scribes with ink stains on their fingers, beggars with bowls dangling from their necks, pickpockets with hands as nimble as squirrels, travellers from Frangistan with a startled look and Venetian spies with honeyed words and astute smiles – everyone inched closer, keen to see.

In a little while, the Sultan's elite guards passed under an arched gateway in full regalia, leading the cavalcade down the acacia-lined thoroughfare, their horses at a ceremonial trot. Following them, mounted on a purebred Arabian stallion, clad in an azure kaftan and a turban so high as to confuse a passing stork on the lookout for a nest, was Suleiman the Magnificent. A collective gasp rose from the audience and mingled with prayers and adulations. Rose petals danced in the air, sprinkled from a hundred windows and balconies.

Behind rows and rows of armour-clad soldiers, some marching, some riding, some pulling their horses by the reins, came the elephant

* A type of syrup widely used in the Middle East.

and the mahout. Initially Jahan had been ordered to sit on the animal's neck and leave the howdah to the Janissary agha. After a few steps in this way, however, the man had asked to be brought down, his face ashen. Accustomed as he was to tempestuousness of all kinds, the elephant's sway proved too much for the Ottoman nobleman. Hence Jahan ensconced himself inside the howdah in the manner of an exiled prince returning home after years abroad. The feeling was strangely sweet. For the first time in days he forgot about the battleground and the stench of death that still wafted from his skin.

Soon it became apparent that the white elephant would be the centre of attention. No one, other than the Sultan, received so much applause and admiration. People everywhere were pointing at Chota, waving, laughing, clapping. A clothier flung strings of ribbons; a Gypsy lass sent a kiss, giggling; a guttersnipe fell down from the branch on which he had climbed, trying to touch the beast's tusks. As Chota sped along, swinging his tail left and right, buoyed by the warm reception, Jahan glided on in a daze of his own. Never had he felt so important, wrapped in the delicious fancy that his presence in this city, if not in this world, filled a unique void. With his cheeks flushed in gratification, he waved back at the spectators.

In the menagerie, Chota was greeted like a hero. It was decided that he would not be sent to the other menageries in the city. He would stay here in the seraglio. His daily ration was doubled and he was allowed to take a bath, every week, in the lily-covered pond at the far end of the courtyard – a privilege that no other wild animal was given. None of the others were permitted to leave the menagerie.

Gradually Jahan forgave the elephant for the way he had behaved on the battleground. He covered his knife-like tusks with two silken balls, and made a new mantle for him with his own hands. He garnished the trims with silver bells and sewed on blue beads against the evil eye. Languid and placid sunsets slipped by. Blissful days these were – though, as too often happens with blissful days, they would be appreciated only when they were no more.

Several days later, while Jahan was cleaning out the barn, Olev the lion-tamer appeared by his side. He said, 'Someone sent you a message.'

'Who?' Jahan asked, a crack in his voice.

'Haven't seen the chap myself. He gave it to a guard so that he'd pass it to you, so I am told.'

Thus saying Olev produced a folded piece of vellum.

'I am illiterate,' said Jahan quickly, as if hoping this would shield him from the contents of the letter. Nor was it exactly true. With the help of Taras the Siberian he had been studying the alphabet. Having discovered the key to the mystery of letters, he had started to wade through books, though handwriting he still found difficult.

'There's nothing to read. I've checked it,' said Olev.

Jahan took the vellum and opened it. There on the smooth surface of the skin was a picture. An elephant, quite badly drawn, but an elephant nonetheless, and on his back a boy with large ears. The animal carried a smile on its shapeless face and looked happy, while the boy had a spear through his heart. Three drops trickled from the end of the spear. Only these had a colour, a deep dark red, for they were made with blood.

'I don't know what this means,' said Jahan, his jaw set tightly, and pushed the letter away.

'Fine,' said Olev after a brief lull. 'In that case we shall destroy it and not mention it to anyone. But whoever this person is, you better start thinking about what you're going to do if he shows up. The walls of the palace are high but not high enough to protect you from evil.'

The second time the Sultana visited the menagerie there was something in her attitude towards the elephant that hadn't been there before: a speck of approval, nigh on appreciation. Again her skirts swished by; again Jahan threw himself on the ground; again her entourage waited to one side, so silent they might have ceased to exist. And once again Mihrimah watched it all with a suppressed smile.

'They say your elephant was brave,' Hurrem remarked without so much as glancing in the mahout's direction.

'Yes, your Highness. Chota fought well,' said Jahan. He did not tell her how the animal had gored soldiers, and how he still felt guilty about having taught him to do so.

'Hmm, but not you, I heard. Is it true you were scared and ran away and came back shivering with fear?'

Jahan's face turned ashen. Who could have whispered such things behind his back? Reading his mind in one swift glance, Hurrem said, 'Birds . . . Pigeons bring me news from everywhere.'

Try as he might to remain indifferent, Jahan believed what she said. In his mind's eye he saw the birds of the aviary flying far and high, carrying in their beaks tidbits of gossip for the Sultana.

'I also heard that your elephant was the people's darling. Everybody loved it. They applauded the white beast more than they applauded the Janissary agha.' Hurrem paused, waiting for her words to sink in.

Jahan knew this was true. Even the commanders in the army had not been showered with as much love as Chota had.

Meanwhile, Hurrem went on. 'I have been thinking . . . Our sons, the two princes, shall be circumcised. There'll be a parade. A big one.'

Uneasiness came over Jahan as he wondered where this was going.

'Your Eminent Sultan and I would like to see the elephant perform.'

'But –'

Already she had turned on her heels. 'But what, Indian?'

Instead of syllables Jahan produced beads of sweat.

'Beware, there're some people who're not taken with you. They think there is something untrustworthy about you. They say you and the beast should be sent to that ruined church to stay with the other big animals. They are right. But I have faith in you, young man. Don't betray my trust.'

Jahan swallowed. 'I won't, your Highness.'

It was a habit of Hurrem's to threaten and sweet-talk interchangeably, breathing down people's necks to make it clear she could crush them should she have the desire to do so, then tossing a flattering remark or two, leaving them confused, beholden. Jahan, however, had no way of knowing this and would learn of it only in time. She strutted away, her chambermaids scurrying to keep up with her. Once again, two figures stayed behind. Princess Mihrimah and Hesna Khatun.

'My Lady Mother seems to be fond of the white elephant,' Mihrimah said witheringly, like a girl imitating her parent's tone. 'If you entertain the crowd well, Mother will dote on you. If Mother dotes on you, you and your beast will be happy.'

'Chota doesn't know any tricks,' Jahan said in a voice so low he wasn't sure if he actually said it.

'I remember you saying that.' Mihrimah gestured to her nursemaid, who produced a dozen circlets from the inside of her long, loose jacket. 'Here, start with these. *Dada* and I will come and check how you are getting along.'

That week Jahan spent every afternoon tossing circlets to Chota, all of which the elephant ignored. Circlets would be replaced by hoops, hoops by balls, and, eventually, balls by apples. Only the latter worked: Chota cared to catch apples so that he could send them to his stomach.

Even so, Mihrimah and her nursemaid came every day. When Chota learned a new trick, the Princess commended him and rewarded him with sweet treats. When the beast failed, she encouraged him with even sweeter words. Once again, the white elephant had brought the Princess and the mahout together. Yet they were not children any longer. Both had grown fast. And, although they tried not to glance at each other in that way, they could not help but notice the changes in each other's bodies. Meanwhile, Hesna Khatun was the sullen, silent witness of all.

Jahan taught the Princess the things he had learned since he had arrived at the menagerie. He showed her how to tell an oak tree's age by counting the rings inside its trunk, how to preserve a butterfly, how resin turned into dazzling amber. He told her how ostriches could run faster than horses or how the stripes on every tiger were unique in the way the fingerprints of humans were. She, too, began to confide in him. Little by little, she told him about her childhood, her brothers and her mother. Being the only daughter amid boys, one of whom was destined for the throne, she had felt lonely, she said. 'They loved me but they never paid enough attention to me. I was different. Because I was different, I was lonely. Can you understand that, Jahan?'

Jahan nodded. That was the one thing he understood well – the loneliness that came with being different.

The one person Mihrimah would never talk about was her father. Both the mahout and the Princess were behaving as though the Sultan wasn't there, in the midst of their lives. Yet, deep inside, they both knew that if he were ever to hear of these garden escapades, all hell would break loose and Jahan would not only lose his job but in all likelihood be sent to a dungeon, where he might be forgotten till the end of time.

Before the circumcision celebrations, the plague arrived. First appearing on the outskirts of the city, in the hovels by the port of Scutari, it spread faster than wildfire, jumping from one house to the next, the curse scattered in the wind. Death settled over Istanbul like a fog that wouldn't lift, seeping through every hole and crack. It fluttered about in the sea breeze, frothed in the yeast of bread, brewed in the thick, bitter coffee. Little by little people stopped going about; shrinking from gatherings, they sank into solitude. The splash of oars and the murmurs of oarsmen could not be heard even on the quietest evenings. No one wished to journey from one shore to the other if they didn't have to. Never had Istanbulites been so afraid of standing out in the crowd. Never had they been so afraid of offending God.

For He had a peevish disposition, the God of the early days of the plague. People were forever worried about the wrong word escaping from their lips, the wrong hand touching their skin, the wrong smell filling their nostrils. They bolted their doors and darkened their windows to avoid the sunrays that spread the disease. Each quarter became hedged in, each street a citadel no one ventured beyond. They spoke in hushed tones, hunched their shoulders and dressed down, wrapped up in modesty. Coarse fabric was substituted for fine linen cloth; elaborate headdresses were abandoned. Golden coins – thrust into jugs, locked into chests – were buried deep. The wives of the wealthy hid their jewellery and slipped into the garments of their handmaids in the hopes of gaining God's favour. Promises were made to go on pilgrimage to Mecca this year and to feed the poor in Arabia. Istanbul was bartering with God – offering habits, offering sacrificial lambs, offering prayers, losing, losing.

Yumrucuk they were called – too pretty a name for the swellings that appeared on the armpits, thighs and necks of the victims. Upon closer inspection, some saw the unmistakable face of Azrael. A sneeze was an ominous sign – people flinched when they heard one. That is how it began. The body broke into boils that swiftly grew bigger, darker. Then came the fever, the vomiting.

It was in the wind, they said; the night air, soiled like grime, was infested with miasma. The rooms in which the victims met their end were scrubbed with vinegar, whitewashed with lime, sprinkled with holy water from Mecca, then abandoned. Nobody wanted to linger in a place with a resentful ghost.

That the rich and mighty were also dying was consolation for some; a sign of hopelessness for others. When a man fell sick, his wives would start quarrelling about who would attend him. Ordinarily, the eldest – or the barren, if there was one – wife would take over. At times a concubine would be sent for. There were men who had four wives and a dozen concubines but still breathed their last alone.

The corpses were carried on carts pulled by oxen, the screech of wheels pulsating on the cobblestones and a sharp tang following along. The cemeteries on the slopes of hills grew over-full, bloated like the sheep slaughtered, skinned and hung from trees on Eid. The gravediggers made each new pit deeper and wider than the previous one, at times burying bodies by the dozen. They kept it to themselves that most of the dead had been neither washed nor shrouded. Some were laid to rest without so much as a gravestone. Grief was an indulgence only a few could afford. Death had to stop harassing the living for the dead to be properly mourned. When the plague had gone, only then would kin and kith beat their breasts and shed their tears to their heart's content. For now, grief was pickled and preserved, kept next to the salted meat and dried peppers in the cellars, to be partaken of in better times.

Ships were sent back without having offloaded their merchandise; caravans were ordered to change their routes. The malady had sprung from the West, like all evils. Travellers, wherever they might be coming from, were met with suspicion. Runaways, itinerant dervishes, nomads, vagabonds, Gypsies – anyone without roots was unwelcome.

Midsummer, the disease seized the Grand Vizier Ayas Pasha – a man believed to be all-powerful. His death unsettled the seraglio. Suddenly, even the walls of the palace were not strong enough to keep the contagion at bay. That same week four concubines got infected, fear darker than kohl swirling in the corridors of the harem. They said Hurrem shut herself in a chamber with her children and refused to see anyone other than the Sultan. She cooked her own food, boiled her own water, even washed her own garments, distrusting the servants.

In the menagerie three trainers died, each in the springtime of life. And Taras the Siberian hid in his shed for days, for everyone hated him, still alive, old and frail as he was. Gone were the days when people didn't want to be seen on the streets. They hurried to mosques, synagogues and churches to pray and repent, repent and pray. Their sins had brought the calamity, the ones they had committed and were sure to commit. It was God's wrath. The flesh was weak. No wonder black roses bloomed on their bodies. Jahan listened to these words, his heart pulsing in the hollow of his throat, believing and disbelieving. Had God created humans, with their foibles, just so as to be able to punish them afterwards?

'We trespassed,' said the imams. 'Sin entered the world,' said the priests. 'Repent we must,' said the rabbis. And the people did, thousands of them. Many turned pious – none more so than the Sultan. Wine was forbidden, wine-makers punished; musical instruments were burned in bonfires, taverns were closed, brothels were sealed, opium dens remained as empty as discarded walnut shells. The preachers spoke only about pestilence and profanity and how they were intertwined, like the plait of an odalisque.

Then, as if in unison, people stopped saying it was because of them. It was *others* who had brought this upon the city, *others* with their impiety and debauchery. Fear turned into resentment; resentment into rage. And rage was a ball of flame you could not hold in your hands for too long; it had to be thrown at someone.

In late July a mob entered the Jewish neighbourhood around Galata Tower. Doors were marked with tar, men were beaten, a rabbi who resisted was cudgelled to death. A Jewish cobbler was rumoured to have poisoned all the wells and cisterns and creeks in Istanbul, spreading the disease. Dozens had been arrested and had already confessed to their crime. That the confessions were obtained under torture was a detail to which no one paid attention. Had the Jews not been expelled from towns in Saxony only a few years ago, and many more burned at the stake in the lands of Frangistan? There was a reason why they carried calamity wherever they went – an ill omen following them like a shadow. They kidnapped children to use their blood in dark rituals.

The charges grew like a river swollen with rain. Finally, Sultan Suleiman issued a *firman*. The local kadis would not be able to give verdicts on blood libel and the few judges who now took on such cases wished not to do so. The accusations waned.

It wasn't the Jews. It was the Christians. They never went to *hamam*, dirty to the core. They did not wash after they coupled with their wives. They drank wine, and, as if this was not sin enough, they called it the blood of Jesus, whom they dared to name God. Worst of all, they ate pork – the meat of an animal that wallowed in its own filth and devoured decayed flesh with maggots. The plague must have been contracted from pig-eaters. The same folk who had terrorized the Jewish streets were seen attacking the Christian quarters later on.

A saddler in Eyup assumed the leadership of the throng. He preached that the Jews and the Christians were People of the Book and, though in error, they were not evil. It wasn't they who were the culprits. It was the Sufis, with their chanting and whirling. Who could be more dangerous than someone who called himself a Muslim and yet had nothing to do with Islam? Did they not say they had no fear of hell and no wish for heaven? Did they not address God as if He were their equal and even said there was God under their cloak? Blasphemy had brought on the doom. Mobs patrolled the streets, wielding truncheons, hunting for heretics. They were neither stopped by the Subashi and his guards nor arrested afterwards.

On Friday, after the evening prayer, they set upon the twisting streets of Pera. Men, and boys as young as seven, with torches in their hands, joined by more along the way, delved into the houses of ill-repute, dragged out the whores and pimps, and set the buildings on fire. One woman, who was so fat she could barely move, was tied up to a pole and whipped, crimson paths on rolls of flesh. A *hunsa*★ was stripped naked, spat upon, shaved from head to toe and dunked into shit. But it was a dwarf woman, they said, who bore the brunt of it, though nobody quite knew why. She was rumoured to be quite close to the Chief White Eunuch and capable of many a contrivance. The next morning, shortly after dawn, stray dogs found her caked in blood and faeces, her nose broken, her ribs crushed, yet somehow still alive.

★ Hermaphrodite.

Only when the mob, now ready to punish the gentry, began to boast of marching to the palace did the Subashi intervene, arresting eleven men. They were hanged the same day, their bodies left swinging in the breeze for everyone to see. By the time the plague left, Istanbul was 5,742 souls fewer in number and the cemeteries were full to bursting.

The same week Jahan received another nasty letter, this one clearly signed by Captain Gareth. With the help of a kitchen boy he sent the seaman the few coins he had put aside, hoping this would keep him quiet for a while. Laden with such worries, he was slow to pick up the new gossip in town.

Lutfi Pasha, the man who had recommended the right builder for the bridge over the River Pruth but then disagreed with him, had taken the place of the late Grand Vizier Ayas Pasha. And the Chief Royal Architect, who had passed away of old age, had been succeeded by none other than carpenter Sinan. It was the talk of the town that two men who did not get along had been promoted, by some twist of fate, exactly around the same time, as if God wished to see whether they would clash – and, if so, who would survive.

Proud and august, for over a thousand years the Hippodrome had seen no end of festivities – always packed, always rowdy. The spectators were men of all ages. Should they like a show, they roared and laughed and sat upright, as though they had a hand in the performance. Should they not take delight in what they saw, they stamped their feet, uttered curses, threw whatever was in their hands. Easy to amuse, hard to please, the audience had changed little since the time of Constantine.

Far off, in the middle of the wooden stalls, stood a terrace adorned with golden tassels. Inside was Sultan Suleiman, seated on a high chair from where he could see and be seen. Tall and lithe, he had a long neck and a short beard. He was attended by the Grand Vizier Lutfi Pasha – who had been married to the Sultan's sister – and other members of the *diwan*. Separated from the Sultan by brocade hangings was the Sultana, surrounded by her handmaidens. Silk curtains and latticed panels shielded the women from the crowd's eyes. Other than those few from the imperial harem, there were no females present.

Foreign emissaries had been ushered into a separate booth. The ambassador of Venice sat upright with a distant look in his eyes and a sapphire brooch on his *zimarra* that had not escaped Jahan's attention. Next to the Venetian were the envoy of Ragusa, the delegates of the Medici of Florence, the podestà of Genoa, the legate of the King of Poland and eminent travellers from Frangistan. They were easy to recognize – not only because of their garments but also because of their expressions, a mixture of disdain and disbelief.

The festivities had been going on for days. At night, flooded with light, Istanbul shone brighter than the eyes of a young bride. Lamps, torches and fireworks punctured the gloom. Caïques glided along the waters of the Golden Horn like shooting stars. Confectioners paraded with sugar-sculptures of man-eating sea-creatures and birds with feathers of every colour. Up and down the streets, giant frames of flowers were displayed. So many sheep were butchered that the creek behind the slaughterhouses ran crimson. Pageboys scurried about, humping trays of rice dripping with fat from sheep's tails. Those who'd had their bellies filled and quenched their thirst with sherbet were treated to *zerde*.* For once, the poor and the rich tucked into the same dishes.

The two princes had been circumcised alongside a hundred poor boys. Sons of candle-makers, lime-burners and cadgers had wailed together with the royal highnesses. Now lying in bed, clad in gowns, 102 of them sobbed whenever they recalled the distress they had gone through, and chuckled at the shadow play being performed to make the memory go away.

Jahan, wide-eyed and terrified, walked in the midst of the frenzy. He had been asked to perform with Chota on the last day. Early in the morning he had brought the elephant to the barns beside the Hippodrome. Much as he hated the fetters around his feet, Chota had settled down, munching apples and leaves. Jahan envied his aplomb and wished some of it would rub off on him. The night before the mahout had slept in fits and starts; his lips had bled from his constant chewing of them.

Other animals made an appearance ahead of them: lions, tigers, monkeys, ostriches, gazelles and a giraffe newly shipped from Egypt. Falconers paraded with hooded birds, jugglers tossed rings, fire-eaters devoured flames and a tightrope-walker crossed a hawser stretched high above. Then came the guilds: stone-cutters carrying hammers and chisels; gardeners pushing carts of roses; architects with miniature models of the mosques they had built. At the head of this last guild strode Sinan, wearing a kaftan trimmed with ermine. When he noticed Jahan, he gave the boy a warm smile. Jahan would have returned one in kind had he not been so anxious.

At long last it was their turn. Praying, Jahan opened the gates, letting Chota out. Passing by a lonely obelisk, brought here from Alexandria by the Emperor Theodosius long ago, they ambled down the track beaten by hundreds of feet and hooves. Light reflected off the tiny mirrors sewn on Chota's mantle – green velvet embroidered with purple patterns, courtesy of the Sultana.

Upon seeing them, the audience hollered with joy. Jahan walked in front of Chota, holding his reins, though the truth was that the

---

* Rice sweetened with saffron and honey.

elephant set his own pace. When they reached the royal terrace, they came to a halt. Jahan laid eyes on the Sultan. He looked solid, imperturbable. To his left was the partition behind which the Sultana and her women had taken seats. Even though Jahan could not get a glimpse of Hurrem, he felt her distrustful eyes piercing him. The thought that beautiful Mihrimah, too, was there, watching his every gesture, doubled his worries. His mouth went dry; his stomach lurched; his legs trembled as he bowed down.

Still shaking, he dug into his pocket and produced a yarn of wool. This he tossed to Chota. The elephant caught it with his trunk, threw it back to him. They repeated the trick a couple of times. Jahan took out the sparkling rings that Mihrimah had given him. He threw them, one at a time, to Chota, who snatched each one out of the air, waving and flinging it aside, as if he didn't care. He then swayed his huge body to and fro, dancing. The audience hooted with laughter. Raising his cane, Jahan scolded him. Chota stood still, ashamed. It was part of the show, like everything else. As a sign of peace the boy handed Chota an apple. In return Chota plucked the daffodil fastened to the mahout's robe and gave it to him. More laughter from the spectators.

Next Jahan balanced a cone on his head. He added another cone, then another, stacking seven of them in total. He shouted, 'Up!'

With his trunk the elephant grabbed him by the waist and placed him above his neck so gingerly the cones remained intact.

'Down!' Jahan ordered.

Slowly, laboriously, Chota crouched. Still on his back, Jahan steadied himself, the wind drying the sweat trickling across his face. Having no knees, elephants found it hard to bend down. Jahan was hoping the Sultan of the Land and the Sea would understand and appreciate. No sooner had Chota managed to squat down than Jahan opened his arms wide and bellowed in triumph. Simultaneously, he saw something coming towards them fast. With a thud it fell on the ground. Jahan jumped off, picked it up. It was a pouch filled with coins. A generous gift from Sultan Suleiman. The mahout bowed; the elephant trumpeted; the audience went wild.

Then came the final act. Chota, representing Islam, would confront a wild boar that stood for Christianity. It was a play habitually performed by a bear and a pig, but, since the elephant was more majestic and clearly the darling of the public, at the last minute the role had been assigned to Chota.

The moment Jahan saw the hog, swinging its tusks, scraping its hooves, his insides twisted into a knot. The brute was smaller than Chota, for sure, but there was a madness in it, a rage whose source he couldn't place. As soon as its chains were removed, the animal made for them like an arrow. It could have gored Jahan's thigh had he not dodged it in time. The audience chortled, ready to side with the hog, should the mahout and the elephant disappoint them.

Jahan wasn't the only one paralysed. To his dismay, Chota was rooted to the spot, eyes half closed. Shouting, Jahan nudged him with his cane. He uttered honeyed words, promising sweet treats and mud baths. Nothing helped. The elephant that had fiercely assailed enemy soldiers and killed several on the battleground had gone numb.

The hog, having lost interest in the elephant, circled then charged Jahan, knocking him to the ground.

'Hey, here!'

Out of nowhere Mirka the bear-tamer appeared, shouting to draw the hog's attention. He carried a spear in his hand, his beast lumbering behind. The two of them were familiar to this game. The bear growled. Furiously grunting, the hog attacked with its mouth wide open. Jahan watched it all as if through a veil. The sounds, though terrible, were muffled by the din of the crowd. The bear – its curved claws sharpened – slashed and ripped, gutting the hog. The animal's intestines gushed out, releasing a sickening smell. Its back legs twitched and kicked. A shriek rose as life abandoned its body, so fierce and unearthly that it pierced the spectators to their very marrow. Stepping on the dying hog with his boot, Mirka saluted his audience. Instantly, he was rewarded with a pouch. As he grabbed it, he looked at Jahan with a smirk he didn't bother to hide. Behind him, small as a mouse, Jahan averted his gaze, wishing with all his heart for an earthquake that would swallow him up.

While the mahout was considering vanishing, the elephant was getting incensed. Some of the spectators had been hurling pebbles at him. Chota flapped his ears and trumpeted. Seeing their success in upsetting so large a creature, the audience began to throw other things: wooden spoons, rotten apples, metal scabbards, chestnuts from a nearby tree . . . Jahan urged Chota to stay calm, his voice no more than a mosquito buzz in the uproar.

All at once, the elephant charged straight for the stalls. Baffled, Jahan ran behind him, waving his arms, yelling. He watched faces in the audience change from astonishment to terror. People scurried left and right, screaming, trampling on those who had fallen down. Jahan caught up with Chota, yanked his tail. The animal might have crushed him, but the mahout wasn't thinking. Guards with swords and spears circled them, though none seemed to know what they were doing. In the commotion Chota tore down the banners, squashed ornaments and ploughed into the booth of foreign emissaries. In trying to get out of the beast's way, the Venetian envoy took a headlong tumble, his precious *zimarra* tearing as someone stepped on it. Jahan saw the sapphire fall off. In a trice he stepped on it and, certain that no one was looking, he grabbed it and hid it in his sash.

When he turned to the elephant again, to his horror he found Chota by the royal terrace. Sultan Suleiman had not budged. He stood erect, his jaw jutting out, his face unreadable. The Grand Vizier was the opposite. Foaming at the mouth, he barked orders here and there. As if he had sensed the man's hatred, the animal moved directly towards the Vizier. He snatched the man's turban off his head and swung it in the air, as if it were another trick he had practised.

'Guards!' Lutfi Pasha shouted.

Out of the corner of his eye Jahan saw an archer aiming at Chota's head. With a cry he dashed towards the man, who, only a second before, had loosed his arrow.

A sharp pain burned his right shoulder and he let out a howl. He wobbled on his feet and collapsed. At his voice the elephant slowed down. So did the people in the first rows. Stunned into silence, they now stared at the mahout bleeding on the ground. It was then that the Sultan, slowly and calmly, stood up and did something no one was expecting. He chuckled.

Had Chota attacked the Lord of the Land and the Sea instead of the Vizier, what might have happened was unimaginable. But, as things stood, the Sultan's mirth saved his life. Someone fetched Lutfi

Pasha's turban, soiled and flattened, and handed it reverentially to him. The Vizier grabbed it from the man's hands but refused to put it on his head. One by one the audience returned to their seats. Oblivious to the wreckage he had caused, Chota stomped towards the exit.

'What've you done, imbecile!' Jahan hollered from the stretcher he was being carried on. 'They'll chop off your balls . . . send you to the slaughterhouse, cook you with cabbage and onions. And they will cast me into the dungeon!'

He would have loved to have kicked a bucket, punched a barrel, smashed a vase. Yet his body felt heavy while his mind spun round in circles. The only thing that outweighed this excruciating pain was his anger – aimed mostly at himself.

A cart brought him to the menagerie, where Olev took one look at him and another at the arrow sticking out of his flesh and nodded at the Chinese twins. Both men disappeared, only to shortly return with a bag of opium.

'What's in there? What are the blades for?' asked Jahan. His neck was damp, his skin pallid, his lips cold.

'Curious lad,' said Olev, as he placed metals of various sizes on a tray. 'I'm going to take that thing out.'

'But how?'

No one answered. Instead they forced him to drink a foul-smelling greenish tea, *maslak*, which was made from dried cannabis leaves. Even the first sip made his head whirl faster. By the time he had finished the cup, the world had acquired a strange luminosity, with colours melting into one another. The opium was mashed into a pulp and spread over the wound. They carried him into the garden so that he could benefit from the remaining daylight.

'Bite this!' Olev instructed.

Dazed, Jahan closed his teeth around the rag they shoved into his mouth. Not that it made much of a difference. When the arrow was pulled out his scream was so loud it sent the birds in the aviary flapping from their roosts.

That evening, as he lay in bed aching all over, Sinan appeared by the door, his gaunt cheeks dim in the shadows. He sank down beside him, the way he had done on that battle's starless night.

'You all right?'

The boy winced in lieu of an answer, his eyes brimming with tears.

'You're not good at performing tricks, are you? Entertaining people is not quite your thing,' Sinan said. 'Still, one has to admire your courage and your love for the elephant.'

'Will I be punished?'

'I think you've been punished enough. Our Sultan knows this.'

'But . . . Lutfi Pasha hates me.'

'Well, he doesn't approve of me either,' said Sinan, dropping his voice a notch.

'Because of the bridge?'

'Because of *defiance*. He has not forgotten. He is used to having everyone worshipping his every word. Those who surround themselves with grovellers who praise everything they do will not forgive the honest man who tells the truth.'

Around them darkness gathered as Sinan asked the boy about his life. Jahan told him about his sisters, his stepfather and his mother's death. For the first time since he came to this city he told his true story, without lies and fabrications. There was no mention of Hindustan.

'Will you go back?' asked Sinan.

'I shall when I'm wealthy and strong. I need to hurry up, as I want to confront my stepfather before he gets too old.'

'So you want to return to revenge your mother?'

'That's right. I swear I will as God is my witness.'

Sinan lapsed into thought. 'That sketch you sent me – whose mansion is that?'

'Oh, it is the Grand Mufti's. I was there the day he tried the heretic. But I made a few changes to the house.'

'Why?'

'I noticed it's quite windy up there, *effendi*. The windows were made small for that reason, but they don't let enough light through. I thought if there was a gallery upstairs, covered with latticework, there'd be more light and the women could watch the sea without being seen.'

Sinan raised an eyebrow. 'I see . . . I thought the drawing was good.'

'Really?' Jahan asked incredulously.

'You'd better learn algebra and measurement. You ought to gain an understanding of numbers. I watched you while we were building that bridge. You are smart, curious, and you learn fast. You can become a builder. You have it in you.'

Pleased to hear this, Jahan said, 'I liked helping with the bridge . . . Chota was happy, too. He doesn't like to be kept in the barn all the time.'

'You are a bright boy, mahout. I want to help you. But there are many bright boys around.' Sinan paused, as if waiting for his words to sink in. 'If you wish to excel at your craft, you have to convince the universe why it should be you rather than someone else.'

What a bizarre thing to say! Jahan blinked, hoping for an explanation, but there was none. Silence poured into the space between them until Sinan spoke again. 'Take a look around. Every man you see here is the son of an Adam. Neither noble nor rich by birth. It doesn't matter who your father is or where you come from. All you need to do to climb up is to work hard. This is the way in the Ottoman palace.'

Jahan lowered his head.

'You are talented, but you ought to be tutored. You must learn languages. If you promise to put your heart into this, I'll help you get lessons at the palace school. Men in the highest positions have been educated there. You have to strive as hard as they did. Year after year.'

'I am not afraid of work, *effendi*,' said Jahan.

'I know but you must let go of the past,' said Sinan as he stood up. 'Resentment is a cage, talent is a captured bird. Break the cage, let the bird take off and soar high. Architecture is a mirror that reflects the harmony and balance present in the universe. If you do not foster these qualities in your heart, you cannot build.'

His cheeks burning, Jahan said, 'I don't understand . . . Why do you help me?'

'When I was about your age, I was fortunate enough to have a good master. He is long dead, may God have mercy on his soul. The only way I can pay him back is by helping others,' Sinan said. 'Besides, something tells me you are not who you seem to be. You and the elephant are like brothers. But you are no mahout, my son. There is more to you, I believe. You have not told me the entire truth.'

'The elephant is my family now,' said Jahan, without quite meeting the architect's eye.

Sinan let out his breath slowly. 'Get some rest; we shall talk again.'

As the master left the barn, a tear rolled down Jahan's face and dropped on to his hand. He looked at it in confusion. He had a wounded shoulder and aching limbs, yet he couldn't tell where his pain came from.

Housed in the third courtyard, the palace school had 342 youths. The brightest *devshirme*★ boys attended the classes. They mastered Islamic law, *hadith*, philosophy, history of the prophets and the Qur'an. They studied mathematics, geometry, geography, astronomy, logic and oration, and learned enough languages to wend their way through the Tower of Babel. Depending on their abilities, they excelled in poetry, music, calligraphy, tiling, pottery, marquetry, ivory carving, metalwork and weaponry. Upon graduation some went into high-ranking posts in the government and military. Others became architects and scientists.

All of the tutors were male, some eunuchs. They carried long sticks, which they did not hesitate to employ to punish the slightest disobedience. The halls were silent, the rules strict. The children of Albanians, Greeks, Bulgarians, Serbs, Bosnians, Georgians and Armenians were taken into the levy of boys, but not the children of Turks, Kurds, Iranians and Gypsies.

Jahan found the classes too hard to follow. He expected to be thrown out at any moment. Yet weeks passed by. Ramadan fell during midsummer. Suddenly days were heavier, nights bursting with smells and sounds. Shops were open longer, funfairs teeming with people went on until late in the evening. The Janissaries, the scholars, the artisans, the beggars, even the addicts – many of whom bolted down on the sly a reddish-brown paste that slowly, very slowly, dissolved in their bellies, helping them to cope with abstinence – were fasting. Even as Eid came and went, no one inquired about him and Chota. It was as if they all had forgotten there was an elephant in the menagerie. Jahan sank into gloom. He suspected the Grand Vizier of being behind this. Clearly, the man had not forgiven Chota for what had happened at the Hippodrome and was biding his time to skin them alive. Little did he know that the dreaded Lutfi Pasha – the second most powerful man in

★ A system whereby the best-looking and most intelligent Christian boys were removed from their families, converted to Islam and recruited to serve the Sultan.

the empire, the royal groom who had married Sultan Suleiman's sister – was in deep trouble.

It all began when, in a house of ill-repute near the Galata Tower, a whore by the name of Kaymak,★ due to the lightness of her skin, refused to sleep with a customer – a brute with money but no mercy. The man beat her. Not satisfied, he took out the scourge that he carried with him and flogged her. Now that – according to the unwritten and unspoken rules of the bagnios of Constantinopolis – was beyond the pale. Ill-treating a whore was understandable; horsewhipping her, nowhere in the book. Everyone in the brothel ran to the woman's rescue, pelting the client with dung. But the man was not one to concede defeat. Foaming at the mouth, he complained to the kadi, who, fearing reprisal from the pimps, sought a middle ground. In the meantime the incident had reached the ears of Lutfi Pasha.

For quite some time the Grand Vizier had resolved to purge the streets of debauchery. Bent on shutting down the bawdy houses, he aimed to banish their fallen inhabitants to places that were so far away they would never be able to return. In the person of the flogged whore, he found the opportunity he had been waiting for. By punishing one he would teach a lesson to all loose women, of which there were too many in Istanbul. Casting aside the kadi's verdict, Lutfi Pasha proclaimed it was the whore who was in the wrong and her genitals should be cut off. She would then be made to sit backwards on a donkey and taken around so that everyone could see what awaited the likes of her.

A punishment of this sort had never been heard of before. When Shah Sultan, Sultan Suleiman's sister, learned about the sentence her husband deemed fit for an ill-starred woman, she was appalled. She – used to having her every whim obeyed – confronted the Grand Vizier, hoping to persuade him to change his mind. She waited till after he had been served with a mouth-watering supper – soup of intestines,

★ Cream.

pheasant stew with onions, Ozbek pilaf with raisins and baklava, Lutfi Pasha's favourite – thinking that if she soothed his stomach, she could soothe his temperament as well.

No sooner had the servants removed the low table, washed the couple's hands with rosewater, poured their coffees and disappeared down the corridors of the house than Shah Sultan murmured, as if to herself, 'Everybody is raving about this prostitute.'

The Grand Vizier said nothing. An orange streak of light seeped in through the window, giving everything an eerie glow.

'Is it true she'll be punished in such an awful way?' asked Shah Sultan sweetly.

'We reap what we sow,' said Lutfi Pasha.

'But is it not too harsh?'

'Harsh? Nay, only befitting.'

'Have you no mercy, husband?' she asked, her voice tinged with contempt.

'Mercy is for those who deserve it.'

Trembling, Shah Sultan rose to her feet and said the words only she could dare. 'Do not come to my bed tonight. Nor tomorrow night nor the ones after.'

Lutfi Pasha paled. His royal bride was surely the bane of his life. People who envied him for having her were fools! Marrying the Sultan's sister or daughter was a curse one could wish only on one's enemy. In order to wed her, he had had to divorce his helpmate – the mother of his four children – of many years, for a Sultan's sister would never be the second wife. In return, had she shown him any gratitude? To the contrary. She carried not a drop of compliance in her blood. Frowning on everything he did, she poured scorn on him day and night, even when the servants were around. Hence, when the Grand Vizier opened his mouth, it was his frustration that spoke. He said, 'Never been keen on your bed anyhow.'

'How dare you?' Shah Sultan said. 'You who are a servant of my brother!'

Lutfi Pasha pulled at his beard, plucking a few strands of hair.

'If I ever hear you've gone ahead with your awful punishment and made this poor woman suffer, be assured that you are no longer any husband of mine!' She strode out of the chamber, leaving him boiling in his anger.

The truth was that Shah Sultan, like many others, had expected the Grand Vizier to spare the prisoner at the eleventh hour. This would be killing two birds with one stone. He would send fear to the hearts of all who sinned and gather respect by showing clemency. Thus Shah Sultan was greatly dismayed when one crisp morning, the sentence was announced by town-criers and carried out. That same day, when Lutfi Pasha came home, he found his wife waiting, fuming.

'Shame on you,' she said, despite knowing that the servants were eavesdropping. 'You are a stone-hearted man!'

'Watch your tongue, wife. That's no way to speak to your husband.'

'You call yourself a husband? You who can only beat hapless women.'

Beside himself with rage, Lutfi Pasha pushed his wife against the tiled wall, and slapped her.

'I will not stay married to a demon like you,' she said, crying, calling him names so contemptible even the gossipers would not repeat them the following day.

Lutfi Pasha made a lunge for his mace. That was when a black eunuch dashed into the room, followed by the maidservants, the drudges, the scullery maids, the cook and the kitchen boys. Together they tied up his hands, gagged his mouth and, with their mistress's blessing, knocked him around.

The next morning Sultan Suleiman heard that his Grand Vizier had attempted to mace his sister. That was the end of Lutfi Pasha. Deposed from his rank, deprived of his wealth, he was exiled to Demotika so fast he did not have time to pack up his things or to bid farewell to anyone.

Back in the menagerie, Jahan listened to all this, bewildered. How soon things changed and how low people fell and from what heights. Even those whom he thought untouchable. Or, perhaps, especially those. It was as if there were two invisible arcs: with our deeds and words we ascended; with our deeds and words we descended.

One afternoon, immersed in thought, Jahan walked back from the palace school to the menagerie. As he approached his shed, he heard a cough that froze his blood. When he entered, he found Captain Gareth waiting for him.

'Look who's comin'! Surprise! I'm back from the deep. I thought I'd better see how my little thief was doing. He must have missed me.'

Jahan said nothing, lest his voice betray his fright. The man had been drinking again. He could smell the rank odour of beer on his breath. His teeth were lined up in his mouth like barrel staves black with tar.

The Captain kept his gaze steadfastly on the mahout. 'What? You look like you've seen a ghost.'

'I thought you were gone. It has been a long time,' Jahan confessed.

'My ship fell through a hole at the bottom of the sea. Lost eighteen men in the devil's worst storm. Lucky me, I survived but fell captive. I contracted ague; they thought I was dead. I've been to hell and didn't like the damn thing, so I returned. What, you're not happy to see me?'

'I am.'

The man flashed him a look of distrust. 'You've been here long enough. What have you stolen? Show me. You must have a treasure trove by now, being the Princess's pet.'

Jahan flinched at the mention of her name. How did he know about Mihrimah? There were spies everywhere. He said, as calmly as he could manage, '*Effendi*, it's not easy. The doors are guarded.'

'I said, what did you get for me?' Captain Gareth sharpened his voice, ready to use it like a weapon. His skin got a shade darker, including the scar on his face.

Jahan had hidden the stolen things under the lilac tree. The Captain immediately confiscated the sapphire brooch, but then made a weird sound, as though he were choking on his tongue. Jahan stared at him in terror, until he realized that the man was laughing. After he'd had a good cackle, he turned sullen. 'Is this all? What do you take me for, an idiot?'

'I'm telling the tru—'

In one swift move the man pulled a dagger from his jacket and held it to Jahan's throat. 'I don't like liars. Never did. Give me one reason why I shouldn't skin you alive.'

The end of the blade piercing his flesh, Jahan swallowed hard. 'I have got news. I am . . . working with the Chief Royal Architect.'

'So?'

'We'll be building mosques . . . for the Sultan. Lots of money comes in.'

The pressure of the cold metal slackened. Captain Crazyhead took a step backwards and regarded the boy as if noticing him for the first time. 'Talk!'

'The Sultan sets great store by the buildings Sinan raises for him and his family. Imagine, he spends more coins on stones than on gems.'

'Fine, then . . .' the Captain said in a rasping whisper. 'You couldn't steal from the palace. Steal from the building works. Earn your master's trust. Be a good lad. Get your hands on the cash. I saved your skin on that damned ship, remember? Don't make me take the favour back.'

'I won't, *effendi*. You won't regret waiting this long. I shall bring you riches. Soon *insha'Allah*,' said Jahan, and in that moment he believed what he said.

By the end of the summer a new disease was clawing at the Ottoman land. Blisters, vomiting, fever, death. *Sheitan's spittle* they called it, those reddish spots. Many perished in a matter of days. Among them was Shehzade Mehmed, only twenty-one years old, son of Suleiman and Hurrem, the apple of their eyes.

The Sultan was devastated. Clad in coarse robes, refusing to see anyone, he devoted himself to prayer. Istanbul mourned with him. Lamps were dimmed, voices hushed. Stores closed early; weddings and bar mitzvahs and circumcisions were kept in abeyance. The fishing boats circling the Serai Gate passed by soundlessly, as if grief were a sleeping baby not to be awakened. The storytellers in the bazaars, the wandering balladeers, the hawkers on the streets, even the minstrels who went to bed with songs and got up with songs – all fell silent. The only thing that disturbed the quiet was the rain. It pelted down in such abundance it was thought the sky was shedding tears for all and sundry. It was on a day such as this that Chota and Jahan were, for the first time, honoured with a visit from the Sultan.

Sunken cheeks, sallow skin, drooped shoulders. The Sultan was so unlike the man Jahan had saluted at the Hippodrome that he might not have recognized him were it not for the guards on his heels. Hastily, he bowed down.

'I remember you and your elephant,' said the Sultan.

Blushing, Jahan flinched from the memory of that ominous afternoon.

'How is your shoulder?'

'It's fine, my Lord.'

'The beast, what does he eat? Tell me about it.'

This Jahan did. He raved about how Chota loved the mud, the water and the food, all the while sensing that Sultan Suleiman needed not so much the information as the distraction from grief. He said if you wished to hurt an elephant you ought to go for the trunk. Having no bones, only muscles, the trunk was many things at once: a nose, an upper lip, an arm, a hand. Breathing, smelling, eating, drinking, sucking up water to shower themselves, scratching their ears, rubbing sleep off their eyes – there was no end to the things elephants could achieve with their trunks. Just as human beings were left- or right-handed, so, too, were elephants left- or right-tusked. Jahan concluded Chota was left-tusked.

'Strange that an animal so majestic has a tail this flimsy,' said the Sultan. 'Do you think Allah is reminding us even the strongest have their weaknesses?'

Not knowing how to answer, Jahan fumbled for words. Mercifully, the Sultan went on, 'The Chief Royal Architect told me you and the elephant would help him.'

'That's right, your Highness.'

'Then be ready. You shall put the beast to work again.'

It was only later on that Jahan would find out what the Lord of the Land and the Sea had meant. He had commissioned Sinan to build a mosque for his deceased son. In a fleeting world, where everything was here today and gone tomorrow, the endowment for the beloved Prince would be of solid marble, solid stone.

And this is how, on the seventh day of September, an auspicious time set by the Chief Royal Astronomer Takiyuddin, Jahan found himself on a construction site, watching the first spade pierce the earth. Forty sheep and forty rams were sacrificed, their blood scattered on to four corners, their meat cooked in cauldrons and distributed among the poor and the lepers. Jahan noticed Ebussuud Efendi, with his high turban and flowing robes, in the crowd. Having become the Shayh al-Islam – the Chief Religious Officer – he carried himself with imperiousness. Seeing him up close sent a shiver down Jahan's spine. He recalled with a lingering ache the heretic Majnun Shaykh – his velvet voice, handsome face and unclouded gaze. He had not forgotten him.

Then they were gone – the Sultan, the members of the *diwan*, the onlookers. Only the labourers were left behind. Hundreds of them. Jahan realized there were two kinds of men on a building site: the ones who never looked you in the eye and the ones who, at times, did. The former were the galley slaves. Shackles on their ankles, whipped into submission. Sailors, peasants, pilgrims or travellers whose lives had been reversed so abruptly they could not tell whether this was a delusion or whether the past had been a dream. Surviving on dried biscuits and thin soup, these Christian slaves erected Muslim shrines from dawn to dusk.

Then there were those who, like Jahan, had volunteered. They were paid two aspers per day, given tastier food and were, overall, treated well. Masons, diggers, carpenters, joiners, smiths, glaziers and draughtsmen — each under his guild. Every expense was written down by a scribe and overseen by a foreman.

Everywhere he turned, Jahan saw a flurry of activity. Steel pulleys, windlasses, winches and hawsers. Earlier Sinan had the carpenters assemble a huge treadwheel crane. Groups of men took turns inside, at times walking, at times running, turning the wheel that hoisted the heaviest stones. Jahan thought there was something about a construction site that resembled the deck of a ship. In both there was the innate knowledge that any individual failure would be the failure of all. And success would be doled out in the smallest portions, shredded like the salted, dried meat in their soup. When putting up a building or sailing in the deep, you learned to watch over one another; an enforced togetherness emerged, a brotherhood of sorts. A tacit understanding ruled across the ranks. You accepted that the task at hand was mightier than yourself, and the only way to forge ahead was by toiling together as one. So you buried the dislikes and the fights, unless a mutiny erupted, in which case the world would be turned upside down.

Workmen were no less superstitious than seamen. One could not whistle, whisper or curse while hammering a nail. All three were invitations to Sheitan, who, once his company was requested, never failed to make an appearance. Should the nail puncture the wall upon Sheitan's arrival, his footprint would be embedded in the edifice till the end of time. It wasn't only Muslims who adhered to these rules. So did Christians and Jews. To ward off the evil eye they left a loaf of bread and a pinch of salt on the highest stone erected. At no stage throughout the construction did they wish to see a pregnant woman pass by — or anyone with red hair or bright blue eyes or a hare-lip. Even Sinan could not convince the labourers to work beside a mason with flame-coloured hair.

Some creatures were unpropitious: frogs and pigs and goats with three legs. Others they didn't mind: snakes, scorpions, lizards, centipedes and worms. Packs of stray dogs came and went. With the exception of those from the Shafi'i sect of Islam, the workmen enjoyed having dogs around, for they were loyal, appreciative. Spiders were treasured, as they had saved the Prophet Mohammed. Killing a spider, worse yet, squashing it underfoot, was a grave sin. One other animal deemed to be a harbinger of good fortune was, much to Jahan's delight, the elephant.

Seeing omens in the sky and the earth, they observed nature, every passing bird, every tree root they hit. If there was a smell in the breeze, sharp and pungent, they suspected someone was brewing a potion. Volunteers combed the area, east and west, occasionally returning with a fisherman, mendicant or crone whom they accused of sorcery and would have persecuted further had Sinan not interceded each time, telling them to let the poor person go.

It was wrong to brag on a construction site. One should never rave about one's achievements and always remember to say *insha'Allah*, because everything was in God's hands and nothing in theirs. Whenever there was a public hanging, some labourers snatched a sliver of wood from the gallows and wore it as an amulet, which Jahan never understood – for how could the misery of one man bring anything good to another?

Sinan did not seem to mind these beliefs, though he clearly did not share them. Even so, Jahan would discover that he was superstitious in his own way. He had a talisman that he wore all the time. Two circles, one inside the other, both made of leather, one light, one dark. He fasted for three days before he embarked on a design. Upon finishing it, no matter how great the building, he would leave within it a flaw – a tile placed the wrong side up, an upended stone or a marble chipped on the edge. He made sure the defect was there, visible to the knowing eye, invisible to the public. Only God was perfect.

One of Sinan's loyal foremen was a Christian Arab from the mountains of Lebanon, named Snowy Gabriel. This man had hair, skin, eyelashes and eyebrows that were as white as alabaster; his eyes, much like a rabbit's, turned pink in the sun. Every now and then a newcomer would refuse to work under him, accusing him of bringing bad luck.

Sinan would vouch for him, saying he had been born this way and was the best foreman in seven climes.

Chota helped, pulling cables, yanking tow-ropes, carrying planks and positioning timbers. Once, while he was hauling up a marble column, the cord snapped, and the load came tumbling down. Snowy Gabriel would have been crushed had he not moved aside at the last instant. Yet, for the most part, the days were uneventful, the work dreary. Every morning the mahout and the elephant left the palace and arrived at this site near the Janissary barracks; they paced the same road once the sun went down. By now the townsfolk had got used to the sight of them. Sometimes they waited en route, children mostly. Some, in their belief that the soil where an elephant trod had healing powers, collected clods of earth after they passed.

Jahan observed closely everyone on the construction site, learning fast. But it was Sinan's apprentices that he was dying to know more about. They were closer to the master than anyone else. The three of them. The first, a slender, olive-skinned Anatolian who limped due to a childhood illness, was called Nikola. He would stare at a building, close his eyes, then draw it down to the tiniest detail. Tall and corpulent, the second was born in a forsaken village near the Iranian border and was raised by his grandfather after marauders had killed his parents. His name was Davud; his mind was sharp as a blade. The third was a mute by the name of Yusuf – a youth who so excelled at numbers that Sinan made him recheck each of his own measurements. His face was hairless, his eyes large and green. Due to an accident as a boy, both his hands had been burned and he wore gloves made of buckskin. There were workers who, if it weren't for fear of Sinan, would have given him a hard time. Knowing this, the mute apprentice, like the galley slaves, kept his gaze on the ground.

At the slightest opportunity Jahan would tiptoe next to these three young men and peek over their shoulders at their designs. When he returned to the menagerie, he would imitate what he had seen, drawing on wet clay or dry sand. One part of him was determined to work hard and be like them. Another part thought only about what to steal, when to run away. And the chasm between was so deep and wide he was finding it increasingly difficult to cross. Sooner or later he would have to choose one or the other.

By January the weather had turned bitter. Icicles dangled from the eaves, dangerously beautiful. Istanbul slept under a thick, white blanket. Still the construction carried on. The galley slaves wrapped rags around their feet. Their toes peeked out from scraps of cloth, aflame, swollen.

On one of those mornings the elephant and the mahout departed from the palace at the usual time. Halfway through the ride a dog came running towards them, barking madly, as if it wanted to show them something.

'Let's go and see what it wants!' Jahan yelled from astride Chota's neck.

With a swerve they began to follow the canine. The dog, delighted in getting the attention it wanted, turned left, heading straight to the embankment, where the water had frozen over the shoreline. The elephant sped up.

'Hey, slow down!'

Before Jahan could finish his words, Chota stepped into the inlet, crushing the ice, sinking up to his belly. They halted, the elephant, the mahout, the dog. There was a corpse in the water, so close they could almost touch it. A concubine in all likelihood. Her skin had turned bluish-purple, her hair danced with the waves. Judging by her clothes and the jewel around her neck, she was from a wealthy household, perhaps the palace.

Jahan ordered Chota to trudge ahead, determined to get his hands on the jewel. He was close to his aim when Chota stopped and refused to move. Perched on an elephant in chilly waters, trying not to panic but panicking anyway, feeling ridiculous, Jahan shouted for help. Fortunately, in a little while a carriage pulled by a donkey appeared. On it were five Gypsies. Quietly, they studied the scene.

'Shall we give a hand, Balaban?' asked one man to the tall figure in the front.

'Yeah, help the woman.'

'Are you daft?' Jahan bawled. 'She's already dead! Save us first.'

The man called Balaban, still holding the reins in one hand, climbed atop the carriage. His face was chiselled, his nose crooked from being broken several times, his hair as long as a hermit's and through his half-open mouth a gold-capped tooth showed. With an egret plume attached to his headwear, he looked crazy and grand in equal degrees. 'Talk to me like that again, I'll chop off your tongue and feed it to the cats.'

Jahan fell silent. He watched as the Gypsies quickly made two swift nooses. They used one to catch the elephant by his trunk and the other to grab the body by its hand, pulling them ashore simultaneously. Chota moved hesitantly. A couple of times he staggered, almost sending Jahan into the water. When they reached land, Jahan jumped down with a sigh. He now remembered what the official had told him the day he and the elephant had arrived in the palace. So these were the infamous Gypsies, the half-tribe. Cautiously, he approached them.

'You saved our lives. We're grateful.'

'We done it for the beast,' said Balaban. 'Got one ourselves. Great animals.'

'You have an elephant?' asked Jahan incredulously.

'Her name's Gulbahar. Yours has a strange colour, though,' Balaban said as his gaze wandered. His men had grabbed the dead woman's necklace and were now sending her back to the waters.

Jahan protested, 'You can't do that. She should be buried properly.'

'A bunch of Gypsies show up with a corpse, you think they're goin' to thank us? They'll say we killed her, throw us in gaol. We leave her here, dogs will tear her to pieces. She's safer in water.' He grinned. 'If you're wonderin' about that necklace, consider it a reward for our troubles. She doesn't need it anyhow.'

Jahan did not tell him he had had the same thought himself. Instead he asked, dropping his voice, 'Do you think she was *murdered*?'

'I should've chopped off that tongue of yours; might do you good. Let me give you two pieces of advice. If you don't know what to do with an answer, don't ask the question,' Balaban said.

'What's the second?' asked Jahan.

'Go take care of your beast. He's got frostbite.'

'What?' Jahan darted towards Chota, whose skin, covered with a flimsy coating of ice, was no longer white but a scary pink. The elephant was shivering.

By now the Gypsies had got back to their carriage. Jahan ran behind them. 'Don't leave, I beg you. I don't know what to do.'

'There's only one cure,' said Balaban. 'He needs strong liquor. *Raki.*'

'*Raki?*' said Jahan. 'Can you find any?'

'Not easy. The beast is large. You need a barrel.' The Gypsies shared a savvy smile. 'If we bring you one, who's gonna pay us?'

'Chief Royal Architect Sinan will,' Jahan said, praying it would be true.

Half a barrel of *raki* and several cups were brought. Were those, too, stolen? Jahan did not dare to ask. Diluting the drink with water, they dipped Chota's trunk into it. Perhaps to set an example to the animal, the Gypsies each downed a cup. Then another. Meanwhile the elephant took a gulp and blew it out, wetting them all over. Yet he must have liked the taste, for he went back to the barrel and drank; this time he did not spew up.

An hour later they reached the construction site – Jahan pulling Chota by the reins, the Gypsies in their carriage, singing merrily.

'Where've you been?' Sinan asked, his eyes darting from the elephant to the Gypsies, from the Gypsies to the elephant.

'We had an accident on the way. These men saved us,' said Jahan.

'Is this animal drunk?' Sinan said, watching the elephant sway. He turned to the Gypsies. 'Are they?'

When he heard the story of the barrel, Sinan chuckled. 'I can't have a befuddled beast constructing a holy mosque. Go and don't come back until he's sobered up.'

'Yes, master,' Jahan said with a dry throat. 'Are you upset with me?'

Sinan sighed. 'You have a way of clinging to life. That's good. But curiosity could be a detriment if not guided. We should expand your training.'

'Expand?'

'You shall continue with your lessons at the palace school. In his spare time Nikola can show you how to draw; Davud will instruct you in geometry; Yusuf in numbers. You'll become an apprentice to my apprentices.'

Not quite knowing what this meant but understanding the privilege, Jahan bent forward to kiss Sinan's hand. 'Thank you, master, I'm –'

Just then a deafening rumble pierced the air. They all ran in that direction, including the Gypsies. Several planks had pulled free of their ropes, causing half the scaffolding to come tumbling down, miraculously not hurting anyone. Timber being expensive, so as to save wood, they had made scaffolding with the help of hawsers and dangled the planks from the abutments.

'Must be the evil eye,' said Jahan, trembling. 'How many accidents in a day!'

'Don't judge too soon,' came a voice from behind. It was Balaban the Gypsy, holding a rope in his hand. When he had everyone's attention, he said, with a perfunctory nod, 'This was no accident. Someone has cut the ropes.'

'Why would anyone do such a thing?' asked Sinan.

Balaban gave a sad smile. 'Who knows? Sheitan never runs out of excuses.'

'There's no devil here,' said Sinan. 'My labourers are hard-working people.'

'If you say so . . .' said Balaban. 'But take my word, *effendi*. No harm in being careful. Maybe there is a traitor among you. If I were you, I'd keep my eyes open.'

The culprit was never found. Between the palace school, the menagerie and the construction site, Jahan had barely any time to sit and think. Even his food he had to eat on the move. He understood that to be apprenticed to Master Sinan meant to have to work incessantly. Lately, the Shayh al-Islam had ordered more mosques to be built far and wide. Decree after decree had been issued to inform the public that those who did not attend the Friday prayers would be made an example of. Every Muslim man, in towns and villages, was urged to pray five times a day and to join the nearest congregation. Since the number of mosque-goers had doubled as a result, Sinan and the apprentices had more work than ever.

No sooner had they finished the Shehzade Mosque than they set about the next construction. Jahan had not yet been able to pilfer any aspers from the coffers. Everything was painstakingly supervised and each expense put in writing. But, while he sought out ways to purloin goods for Captain Gareth and dreamed of inflicting harm on his stepfather, he had, unknowingly, become engrossed in the world of draughtsmanship.

He could not get any news about Mihrimah, let alone see her. Oddly, in her absence her significance had grown. Folding his heart like a handkerchief, he kept inside the memory of the afternoons they had spent together. He revealed his longing only to Chota, who was getting heavier by the day, his appetite bigger than his shadow.

In the summer Sinan and the four apprentices began to work on their biggest venture yet: the Suleimaniye. The mosque that the Sultan commissioned for himself would glorify his name for eternity. Long before he settled on where to lay the first stone, Sinan had butchers haul carcasses of cows and sheep. These were suspended from iron rings and left to rot at various locations. Every few days Sinan inspected the meat. Where the decay was faster, the humidity was higher. Since damp gnawed into buildings the way moths ate into fabric, he avoided such spots. He went for a place where the air was dry and the earth solid enough to hold through an earthquake. Settled atop a hill, the mosque, like the sovereign after whom it was named, would keep an eye on the entire city.

Each of the materials was chosen with care. Lead and iron were brought from Serbia and Bosnia, timber from Varna. The marble was from Arab lands, and from the site where King Solomon's palace had once been, the polished surfaces still reflecting the beauty of the Queen of Sheba. One giant column was from Baalbek, the Sun City. Seventeen pillars were removed from the Hippodrome, disturbing the angry ghost of the Empress Theodora.

There were hundreds of them: galley slaves and hired men. Almost half were Christians, a small number were Jews and the rest Muslims. Sinan had appointed a foreman to each division of workers to see to it that things ran smoothly. Even so, he constantly had to cross the site from one end to the other to make sure everything was in order.

'Master, why don't you ride Chota?' Jahan asked. 'He can carry you wherever you wish.'

'You want me to sit on the beast?' Sinan said, amused.

Despite his hesitation when Jahan put the howdah on Chota and invited him to a ride, he did not decline.

Before they set off, Jahan had a quiet word with the elephant. 'Be kind with the master. Don't shake him much.'

In a steady rhythm they clomped around the construction site, and down the gravel path towards the sea, until the sound of hundreds of people working alongside one another had turned into a distant hum. Finally they stopped, watching a wispy fog rise from the shore. Sinan, a childish joy in his voice, said, 'I can ride, it seems.'

From then on, day after day, the architect and the elephant would inspect the site together, the sight of them making the labourers smile. Everyone worked hard. The air hanging over their heads was thick with sweat and dust. But Istanbul was thousands of mouths backbiting, slandering, never satisfied. Such awful things they said. That Sinan had no aptitude for finishing such a lofty task. That he was embezzling wood and marble to enlarge his own house. That, having been born and raised a Christian, he could not put together a holy mosque of such massive proportions – and, even if he did, the dome would collapse on his head.

Their lies harrowed Jahan's soul. Time and again he felt like shouting at the top of his voice on to the rows of houses below, telling them to still their tongues. Every dawn he would wake up hoping the wind would disperse yesterday's rumours; every night he went to sleep crushed under the weight of new accusations.

One afternoon, they had a visit from the Sultan. As soon as Jahan heard the hoofbeats, he knew the gossip had reached the sovereign's ears and tainted his heart. The racket of mallets, saws, axes and hatchets came to a standstill. Into this silence, the Sultan rode like the wind. Pulling the reins of his horse, he glowered from high upon his stallion. He was attired in a modest robe of brown wool – gone were his kaftans of atlas in dazzling colours. With age and gout he had become more pious. Leaving off wine, giving up pleasures, he had ordered the remaining musical instruments in the palace to be burned. By a decision of the *diwan*, the taverns, houses of ill-repute and the recently opened coffee-houses had been closed down; all fermented drinks, including *boza*, which was always in vogue, were forbidden. He frightened Jahan, this new Suleiman.

Bowing, Sinan greeted him. 'Your Highness, you have honoured us.'

'Is it true what I've heard about you? Answer!'

'Could my Lord tell me what he heard about this humble ant?' Sinan said.

'They say you've been wasting precious time with trims and frills – is that true?'

'I can assure my Sultan that I spare no effort for the outside and the inside of his mosque. I intend to build with the finest craftsmanship and –'

'Enough!' the Sultan cut in. 'I've no regard for decorations. Nor should you, if you're wise. I order you to finish at once. Not a day's delay! I want to see the dome, not the embellishments.'

Scolded in front of his workers and apprentices, Sinan paled. Yet when he spoke he sounded calm. 'They are inseparable, the dome and the embellishments.'

'Architect! Have you not heard what happened to the draughtsman of my forefather Mehmet Khan? He had the same name as you. An omen of things to come, you say?'

Sinan answered carefully, as though talking to a surly boy. 'I'm aware of his sad fate, your Highness.'

'Then you know what lies in wait for those who don't keep their promises. Make sure you're not one of them!'

When the Sultan left, they took up work again. Even so, it wasn't the same. There was something new in the air, the smell of despair. Although they neither shirked nor slowed their work, they felt daunted. If they would not be able to please the Sultan, what was the use of keeping their noses to the grindstone? Why work so hard when that work went unappreciated?

During the next days Jahan waited for a chance to talk with Sinan. Only towards the end of the week was he able to approach the master. Surrounded by scrolls, his back hunched, he was drawing. Upon seeing him, Sinan gave a tired smile. 'How are your lessons coming along?'

'I hope I can make you proud, master.'

'I know you will.'

'Master, the other day the Sultan mentioned an architect. The one who had the same name as yours. What happened to him?'

'Oh, Atik Sinan . . .' He paused, as if that said it all.

Then he told the story. Atik Sinan had been the Chief Royal Architect of Sultan Fatih, the Conqueror of Constantinople. Diligent and dedicated, he had excelled at his craft. All had gone well until he started to build a mosque for the Sultan. Fatih wished his mosque to be the most majestic building ever raised. That included the Hagia Sophia. For this purpose he had brought over the tallest columns he could find in seven climes. When he heard that his Chief Royal Architect had shortened these columns without first asking him, he was furious. He accused the architect of deliberately obstructing his aims. Poor Atik Sinan tried to explain: as Istanbul was a city of earthquakes, he had to keep safety in mind, and had shortened the columns to make the edifice stronger. Fatih did not like this answer. He had the architect imprisoned in the worst dungeon, where his hands were chopped off. He was then beaten to death. This talented craftsman of the Ottoman land died alone and in pain in a dark prison cell by the sea. Whoever doubted this story could go and read it on his gravestone.

Jahan's bottom lip trembled. Until then he had always believed it was thieves and miscreants who lived on the edge of danger. Now he saw that even honest artisans dangled from the thinnest of cotton threads. Should the sovereign get upset, he would have them sent to the gibbet. How could one work under such strain?

Sinan, watching him, put a hand on his shoulder. 'Talent is a favour of the divine. To perfect it one must work hard. This is what we must do.'

'But aren't you afraid –'

'My son, I dread the Sultan's wrath as much as you do. Yet that is not why I toil. If there were no hope of reward and no fear of punishment, would I work less? I don't believe so. I work to honour the divine gift. Every artisan and artist enters into a covenant with the divine. Have you made yours?'

Jahan made a sour face. 'I don't understand.'

'Let me tell you a secret,' said Sinan. 'Beneath every building we raise – it doesn't matter whether it's small or large – just imagine that below the foundations lies the centre of the universe. Then you will work with more care and love.'

Jahan pursed his lips. 'I don't understand what that means.'

'You will,' said Sinan. 'Architecture is a conversation with God. And nowhere does He speak more loudly than at the centre.'

Jahan was intrigued. 'Where is this place, master?'

Yet, before Sinan could answer, Snowy Gabriel came running in, his face ashen. 'My Lord, we are doomed, the delivery –'

For weeks on end they had been waiting for a consignment of marble from Alexandria. Finally, the ship had arrived – but without the precious delivery. When questioned, the Captain explained they had been caught in a storm so awful they'd had to dump half the freight. Nobody believed him but nobody could prove otherwise either. Sinan had to make changes in his design, reducing the number of pillars.

In his palace Sultan Suleiman was getting more impatient with every passing day, as the mosque that was to bear his name fell further and further behind schedule. In the meantime, the splendid columns intended for the Suleimaniye Mosque lay at the bottom of the Red Sea, castles for fish.

'Mahout! Where are you?'

Jahan ran out of the barn and held his breath at the sight of her. Dressed in her customary silks, dyed in rich blue, and, for once, alone, she gave him a look that was so tender he trembled slightly. 'You have honoured us with your visit,' he murmured as he knelt down.

'I have news for the elephant,' she said and paused for a moment. She enjoyed watching him squirm with curiosity. 'The Austrian ambassador brought a painter to the court. An ambitious man, so I heard. They have asked my father's permission to make the beast's painting.'

'What did our noble Sultan say?'

'Well, he was going to say no, but after I spoke with him, he changed his mind. A painting would be nice, I persuaded him. In the courts of Frangistan kings and queens, they are accustomed to having their likenesses made. Even lowly merchants do so.' Mihrimah added softly, 'Ladies, too, imagine.'

Detecting a trace of longing in her voice, Jahan asked cautiously, 'Would your Highness like to have her likeness painted some day?'

'What a stupid question!' she said. 'You should well know that is impossible.'

Jahan apologized in panic, unsure whether he had crossed a boundary or discovered a piece of information he was not meant to possess. How he wished he could tell her that he had, in fact, carved every inch of her face into the infinite space within his mind, so that each time he closed his eyes he saw her, talking, frowning, laughing, her moonlike face in its many moods.

'I am no painter but I can make a sketch of you, your Highness,' Jahan said with a surge of courage. 'No one will know.'

'Are you trying to tell me you will shamelessly draw my face and expect me to be happy about it?' she said.

From her tone Jahan could not fathom whether she was infuriated or mocking him. Yet the thought of them sharing a secret was so delicious he could not help but believe it to be true.

She took a step closer. 'Why would I allow such insolence?'

'Because, your Highness,' said Jahan, his voice now trembling, 'nobody sees you the way I do.'

He closed his eyes, waiting for the punishment that was sure to come. But Mihrimah remained strangely silent.

Busbecq, the Austrian ambassador, was an inquisitive man. Every time he was invited to the palace to discuss matters of state, he asked to be taken to the menagerie to see the animals afterwards. Such was his love for, and interest in, animals that he had filled the embassy grounds with as many of them as he could obtain. The locals called his garden Noah's Ark. He kept flat-horned stags, weasels, sables, lynxes, eagles, monkeys, reptiles with odd names, deer, mules, a bear, a wolf and, to the horror of his Muslim servants, a pig. His favourite animals were tigers – and Chota.

It was Busbecq who introduced Melchior Lorichs to the Ottoman court. Since he had arrived in the Ottoman land, the painter had drawn Janissaries with muskets, camels with war drums, porters bent under their loads or ancient roadside ruins. He had two remaining wishes: to paint Ottoman women in their mantles and *yashmaks*; and to draw Sultan Suleiman's elephant. Now that he had received permission from the Sultan to pursue his second wish, life changed for Jahan and Chota. Twice a week the mahout would bring the elephant to the ambassador's residence.

Busbecq believed there were two blessings in life: books and friends. And that they should be possessed in inverse quantities: many books, but only a handful of friends. When he realized Jahan was not the ignorant tamer he had taken him for, he began to chat with him, one foreigner to another.

'The Turks have a great respect for paper,' said Busbecq. 'If they see a scrap of it on the ground, they pick it up and put it somewhere high, so that it won't be trodden on. But isn't it odd that, while they revere paper, they don't have an interest in books?'

'My master does,' said Jahan.

'Yes, and we shall pray for his good health,' said Busbecq. 'Here's another thing that I find odd: the Turks have no sense of chronology.

That's the first thing every foreigner needs to learn in this land. They muddle up historical events. Today succeeds tomorrow, and tomorrow might precede yesterday.'

From him Jahan heard a surprising thing. There was an elephant in his King's court. And he was named Suleiman!

'It's not an insult,' Busbecq assured. 'A sign of respect, I'd say.'

As Jahan listened to Busbecq prattle on about animals and their ways, Melchior, wearing a verdigris robe and with a hard stare in his eyes, took Chota into the garden. Despite Jahan's reservations he insisted on having the elephant pose under an acacia tree. He seemed a good man, and talented, yet a bit too full of himself, as artists tended to be. He had chosen his vocation over the objections of his parents, and his brows were drawn in a perpetual frown, as if somewhere in his mind he was still quarrelling with them. No sooner had he positioned Chota and placed his easel across from him than the elephant reached out and grabbed a branch.

'Hey, stop!' yelled Melchior. Seeing what little effect his words had on the elephant, he turned to the mahout. 'Is the beast starved?'

'He's not. He's had a hearty breakfast,' Jahan said.

'Then why is he eating the leaves?'

'He's an animal, sir.'

Melchior eyed Jahan coldly, trying to assess whether he was mocking him. 'Next time before you come here, feed him better.'

Jahan did. Chota would eat double the amount of his daily morning ration; then, upon reaching the ambassador's residence, he would devour the acacia leaves. After a few more attempts the artist agreed to alter the setting. This time Chota was posed outside against a snaky, sleepy street with rickety houses. Busbecq watched them from the window of his room upstairs. Relations between the two empires had swiftly deteriorated, and the ambassador was now kept under house arrest. While Melchior worked with Chota, Jahan kept the ambassador company, benefiting from his wide knowledge of flowers and herbs.

Two months later Melchior finished Chota's portrait. To celebrate, Busbecq invited a number of guests. Pashas, viziers, emissaries. Jahan was surprised to see that, although the ambassador was still forbidden to go out, people had no hesitation in visiting him. The easel was covered with a thick, white cloth. It stood in a corner, waiting for its moment. Melchior was wearing a robe of blue velvet, beaming with pleasure. Jahan wondered, not for the first time, if all artists were like this. Thriving upon a drop of praise. Chota was at the end of the garden. The artist had insisted that the elephant should be part of the celebration. Jahan tethered him to an old oak tree to prevent him from stepping on someone.

Before long, the ambassador announced it was time to unveil the painting. A murmur rose as the guests drew near. Since it was not a portrait of a human being, even devout Muslims were curious to see it. The cloth was removed and underneath Jahan saw the most bizarre image.

Chota didn't seem like Chota. His tusks were larger and sharper; he had a ferocious look on his face, as though ready to jump out of the frame and attack. The street and the houses and the sky were so real one could almost touch them. The painting exuded warmth. Impressed, everyone applauded. Busbecq rewarded the artist with a pouch. He also tipped Jahan, thanking him for his help in bringing about a work of art. Melchior, reeking of wine, embraced the boy as well.

An hour later, ready to leave, Jahan paused in front of the easel. That was when he saw, to his horror, that the top part of the painting was missing. Where there had been a fluffy cloud a while ago, there now was a large hole. Jahan turned to Chota, his heart hammering. The animal's rope had snapped. Whatever doubts he may have had about Chota's culpability disappeared when he noticed a smidgen of blue paint on one of his tusks. Wordlessly pulling Chota's reins, Jahan left the ambassador's residence. They closed the gate behind them, throwing themselves into the evening breeze. Jahan would never see Melchior again. He later heard that the painter had gone back to his own country and made quite a name for himself with his Oriental collection, though a painting of Sultan Suleiman's white elephant was not among his works.

By the time Sinan and the apprentices were near the end of the Sulei-maniye Mosque, the Sultan's gout had become so severe that his legs, swollen and oozing from open sores, had to be swathed in gauze. He had on his hands the blood of those once dear to him – of his first Grand Vizier, Ibrahim; and of his eldest son, Mustafa. Both men had been the apple of his eye and yet were executed, one after the other, by order of the Sultan. Istanbul seethed with plots and conspiracies.

Jahan thought they would not hear from the Sultan for a while. How wrong he was. Despite his grief and his illness he kept sending messages, his tone terse, restless. Then, one day, he was at the site again, in pain but glowering. He glanced at the half-finished mosque as if it were invisible to him. On his horse he cantered towards Sinan.

'Architect, too much time has gone by. I'm losing patience.'

Sinan said, 'I assure your Majesty that I shall complete his mosque, God willing.'

'How much more time do you need?'

'Two months, my Lord.'

The Sultan stared at the site, his eyes hard. 'Two months it is! Not a day more. If the key is not delivered by then, we shall talk again.'

Once he had gone, the workers exchanged nervous glances. Nobody knew how they could possibly meet his demand in so short a time. Unrest boiled up like stew in a pot. Fretting that at the end of the two months the Sultan would punish them, the labourers started to talk about deserting.

One day, as things were getting increasingly out of hand, Sinan asked Jahan to help him into the howdah. He was going to give a speech – from atop the elephant.

'Brothers! There was a bee flying around this morning. Did you notice it?'

No one answered.

'I thought to myself, if I were that tiniest of creatures and if I could land on every man's shoulder and listen to the sounds in his head, what would I hear?'

The crowd stirred somewhat.

'I think I would hear worries. Some of you are uneasy. If we don't finish the mosque in time, we'll be in trouble, you say. Rest assured this won't happen. If our Sultan is not pleased, none of you will be worse off. Other than me.'

'How do we know our heads will not roll off next to yours?' a worker asked without revealing his face. Instantly a murmur of assent rose.

'Hear me out. This place was a bare field. With us the holy mosque rose, stone upon stone. Winter and summer, we slogged together. You saw one another more often than you saw your wives and children.'

Whispers rippled throughout the site.

'People will come here after we are dead. They won't know our names. But they will see what we've achieved. They shall remember us.'

'So you say!' someone shouted.

Sinan said haltingly, 'If I fail, I fail alone. But if I succeed, we all succeed.'

'He thinks we're stupid,' someone else ventured.

They did not believe him. The man whom they had obeyed and respected all this time was suddenly seen as someone who was putting their lives in danger.

'Brothers!' said Sinan finally. 'I see I cannot convince you. I shall put in writing everything I have said and seal it. Should anything happen, give my letter to our honourable Sultan. As a reward for your trust we will distribute tips.'

Their silence was approval enough. Thus Sinan wrote, in his elegant handwriting, that he was the sole person responsible for any failures related to the Suleimaniye Mosque. The success belonged to God – and then to the workers. The letter was signed and sealed, and buried outside the walls. If things went wrong, they all knew where to find it.

The next morning no one failed to turn up. *Baksheesh* were given out. Jahan managed to benefit from the disruption, snitching fifty aspers from the coffers. He silenced the guilt-ridden voice inside by reminding himself that he was not stealing from his master, but from the Sultan, who already had plenty.

They picked up where they left off, working till late hours. Dozens of hands were brought in. Every unemployed stonecutter in the city was asked to join, every carver, etcher, draughtsman. Just when everyone thought he would be frozen with fear, Sinan was moving heaven and earth. His frenzy was contagious. Seeing him so driven, his apprentices strove harder. The expenses soared. Suleimaniye Mosque would cost the treasury 54,697,560 aspers.

Even amid the whirl there was not a single feature the Chief Royal Architect had not considered at length. The tiles, made in the ateliers in Iznik, were in vivid colours – turquoise, red, white. The beautiful *thuluth* that spelled out Allah, Mohammed and Al was completed by the Court Calligrapher, Molla Hasan. While people adored the decorations inside, most failed to understand how the buttresses had been incorporated into the walls. Very few saw how the side walls, freed from the burden of having to carry the dome, were dotted with numerous windows, so that the light poured in as warmly as milk from the breast of a mother to her infant. And even fewer were aware that each jutting stone inside the mosque was placed in such a way as to make the sounds in the mosque reverberate, allowing every member of the congregation to hear the sermons, regardless of how close or how far he might be seated from the imam.

Murano-glass oil lamps and mirror globes hung from the ceilings. Among them were ostrich eggs, dainty and delicate, tastefully painted, decorated with silk tassels, suspended from iron hoops. Miniature mosques of ivory were planted inside glass globes that dangled alongside each other. In the centre was a massive gilt ball. After dusk, when the lamps burned and the mirrors cast back their light, the entire mosque looked as though it had swallowed the sun. And carpets . . . hundreds of them. In countless homes in Cairo and Kure, women and girls of every age had been weaving the carpets of Suleimaniye.

The mosque was colossal, its dome majestic; its double-storeyed gallery was unusual, and its quadruple minarets pierced the sky. The central baldachin's red-granite columns were four in total, and were likened to the friends of the Prophet – the caliphs Abu Bakr, Omar, Osman and Ali. Every verse from the Qur'an that was displayed inside was chosen by the Shayh al-Islam Ebussuud. The calligraphy reminded Muslims to pray five times a day and never to deviate from the beliefs of the congregation. At a time of conflict with Shia Iran, the Ottoman rulers were adhering scrupulously to Sunni Islam, and becoming, at least on the surface, more and more pious.

Erected upon layered terraces, and surrounded by a college, library, hospital and shops, the mosque site viewed from below was impressive. In addition to a madrasa, there was a convent for dervishes, guest rooms, a kitchen, a bakery, a refectory, a hospice, a medical college and a caravanserai. By the time Sinan and his apprentices had laid the last stone nothing was the same – neither the city nor the throne. Between the time of its inception and its completion the world had become a darker place and the Sultan a sadder man. That was the thing about colossal buildings. While they did not change, the people who ordered, designed, built and eventually used them constantly did.

Everyone came to see the Suleimaniye, the mosque that surpassed all other mosques. The Bailo, the ambassadors, even Shah Tahmasp's envoy, though no real peace had been achieved between the two kingdoms, only a respite from enmity.

The Sultan, his eyes brimming, said, 'My architect built me a mosque that will survive till the Day of Judgement.'

'When Hallaj Mansur rises from the dead to shake Mount Damavand, he might shake the mountain but not your dome, your Highness,' Sinan responded.

The Sultan held the gilded key in his hand and addressed the crowd. 'Who among you is the most worthy? I want that man to take this key and open the door.'

Jahan looked around. All the people who had been gossiping about his master were now silent, smiling.

'None among you deserves this more than the Chief Royal Architect,' the Sultan said. He turned to Sinan. 'You have not let me down. I'm pleased with you.'

Sinan, his face flushed, lowered his gaze. He took the key, opened the gate and invited the Sultan in. One by one the others followed. Jahan wormed his way through the crowd, determined to make the most of this day. Encircling him on all sides were the wealthiest men in the empire. Gems shone on their fingers, pouches bulged from under their elegant robes. To his left he saw a figure of ample proportions, a kadi from Rumelia, talking fervently with another officer. A deep crimson rosary dangled from the man's hand, his prayers made of rubies.

As they poured towards the entrance, Jahan propelled himself against the man, wearing a contrite look as if being helplessly shoved in the commotion.

'*Effendi*, I beg your pardon.'

The kadi glowered, looking over Jahan's shoulder. He was swirled with the others through the door, unaware that the young man had snatched his rosary. To avoid encountering him again, Jahan moved in the opposite direction, allowing people to pass him by. He waited to one side for a while. Thus it was some time before he entered the Suleimaniye Mosque. By then most of the guests had left the mosque itself and were touring the complex.

Feeling the gems under his fingers, Jahan walked into the mosque. His buoyant mood changed to dismay when he remembered Captain Gareth. The man was away on another voyage that would take at least a couple of months. Jahan had to keep his booty somewhere safe and give it to him upon his return. Even so, he wondered if he could sell the rosary and buy a gift for Mihrimah. Perhaps a haircomb made of mother-of-pearl and tortoiseshell. Secretly, he had been working on her sketches, over and over again, unsatisfied with the results. He had never expected it to be so hard to put on paper an image that was already etched indelibly in his mind.

With these thoughts he stepped over the threshold and stopped. Inside, a strange rainbow spilled from the windows. Crimson, cobalt-blue, vermilion. He remembered, suddenly, how as a boy he would lie under birch trees and stare up, as though in search of heaven. Should the sky fall down the trees would hold it up, he would reassure himself. He had done this many times but once had an odd experience. On that day the sky was lurid, the clouds so close he could reach out and tickle one. As he looked up, the green of the leaves had melted into the blue beyond. The feeling was so remarkable it had almost choked him up. It had lasted no longer than the blink of an eye, but he still remembered, after all these years, the taste of that elation.

Now, as he stood admiring the dome they had built on four giant piers, seeing it for the thousandth time but almost seeing it anew, he felt the same thing. The dome had blended with the firmament above. He fell on his knees, without a care as to who might be watching him. He lay down on the carpet, eyes closed, arms and legs open wide, once again that boy under the birch trees. Alone in the mosque, only a dot in this vast expanse, Jahan could think only of the world as an enormous building site. While the master and the apprentices had been raising this mosque, the universe had been constructing their fate. Never before had he thought of God as an architect. Christians, Jews, Muslims, Zoroastrians and people of myriad faiths and creeds lived under the same invisible dome. For the eye that could see, architecture was everywhere.

Hence, with a stolen rosary in his hand and an inexplicable gratitude in his heart, full of conflicts and confusions, under the majestic dome of the Suleimaniye Mosque, Jahan stood, a most intelligent animal-tamer and a most perplexed apprentice. Time, too, stopped with him. It seemed to him that in that instant he had, unknowingly, come a step closer to the centre of the universe.

Every now and then Master Sinan sent the apprentices and novices on odd errands – from buying a pot of ink at the bazaar to rummaging around the ruins of an ancient church and reporting, upon their return, why some parts had fallen into decay while others had lasted; from digging in various hills to see which types of soil crawled with worms to spending a day with the *ney*-makers and observing how a simple musical instrument could be made to capture sounds of such immensity. They were instructed to carry out these orders to the best of their ability, however trifling they seemed to be. Yet, in truth, each always weighed their assignments against those of the others, judging, begrudging. Having never been assigned such tasks, Jahan had been spared this contention.

That changed one Thursday afternoon. As if to make up for lost time, Sinan gave him not one but two tasks. First, Jahan was to visit a couple of ostrich-egg vendors to inform them that Sinan would soon be in need of their merchandise. Then, he was to drop round a bookseller's to purchase a book. Sinan hadn't said which book. He said when he got there he would know. This last detail Jahan found strange, but he didn't mind. Child's play, he thought to himself as he got ready to leave the site. He was bent on accomplishing his tasks so fast and so flawlessly that the master would have to entrust him with more serious duties the next time.

'Well, what is it?' came a voice from behind.

When he turned he found the other three apprentices watching him.

'Oh, naught. Ostrich eggs and a book.'

'A book?' Nikola asked. 'Is it from the bookseller in Pera?'

When they saw Jahan nod, their faces clouded over. Davud said, 'Congratulations, novice! The master only sends his favourites to the old goat.'

As pleased as he was to hear this, Jahan felt a pang of unease.

'Don't be humble next to him,' said Nikola. 'Show him how much you know. He'll like that.'

Yusuf smiled in agreement.

'Don't forget to shout. Simeon is deaf as a log,' said Davud.

Jahan thanked them for their advice. Much as he hated entrusting Chota to the care of others, he made provision for him. Before noon he set off with a horse – a lazy, listless creature – and a pouch of money that had been provided for him. Passing by fields covered in lush vegetation and cemeteries lined with cypress trees, he and the horse picked their way towards Unkapani. Once there, though it was the longer route, Jahan went via the quay. He enjoyed going there whenever he could, as though to reassure himself that if things got too dreary, he could jump on board one of the vessels and return to the home that, deep in his heart, he still believed awaited him.

The port was teeming with sounds and smells. The soughing of waves, the shrieking of seagulls and the barking of orders mingled with the clanking of chains and the cracking of whips. A tang of seaweed permeated the air, and the reek of sweat and excrement wafted in from hundreds of bodies trudging in tandem – the captives from the recent naval victory. Children, the elderly, women and men – people who weeks ago had names and families of their own. With their ankles shackled, looking about but unseeing, they were here and not here. Jahan jumped off the horse and joined the multitude watching this grim procession.

They were all covered head to toe in grime. Some wore garbs that had once been elegant, which they had arranged to retain some semblance of dignity. These, Jahan supposed, were the gentry. Others were clad in tatters that the beggars of Eyup would slight. Regardless of who they might have been in their previous lives, they were now subject to the whip, which descended at random, less to quicken their pace than to snatch them back from any daydream in which they might have momentarily taken shelter.

Jahan hopped back on his horse and set out for the bazaar. He spoke with several merchants who traded in, among other things, ostrich eggs. He told them Sinan would soon have need of their stocks. The Chief Royal Architect used these eggs to keep the spiders away, so as to prevent cobwebs from gathering in the mosques. When a hole was pricked in each end of the egg and it was suspended from the ceiling, it would release a smell that would not bother humans but would surely keep all insects at bay.

The vendors listened. But when Jahan inquired if the goods would be ready in a month's time, all they said was *Insha'Allah*. Not quite sure whether he had fulfilled his first assignment, Jahan proceeded to the second one.

When Jahan arrived at the bookseller's, a two-storey wooden house that had seen better days, the horse looked as happy to be rid of him as he was of the horse. Remembering what the apprentices said, he pounded hard. The door opened and a doddering man appeared, looking enraged.

'You want to break my door or what?'

'*Selamun aleikum*, I was sent by the –'

'Why are you shouting? You think I'm deaf, you dolt!'

Puzzled, Jahan stammered, 'No, *effendi*.'

'Who sent you here?' asked the bookseller stiffly, but when he heard Sinan's name his face softened. 'Come on in, then.'

Inside, the smell of a freshly baked loaf wrapped round them like a blanket. Sitting in a corner was a woman, gaunt and old, hunched over her sewing. Simeon said, 'That's my wife, Esther. Let's not disturb her.'

They pottered down the dark, draughty corridors. The house was a maze. Inside were shelves laden with volume after volume of leather-bound books, mostly in hues of brown and black. Some had been looted by corsairs from remote islands, port towns or enemy vessels. Knowing Simeon's delight in such articles, the sea dogs brought them over in return for a decent sum. Others had been gathered in Frankish kingdoms. Among them were medical treatises by Spanish physicians and volumes by French noblemen. Still others had been printed in Istanbul or Salonika. The Sephardic Jews, with permission from the Sultan, published their own books. In one corner there was a compendium of mathematical manuscripts, which, Jahan learned, were once owned by a scholar called Molla Lutfi; drawings of the winds and the airstreams, stars and heavenly bodies, were incorporated into the borders of each page. There was *The Book of the Knight Zifar*, freshly arrived from Spain; a pile of wooden engravings by Antonio da Sangallo; a treatise titled *Regole generali di architettura* by a certain Sebastiano Serlio, a Bolognese architect; and a gilt-edged manuscript in Latin, *De Architectura*, by Vitruvius. The last, found during the conquest of Buda, had ended up in Istanbul. A tract by a Leon Battista Alberti was titled *De re aedificatoria*, which Simeon translated as *The Art of Building*. There was a tome by a man with an awkward name – Ibn Maimon. Its title was *The Guide for the Perplexed*, which Jahan thought was well suited to himself.

They arrived at a large, dim room at the back. A cupboard with dozens of drawers, its doors intricately carved and fretted, stood in the middle. Simeon gestured to the boy to sit in the only chair.

'How's your master? Haven't seen him in a while.'

'He sends you his regards,' said Jahan. 'He wanted me to choose a book. But didn't say which.'

'That's easy. First, tell me, honestly, are you a learner?'

Jahan gave a surprised look. 'I attend the Palace School and –'

'I didn't say are you a student. I asked, are you a learner? Not every pupil is a learner.'

Remembering Nikola's counsel, Jahan decided this was his moment to stand up to this grumpy man. 'Working on construction sites all day long, one learns whether one wants to or not.'

The expression on Simeon's face was one of belittlement. 'Our Sultan, may the mercy of God be upon him, should levy a tax on idiocy. If he could collect a coin for every stupid word uttered, his treasury would be full.'

It suddenly dawned on Jahan that his fellow apprentices had misled him. Everything he did or said only helped to annoy the old man. He said meekly, 'The others have been here before, have they?'

'Oh, yes, many times,' said Simeon. 'Lucky you, being a novice to a man like Sinan. Are you aware of your good fortune?'

Jahan averted his eyes, feeling like an impostor. What would the man think if he heard that Jahan was trying to steal from construction sites? Slowly, he said, 'I do my best, *effendi*.'

'Masters are great but books are better. He who has a library has a thousand teachers. Your Prophet said, "Seek lore, even if it be in China." Mine said, "God created us because He wanted to be known." Ignorant men think we are here to fight and make wars and to couple and have children. Nay, our job is to expand our knowledge. That's why we're here.' Simeon paused. 'Tell me, do you talk to God?'

'I pray.'

'Didn't ask do you *pray*, dunce. You want to become an architect, you have to speak to something bigger than you!'

Jahan lowered his gaze. 'I wouldn't bother God with my worries. But I talk with my elephant. Chota is bigger than me and wiser. He is young, but I think he was a hundred years old when he was born.'

When Jahan lifted his head there was something in the old man's stare that wasn't there a moment ago. A trace of appreciation. 'You seem like a kind soul but your mind is confused. You are like a boat with two oarsmen rowing in separate directions. That means you have not found the centre of your heart yet.'

Remembering his master's words the other day, Jahan shivered imperceptibly. Simeon went on, 'Now, tell me, what do you like to build best?'

'I like bridges.'

It began to rain. From the depths of the corridor came the rustle of a page being turned. Was it Simeon's wife who was reading? Or was there someone else in the house? In that moment Jahan had a suspicion that one of the apprentices was there, hiding, listening. He glanced at the bookseller, as though for confirmation. But the man was busy fumbling inside a chest. Finally, he produced a sketch. 'Look. A bridge on the Golden Horn. It was made by Leonardo.'

Having heard of this name from his master, Jahan was quiet.

'Sultan Bayezid had sought his help. Leonardo sent him his drawings. Not a humble letter, in my opinion. He said he could make the bridge. Not only that, he'd make lots of other things in our city. A movable bridge across the Bosphorus.'

Simeon opened another chest. Inside were sketches that he said were by Michelangelo, most of them of domes – belonging to the Pantheon, Florence's cathedral and the Hagia Sophia. 'Michelangelo was bent on coming here. Said so in his letters.'

'You corresponded with him?'

'Long time ago. He was a young man. So was I. He wanted to work in the Levant. I encouraged him. The Sultan was open to it. I was their dragoman. Me and the Franciscan friars. But not sure they helped; they don't like the Turks.' Simeon lapsed into thought. 'He was going to build a bridge across the Golden Horn. It would have had an observatory inside. And a library. I'd have been in charge of that.'

Jahan heard the disappointment in his voice. 'What happened?'

'They convinced him not to. They said it was better that he should die at the hands of the Pope than be rewarded by the Sultan. That was the end of it. Rome is Rome. Istanbul is Istanbul. Nobody is talking about bringing the two cities closer any more.' Simeon sighed wearily. 'But they are always watching.'

'Who, *effendi*?'

'The eyes of Rome. Watching your master.'

Jahan felt uncomfortable. He thought about the falling scaffolding and the cut ropes; he thought about the marble that was never delivered . . . Behind all these accidents and misfortunes, could there be a hidden force? *The eyes of Rome.* He composed himself. His mind had run wild again.

Meanwhile the man had already walked over to a shelf and pulled out a tome with woodcut illustrations.

'This is yours. Tell your master this is the book that I chose for you.'

Without so much as a glance at the cover Jahan opened his pouch but the bookseller refused. 'Keep your coins, young man. Learn Italian. If you are a man of bridges, you ought to be able to speak sundry languages.'

Tucking the book under his arm, lost for words, Jahan walked out. The horse was waiting. Only when he arrived at Sinan's house did it occur to him to examine the gift. It was *La Divina Commedia* by a gentleman called Dante.

When Jahan showed the book to Sinan, his face broke into a smile. He said, 'Simeon seems to have liked you. He gave you his favourite book.'

'He said I ought to learn Italian.'

'Well . . . he's right.'

'But who is going to teach me?'

'Why, Simeon himself of course. He also taught Davud, Nikola and Yusuf.'

Jahan felt a twist of jealousy. Until then he had believed that the old bookseller had liked him more than the others. Sinan said, 'When you master a language, you are given the key to a castle. What you'll find inside depends on you.'

Liking the imagery of entering a castle to collect the riches within, Jahan beamed. 'Yes, master.'

That was how the novice came to spend many hours of his youth in the bookseller's shop, which would, by and by, become a haven, a home. He was no outsider inside those walls. Lost among books, he found himself. As his knowledge of Italian grew, he began to dabble in Latin and French; and, as his knowledge of drawing grew, he inched his way up from novice to apprentice, and at last found himself welcome in Sinan's own library. There was another collection at the headquarters of the royal architects in Vefa. Over the years Jahan would visit it on many occasions, but nothing would give him such pleasure as being in Simeon's house, surrounded by the smells of ink, leather and baking bread.

Trumpeting, rumbling, Chota paced up and down. He had been in a similar state twice before, but each time the craze had come and gone. Only now it was not going anywhere. Unruly and ill-tempered, he had so scared the servants the other day that Jahan had to have him chained. In the morning, the beast broke his chains and charged into a tree. The glands on the sides of his head dripped a smelly, oily substance, which, Jahan knew, could mean only one thing: the elephant was in heat.

Trying to find a lady friend for Chota in Istanbul was like wishing for snow in August. Jahan searched high and low. It all came to naught. Wherever the mahout went, doors were closed in his face, but not before someone had a good laugh at his expense. Even Olev the lion-tamer did not know what to do, for once.

When Mihrimah appeared in the garden with her nursemaid and asked to see the elephant, Jahan broke into a sweat. The shame of explaining to her why she could not see Chota in this state was so heavy he almost choked.

She laughed at his panic, but when she spoke there was a trace of sadness in her voice. 'Well, the elephant has grown up. No longer that cute calf. The innocence of childhood leaves all of us eventually.'

Jahan was dumbstruck with worry. He could only muster a meek protest. 'Your Highness, this season will come and go. Chota is the same as always. You should not stop visiting him, I beg.'

She turned her head, unwilling to look at him, facing the sun. 'Can you catch the wind, mahout? Can you bring down the moon? There are things we cannot change. I have accepted this truth, and, one day, so will you.'

As if he had heard the exchange and wished to interject, Chota began to bellow. He made so much noise, yanking at his chains, that Jahan had no time to take in Mihrimah's words.

After the Princess and the nursemaid left, Jahan had an idea. He remembered the Gypsies who had saved them from the ice. Had they not said they had an elephant? When he shared his hope with the other tamers, they shook their heads. 'The Gypsies wander round all year. How are you going to track them down?'

In the end it was Master Sinan who helped him. The architect not only gave his apprentice time off from work but also provided him with a carriage and a silver coin, and said, with a smile, 'Go and find the beast a pretty wife and make him happy. Only God is alone.'

They rode in silence through the Gate of the Spring, the coachman and Jahan, watching the clouds turn light pink far ahead. It took hours to find the Romanies. Finally they saw wagons in the distance, bedrolls and clothes strewn on the hedges, punctuating the dull landscape with their brash colours. The coachman refused to go near. He had heard too many stories about these roamers, and had no wish to meet any of them.

'Be careful,' he said to Jahan. 'If they offer you a drink, refuse. Not a sip from their hands. Remember, Satan, *djinn* and Gypsies, they will all steal your soul.'

Waving at him, Jahan left the carriage and quickly set off towards the camp, fearful that if he dithered he would lose courage. His boots crunched on the path as he approached a bevy of children, their noses snotty, their feet bare. One woman was suckling her twins, a baby latched on to each teat. Catching him staring at her bosom, she glared at him. Ashamed, Jahan averted his gaze.

He approached one of the boys. 'Is your chief here?' The child stood so still that Jahan doubted he had heard him.

'What do you want?' A husky voice came from behind so suddenly that Jahan almost jumped out of his skin. Upon turning round, he saw two men scowling at him.

'I need to see your leader . . . Balaban,' Jahan said.

'How do you know him?'

'He . . . he saved me once,' was all that Jahan could come up with.

He was taken to a tent in a shade of indigo so bold that even the blue jay in the aviary would envy it. On the walls were carpets with pictures of animals and flowers, and one with Abraham catching a ram to sacrifice in place of his son. In one corner, sitting by a stove, was a group of men and in their midst was none other than Balaban.

'Look who's here!' Balaban said. 'Why have you come, tell.'

'I need help. My elephant's lost his mind. He's in rut. I remember you said you had a female –'

Before he could finish his sentence Balaban grabbed him by the robe, pulled out a dagger and held it against his jaw. 'Rascal! Scamp! You've got the guts to ask me to be your pimp! D'you want me to spill your blood here or shall we go outside?'

'No, *effendi*. I intend well. It's for the animals' benefit,' Jahan said in a grovelling voice.

Balaban pushed him away. 'What's in it for me?'

'If your elephant gets pregnant, you will have two animals,' Jahan said. 'You could make use of them both.'

Balaban weighed this up, unimpressed. 'What else?'

Jahan showed him the coin Sinan had given him, but Balaban again said, 'What else?'

Deciding to take another path, Jahan said, 'This elephant belongs to the palace. If you don't help me, the Sultan will be furious.'

'The Sultan, you said?'

Jahan nodded vigorously, confident that he had him now.

'You wretched toad!' Balaban kicked a cushion, which went flying to the wall, where it hit Abraham's ram and bounced back. 'Is this the Sultan's generosity? A chipped coin?'

'I beg you. Architect Sinan needs the elephant to work.'

The silence was unbearable. After a moment, and an exchange of glances, none of which Jahan could decipher, Balaban shrugged. 'Gulbahar is pretty as a lotus flower. You must earn her hand.'

'What do you want my elephant to do?' Jahan asked suspiciously.

'Not your elephant. You!'

Jahan tried to maintain a brave countenance but his voice cracked. 'Me?'

Just then the woman who had been suckling the twins appeared, carrying a tray with drinks and fried dough covered in syrup.

'First take a bite. He who shares my bread and salt is not my enemy,' said Balaban.

Jahan hesitated for a moment. He popped into his mouth a dough ball, savouring the sweet taste.

'Now have a drink. Can't walk straight when the road is crooked.'

'May our wives die if we don't knock these back in one go!'

Like them, Jahan downed the mud-coloured fluid in one gulp; like them, he brought down the cup with a thud on the wooden table; like them, he wiped his mouth with the back of his hand. Although the drink was pungent, burning all the way down to his stomach, it was surprisingly enjoyable. Then they told him, in waggish detail and with boyish mirth, what they were daring him to do.

'Up to you!' Balaban said. 'Take it or leave.'

Whether it was his love for Chota, or his bull-headedness, or the drink, Jahan said, after a pause, 'Fine, I'll do it.'

The men walked out, leaving him with the women. Brazen, pert, they helped him to dress up as a dancer. A purple *shalwar* and a short embroidered vest that revealed his belly. They painted his face with a whitish powder that smelled of rice. They put kohl around his eyes, and reddened his cheeks and lips with crushed beetles, or so he was told. They reddened his fingers with henna and sprinkled rosewater down his neck. And on his pate they placed a horse's tail, giving him the strangest hair.

Balaban and his men came back, accompanied by musicians who, it turned out, could not play a tune without sniggering. They strummed on their instruments and blew their horns a bit, and then one of them burst out laughing, the others following gleefully. Still, Jahan danced, if his clumsy moves could be called dancing. The Romanies watched, drinking, cackling with delight. When one of the men tried to hug Jahan with no decent intentions, Balaban hit his head with a wooden spoon and shouted, 'Behave!'

From then on Jahan danced more willingly, trusting that if he kept his part of the deal, so would they. Hours later, when he walked out of the tent clad in his old clothes, though with henna on his hands and kohl on his eyes, the coachman was nowhere to be seen. Jahan didn't mind. He did not have to make his way back on foot. He had a female elephant to take him.

Four days later Jahan returned Gulbahar. It took him a whole afternoon to locate the Gypsies, as they had moved again. The old women huddled in a corner greeted him with a smirk, which Jahan pretended not to notice.

'The dancer is back,' yelled a small boy. A cackle rose from behind him. It was Balaban.

'Felicitations,' said the chieftain, 'your elephant is no longer a virgin.'

'Gulbahar made Chota the happiest elephant in the world,' Jahan said with a bashful smile. Then, with a new realization, he added: 'You've done it again, Balaban. You've saved my skin.'

Every Wednesday, Master Sinan gathered his apprentices in his house and instructed them to design a building – an aqueduct, a madrasa, a bath house or a *bedestan*. The young men took these assignments with the utmost seriousness, seeing a chance not only to display their talents but also to outshine their rivals. Sometimes their task would be as straightforward as drawing a one-roomed hut. At other times a more demanding exercise would be set: how to reduce the number of columns in a mansion without diminishing its strength and solidity; how to make the best use of mortar, which, although it bonded well, led to nasty cracks as it dried; how to assemble a criss-cross of water channels above and beneath the ground. Such exercises they were expected to tackle on their own. It was permitted to share the finer points of technique; but under no circumstances were they to see one another's designs.

'Architecture is team work,' said Sinan. 'Apprenticeship is not.'

'Why don't you want us to look at each other's drawings?' Jahan once asked.

'Because you'll compare. If you think you are better than the others, you'll be poisoned by hubris. If you think another's better, poisoned by envy. Either way, it is poison.'

One such afternoon they had each finished drawing a dervish convent when a servant announced that the master was waiting for them in the library. Putting their pens aside, they walked out wordlessly, burning with curiosity. Upstairs they found the master with scrolls unrolled and spread open to his left and his right. In the middle of the room, upon an oak table, was a wooden model.

'Come,' Sinan said.

Timid and awkward, the four stumbled forward.

'Do you know what building this is?' Sinan asked.

Davud, examining the model with a frown, said, 'It's an infidel temple.'

'The dome is admirable,' said Nikola.

'Where is this place?' asked Jahan.

'In Rome,' Sinan replied, waving his hand as if Rome were outside the window. He said it was called San Pietro, and when finished it would possess the largest dome in all of Christendom. Several architects had worked on it, some aiming to demolish the old basilica and start anew; others to restore it. The last draughtsman, Sangallo, had passed away. The construction, at the behest of the Pope, had been assigned to Michelangelo. Recognizing the name the bookseller had mentioned, Jahan pricked up his ears.

Sinan said that Michelangelo, who was not young any more, had two choices. He could either disregard the existing designs or build on them. The decision would demonstrate not only his talents as a craftsman but also his character. Sinan spoke with such fervour that a surge of excitement ran through his apprentices. Yet all the while a thought tugged at the back of their minds: why was the master telling them this?

Reading their mood in one glance, Sinan said, 'I'd like you to see San Pietro. Study its design. Compare what they've done over there with what we're doing here. If you aim to excel in your craft, you ought to study the works of others.'

It took them a moment to grasp the full weight of his statement. 'You . . . want us to travel to the land of Franks?' Davud faltered. 'And see the churches?'

'We follow our Prophet's advice: we seek lore near and far.' Sinan told them he had learned much from his travels in the lands of the Franks, in the Balkans, Anatolia, Syria, Egypt, Iraq and eastward into the Caucasus. 'Stones stay still. A learner, never.'

'But master, should we not teach *them*?' It was Davud again. 'They are Christians. Why should we learn from their ways?'

'Every good craftsman is your teacher, no matter where he may be from. Artists and artisans are people of the same faith.'

And, so saying, Sinan brought out two velvet cases, one thin and long, the other plump and round. Inside the first was an oversized silver pin and in the second an inward-curved lens, the size of a ripe apple.

'What is it?' Nikola asked, dropping his voice to a whisper, as though he were staring at some dark sorcery.

'It's a prism,' Sinan explained. 'We use it to observe how the sun's rays travel inside buildings. In a cathedral it would work well.'

'And this?' Jahan said, holding the pin on his palm like a baby bird.

'That's for the sound. Enter the buildings when there are few people inside. Hold the pin at the level of your head and drop it. Does the sound die off right away? Or does it reach the furthest corners? If so, ask yourself how did the architect achieve this? Can one make the sound flow like water, back and forth, in a gentle tide? In cathedrals this is done through the creation of a whispering gallery. Go and listen: you'll hear how the smallest sound is carried.'

Sinan spoke as fast as a pelting storm of hail. They had never seen him like this before, his eyes sparkling, his face lit up. He said there were three fountains of wisdom from which every artisan should drink abundantly: books, work and roads. Reading, practising and travelling. He went on, 'Unfortunately, I can't send away all of you. We've work to do. You need to decide among yourselves who will go. A trip for about five weeks.'

Nikola, Davud, Yusuf and Jahan stole furtive glances at one another, shoulders stiff. The desire to impress their master with their audacity clashed in their hearts with their wish to stay where everything was familiar. It was Yusuf who came forward first, shaking his head. He didn't want to go. Jahan was not surprised to see this. Like a small planet orbiting a bigger one, Yusuf always wished to be close to the master.

'How about the others?' Sinan asked.

'I can't go either,' said Jahan. 'Who would take care of the elephant?'

He wasn't exactly telling the truth. Another tamer could easily substitute for him, should the master arrange it with the palace officials. Yet Chota was only one of his concerns. He needed to stay close to Mihrimah. Lately she had been visiting the menagerie more often, wearing a troubled look in her beautiful eyes, as if she had something to tell but couldn't.

'My parents are old,' said Nikola. 'It'd be hard to leave them for that long.'

All heads turned to Davud. He sighed. 'I can go, master.'

Sinan gave an appreciative nod and said, to no one in particular, 'If any one of you changes his mind, let me know in a few days' time.'

The following afternoon, Mihrimah did not come to see the elephant. Nor the one after that. Instead Hesna Khatun arrived with the latest news from inside the seraglio.

'Don't wait for her,' she said. 'Your Princess is getting married.'

'What are you saying, *dada*?'

Her whole body suddenly convulsed with an asthma attack; she took out a pouch and inhaled its contents. A sharp smell of herbs wafted in the air. 'Don't call me that. Only she can.'

'Tell me,' said Jahan, ignoring all pretence at etiquette.

And she did. Mihrimah had been betrothed to Rustem Pasha, a man of forty winters and infinite ambition. No one liked him, but the Sultana did, and that was enough.

After the nursemaid left, Jahan worked on a new design, swept the barn floor, washed the troughs, burnished the elephant's armour, applied oil to the elephant's skin, destroyed the design he was working on and started another, greased the hinges on every door, made another sketch and destroyed it immediately, and forgot to feed Chota.

The menagerie was engulfed by gossip about the wedding throughout the entire evening. At midnight, Jahan could stand no more, and he sneaked outside. His legs and arms throbbed with tiredness, and his chest with a pain he had not known before. He walked until he reached the walls separating the menagerie from the inner courtyard, and once there, not knowing what else to do, made his way back again. He arrived at the lilac tree she had sat under as he had told her the story of Chota's birth and their journey from Hindustan.

The tree glowed in the dark, as though it were a gateway to a better world. He put his ear to its trunk, trying to hear what the earth was telling him. Only silence. Stubborn, scabby silence. The wind picked up, the air got chilly. A fog of sadness fell over the palace. He continued to sit, waiting for the night's cold to envelop him, numbing his senses. It didn't work. He still felt. It still hurt.

The next morning he sent a letter to his master. A short message.

Esteemed Master,

If you still wish me to go, I will gladly accompany Davud to Rome.

Your humble apprentice,
Jahan

Rome, the city where memories were chiselled in marble. The day they arrived it was raining – a drizzle as light as a caress. Slowing down their horses to a trot, they rode aimlessly for a while. Each face was unfamiliar, every street more baffling than the previous one. Occasionally they passed over a bridge, under an arch – round or lancet – or through a piazza teeming with pedlars and their customers. Jahan could not say what he had expected, but the city was large and lively beyond his ken. He and Davud, rigid and ill at ease, wove their way through the crowds. As they came upon the ruins of an ancient forum, they stopped and stared in awe. They saw friars wearing robes of black, mercenaries marching in pairs, beggars looking no different from the beggars in Istanbul. Women wore perfume pendants round their necks, and they cared to cover neither their hair nor their bosoms. Davud, blushing up to his ears, averted his eyes every time they ran into a gentlewoman with puffy sleeves and her handmaids. But Jahan looked, secretly. By mid-afternoon they reached the address Simeon the bookseller had written down. They found it with ease after asking a couple of passers-by, who directed them, albeit with a hard stare, to the Jewish quarter.

Leon Buendia's shop in Rome bore an astonishing resemblance to Simeon Buendia's shop in Istanbul. Here, too, was a house on a cobbled, cluttered street; a faded, ancient wooden door; and, behind that, room after room of books and manuscripts. Here, too, lived an elderly man with oversized ears and flaring eyebrows, perhaps not quite as ill-humoured as his brother.

'Simeon sends his regards,' Jahan said in Italian when they had been ushered in, seated around a table and offered a sweet paste of almonds.

'How is my little brother doing?'

Jahan said, 'Working, reading, grumbling.'

Leon broke into a smile. 'He was always a surly one.'

'He wants you to move to Istanbul,' Jahan commented.

'He thinks it's better over there. I'd like him to settle here. We're mortals. Decisions are sheep; habits, the shepherd.'

Jahan was reflecting on this when Davud said: 'We'd like to visit Michelangelo.'

At this the bookseller shook his head. 'I have enormous respect for your master. But you must understand that's not easy. Il Divino accepts no one. After two years, he's still grieving.'

'Oh, who died?' Jahan asked.

'His brother, first. Then, his favourite apprentice. That destroyed him.'

Jahan could not help but wonder how long their master would mourn if something happened to one of them. Meanwhile, the bookseller said that the apprentice, whose name was Urbino, had been with Michelangelo since he was fourteen years old. For twenty-six years the two of them had been inseparable. Such was the master's devotion to his talented apprentice that in the last months of the latter's illness he had not allowed anyone else to take care of him, nursing him day and night. After Urbino's death, Michelangelo, always a peevish man, had become resentful, ready to explode at the slightest bother.

'Il Divino doesn't like people. The few he does, he loves too much.'

Jahan arched his eyebrows. Their master wasn't like this. Sinan neither loathed nor shunned people. Balanced and well-mannered, he was kind to all. Yet perhaps there was a short distance between accepting everyone and not being too keen on anyone. If so, wouldn't it be better to assist a master who was unkind to everybody except *you* than a master who was kind to everybody including *you*?

Leon continued, 'Il Divino's dislike of human beings is reciprocated, surely.'

'He's got enemies?' Davud asked.

'Oh, indeed. There are those who worship him and those who loathe him. Even God doesn't know which side outnumbers which.'

Leon said Il Divino already had plenty of rivals when he took over, unwillingly, the construction of San Pietro. Since then his admirers and adversaries had doubled. Although he had utilized much of Bramante's plan, he openly disparaged his predecessor, which had not helped to endear him to his enemies. 'He said Sangallo's design was badly done, poor in light. He said it'd make a good meadow.'

'Meadow?' Jahan asked.

'For grazing. He said Sangallo's design was for dumb oxen and sheep who knew nothing about art. That didn't go down well with those who were fond of Sangallo.'

Jahan sighed. Here, too, his master differed. For the life of him he could not imagine Sinan pouring scorn on another architect, dead or alive. He said, cautiously, 'We heard the Pope backs Michelangelo.'

'Well, true. If it weren't for His Holiness, the artist would be torn to pieces,' Leon remarked, shifting in his chair and, momentarily, blocking the candlelight. Just as his face sank into shadow, he said, 'Your master must have enemies, too.'

Davud and Jahan looked at each other. It was a strange thing to say, yet so true.

'He does,' Davud said, giving the smallest of nods.

Leon told them that at the head of Michelangelo's foes was a man named Nanni di Baccio Bigio – architect and sculptor. 'Strange, isn't it? The more like kindred a man seems, the more likely he is to become your enemy.' No sooner had Leon uttered this than his face crumpled, as though he realized he had said too much. He squirmed in his chair.

Watching him, Jahan said, 'We've tired you. We'd better leave.'

'I'd have liked to put you up, but . . .' Leon said, drawing in a breath.

There was a curfew in the Jewish quarter, he explained. Once the gates were locked, no one could go in. If they had visitors, they would have to inform the authorities. Having no intention of burdening the old man with their presence, they asked him to recommend somewhere where they could stay. Leon called his servant boy, who seemed to be about eight years old, and instructed him to take the Ottomans to a guest house, where, he said, they would be among fellow artists.

Thus they were on the streets again, pulling their horses by the reins as they trod behind the lad. They passed by wealthy houses with glass on the windows. They crossed markets where they saw pigs roasting on spits. Jahan had a suspicion the boy was not taking any shortcuts. Not because he wanted to show the city to them, but because he wanted to show them to the city. They were so obvious in their garments. Once, as Jahan turned back to talk to Davud, something, an intuition more than a concrete sight, stopped him cold. He feared they were being followed. He glanced left and right, unsure. Finally they arrived at a two-storey house that reeked of sausage and sweat. Their room and their pisspot they shared with three others – a painter, an anatomy student and a gambler.

The first thing next morning, they went to Il Divino's house. Finding its location was easy. Even children knew where the great man lived. Getting through his door, however, was beyond the bounds of possibility. They introduced themselves to his assistant, explaining they had been sent by the Ottoman Chief Royal Architect. In return, they were told, politely but firmly, that Michelangelo did not wish to see anyone.

'Who does he think he is?' Davud bellowed once they were out of earshot. 'He's belittling us.'

'You heard what everyone said; the man doesn't even see his own Pope.'

Davud clucked his tongue. 'I tell you, these infidels need a lesson. They can't treat us like this.'

In the ensuing days, they visited churches, as Sinan had asked them to do. The lime in Rome was of a warm shade, albeit inferior in nature. The locals mixed it with a brownish substance called pozzolana to produce mortar. When dry it turned fine and powdery, and they used it profusely in their building works; but over time it became covered by an ugly mould. Jahan and Davud took notes, sketched the buildings. Many times they became lost in a maze of alleyways, only to find themselves staring in wonder at a basilica. But it was the construction of San Pietro that impressed them beyond anything. A circular shrine in the cold morning light, elusive and enticing like the remains of a dream slipping away. It was far from being finished, but, having studied every model they could lay their hands on, they were able to fathom how massive and majestic it would be – the base, the drum, the dome and the cupola. Its smell of stone, sand and newly sawn wood would cling to their robes and stay with them.

Jahan thought that there were two main types of temple built by humankind: those that aspired to reach out to the skies and those that wished to bring the skies closer down to the ground. On occasion, there was a third: those that did both. Such was San Pietro. As he stood there watching, completing the structure in his mind's eye, he had the strange sense that here, too, was the centre of the universe.

The labourers were waiting for a delivery that had been delayed due to bad weather in the south. This was fortunate for Sinan's apprentices, because it enabled them to walk around without being seen by too many. Positioning themselves on a hill, they completed dozens of drawings. The lower choir walls, the giant pilasters, the crossing piers, each an ode to perfection.

Every day without exception they went to see Michelangelo, only to be stopped before they crossed the threshold of his house. The same apprentice – a painter and a nobleman of some kind – stood sentinel by the entrance, bent on not allowing anyone in. His name was Ascanio. Jahan had never met an apprentice so protective of his master.

'Il Divino is not a man of this world,' Ascanio said, staring at them intently. He explained how his master spurned his meals, surviving on pieces of bread. 'Even if you poured upon his head all the scudi in Rome, he'd still be living in penury.'

'Why live poorly in the midst of riches?' Davud said.

'Simple. He's not interested in earthly trinkets.'

Davud seemed determined to rub Ascanio up the wrong way. 'Is it true that he sleeps in his boots and never takes a bath?'

A flush of crimson crept over Ascanio's cheeks. 'Don't believe everything you hear. This city is cruel.' He said Michelangelo's friends in Florence had called him back, but, out of his love for his art and because he was a man of his word, he had not abandoned Rome. 'Do they appreciate it? Not even a crumb of gratitude! The more you give them the more they ask. You know what my master says?'

'What?' Jahan duly asked.

'Greed puts gratitude to sleep.'

What Ascanio didn't say was how the townsmen fretted that Michelangelo would die before he finished San Pietro. In old age his spirit was low, his body frail, though his mind was sharp as a blade. He suffered from sundry other ailments – trapped wind, a pain in the abdomen and kidney stones so severe he could barely take a piss sometimes. Jahan wondered if his master, too, feared death. A diligent and dedicated craftsman such as Sinan might have a hard time accepting his mortality.

He raised buildings that would remain, while his own transience loomed more heavily in his heart each passing day. It was a thought that came and went. He would remember it again, years later.

One afternoon, after another failed attempt to see Il Divino, they entered an eatery that smelled to high heaven of smoke and grease. They ordered eel pie, roasted quail and some sweet called *torrone*. That was when Jahan noticed a stranger watching them: his cap pulled down to his nose, his face half hidden.

'Don't look. Somebody is following us.'

'Who?' said Davud, instantly turning around.

The man sprang to his feet, pushed away his table and darted outside as if possessed. Sinan's apprentices exchanged a puzzled glance. Davud said with a shrug, 'He must have been a pilferer. He knows we are foreigners – probably wanted to nick our money.'

On the tenth day, they visited Michelangelo for the last time. Ascanio had left on an errand and not yet returned. Another apprentice had taken his place, someone younger and, seemingly, kinder. They introduced themselves as if this were the first time and asked the apprentice to inform his master of their presence. To their surprise he nodded amiably and went inside. In a little while he came back and said that Michelangelo had agreed to see them. Trying not to show their astonishment, they followed him. It dawned on Jahan that Ascanio might have never asked Michelangelo whether he would like to see them, certain that Il Divino did not want to be disturbed. Apprentices who regarded their masters like their fathers tended to be overprotective, he decided.

They were ushered into a large room. A clutter of paints, canisters, chisels, hammers, scrolls, books and clothes was scattered about. Most windows were covered with heavy, bright-hued curtains to block the noise from the street, giving the entire place an aura of unearthliness. In the midst of the jumble stood an elderly man, stiff and slender, working on a sculpture – a male head and torso – by the light spilling from candles made of goat's tallow. He had another burning candle strapped to the metal band on his head. He was neither tall nor solidly built, except for his shoulders, which were broad, and his arms, which were muscular. Small and dark were his eyes, solemn and sallow his countenance. His nose was flat, and, as for his beard, black bristles streaked with white, Jahan did not find it impressive. It was his hands that he was drawn to – long, bony fingers, pale at the tips; chipped and chewed fingernails covered in dust and dirt.

'Thank you for seeing us,' Jahan said, bowing.

Without turning around, Il Divino said, 'I once got a letter from your Sultan.'

'That must have been the late Sultan Bayezid,' Davud ventured.

Ignoring the remark, Michelangelo said, 'You don't make sculptures. How you can call it idolatry, I'll never understand. But your Sultan was generous. I was keen to come. It would have been my *grandissima vergogna*.* It wasn't meant to be.'

Gruff and throaty, like a man used to living inside his mind, he spoke so fast that Davud and Jahan had trouble following him with their limited Italian. He asked, 'How is your master?'

Only now remembering why they had come here in the first place, they presented the letter Sinan had entrusted to them. Wiping his palms on an apron dirtier than his hands, Il Divino broke the seal. When he finished reading, there was something in his eyes that wasn't there a moment ago – a kind of restlessness.

Davud told him they would be happy to carry any message he might wish to send to Sinan. Nodding, the artist strode to a table piled with oddments of all sorts. Shoving things on to the floor he cleared a space for himself and sat down to compose a letter, his forehead furrowed in thought.

Not knowing what to do meanwhile and not having been asked to sit, Jahan and Davud inspected their surroundings. On a workbench stood two models, both of San Pietro – one wooden, one clay. They noticed Michelangelo had redesigned the facade and got rid of the portico. He had also changed the shape of the main piers bearing the dome. The small windows were gone, replaced by fewer but larger windows that invited more light.

A crash pulled them out of their trance. Michelangelo, having

* The utmost disgrace.

finished his letter, was searching for his wax. Frustrated, he had pushed aside a couple of scrolls, breaking a flask.

They looked under books, in drawers, over boxes. At long last the lost item was found under a cushion, half crushed from being stepped on. Michelangelo melted the wax, put his seal on it, tied a ribbon round the letter. He must have seen their interest in the San Pietro models, for he said, 'Sangallo took years to complete his design. I've done mine in fifteen days.'

Jahan was surprised to hear the anger in his voice. He, the most revered artist in Rome, was competing with a ghost. It occurred to Jahan that perhaps sculpture suited Michelangelo's temperament more than architecture. He didn't say this. Instead, having seen an exquisite drawing of a horse he remarked, 'You like animals.'

'I study them.' Michelangelo explained that he dissected corpses and goitrous animals to see the muscles, the nerves, the bones.

'I've a white elephant,' Jahan said proudly. 'We work on construction sites.'

'Your master employs an elephant? Maybe I should have one, too.'

He asked them about the Suleimaniye Mosque, commending Sinan on his work. Where did Michelangelo's knowledge come from, Jahan wondered. He was searching for some delicate way to inquire when the artist lifted his hand and said, *'Altro non mi achade.'*★

They left quietly.

★ 'I think that's all.'

169

That same week they set off for Istanbul, making the journey on two
stallions. Fond as he was of his mount, Jahan missed Chota. He could
not help but worry that the tamer who had replaced him had not done
his job properly or, even if he had, the animal had refused to eat, as
elephants sometimes did, when they felt lonely or forlorn. But the
closer they got to Istanbul the more distraught he felt. In Rome he had
managed not to think about Mihrimah but now the memory of her
came back with a vengeance, like rapids smashing the barrier that had
trapped them.

When they stopped to rest and relieve themselves, Jahan noticed
that Davud looked pensive. As he knew his companion was an orphan
and had been raised by his grandfather, he asked him about his childhood. 'What is there to tell?' said Davud gently. He had been a lost,
angry boy until Master Sinan had found him, educated him and
changed his destiny.

Afterwards they made their way to Adrianople wordlessly, each
drawing into his own thoughts. Darkness descended; they galloped.
Only when their backs could take no more and the horses were foaming at the mouth did they slow down. There was an inn nearby and
that was where they decided to spend the night.

Inside, it was teeming. The dining hall was ample, though with
ceilings so low that unless you sat you had to stoop. In one corner, in a
fireplace hollowed out of stone, a cauldron blackened with soot simmered. At the long, wide wooden tables customers were perched –
men of every age and religion.

The instant Jahan and Davud entered every head turned in their
direction, and the noise slackened. Nobody welcomed them. Spotting
an empty place at the end of one table, they squeezed in. Jahan glanced
around. To his left sat a gaunt and greying man, perhaps a scribe, since
his fingers were stained with ink. Across from them was a Frank with
hair the colour of straw, warming his hands over a steaming bowl. He
doffed his hat towards them as though in salute.

'Do you know him?' Jahan asked Davud.

'How could I know anyone in this hole?'

A dwarf passed by carrying a tray of drinks. As he purposefully made his way, somebody tripped him. He fell down, the cups rolling along the floor. Peals of laughter erupted. The dwarf stood up, blushed but calm; the customers went back to their food, as if it had been someone else howling a moment ago.

They ate in silence. After supper Davud went upstairs for the evening prayer. Jahan decided to stay a bit longer. A kind of tranquillity such as he had never encountered before came over him. He was lonely as an abandoned lighthouse, yet in that moment he felt in company, though of what or whom he could not tell. For the first time the aching over Mihrimah's wedding stopped.

'Your friend's gone?'

Lifting his head, Jahan saw the man with the straw-coloured hair gazing at him.

'May I sit?' he asked, and without waiting for an answer did so. With a flick of his fingers he signalled to the dwarf. A minute later they had a jug on the table between them.

'Let's drink!' the stranger said.

The wine tasted of tree bark and roses left to dry. The traveller, whose name was Tommaso, struck Jahan as an intelligent man. An Italian, he said he was going east, as he was dying to see the Hagia Sophia. Glasses were renewed. Then the jug. They talked amicably, though afterwards Jahan would not remember half of what was said.

'Our master sent us to Rome,' said Jahan. Tipsy as he was he was careful not to mention the letter they were carrying. 'He wanted us to expand our knowledge.'

Like a man who had not spoken for a few days, Jahan talked about the things he was bent on achieving. Words dripping with wine. Since he had heard of Mihrimah's marriage, something in him longed to climb up fast.

Tommaso regarded him over the brim of his cup and said, very slowly, 'Does what we do in life matter so much? Or is it what we don't do that carries weight?'

'What do you mean?' asked Jahan after he knocked back his drink.

'Say you are passing through the woods and you see this woman. All alone. You could have her there, but you don't. That shows what kind of a man you are. A man swears at you. You could land a punch on his nose. If you don't, that is who you are.'

Jahan said, 'So not doing something is a feat, then?'

'True,' Tommaso said with a smile. 'You build with wood, stone, iron. You also build with absence. Your master knows this well.'

Jahan got a sick feeling in the pit of his stomach. 'How do you know him?'

'Everybody knows your master,' said Tommaso as he stood up and threw the dwarf a coin. 'Need to go, my friend.'

Secretly, Jahan was glad that Tommaso had paid. He would have felt guilty if he had had to spend his master's money on wine.

Tommaso said, 'If you want to thrive, that's fine. God bless you either way. Just don't become one of those wretched souls.'

Upstairs, Jahan found Davud sleeping among a dozen travellers. He tottered over to a window and opened it. A cricket chirruped outside. An owl hooted. It was an enchanting evening, the moon a golden sickle. Stretching out before him like a fan was a garden lined with stone-edged beds, wafting a smell so delicious he could have gobbled it up. As he was inhaling that sweet smell he remembered. Only then. Those words came to him. He had read them before. They were from Dante. *Inferno.* *Don't be one of those wretched souls who live without blame or without praise.*

The next morning, when Jahan and Davud woke up, they discovered they had been robbed. Their boots, the coins left in their purses, the silver pin, the crystal ball and the sack where they kept their drawings – all had vanished. So had Jahan's leather-bound diary and the ring he had hidden inside. Every sketch they had meticulously made throughout the journey had been carried off. Gone, too, was Michelangelo's letter.

'What kind of bandits would steal architectural drawings?' Jahan protested.

'They must have mistaken them for valuables,' Davud said sadly.

Oddly, nothing had been stolen from the other travellers. The thief, whoever he was, had targeted only Sinan's apprentices. They sobbed and wailed like children. They searched again and again. It was no use. Worried, mortified and broken, they left the inn. Each was accusing himself: Jahan for drinking the night before and Davud for falling asleep so early and so heavily.

They would never get to know what Il Divino had written to their master. The correspondence between the Chief Architect of Rome and the Chief Royal Architect of Istanbul was severed, and not for the first time. The apprentices arrived at the house of Sinan with nothing to offer him. It was as though nothing remained from their long journey, except the ache in their limbs and the memories of San Pietro, already withering away.

Captain Gareth arrived, an acrid smell of salt, sweat and liquor clinging to him. He seemed to pass through the palace walls as easily as a ghost. Nobody liked him, but nobody dared to upset him either. As a result, everyone gave him a wide berth – exactly what he wanted.

Jahan noticed the man didn't look well. His skin, which usually was a shade of bright pink not found among Ottoman men, had turned sallow. His lips were chapped, his cheeks sunken. Jahan suspected he might have contracted a disease on one of his voyages. Either that or treason had finally started to poison his soul.

'Well, well. It's been a long while. The other day I said to myself, I should go to visit the fake mahout and give him a piece of my mind. I get here and what do I hear? Oh, no, they say, he's in Rome! Rome? What a lucky lad you are. So how was it in the brothels? Would love to have a taste myself. Alas! Nobody sends me to Rome! Where's my compensation? Tell me, what did you bring for an old friend?'

'We have been robbed on our way back to Istanbul,' Jahan said.

'Oh, yeah? I love trumped-up stories.'

To shut him up, Jahan gave him the sapphire rosary he had stolen at the opening of the Suleimaniye Mosque. He had planned to sell it and buy a present for Mihrimah. What a dolt he had been.

One glance at the booty and the man's face fell. 'Is this all, you sluggard?'

It wasn't. Buried deep under the same tree, Jahan had another box: silver cutlery from the imperial kitchens, a pearl that had fallen off from the hem of Mihrimah's gown, a gold-nibbed pen, a jar of honey from the royal pantry and a hairpin that belonged to Hesna Khatun. The nursemaid had been giving him another roasting when she'd had an asthma attack and had bent forward so close to Jahan's finger-tips it would have been a sin not to snitch the hairpin. Jahan hadn't intended to hand any of these things to Captain Crazyhead. He had wanted to keep them to himself in case something went wrong and he needed to take flight.

But the Captain was no fool. 'I'm losing patience. Pity, you're still young. When they learn what kind of lies you've been telling, they'll skin you alive.'

Jahan shuddered at the thought, but he was also aware that the man had neither given him a drubbing nor pulled a dagger on him. Something was making him hesitate.

'Your Princess is miserable, they say. Poor thing. She has all the riches in the world but no love to cuddle her.'

'I haven't seen her in a while,' Jahan said uncomfortably.

'Oh, you will, I'm sure. Since she dotes on the white elephant . . .'

Jahan understood. Captain Gareth had heard that Princess Mihrimah was unhappy in her marriage. He had learned, just as the entire city had, that she spent many afternoons crying on her own in her beautiful, lonely house. Knowing that she was fond of Chota, and perhaps of the mahout, too, the Captain had guessed that it wouldn't take her too long to reappear in the menagerie. Jahan was the goose that would lay golden eggs for him. He didn't wish to butcher him too soon.

Suddenly Jahan felt heartened. With a grin he said, 'You should go now. The Chief White Eunuch might come by at any moment. I wouldn't want to be in your shoes if he finds you here.'

Captain Gareth's bottom lip sagged, unsure what to say. Jahan added hastily, 'Go! When I have something to show you, I'll send word.'

Although the man gave him an icy stare, he didn't object. For the first time he took his leave without uttering threats. And thus Jahan discovered something about wretches like him – that, as scary as they were, they thrived upon other people's weaknesses. If Jahan was determined to survive in the seraglio, he decided, he had to build an internal harem and put under lock and key every fear, worry, secret and heartbreak that had marred his soul. He would be both the Sultan and the eunuch of that harem. He would not allow anyone to take a peek inside. Including his master.

The Dome

Jahan would always remember 1562 as the year of happiness. Everyone had one such year in their lives, he believed. It grew, it blossomed, and, just as he started to think it would always be like this, it was over. His time of joy started when they set out to build a mosque for Mihrimah. Now that her father had given her vast lands and ample revenues, she had become the richest woman in the empire – and the most commanding. People were frightened to upset her. Including the apprentices. Even Master Sinan was rather uncomfortable in her presence. She sent everyone into a cold sweat. Except Jahan. He was too besotted with her to remember to fear her.

Thus, while the other apprentices were timid and reluctant to say anything new, Jahan was bursting with ideas. He worked so hard that, even though he was still no more than an apprentice, his master valued his eagerness. Sinan began to take Jahan with him whenever he visited the Princess to inform her about their progress.

All throughout those early months, no matter what Jahan did or where he was, he thought about the layout that Sinan had drawn so neatly. At night in bed he racked his brains to figure out how to perfect it. Even in his sleep he carried stones to Mihrimah's mosque. Then one day, overstepping a boundary, he drew a porch of seven domed bays and handed it to the Chief Royal Architect.

'You put aside my layout and drew your own,' said Sinan, sounding more incredulous than upset.

'Master, forgive me, I meant no disrespect. I believe the entrance to the mosque should be overwhelming, unexpected.'

Sinan could have scolded him then and there. He didn't. Instead he inspected the sketch and asked, 'Why seven?'

Jahan had already thought of an answer. 'It is the number of the layers of earth. And the circles a pilgrim makes around the Kaaba. It's a holy number.'

Sinan remained thoughtful for a moment. Then he rolled up the scroll and said, 'Come back with new designs. Do a better job, if you want me to take you seriously.'

Jahan did. He kept drawing, measuring, dreaming. At no stage did he confess to himself that he wanted the mosque to remind Mihrimah of the day they had met. When she was still a girl escaping from a wasp. When she had worn a necklace with seven pearls. In his plans he chose the lightest marble and granite for the columns, the colour of her dress and veil. Four towers would support the dome, as they had been four in the garden that afternoon: the Princess, Hesna Khatun, the mahout and the elephant. And a single minaret would stand high, slender and graceful, just like her. Her mosque would have lots of windows, both on the dome and in the prayer hall, to reflect the sunshine in her hair.

After weeks of this frenzy, Sinan pulled Jahan aside and said, 'I have been watching you toil away. Although you are not fully ready, I believe you have the strength and the grit. I'm going to give you more responsibility for Princess Mihrimah's mosque. I'll let you make those changes.'

Jahan kissed his master's hand, put it on his forehead. Whatever life had been like for him until then, it would never be the same afterwards. On no other construction site would he work this hard, exhausting himself with every detail.

Meanwhile, Jahan's tireless dedication was a source of irritation for the other apprentices, although this he wouldn't realize until it was too late.

As they neared the end of Mihrimah's Mosque, the master and the apprentices found themselves in a quagmire. For some time now the ancient aqueducts had been in need of repair. Lined up like defeated giants, they loomed over the city, aged and drained. As the population of Istanbul grew, so did the demand for water. Deep under hospitals, inns, slaughterhouses, *hamams*, mosques, churches and synagogues, holy springs percolated through the soil – except, it was not enough any more.

Sinan was ready to embark on the task. He did not just want to restore what had been done back in the days of the infidels: his intentions were bigger, more daring. He yearned to bring water to the entire city by building a succession of stone bridges, sluiceways and subterranean tunnels. Cisterns – open and covered – would supply provisions for dry summer seasons. It was a major venture and one that earned him adversaries aplenty – but none was powerful as Rustem Pasha: the royal groom, the new Grand Vizier and Mihrimah's husband.

Rustem had opposed Sinan's plan from the beginning. Fresh water meant fresh migrants – more congestion, more hovels, more pestilence. Istanbul was crowded enough and could do without new settlers, each of whom would arrive with a bundle of dreams and disappointments.

Many sided with Rustem, though for reasons of their own. Rival architects who begrudged Sinan his talent did not wish him to undertake such a colossal commission for fear that he might succeed. Laymen insisted no mortal could fetch water from the mountains – unless he was Ferhad bursting through Mount Bisutun to carry milk to Shirin. Preachers said the earth should be left undisturbed, lest the *djinn* awaken and heap calamities on mankind. While everyone sniped, Sinan went on working as if there were nothing to fret about. How he held on to his faith amid treachery and remained quiet in the face of malicious gossip was beyond Jahan's grasp. Not even once had the master returned slander with slander. He reminded Jahan of a turtle that, upon being prodded by children, retreats into its shell, waiting for the madness to pass. Yet the turtle that was Sinan kept working, working, all the time that he remained still.

Nikola and Jahan were to assist the master in the water scheme. It was their responsibility to take the measurements, calculate the angles of the slopes, perfect the designs, and inspect where the Byzantine waterways had failed and how they could be improved. Once they had all this information, they would present their findings to the Sultan.

Entrusted with a task this big, Nikola and Jahan were thrilled and anxious in equal measure. Of all the jobs they had undertaken over the years, this was by far the hardest. Even so, they slogged away less to impress the Sultan or to defeat the Grand Vizier than to avoid embarrassment for their master. One by one they detected the springs and boreholes, creeks and streams, well-heads and reservoirs, marked them on the map and ruminated on how to connect them through channels both above and below the ground. Finally, one Thursday afternoon, the master and the two apprentices, spruce and spirited, headed to the palace, laden with designs and hopes.

It was Rustem who welcomed them, courteously but coldly. Jahan dug his fingernails into his palms so as to stop from shaking in front of the Croatian who had stolen Mihrimah from him. The Grand Vizier did not notice a thing. With his tall body, cunning mind and resilient nature, he had won a great many accolades – and today it seemed likely that he would do his best to obstruct Sinan. So deep was his dislike of the migrants from Anatolia that, in order to prevent them from coming, he was willing to sacrifice the prosperity of everyone in the city.

Upon being ushered into the Audience Chamber, they found Sultan Suleiman on his throne, which was covered in gold cloth and studded with gems. A fountain trickled in one corner, its sound breaking the silence in the room. The Lord of Worlds, wearing a robe of yellow satin with black sable, greeted Sinan warmly, though the hardness in his voice was lost on no one. He had put on bright colours for the first time in weeks. His two sons had become each other's worst enemy, but it was the loss of Hurrem that had shattered him like nothing else. The woman to whom he had written love poems, the mother of his five children, the queen who was both hated and adored, the concubine who had climbed higher than any other harem girl, the laughing one, was gone. She had died without seeing one of her sons on the Ottoman throne.

After prostrating themselves three times on the ground, eyes cast down, the apprentices trod behind their master, the carpet soft and lush beneath their feet. Later on, Jahan would remember the light spilling from the sconces, and the smell of the linden tree outside the window that he dared not peek at but was comforted by all the same.

'Chief Royal Architect, defend your plans,' ordered Sultan Suleiman.

Sinan gave his apprentices a nod. They had drawn their sketches on panels of camel skin, so thin as to be transparent. Four in total. Nikola and Jahan, each taking an end, unrolled and displayed the first design. Sinan, meanwhile, gave an account of what he intended to do, pointing every now and then at some detail. Neither the Sultan nor the Grand Vizier uttered a word.

They swiftly proceeded to the second and third drawings – aqueducts of various sizes and at various locations. The fourth – that of a warren of underground conduits that would link several sources, the plan that most excited them – Sinan put aside. Had he found a more receptive audience, he would have shown it. Now, however, instinct told him to keep it to himself. Instead, he said that, with the help of ducts, he would make the water flow to gardens, courtyards and vineyards. He said there was nothing as noble as relieving the thirst of the parched. When he finished, Sultan Suleiman hemmed and hawed for a while. Turning to the Grand Vizier, he asked his opinion.

Rustem had been waiting for this moment. He spoke gingerly, as if what he were about to reveal caused him pain, yet he had no other choice. 'Architect Sinan is a skilful man. He came here with a sublime idea. But I'm afraid he doesn't understand this will only bring us trouble.'

'What kind of trouble, Vizier?'

'My Sultan, this is costly. It'll strain the treasury.'

When asked what he had to say to that, Sinan said, 'There are ways to cut expenses. Where we can, we'll choose the shortest route and use suitable materials.'

The Grand Vizier said, 'What will you have achieved then? More migrants! Say there is a fire – how will you put it out if you have houses planted side by side like wild mushrooms?' Not expecting an answer, he produced a handkerchief and wiped his forehead. 'This city is full to bursting. We need no more.'

A shadow crossed Sinan's face. 'How many will arrive is a question that can be settled by our Sultan. But the people who are here ought to have water.'

This went on for a while. The Chief Royal Architect countered the Grand Vizier, the Grand Vizier countered the Chief Royal Architect. Finally, bored with the parley, the Sultan declared, 'That's enough, I've listened to both sides. You shall learn my decision!'

Sinan and his apprentices, walking backwards, left the chamber. Rustem stayed behind, which Jahan thought unfair. Surely in their absence he would try to persuade the sovereign. Jahan racked his brains to try to save the situation. If one of them could spend a bit more time alone with the Sultan, without the interference of the Grand Vizier, he might be brought round. Otherwise, they stood no chance.

That evening, enervated by the events of the day, the apprentices stayed in Sinan's house. Jahan had hoped to discuss things, but the master, never one for idle ramblings, made them study. Exhausted, they retreated to bed following supper. It was there, as he lay on his mat, tossing and turning in the dark, that Jahan came up with a plan.

Unable to wait till the morning, he groped his way to the other side of the room, where Nikola was sound asleep. He shook him by the shoulder.

Jolted out of whatever dream he was having, Nikola said, 'Who is there?'

'Shh, it's me.'

'Jahan . . . what's happened?'

'Can't sleep. I keep thinking about how it went today.'

'Me too,' he said, even though he had been dead to the world a moment ago.

'How can our Sultan reach a just decision when the Vizier is with him all the time? Master sees the Sultan only once in a while. Rustem has access to him every day.'

'True, but there's nothing we can do.'

'Maybe there is. I've an idea,' Jahan said. 'There is one place where the Grand Vizier will never bother the Sultan.'

Nikola gasped. 'You are going to enter the harem?'

'Nay, dim-witted one,' Jahan said, chuckling despite himself. 'There's *another* place the Vizier would not accompany him. Guess!'

'Ogh, I can't,' Nikola pleaded. 'Tell me.'

'Hunting. When the Sultan goes hunting, I'll follow him and explain our intentions. Without that nosy Vizier around, he'll think more clearly.'

'Brother, that's a brilliant plan,' Nikola said.

They both knew the Grand Vizier detested the chase. Being hopelessly clumsy, he could not move at the same pace as the others, let alone track a prey up and down the hills.

'This'll be our gift to our master,' Jahan said. 'Don't tell him anything yet.'

Nikola's voice dwindled to a whisper. 'What if it's dangerous?'

'Why should it be? If the Sultan does not want to listen, I'll leave.'

'Shall I come with you?'

'Better if I go alone. When I get back, I promise I'll tell you everything.'

'But . . . be careful.'

'Don't worry, it's going to be fine.'

Despite his confidence, Jahan's mind was a beehive the rest of the week, his nerves in shreds. He constantly rehearsed, word by word, what he would tell the Sultan. Thanks to his companions in the menagerie, he knew where the Sultan would be hunting and when. Here began the second part of his plan, which he had not shared with Nikola. He would take Chota with him. So far all his efforts to endear the animal to the Sultan had been for naught. Now, Jahan thought, both the elephant and the mahout had a chance to win him over.

The day, at last, arrived, and the morning saw Jahan, atop the elephant, a leather bag strapped to his back, reaching the enormous Bab-i Humayun Gate in the direction of Hagia Sophia and saluting the guards.

'Where are you going?' one of them asked.

'Our Sultan, refuge of the world, forgot his lucky bow. I've been ordered to take it to him.'

'Why didn't they send out a horseman?' demanded a second guard.

'Because elephants are faster than horses,' Jahan said without missing a beat.

They sniggered. The first guard said, 'Maybe I should go to check.'

'Sure, I'll wait. If the Sultan notices he doesn't have his lucky bow and gets upset, it won't be my fault.'

Chewing their moustaches, the men regarded him. Jahan's seriousness had given them pause for thought. Then, as if linked to each other through an invisible string, they both moved aside.

'Go!' said the second guard. 'You'd better hurry that elephant up.'

And so Jahan did, though not until the city was behind them. He didn't want Chota to trample anyone. As soon as the sights and sounds of Istanbul had vanished, he ordered the elephant to run.

They reached the pinewoods north of the city. Jahan had learned that whenever the Sultan went hunting, he would drive his prey towards the edge of a certain precipice. That's where Jahan waited. A long time went by – or so it seemed to him. He began to worry. They might be hiding somewhere behind the bushes, for all he knew, and shoot him accidentally. He was inventing new fears when he heard the distant barking of dogs. There were half a dozen of them, drawing swiftly near.

Then Jahan saw it – him. A stag. Out of the forest he sprang, reeling. An arrow had pierced his neck and a second one his heart. It was a miracle that he was still running.

As Jahan got off the elephant, the stag came closer, its antlers glittering in the sunset. It was a magnificent animal – large liquid eyes, wild to the point of delirium. Disturbed by the smell of blood, Chota swung his tusks. But the stag had reached a point beyond threats. He widened his nostrils and, opening his mouth, as though he wanted to say something, collapsed.

Jahan sprang towards him, tripping over a tree root. By the time he reached the deer, five greyhounds had appeared out of nowhere, barking with all their might. They circled the carcass, not letting him get close.

On an impulse Jahan turned around. The Sultan, sitting astride his horse, was staring at him. Trembling, Jahan threw himself to the ground. 'My Lord.'

'What are you doing here – you and the elephant?'

'This humble servant came to see you, if you'll allow me to say a few words.'

'Aren't you my mahout?'

'Yes, my Lord,' Jahan said. Just the other day he had stood a few steps away from him, showing their designs. But apparently he had forgotten. 'I'm also an apprentice to Master Sinan. It's on this matter that I came to plead to your Highness.'

While they were speaking, servants had loaded the carcass on to a cart pulled by two horses. The greyhounds, still barking their triumph, followed noisily.

'You have taken a royal elephant without permission?' the Sultan asked. 'Do you know you could be flogged for less than that?'

'Your Majesty, I ask your forgiveness. I had to see you. I hoped if I came with the elephant you would notice me.'

If Jahan had dared to look up, he would have seen the Sultan's eyes crinkled in a smile. 'You must have a reason for such a misdeed.'

'My Lord, if you'll allow me . . .' Jahan couldn't help the quiver in his voice.

Slowly, Jahan unrolled the camel skin they had not had the opportunity to show the other day. He explained how important Sinan's scheme was for the city and how many people – old, sick, frail and poor – would pray for the Sultan every time they quenched their thirst. Sultan Suleiman listened and asked questions. Jahan was delighted to see he had been right to assume that outside the palace walls the sovereign would be a different man – a kinder man.

The Sultan said, 'Does your master know you are here?'

'He does not. He'd be upset at me if he knew.'

'I should be upset with you, but I'm not. You revere your master, clearly. If all of Sinan's apprentices are as devoted as you, he's a fortunate man.'

Jahan felt a smile tug at the corners of his mouth. Of such unbidden vanities are perhaps spun life's gravest delusions. It is at moments like this that Sheitan taps on our shoulders and whispers in our ear, asking, naively, why we should not want more.

'Your Majesty, may I show you one more thing?'

The Sultan gave the slightest nod. Jahan took out the parchment he had kept inside his robe. It was a design of his own – for a stone river-bridge with seven arches.

It would have stone projections facing upstream to protect the piers from the force of the water and walkways above for pedestrians and animals. Its massive drawbridge would make it possible to control the flow of goods and passengers. If the Sultan accepted his bridge alongside Sinan's waterways, Jahan would make quite a name for himself. 'Architect of water' they would call him. Or, better yet, 'Sinan's prodigy.' He might even be accepted into the guild, who knew. As a rule an apprentice made his way up no faster than a snail would inch across a meadow, but why shouldn't Jahan be an exception? His success would surely reach Mihrimah's ears.

Casting no more than a glance at the design, the Sultan grabbed his stallion's bridle. 'I like your courage, young man. But courage is a dangerous thing. Remember, a ruler considers many aspects before making a decision. Go back, wait to hear from me.'

Off he rode, tailed by men, dogs and horses. Even after they had disappeared, Jahan could feel their wind on his skin. He heaved a sigh of relief. Everything had gone smoothly. He thanked the skies.

The next day, on the construction site, Nikola came running. 'What happened? How did it go?'

'I saw him. I talked to him.'

Nikola's eyes grew wide. 'You did?'

'Yes!' Jahan said with a feeling of triumph he could barely contain. 'If you ask me, our Sultan wants us to build a new aqueduct and a bridge.'

'What bridge?'

'Oh, I mentioned this bridge I designed.'

'Without consulting the master?'

Feeling uneasy, Jahan didn't answer. All day he waited for a chance to speak with Sinan. It did not come. Instead, shortly before sunset, four Janissaries arrived.

Sinan greeted them. '*Selamun aleikum*, soldiers, what brings you here?'

'We came to get one of your men, Architect.'

Sinan said, 'There must be a mistake. My labourers are honest people.'

'Not a labourer. An apprentice!'

Having overheard the conversation, Jahan walked towards them, sensing the inevitable. Just then Sinan asked, 'Which one?' A soldier gave Jahan's name.

Baffled, Sinan blinked. 'He is a good student.'

'The Grand Vizier's orders,' said the head of the soldiers, who respected the master and did not want to upset him by dragging off his apprentice.

'He didn't do anything wrong, did he?' Sinan insisted.

No one volunteered an answer. Into the awkward silence, Jahan muttered, 'I'm sorry, master.'

Sinan's face crumpled as he realized there were things about which he did not know. Placing his hands on Jahan's shoulders, he squeezed hard, as if he wanted to pass on to him some of his faith. He said, 'Whatever happens, I shall not leave you. You are not alone. God is with you.'

Jahan's throat constricted. He dared not open his mouth for fear a sob would escape his lips. The soldiers, respectfully, walked on either side of him. As soon as the sounds of the construction site had been reduced to a faint murmur, they manacled Jahan's hands. In this state he was taken to the Grand Vizier.

'You!' Rustem Pasha said, pointing a finger. 'You had the effrontery to ambush the Sultan. Like a snake you slithered behind my back!'

Jahan felt sweat dampen his neck; he was trembling.

'You intend to bring doom on the treasury, that's it! I inquired about you. You seem to be full of lies! Are you an Iranian spy?'

'My Vizier,' Jahan said, his voice breaking, 'I swear on the Holy Qur'an, I am no spy. I had no bad intentions.'

'We'll see about that.' Rustem called the guards.

This was how Sinan's unruly apprentice, in an effort to help his master bring water to the city, found himself being taken to the dark dungeons of the Fortress of Seven Towers – where hundreds and hundreds of souls had gone before him but only a handful had come out alive.

'Your name?' the scribe asked for the second time.

Jahan was doing himself no favours by refusing to answer. Even so, something inside him resisted having his name added to that parchment, which included the name of every lowlife who had ever been caught in Istanbul. He was seized by an increasing fear that once you were written down, you would be entombed in this hole till the end of time.

The scribe glared at him. His accent, in contrast with his handwriting, lacked the slightest grace. 'I ask, you answer. If you don't, I chop off your tongue.'

The head warden, who had been watching them, interjected, 'Now, now. No need to frighten the hen.'

'A royal hen, *effendi*!' said the scribe.

'We shall see. All hens are the same with their feathers plucked.'

'That's right, *effendi*!'

Regarding Jahan with a deadpan expression, the head warden did not laugh. Thin-faced and round-shouldered, he reminded Jahan of a boy in his village who used to catch toads, tie them on a stick and dissect them with his knife – all the while his face unchanging, his stare vacant.

'We never had anyone like him, did we?' said the head warden, as if Jahan weren't in the room.

'Yeah, quite a catch, this one.'

'The Grand Vizier's catch!'

Jahan understood that they already knew everything about him. Asking his name – just like holding him in fetters when it was clear that he wasn't going to take flight – was for the sheer pleasure of annoying him. By remaining silent he was only prolonging the mockery. His voice came out hoarse when he spoke. 'I'm our Sultan's elephant-tamer and apprentice to the Chief Royal Architect.'

A brief silence followed, pricked by the scratching of the scribe's plume. When he finished, the scribe said, 'He's a sorry man, isn't he, *effendi*?'

'Sorry, for sure. Small man with a big enemy.'

Jahan swallowed hard. 'My master will get me out of here.'

The head warden came so close that Jahan could smell his sour breath. 'Every man who rotted in here had a master. It did them no good. Those masters did not even go to their funerals.'

The scribe chuckled. Jahan insisted, 'My master is different.'

'A cock that crows too soon is calling the butcher,' said the head warden and, raising his voice, he said to the guards, 'Take this prince to his palace.'

The guards shoved Jahan through a dingy, damp corridor. They went down a flight of stairs and entered a passageway so narrow that they had to proceed single file. Jahan could not help but notice the cracks on a wall where slimy, green moss had gathered. They descended to another floor, then another. The stench got thicker, the gloom heavier. He stepped upon something that he knew instinctively had once been alive.

They were in the belly of the tower. Save for a few sconces, it was so dark that if Jahan hadn't known it was morning when he had been brought here, he would have believed night had fallen. There were cells left and right, carved out like missing teeth in a mouth. Then he saw *them*. Hollow-cheeked, raw-boned, short and tall, young and old. Some were watching him, their foreheads resting against the iron bars. Others ignored him, turning their backs. Still others were lying on coarse mats. Every now and then, Jahan caught sight of a bony arm reaching out for a ladle of water, a haggard face peeking out from the shadows, turds piled beside buckets filled to the brim with excrement.

One inmate cried out in a gravelly whisper, and when Jahan turned to hear what he was saying, he spat on his face. Unable to move his hands, Jahan tried to wipe off the phlegm with his shoulder. The prisoner laughed. Even when his lips had stopped moving, the laughter continued – low, creepy. In that moment Jahan felt like the tower was jeering at him. His knees gave way. True, he was a thief, but not like them. These people were bandits, murderers, rapists, marauders and brigands. He should not have been among them. Bitterness rose in his throat like bile, almost choking him.

'Walk!' barked a guard.

Ahead of them something squeaked. The guard shone his torch on it. A bat. Jahan wondered how it had got in. There was no time to ponder. Opening a rusty gate, the guards pushed Jahan into an empty dungeon.

'Here's your throne, your Highness!'

Jahan waited for his eyes to get used to the dark. There were slivers of light from openings high above, no more than half a dozen and each no larger than a coin. This was where fresh air entered, if it did at all. He saw stone walls, a dirt floor, a threadbare mat and two wooden buckets – one of which was caked with faeces, and the other filled with water in which a few dead insects floated.

'Hey, why didn't you bring him here?' someone yelled from across the hall.

The man raved about what he would do to Jahan. At each lecherous remark his mates hooted with laughter. They went on in this vein for a while, he shouting obscenities and smacking his lips, the others jeering. Soon they were singing a song – banging, clapping, stomping their feet. Such was the noise Jahan could not help but steal a glance at their cell, which, in contrast to his, was bright with candles.

One of the inmates – a lad with curly hair, almond eyes, dimpled cheeks – began to dance while the others whistled and cheered. With a slow sway, he pulled his shirt up, exposing his bellybutton, on which shone a tiny pearl. Underneath, a word was tattooed in letters large and legible enough for Jahan to make it out – *Beloved*.

'Come on, Kaymak!'

'Shake that sweet rump!'

Emboldened, Kaymak began to joggle his body. The harder he jerked and jiggled the more ribald the taunting became. The other inmates – there were four of them – cackled, though Jahan noticed they were frightened of the bully. What struck him was that these prisoners were unchained, unlike himself and pretty much everyone else whom he had passed along the way. How they had obtained this privilege, Jahan could not possibly imagine.

As Jahan was observing the lad, the bully had been observing him. Suddenly, he grabbed Kaymak from behind and thrust himself forward as if mounting him. His cronies roared. Blushing, Kaymak broke into a nervous smile. The ruckus must have been heard from everywhere but the guards had disappeared.

The bully produced a blade from out of his boot. He licked its cold, sharp end and held it against Kaymak's throat. The lad's Adam's apple bobbed up and down, but he continued swinging. For a while the three were locked in a world of their own – the bully, the dancer, the blade.

The bully stepped aside, rolled up his sleeve. His left arm was covered in bruises and lacerations: some of the latter had scabbed over, while others seemed to be recent. With one quick move he slashed his flesh from wrist to elbow. Trickles of blood dropped on to the floor, which, Jahan only now realized, was flecked with black stains. Try as he might to appear indifferent, Jahan went limp. It occurred to him that he could kill this man.

That was when a voice penetrated the air. 'Enough, you lot!'

The command, unreal as it sounded, echoed off the walls and muted the commotion at once. Jahan glanced to his right, towards the cell at the end of the corridor. At first he saw nothing. Then, slowly, out of the dusk, strode a familiar face. Balaban.

The bully gave a grunt. 'The chaps were havin' a bit of fun.'

'Yeah? Tell 'em they're giving me a headache.'

The bully gestured to his men. They retreated to the corners of their cell, including the lad, who reluctantly strutted away.

'One more thing,' called Balaban.

'Hmmm?'

'Stop cutting yourself, Abdullah. Don't want to see blood everywhere.'

'It was for the newbie,' Abdullah said, sounding offended that his gore wasn't appreciated.

'Well, the ceremony is over,' Balaban said. He approached the iron bars of his cell, only now glancing at Jahan. 'What do you know! It's the Indian guy.'

There were five Gypsies with him in his dungeon, loyal to the core. One by one they bobbed their heads and saluted Jahan.

'How did you end up in this shithole?' asked Balaban.

'I have upset the Grand Vizier,' said Jahan. 'And you?'

'Me? I've done nothing. Just gave a kadi a little tickle!'

Balaban had been arrested for stealing a coach that belonged to a judge. This man had thrown Balaban's distant cousin into gaol and sent his great-uncle to the gallows-tree. Determined to avenge his family,

Balaban and his mates had purloined the kadi's jewels and kaftans, cooked the peacocks in his courtyard, kidnapped his fourth wife and set his stables on fire. Only when they set their sights on his brand-new coach – brought from Frangistan and previously owned by a seigneur – had they been caught.

In the dungeons of the Fortress of Seven Towers, Balaban was king. Amid the misery and wretchedness he had made an oasis – soft, silk cushions, a brazier for warmth, a brass pot to brew coffee, the carved oak chair that was his throne. The inmates either revered or avoided him, careful not to tread on his toes. For they all had loved ones outside – parents, wives, children. Even the fiercest prisoner was aware that, should he wrong Balaban, a member of the Gypsy kith and kin would strike back. For Balaban was the head of an enormous tribe, the size of which was a mystery even to him. But this wasn't the only reason why he was held in the highest regard. Inmates and guards dreaded the Romany jinx, which, if cast on a full moon, could be purged only in seven generations' time. Even after the culprit died, his grandchildren would suffer the consequences.

All this Jahan learned fast. He suspected that behind the legends about Balaban was none other than Balaban himself. Next to Sinan, he was the most intelligent man Jahan had met. But whereas his master's wit was a calm, bottomless lake, Balaban's was a turbulent river, slopping and sloshing over, too tempestuous to follow a course.

At night Jahan wrapped around himself a flimsy, moth-eaten blanket that reeked of every soul who had used it. Often it got so chilly his teeth chattered; the clatter reminding him of chisels chipping away at stone. Through the cracks in the walls the wind howled, insects scuttled, rats scurried. The thought of one of these creatures entering his ear or chewing up his nose was so terrifying he slept in fits and starts, awaiting the break of dawn, his head aching from clenching his jaw. He missed Chota. He longed to see Mihrimah once more, hear her satin voice. His previous life now seemed like a tale he vaguely knew because he had once heard it from someone else.

The guards were spiteful, the weeks painfully slow. Time became a winding staircase that reached nowhere. Loneliness, he could cope with; desertion he could not. Try as he might to find excuses he could not comprehend why Sinan had not even sent him a message.

In the early days, whenever he heard footsteps down the corridor, he had expected the guards to release him. Not any more. Surely he was forgotten. He imagined them – Yusuf, Nikola, Davud and his master – working as usual, unaffected by his absence. He saw Mihrimah with her handmaidens, contemplating her face in a Venetian mirror, silently mourning, silently but not deeply. He thought about Chota and the animal-tamers in the palace, each in his own world. Resentment and rage infested his soul, multiplying faster than the lice crawling on his head.

Once a day they were given a piece of mouldy bread and a gruel with bits of gristle, none of which Jahan could cram down without retching. Hunger did strange things, he found out. No matter what time of the day, he dreamed of food – all kinds of provisions. He talked to himself, arguing with those who had hurt him in the past. Captain Gareth, Carnation Kamil Agha, the bear-tamer Mirka . . . Awake or asleep, he quarrelled with each of them. In his cell Abdullah watched him with a wry smile, as though to say they were now beginning to look alike.

A month into this, the guards brought in a boy with a face too pretty for his own good – a pilferer, as it turned out. He could barely walk, having received a hundred strokes on each foot. Afterwards he had duly kissed the hands of his punisher, thanking him for teaching him the way of righteousness. He was asked to pay the man who had flogged him in return for having tired him so. The boy had not a single asper to his name. He was beaten again, and sent to the Fortress of Seven Towers.

There was plenty of space in Jahan's cell, but the boy was put in the one opposite. It didn't take Abdullah long to start harassing him. The boy resisted fiercely. Every so often Jahan heard his reedy voice, infused with fear. Dark circles appeared under his eyes. Jahan suspected he could not lay his head down to rest for having always to be alert.

One morning, having only just passed out at dawn, Jahan awoke to muffled sounds. He noticed Kaymak first, plucking his eyebrows in one corner of his cell. The others were playing a game of dice, yelling and swearing. Then he saw them: Abdullah had propped his blade against the boy's throat, forcing him to be quiet as he pulled his breeches down. Everyone was feigning ignorance.

Jahan ran to the bars and shouted at the top of his voice, 'Balaban!'
Not a sound. 'Balaban, hey!'

'What?' came a grumpy response. 'Why are you braying like a horse?'

'The boy is in a bad way!'

'So?'

'Help him!'

'If I were to help every witless lad, I wouldn't have time to shit.'

'He's only a child.'

'So? If you're a mallet, knock; if you're a peg, bear the knocking.'

Jahan bellowed, 'Damn you! Do something or else . . .'

The sentence dangled in the air, unfinished. Jahan hesitated, swallowing hard. With what could he possibly threaten him? He added, wearily, 'It means you are no different than Abdullah.'

'Never claimed I was,' Balaban replied.

Abdullah chuckled. His hands fondling the boy's haunches, he said, 'You want to save him? Come, swap places!'

An awkward silence descended as Jahan considered what to do. Balaban, Kaymak, the boy, the inmates down the corridor – it felt as though everyone was waiting for his response. Jahan felt a burning shame and yet also the need to say something remarkable. 'I've an elephant. He's trampled many a man. When I get out of here, I swear he'll kill you.'

'What is an elephant?' said Abdullah, sounding confused.

'A wild beast. Larger than a house.'

Abdullah scoffed. 'Did you swallow hashish, eh? Where did you find it?'

'It's true. Elephants are the biggest animals on earth. Mine will make a hash of you.'

'That's a lie!' Abdullah said.

'You better believe him,' Balaban broke in. 'Got an elephant myself. His elephant and mine are husband and wife. Clever animals. Smarter than you, for sure. They could squash you like a toad.'

Now that Balaban had sided with Jahan, Abdullah took the threat more seriously. Frowning, he asked, 'What do they eat?'

'Human flesh,' Jahan said.

'Liar!' Abdullah said, though less certain this time.

In that fleeting moment the boy freed himself from Abdullah's

embrace and ran to the other side of the cell. He did not speak a word all day. Fortunately for him, he would soon be released. Glad as Jahan was to see him safe, he could not rise from his own mat to bid him farewell. He felt tired. And thirsty. And cold. Time had come to a stop for him. In fits of delirium, he kissed Mihrimah, laughed with Sinan, walked beside Nikola, Yusuf and Davud. He saw a few *ghuls* and *ifrits**★*
as well. One of them was quite pesky, insisting that he swallow a brew.

'I don't want anything from an *ifrit*,' Jahan said.

'I'm no *ifrit*, you idiot.'

Jahan forced his eyes open. 'Balaban?'

'Yeah, come on, drink! You're burning up.' Holding the cup in one hand, Balaban helped Jahan to sit up and rest his back against the wall.

'What are you doing here?'

'Looking after you.'

'How did you get in?'

'I've the keys to every cell in this corridor.'

'You what?'

'Shh, we'll talk about that later. Say, do you have a wife?'

'Nay.'

'How about a lover, eh? Big bosom, warm arse. Imagine she made a sherbet for you. Take a sip, don't break her heart.'

For the life of him Jahan could not think of Mihrimah preparing for him – or for anyone else – *sherbet*. Closing his eyes, he muttered, 'I don't want –'

'Trust me and drink this.'

'Trust *you*? You didn't help the boy.'

Balaban sighed. 'That boy was not one of ours. He had not sworn allegiance. If I protect everyone, how will I keep my own people loyal? I've enough to worry about. You know what they say, where there are two Gypsies, there are three opinions.'

'So you only protect yours?'

'Yes, only family!'

'Damn your family!'

'Watch what you say, brother. Why should I help every rogue in this hole?'

★ Types of *djinn*, huge winged creatures of fire.

'Why are you helping me? I was wrong. You're worse than Abdullah.'

'You talk to me like that and I'll rip out your tongue.'

'Do it,' said Jahan. 'Doesn't matter any more.'

'Unless . . . you are family. Then you can talk to me like that.'

Seized by a fit, Jahan coughed, his shoulders convulsing. When he found his voice again, he asked, 'What are you talking about?'

'Let's make a deal. You drink this, get well. I throw a feast come this spring. I make you an honorary Romany. I don't have to chop out your tongue.'

A ripple of laughter came from Jahan's lips. Balaban glowered at him. 'You think it's funny?'

'Nay, it's not that,' Jahan said. 'I'd be honoured. It's just . . . I don't think I'll get out of here.'

Abdullah, having eavesdropped on them from his cell, yelled, 'Let him rot!'

'Shut your trap!' Balaban shouted. Lowering his voice, he said to Jahan, 'You drink this, I make you a Gypsy. This is an excellent brew, *Daki dey*'s* recipe.'

In his state it didn't occur to Jahan to ask who that was. As soon as he took a sip, he spat it out. 'Ughh. What's this? Disgusting.'

Balaban sighed. With one brisk move, he pulled Jahan's head back, pressed it against his shoulder and poured the liquid down his throat. Spilling and gasping and coughing and retching, Jahan nevertheless swallowed half of it.

'Good,' Balaban said. Taking out a handkerchief from inside his waistcoat, he tied it around Jahan's head. 'This spring, you become family.'

Whether it was the magic of the brew, which Jahan consumed three times a day for the next week, or sheer luck, of which he didn't think he had much, he overcame the illness. He even found the strength to start designing again.

* Maternal grandmother.

In the Fortress of Seven Towers, if hope was a scarcity, shit was a superfluity. The buckets were seldom emptied and Jahan's was no exception. A pile of excrement had accumulated in one corner. In days of old, architects had scratched their designs into plaster tracing-floors. Jahan drew on his floor with a twig and used shit as ink.

First he designed a caravanserai. Wiped it off, tried a manor house, one worthy of Mihrimah. His masterpiece was a prison building. Not vertical but horizontal. Through large openings in the ceiling it would get lots of light and fresh air. In his prison he would never place the young convicts with the old. Nor would he keep anyone in chains. The convicts could work in ateliers, learning carpentry or masonry. There would be workshops adjacent to the master building. Until this day Jahan had enjoyed designing buildings but had never really given any thought to those who would be using them and to how they would feel. Now it was different. He cared about people as much as he did about buildings.

'What are you doing?' Balaban asked the next time he came to check on him.

'Drawing an alms house. This part is the kitchen. And here is the library. If every wise man in the city would teach there for a day, imagine how even the destitute could thrive.'

'Poor thing, you've gone mad,' said Balaban; but he couldn't help asking, 'How about the other?'

'That's a hospital,' said Jahan, pointing at the second drawing. 'For people madder than me. The building will contain them but without incarcerating them.'

'Well, do your drawings outside. I've got news. The Grand Vizier pardoned you.'

'How do you know?'

'I have family in the palace.'

A shadow crossed Jahan's face. 'But why? What has changed?'

'What's wrong with you?' said Balaban, throwing up his hands in exasperation. 'Fall on your knees and thank Allah. Why are you always asking questions? When you are drowning, you grab on to a snake. You don't say, Are you a good snake or a bad one, let me take a look at you first.'

Shortly before dawn, Jahan heard footsteps; then the key turned in the lock to his cell. Two guards entered. They took off his chains, helped him to his feet. Despite what he had heard from Balaban, the first and only thing that came to his mind was that they were going to execute him. Seeing his reluctance, they pushed him, though more gently than they had on other days. Their compassion confirmed his fear.

'Are you going to hang me?'

'Nay, imbecile. You're free to leave.'

In disbelief Jahan walked towards Balaban's cell. The Gypsies were asleep. It upset him to go without saying goodbye; he took off the handkerchief the chieftain had wrapped round his head and tied it to the iron bars. He glanced at Kaymak, who just then muttered something inaudible. Lying nearby, Abdullah was sleeping peacefully, seemingly incapable of the violence that was within him.

They strode along the corridors, up the stairs. As they ascended the floors, all Jahan could think about was who had saved him and why. Outside there was a carriage waiting for him.

'Where are we going?' he asked the coachman.

'I've been ordered to take you to My Lady Mihrimah.'

Thus he discovered who had rescued him. From the coach window he stared at the haze over the sea, the dark green of the pine trees, the kites with their forked tails soaring high on a breeze. Everything was as he had left it. At the same time nothing was the same. When one underwent a sudden change, one expected the world, too, to somehow have become different.

Poking out his head, he called to the coachman, 'I can't go in this state. I beg you, take me to a *hamam*.'

'No, I've got orders to take you to my Sultana straight away.'

'*Effendi*, have mercy. How can I let her see me like this?'

The coachman shrugged. He didn't care. 'You should have thought of that earlier,' he said harshly.

At these words Jahan was incensed. He no longer had any patience for heartless people. 'Now you listen to me. I have just walked out of a dungeon. If need be, I'll walk back into it. But before that I'll kill you!'

The coachman grumbled. Even so, fearing an ex-convict, he stopped the carriage at the next square and swerved into a side street, looking for the nearest *hamam*.

The *hamam* owner did not want to let Jahan in and did so only after being bribed by the coachman. The moment the hot water touched his skin, Jahan winced with pain. The warmth of the marble against his toes felt like walking on clouds. He shaved for the first time in six weeks. The *tellak*, a hulky Kurd, was either irate at an injustice he had suffered just that morning or had consumed too much spice, for he scrubbed too hard – his fingers working swiftly, scarlet rings forming around his wrists from the exertion. When he was done, Jahan's skin was as red as poppies. The odour and filth of the dungeon seeped out of his skin in black specks. Dizzy, he stood up and tottered through the mist towards the dais outside. It felt cool and fresh after the steaming hot inner chamber.

They offered him wild strawberry sherbet. While sipping his drink, for want of anything better to do, he glanced around. There was a stout man with a ruddy complexion, a merchant probably, half asleep. Another man with darting eyes and a scar that ran down his cheekbone was sitting on the edge, dangling his legs, which were covered, for the most part, with a *peshtamal*. The Kazakh next to him scrutinized Jahan and, not finding him of interest, turned his back.

In a while two boys appeared – their faces devoid of hair, their eyes big and bright. It was the stocky man who had summoned them. Jahan knew what was going on. In the private rooms boys performed services for chosen customers. Jahan thought of Kaymak and Abdullah. His back tightened, his mouth twisted into a grimace.

A voice muttered in his ear, 'You don't like boys.'

A man had plumped himself down on the marble beside Jahan. His chest, arms, legs, even his shoulders were covered by dark tufts of hair.

'I don't like what's happening,' Jahan said.

Though he nodded as if in agreement, the man responded with a grin. 'You know what they say: "Boys in the summer, wives in the winter to keep you warm."'

'I'd rather get a thin blanket in the summer and a quilt in the winter.'

The man chuckled but said no more. Before he left the *hamam* Jahan put on the robes the coachman had arranged. He saw the two boys outside, whispering, one of them holding an akce as though it were the key to a secret world.

That same afternoon, as he entered Mihrimah's mansion on the shores of the Bosphorus, he was engulfed by a nervous excitement. So it hadn't gone numb, his heart. Taking short breaths to steady himself, he knelt before her.

'Look at you!' Her hand flew to her mouth. 'You are all bones.'

Jahan dared to glance up at her. Around her neck was a rope of pearls that caught the sun every time she moved. Her dress was of pure sarsenet, the colour of an evergreen. A married woman, she carried herself differently now. Behind her light veil she was beautiful – and sad. Never had anyone's sorrow been so sweet. She was worried for him. Perhaps she even loved him. He felt as if his heart would break.

Ordering dish after dish, she urged him to taste everything. Stewed mutton, stuffed vine leaves, prunes in syrup, sugared almonds of various colours. There was something on a tiny plate Jahan had never had before – caviar. Fate was odd. The day before he was drawing designs on the floor with shit. Now he was perched on silk cushions, eating caviar from the hand of his beloved. And as he closed his eyes for a moment, he could not tell which was real and which someone else's life.

'You used to tell me stories,' Mihrimah said, in a voice that barely rose above a whisper. 'Do you remember?'

'How could I forget, your Highness?'

'Everything was different back then. We were only children. One needs to be a child to revel fully in a tale, don't you think? Still, even as adults we can –'

She was about to say more when her words were interrupted by the sound of footsteps on the great staircase. Jahan's back straightened, as it occurred to him that it could be her husband, Rustem Pasha. When he turned his head he saw Hesna Khatun with a little girl by her side. The child made a deep obeisance before her mother and fixed her large brown eyes on Jahan.

'Aisha, my delight, I want you to greet our guest. He is a talented architect. He and Master Sinan made those beautiful mosques that we always talk about.'

'Yes, Mother,' the child said without a trace of interest.

'He has also taken care of the white elephant,' Mihrimah added.

Aisha's face lit up. 'Are you the one who helped the elephant to drink his mama's milk?'

Jahan drew in a breath. The stories he had once told Mihrimah, she must have recounted to her daughter. The realization made him smile, as if he had penetrated the intimacy of this house and become a part of its bedtime conversations without even knowing. Over the child's head his eyes met Mihrimah's. An understanding passed between them, like a soft rustle of wind.

'Would your Excellency like to come to see the elephant some day?' Jahan asked the girl.

Aisha pursed her lips, as if to say she might or she might not. Instead of looking at her mother for permission, she glanced up at Hesna Khatun, who had been in the background, silently watching them.

Jahan's eyes moved to the nursemaid. She had aged: her cheeks had shrivelled up like withered leaves. But even the unmistakable sternness of her gaze didn't disrupt Jahan's line of thinking. This was what his life could have been like if only he had been fortunate enough to be in Rustem Pasha's shoes – this girl would be his daughter, these walls his shield against the world, this splendid view from the window the reality he woke up to every morning and the Princess he secretly loved his official wife. Never before, not even in his darkest hours in the dungeon, had he wished for another man's death the way he did now.

He caught a blur of movement. Hesna Khatun was staring at him with unblinking eyes, her lips moving fast, as if she were talking to someone. Jahan's skin turned to gooseflesh. He knew she had read his mind, though he couldn't explain how – and that she would find some way of using this against him.

The day after he was released from prison, Jahan woke up with heaviness in his heart. He blinked a few times, unable to grasp where he was. The tamers were up and about, and, from behind the closed door, he could hear the growl of a leopard. Dragging himself out of the bed, he lurched into the courtyard and splashed water on his face from the fountain. A drizzle fell on the heather, pearly drops like dew. There was a fresh smell in the breeze, and the animals paced lazily in their cages. Though he had spent time with Chota the preceding evening, he was eager to see him again. Later on in the day he would visit his master. He was both exuberant and nervous. He would ask Sinan why he had not come to visit him in the dungeon, and if, for some reason, he was not able to, why had he not sent a letter.

By midday he reached his master's house. His melancholy oozed away as soon as he saw Sinan and the affection in his gaze. He wondered if the father he had lost had ever regarded him like that. He stooped to kiss his master's hand, but Sinan pulled him towards himself and held him in his arms. His voice breaking, he said, 'Let me look at you. You are so thin, son.'

In a little while the blind *kahya* entered the room. Her son was now being taught all of his mother's duties, and Jahan knew that one day very soon the man would be called upon to take her place. The apprentice felt a harrowing sadness, and hoped he would be able to say farewell to the old servant when the time came and ask for her blessing.

'He needs to eat,' Sinan said from his seat to the *kahya*.

'The poor boy,' the old woman exclaimed and, moving as quickly as she could, went to give orders for the meal.

The servants bustled in, carrying a low table, towels and wooden spoons. They placed in front of him bowls of honey, butter, cream, flattened bread, sour-grape molasses, halvah and a jar of yoghurt drink with mint and raisins.

'Eat! Drink!' Sinan ordered.

Jahan complied, though he felt no hunger. When he could not take another bite, Sinan, who had been watching him, said quietly, 'They punished you in order to get at me. Everybody knows that.'

Jahan was lost for words. Unaware of the bitterness fermenting in his apprentice's heart, Sinan carried on. 'His Majesty wishes to reconsider the water design. I'd like you to come with me to the palace. We need to clear your name.'

'I don't even know what I've been accused of,' said Jahan.

A pause. 'Treachery.'

It wasn't horror Jahan felt in that moment, only a deep sadness. 'Will Rustem Pasha be there?' he asked. Seeing the Grand Vizier's ugly face was the last thing he wanted.

'No doubt. You'll have to kiss his hand, ask his forgiveness. Can you do that?'

Jahan could not answer. Instead he inquired, 'I don't understand this sudden clemency. What has changed?'

'That's what I've been wondering myself. There must be a reason, but I can't fathom it. All I know is that our Sultan has expressed his wish to see me.'

Jahan remained silent. It must have been Mihrimah. She must have talked to her husband and pleaded with her father, begging him to listen to the architects one last time. Hints delicate as tufts of dandelions in the wind. Everything suggested that she cared for him. Jahan lowered his head for fear his master could read his thoughts.

On the day of their visit Jahan put on new robes – light cotton *shalwar*, linen shirt, leather shoes, pointed at the toes. His master had bought them to help him look his best. Sinan, too, had carefully dressed in a russet kaftan and bulbous turban. The *kahya* muttered the prayers she had learned from her mother almost a century ago and sprinkled rosewater blessed by seven imams on their heads.

They had been sent a royal carriage – a propitious sign, no doubt, indicating that the Sultan had some regard for them. Inside they sat, the master and the apprentice, scrolls in between them. Their stomachs tied in knots, they found it hard to talk. It was in this mood that Sinan and Jahan entered the palace.

Sultan Suleiman welcomed them. On one side of him stood the hefty figure of the Grand Vizier. On the other, the Shayh al-Islam and the Chief Janissary Agha. Their hands tightly clasped, they eyed them with a coldness they felt no need to mask.

The Sultan said, 'Chief Royal Architect. Each of these honourable men has questions for you. Are you willing to answer?'

Sinan bowed. 'I'm honoured, your Felicitous Majesty.'

The Shayh al-Islam, Ebussuud Efendi, his face as unreadable as a faded manuscript, spoke first. 'In our glorious city there are bridges from the time of the infidels that have not survived. They collapsed because they were built without true faith. Do you agree?'

Sinan took a breath. 'God gave us a mind and told us to use it well. Many ancient bridges are in ruins because they were not built upon firm ground. When we raise a bridge we make sure the water is shallow, the earth is solid, the tides favourable. Bridges are built with faith, true. But also with knowledge.'

Sultan Suleiman made a gesture to his left, the signal for the Chief Janissary Agha to speak. 'Majesty, your vassal Sinan seems to think he can predict how much water there is seven layers under the ground. How is that possible? We thought he was an architect, not a necromancer. Does he also profess mastery of the occult?'

Jahan blenched at the innuendo, aware of the implications of being accused of black magic.

Sinan replied, 'I have no experience in divination. The amount of water under the earth can be measured through the right use of instruments.'

'These instruments he mentions – do they come from Allah? Or from Sheitan?' said the Chief Janissary Agha.

'Surely from God,' replied Sinan. 'He wants us to expand our knowledge.'

The Shayh al-Islam interjected: 'Al-Khidr, may he rest in Paradise, discovered water. Do you claim to be a holy man like him?'

'I'm not worthy of the fingernail of a holy man,' Sinan said. 'Al-Khidr travelled with the Prophet Moses and unravelled the secrets of the universe. Next to his knowledge, mine is a droplet of water. But I believe, using the right measurements, we can locate the invisible sources.'

The Sultan turned to the Grand Vizier. 'What do you say, Pasha?'

Rustem gave a dry cough. 'I'd like to learn how much the Chief Royal Architect is planning to spend. Our treasury cannot be emptied.'

Expecting this question, Sinan said, 'There are two choices. The spending will differ, depending on the wishes of my Sultan.'

Suleiman was intrigued. 'What do you mean, Architect?'

'Majesty, our aim is to bring fresh water to the city. We need labourers, hundreds of them. If you prefer, we will employ galley slaves. Then you won't have to pay them. You'll have no end of vassals.'

'What is the second way?'

'We hire skilled craftsmen. They'll be paid, according to their ability and service to his Majesty. In return they will give their sweat and their prayers.'

'So he thinks he can fill the coffers with sweat and prayers?' Rustem said.

Ignoring the remark, the Sultan asked Sinan, 'Which would *you* suggest?'

'I believe we should pay them and get their blessings. The treasury might not be all that it was, but it's better for the throne and for the people.'

Jahan went pale, expecting the worst. At last, after a long, awkward silence, the Sultan raised his hand and said, 'The Chief Royal Architect is right. Water is a charity and must be distributed generously. I shall give water to the people and I shall pay my workers.'

But with the next breath Suleiman said to Sinan, 'Even so, I'm not allowing you to build a new bridge. Renovate the aqueducts – that's enough.'

The chamber stirred as each man reflected on who, if anyone, had won the argument. Sinan said, 'My Lord, with your permission, my Indian apprentice will help me with the renovation.'

The Sultan ran a finger through his beard as his eyes took in Jahan. 'I remember him. It's good you have such a dedicated apprentice.' He paused. 'What do you say, Pasha – shall we forgive him?'

The Grand Vizier, a sparkle in his eyes, extended his arm. Sinan nodded encouragingly at Jahan. Showing more determination than he felt, Jahan took a step forward as through a mist and kissed the plump hand with rings, put it on his forehead. He would have loved to swipe one of those rings, he thought. A recompense for his sufferings.

'May God bless your efforts,' said Rustem, his icy glare at variance with the sweetness in his voice.

On the way back they passed through marble corridors, the master and the apprentice. The elation that came over them was so intense that they found it hard to stay silent. Jahan knew that not only his heart had been pounding: his master, too, had been scared. Once again, Sinan had found himself in a tight spot when all he wanted to do was his work. Once again, as though aided by an obscure well-wisher, he had been reprieved. Perhaps he had a protector, Jahan thought, a mysterious patron who interfered on his behalf each time things got too thorny, an invisible guardian angel always by his side . . .

Back in the menagerie, Jahan found the animal-tamers waiting for him with a smirk on their faces.

'Come with me,' said Olev, folding his arms over his chest.

'Where are we going?' said Jahan.

'Don't ask,' said Olev and pulled him by the elbow. 'A man who's just come out of prison is a man in need of joy.'

To Jahan's surprise, Olev led him towards the stables of the favoured horses. Here they kept the best thoroughbreds, each of which wore round its neck a blue amulet against the evil eye. Upon seeing them approach, the Chief White Eunuch's beloved stallion, Tempest, neighed softly. Noble, majestic, alone. Olev patted the animal, speaking sweet words in his ear.

'Will somebody tell me what's going on?' inquired Jahan nervously.

'You always wanted to ride this horse, didn't you? This is our gift to you.'

'But Kamil Agha —'

Olev cut short his words with a raise of his hand. 'Don't worry, it's all arranged. He's not in the palace tonight. He's out visiting the *hamam* of sorrows. Don't ask me where that place may be, I cannot tell.'

'But what do you expect me to do with the horse?'

'Nothing,' Olev responded, giving a wink. 'Just go and ride down the hill.'

A little while later, a shadow shot out of the stable gates: Jahan, lying so low his body was level with the horse's back, riding Tempest into the dark. The two guards by the gates, having been bribed beforehand, couldn't care less. He galloped in the direction Olev had mentioned, enjoying the wind on his face, feeling free and reckless for once. After a bit he slowed down. There, in the near-distance, was a cart and huddled together on it were the Gypsies!

'What on earth?' Jahan exclaimed. 'When did you get out of prison?'

'Oh, we'd all been released about a month before you. We just waited with you until you were pardoned,' said Balaban.

'What? Why didn't you tell me?' stammered Jahan. 'What are you doing here at this hour?'

'The lion-man sent us word,' Balaban said, as he tethered Tempest's reins to the back of the cart. 'Your friends had a chat about you, it seems. They think it's time for you to have a bit of pleasure. You deserve it.'

'What does that mean?' Jahan said suspiciously.

The glance that the Gypsies exchanged was one of amusement.

'You'll see,' said Balaban, and before Jahan could object he whipped the donkey. The cart set off, followed by Tempest.

The cart rattled along, passing through the country lanes and the field tracks. Though it was a crisp autumn evening, with the sky a velvety black, patches of mist were rolling up northwards, edging towards the outer ends of the city. A blanket of fog swallowed the winding streets and arching bridges, and Istanbul swallowed them. They passed through alleyways, many of which were so narrow – with wooden houses on both sides buckled like saplings bent in a gale – that their axles scraped the walls as they rode by. Each neighbourhood they left behind seemed quieter, mustier and more doleful than the last. Balaban fell silent. All they heard for a long time, other than the occasional squawk from a seagull, was the clatter of hooves and wheels on the cobblestones.

The wagon came to a halt and they climbed off. Taking a breath to steady himself, Jahan jumped down from the horse, looked around for a familiar sight and found none.

'Come on,' Balaban said, nudging him. 'Movement is a blessing.' Putting his right hand on his heart, the chieftain turned to his men. 'You go, God go with you.'

Jahan trod behind Balaban. At each step the street smells intensified – traces of jasmine mingling with the tang of the sea and the whiffs of food, briny and garlicky. Tamers learned a lot from their animals and there was one thing Chota had hammered into him: how to sniff better. So he paid more attention to these scents in the breeze, and after a while he caught a hint of perfumed oils from a house nearby.

'What is this place?' whispered Jahan.

Balaban chuckled. 'Don't you get it? We've brought you to the bawdy house!'

Jahan paled. 'I refuse to go.'

'What? You afraid of the wenches? We'll just go in and take a look. If you don't like what you see, we'll leave. May my blood redden the soil under your feet if I lie. Come on, Indian. After all we've gone through in the gaol, listen to me.'

Jahan dithered. He could neither accept nor refuse. Balaban pushed him, ceaselessly talking to assuage his fear. He explained that a brothel in Istanbul was a bit like the beginning of a Turkish tale – *Once there was, once there wasn't*. Several harlots could dwell under the same roof for months, and, just when you thought they would be there forever, they'd vanish into thin air, the house an empty shell. Then there were the wives, as poor as a mouse in a looted larder, their husbands gone to war or good for nothing, who would become strumpets – though only on certain occasions, few and far between.

In most neighbourhoods the women who were thought to be of easy virtue were pelted with curses and stones. Often they woke up with tar rubbed on the thresholds of their homes, slanders scrawled on their walls. At times these women could be arrested, even imprisoned. Strumpets were made to sit backwards on mules and to ride through the streets so that everybody could see what was due to the likes of them.

But the kadis were a varied bunch and just as confused as everyone else, Balaban said. As much as they loathed the harlots, they saw the trade as an evil bound to happen and a boon for the treasury, since it was taxed. The only time it was strictly forbidden was in the month of Ramadan. During the rest of the year, whoredom was the only transgression that both was and wasn't a crime.

The district of Eyup had, a little while back, become strict and issued a number of decrees. Taverns were closed, as were whorehouses and coffee-houses that allowed gambling. All ladies of ill-repute were banished, even those who had given up the life and married. To avoid the same fate, the painted women moved from one place to another, depending on the weather.

'Harlotry is like the wind,' said Balaban; 'if you try to clap it in irons, it will slip away through the holes.'

With that they reached the door. It was opened by a black man. Upon seeing Balaban, he bowed and said, 'Master, welcome.'

'You own this place?' Jahan muttered in surprise.

Balaban gave the servant a frosty glance. He turned to Jahan and, raising both hands, he said, 'I'm a poor Romany. D'you think this a house on wheels? How can I own it? Come, let's not waste time.'

They were ushered upstairs, where an elderly woman, her face as wrinkled as a walnut, greeted Balaban with much esteem. Next to her was a basket, inside of which was a mother cat with six kittens, curled in balls, all with the same thick, smoke-grey coat. 'They were born here,' she said. 'Each named after one of my girls.'

Those girls, Jahan learned, were: Arab Fatima; Nefise the Venetian; Kurd Kamer; Narin the Circassian; Zarife the Turk; Leah the Jewess; and Ani the Armenian.

To their left and right, there were closed doors, from behind which Jahan could hear an occasional murmur. Balaban pushed Jahan into one of the rooms, made him sit on cushions, said he'd better go to check on the musicians and disappeared.

A maid appeared carrying a tray. She had flaming hair and sad scars on both sides of her face. Her eyes had a distant look, as if in search of other, long-ago evenings. She brought him water, wine and plates piled with goat's cheese, sweetened figs, roasted almonds, pickles. Placing them on a low table, she asked if there was anything else he would like. Jahan shook his head, fixing his stare on the patterns of the carpet. As soon as the maid left, two women walked into the room on each other's heels. One was so fat she had three chins. Her cheeks were round and bright red. It occurred to Jahan that if Chota had been there he would have gulped them down for apples. The thought made him smile.

She beamed. 'You like me?'

'No,' Jahan exclaimed. Not wanting to appear rude, he added hastily, 'Well, yes, but not like that.'

They giggled – she more than the other. The flesh on her belly bounced up and down. Smacking her lips, she leaned forward. 'I've three breasts and there's a monster in my belly that comes out when I'm hungry. I eat men!'

Jahan looked at her in horror. They broke into another peal of laughter.

'Could one of you call Balaban?' Jahan said. 'I need to see him.'

They exchanged glances, fearing their teasing might have gone too far. The room felt hot, fusty. Rising to his feet, Jahan mumbled an apology and, like an arrow, shot out of the room. At the last moment he noticed that the women, too, had stood up and were following him. Swiftly, he closed the door and slipped the bolt on it. Outside, by the stairs, he careened into the maid, who had been carrying the tray.

'Are you all right?' she said. 'You going?'

'Yes, Chota's waiting.'

'Is that your wife?'

Despite himself Jahan smiled. 'Nay, he's my elephant. Huge animal.'

Her dark eyes brightened. 'I know what an elephant is.'

All at once the women locked in the room began to pound on the door. Jahan paled. The last thing he wanted was to be caught. He looked around in panic.

'Come with me,' the maid said, taking him by the hand.

Through a hatch at the back they reached a flight of creaky stairs. She led him to her room in the attic, where the ceiling was so low they had to stoop. Yet, under the half-moon, the view out of the window was charming – a forest of tall pine trees and, beyond that, the sea in stripes of black. From up here the water seemed like something else, soft and solid, a massive silk shawl spread round the shoulders of the city.

Jahan told her what had happened downstairs, which amused her greatly. She said her name was Peri. She'd been a camp-follower in times past, but not any more. After her face had been marred – by a soldier who had seen such things on the battlefield that he had become sick in the head and took out his anger on harlots – no one desired her.

'It's not true no man will want you,' said Jahan. 'You're prettier than those women downstairs.'

She kissed him and he kissed her back, the taste of her tongue lingering in his mouth. She caressed his hair, her fingertips soft and warm against his forehead, which was creased with worry. 'You have never done it, have you?' she asked.

The deep blush on his face was enough of an answer for her. She made him lie down and slowly took off his clothes. At the touch of her lips on his skin, desire surged through him. Jahan had never known that such a kingdom of pleasure existed. Only years later would he understand how lucky he had been for having someone like her to show him the way.

In the dark, while he slept next to Peri, he saw himself in an unknown land riding Chota. They pranced on top of mansions, hopping from one roof to another. Then he saw Mihrimah in the distance, wearing a dress of white linen, her hair fluttering in the wind. 'Wait!' he yelled. She did not hear. He shouted again. Every time he opened his mouth it was yet another lost scream.

'Shh, wake up.'

It took Jahan a moment to remember where he was, and when he did he was drenched in cold sweat. Dressing fast, he mumbled, 'I ought to go.' He stopped, noticing that her face was clouding over. 'I'm sorry. I don't know . . . this, I . . . pay you?'

Peri turned her head. 'You don't owe me anything.'

Jahan went close, caressed her hair. Inside him confusion was fermenting, soon to turn into the sharpest guilt. He knew he had to leave before that occurred. He didn't want Peri to witness what had happened between them changing into regret.

'You've been talking in your sleep,' Peri said as she opened the door.

'Did I disturb you?'

Peri ignored the question. 'She dwells in your heart, clearly. Whoever she is. Does she know you love her?'

Dazed, discomfited, Jahan left the house. He would never have dared to call this thing he felt for Mihrimah love, and yet when it was uttered, unveiled, by someone else, he carefully picked up the word and hugged it to his chest, not willing to let go.

A hundred and thirty hands were hired for the repair of the aqueducts. They worked in two teams – the first on the west wing, the second on the middle part, where the decay had been most severe. In the meantime the four apprentices, with the help of an astrolabe, measured the depths of valleys and the heights of peaks. As was his wont, Sinan ordered them to research the methods undertaken by the craftsmen of the past. They needed to understand how the Byzantines had succeeded and how they had failed if they wished to do better themselves.

Davud and Yusuf, adept at the science of geometry, took the measurements of the waterways. Nikola and Jahan, trudging up and down the hills, logged all the broken canals and the clogged runnels. In some places the water rushed through a gorge because the conduits had fallen into disrepair. Water was dispersed amid green meadows, returned to the earth without having been of use to human beings. In other parts they had to find the source of the stream and excavate the conduits. They dammed the water to make it flow in a single direction, towards the city. Then, with the aid of a new ditch, they made it run the length of the dale. At every stage they measured the quantity – using brass spouts attached to tanks with sluices – calculating how much water had accumulated along the way.

A week later Jahan began to notice something strange. The labourers were giving them a wide berth, reluctant to carry out the orders. The more he observed them, the more he was convinced that they were looking for excuses not to hammer a nail, carry a plank, or do the slightest thing, which, when added together, was enough to hold everything back.

He pulled aside one of the draughtsmen – a Kurd named Salahaddin. His wife had recently given birth to twin boys. Knowing him to be an honest man, Jahan expected him to tell the truth.

'What's going on? Why's everyone slow?'

Salahaddin averted his gaze. 'We're workin', *effendi*.'

'You are falling behind – why?'

A little blush crept into his cheeks. 'You didn't tell us there was a saint here.'

'Who says that?'

The man shrugged, refusing to give names.

Jahan tried another question. 'How do they know there's a saint?'

'They have seen . . . an apparition,' Salahaddin replied, glancing at Jahan, as if for confirmation.

It was the ghost of a martyr – a mettlesome Muslim soldier who had met his end while fighting the infidels. An arrow had pierced his chest and entered his heart, yet he had kept on fighting relentlessly for two more days. On the third morning he had fallen and was buried in this area. Now his soul, disturbed by the hustle and bustle of the construction, was appearing to the labourers, who fretted that the ghost would put a curse on them.

'Nonsense. Whoever is spreading this story wants to harm Master Sinan.'

'It's true, *effendi*,' said Salahaddin. 'People have seen it.'

'Where?' Jahan said, throwing up his hands in exasperation. 'Show me!'

To his surprise, the man pointed with his chin at the scaffolding.

'Has the ghost set up home there?' Jahan asked teasingly.

But Salahaddin was solemn. 'That's where he was seen.'

During the rest of the afternoon Jahan prowled around the scaffolding, checking the planks, tightening the ropes, making sure it was safe, scowling at every man who so much as threw a glance at him.

'You are not paying attention,' said Davud, when they were studying the measurements the next day.

'I'm sorry. My mind –' said Jahan and gasped. In that moment something had caught his eye – on the raised wooden platform, down along the third tier. A few labourers were working there, one of them carrying a bucket. He watched the man sway on his feet, as if pushed by an invisible hand, then regain his balance. The hairs on the back of Jahan's neck stiffened. In the past, whenever timber was scarce, they had used platforms dangling from abutments above to save wood. But this one rose from the ground and was attached to the walls, supported by struts and trusses. For it to move to and fro, the ropes must have come loose and a part of the edifice must have been hanging free – a part or all.

'Are you all right?' asked Davud, following his gaze.

A scream of panic shattered the hum of work. They watched a board flip in the air, whirling as though it were a leaf in the wind, and plummet to the ground. Another board hit a mason, landing on his head with a sickening thud. People ran left and right as timber and metal rained from above.

'*Kiyamet, kiyamet,*'* someone wailed.

Oxen bellowed in pain, a horse with a broken leg lay on its side, its body twitching, its nostrils flaring. Jahan could not see Chota in the commotion. In the blink of an eye the scaffolding they had proudly put up only weeks before had come tumbling down. The workers on the higher tiers in the middle section suffered the worst falls, along with those down below who had been hit by the planks. Of these, eight would not survive. Among them was Salahaddin.

* Apocalypse.

Sinan and the four apprentices approached the *gassal*.★ 'May we stay next to you while you wash him?'

The man hesitated. Then, either because he had recognized the Chief Royal Architect or because he had confused him with a bereaved relative, he said, 'That's fine, *effendi*.'

Turning to his apprentices, Sinan asked, 'Would any of you like to join me?'

Yusuf avoided his gaze, a light blush rising to his cheeks. Nikola, who wasn't a Muslim, said the man might not have wished him to be present at the washing. Davud, suddenly waxen, said he had still not forgotten the corpses he had seen as a child and did not wish to encounter another until the day he died. Being the only one left, Jahan nodded. 'I'll come.'

Lying on cold marble was Salahaddin's naked body. Bruises of various sizes and shades covered the left side of his head and chest where he had been hit by the falling timbers. Even so, Jahan had the strange sensation that the injuries had been painted on rather than etched into Salahaddin's frame, and that if they washed them off, he could, at any moment, show signs of life.

'God has built the palace of our body and entrusted to us its key,' Sinan said in a voice so quiet that the *gassal*, standing behind, bowed his head, assuming he was praying.

The palace of our body . . . What a peculiar thing to say, Jahan thought. All he saw was a pile of wounded flesh. As if he had read his thoughts, Sinan asked Jahan to come closer.

'Man is made in the image of God. At its centre there's order, balance. See the circles and the squares. See how proportionately they have been arranged. There are four humours – blood, yellow bile, black bile and phlegm. We work with four elements – wood, marble, glass, metal.'

Jahan and the *gassal* exchanged a glance. Jahan knew what the man was thinking, for he'd had similar thoughts himself. He feared that his master, out of sorrow or weariness, had lost his mind.

★ Washer of the dead.

'The face is the facade, the eyes are the windows, the mouth is the door that opens into the universe. The legs and the arms are the staircases.' Then Sinan poured water from a ewer, and, by drawing circles with his hands, began to wash the body with such tenderness that the *gassal* dared not move.

'That's why when you see a human being, slave or vizier, Mohammedan or heathen, you ought to respect him. Remember, even a beggar owns a palace.'

Jahan said, 'With much respect, master, I don't see perfection. I see the missing teeth. This crooked bone. All of us, I mean, some are hunchbacked, others –'

'Cracks on the surface. But the building is flawless.'

The *gassal*, craning his neck over their shoulders, bowed his head in assent, perhaps convinced more by the lull of Sinan's voice than by his views. After that they were silent. They washed the deceased twice – once with warm water, once with tepid. Then they wrapped him head to toe in a milky-white shroud, leaving his right hand outside. This they held, gently, and placed on his heart, as though he were saying his goodbyes to this world and his salaams to the next.

The funeral prayer was led by an imam with a goitre so large that it pressed on his windpipe, making his breath come out in raspy gasps. He said it was of great consolation that they had died on a construction site. The men had not been leching after women of ill-repute or imbibing or gambling or uttering blasphemies. Death had found them in an hour of honest, hard work. When the Day of Judgement arrived, which it was sure to do, God would take this into account.

He said Salahaddin had departed this mortal life while building a bridge for the Sultan – no one dared to say that it was in fact while repairing an aqueduct. In return, in the other world, when it was his turn to cross the Bridge of Sirat – thinner than a hair, slimier than a thousand eels – a pair of angels would assist him. They would hold him by his hands and not let him fall into the flames of hell underneath.

The casket was transported to the cemetery amid wailing and keening. Salahaddin's family were poor, so Sinan had paid for his tombstone.

The father of the deceased, brought low by age and grief, trudged towards them. Touched and honoured that a man like Sinan should attend his son's funeral, he thanked each of them. Salahaddin's brother, meanwhile, kept his distance. It wasn't hard to see he was holding them responsible for his loss, this lad who was no more than fourteen. One glance at him and Jahan knew they had made themselves yet another enemy. When, after throwing spadefuls of earth on to his brother's coffin, he moved towards the back of the crowd, Jahan followed him.

'May God welcome your brother into Paradise,' Jahan said as soon as he caught up with him.

No response. An awkward moment passed between them, as each waited for the other to speak. In the end, it was the lad who broke the silence. 'Were you with him when he died?'

'I was nearby.'

'The ghost pushed them. Did you see it happen?'

'Nobody pushed them. It was an accident,' Jahan said nervously. Even he couldn't deny the bizarreness of the incident.

'The ghost wants you to stop. There'll be no end to disaster if you disturb him, but your master doesn't care. He has no respect for the dead.'

'That's not true. Master is a good man,' said Jahan.

The boy's face darkened with rage. 'Your friend was right. You are befouling a sacred place. What with your hammers and donkeys. You are all condemned to hell.'

The crowd began to disperse. Amid the mourners inching towards the gate, Jahan noticed Sinan moving listlessly, as though pulled by invisible strings against his will. Jahan said weakly, 'Don't blame my master.'

As they left the cemetery, the wind blustered, tufts of dust and dirt rolling in their direction. Later, much later, it would dawn on Jahan that in the commotion he had not asked Salahaddin's brother who this *friend* he had talked with was and why he had uttered premonitions so dire.

The next day only half of the labourers turned up for work.

'So much for paid workmen!' Davud exclaimed. 'Had we hired

chained galley slaves, none of this would have happened. See where kindness gets us?'

'Master will find extra hands,' Nikola said.

He was right. Determined to complete what he had started, Sinan took on new labourers. It wasn't hard to obtain them. There were many in need of a job in this city. The misery of hunger prevailed over the fear of a saint's curse. For a while, things seemed to improve. The work proceeded without incident. Autumn drew in, the air chilled.

Then came the flood. Sweeping down houses, taverns, shrines and sheds, it gushed through the valleys. Because they had not been able to fully unclog the channels leading to the aqueduct, the waters washed away the scaffolding and crumbled the watercourse as if it had been a wafer. The flood had caught them unprepared. No one was injured. But they lost weeks of work and materials of value. The disaster gave credence to the gossip-mongers' rumours, and even those who had previously been unsure now became convinced that Sinan and his apprentices were accursed.

Their spirits sank. Until this point their master had overcome every obstacle, no matter how great or daunting. Yet this was different. How could Sinan possibly defeat a ghost?

The renovation work stopped. Hard as Sinan tried, he could not convince a single soul to keep on working. The labourers accused the Chief Royal Architect of putting them in danger in order to win the Sultan's favour. Who needed water when the water was jinxed? The aqueducts dated from the days of the infidels. Why repair them if not to spread idolatry?

Jahan was surprised to hear they had already forgotten about the ghost of the Muslim martyr. They had found new fears to cling to and cling they did. Silent and compliant on the surface, they whispered malicious gossip as soon as the apprentices turned their backs.

After a week of this Sinan appeared with a small, wiry visitor by his side. The two of them climbed up on to the newly built scaffolding.

'Workmen! Foremen! We are fortunate to have a respectable *hodja** with us.'

Sinan extended his hand to the stranger. The man took a step forward, ashen and drawn, unused to heights. Closing his eyes, he chanted verses from the Qur'an. He was called the Nightingale Hodja, they learned. Born in Bosnia, he could commune with God in seven languages and knew the ways of many creeds and sects. There was something in the voice of this man, who otherwise looked very ordinary, that enchanted the labourers. He told them to move on and never speak evil of others, for if Sheitan could fly so high, it was thanks to two wings: sloth and slander.

The *hodja* came every day, stood with them from dawn to dusk, dust in his hair, mud on his shoes. He sprinkled blessed water and uttered the prayer of *Cevsen*, which he said the Archangel Gabriel had revealed when the Prophet Mohammed was afraid and in need of protection – for prophets, just like common men, could be frightened of the dangers of this world – and he sanctified the aqueducts, calming the fears of Jews, Christians and Muslims alike. Then he concluded, 'It's clean now. This site is as pure as your mother's milk. Go back to work.'

*Religious teacher, preacher.

So they did. Little by little. They finished the renovations so perfectly that even those who hated Sinan more than any soul on earth
could not raise objections. Sultan Suleiman was pleased. He honoured
his architect with gifts and praises, calling him *Al-insan al-Kamil*.★

It was after this incident that Jahan understood his master's secret
resided not in his toughness, for he was not tough, nor in his inde-
structibility, for he was not indestructible, but in his ability to adapt to
change and calamity, and to rebuild himself, again and again, out of
the ruins. While Jahan was made of wood, and Davud of metal, and
Nikola of stone, and Yusuf of glass, Sinan was made of flowing water.
When anything blocked his course, he would flow under, around,
above it, however he could; he found his way through the cracks, and
kept flowing forward.

★ The one who has reached perfection.

What an awful night it was! Chota was in pain. Roaring, bellowing, growling till the first light of the day, he swayed his trunk this way and that, exhausted. Such was his discomfort that Jahan had to sleep next to him, if sleep he could. One peek into the animal's mouth and he saw the reason for his torment: the molar at the back of his left lower jaw was a nasty black colour and the gum had become swollen with pus.

Jahan recalled how the summer before he had had a terrible toothache himself, and the barber who shaved the Overseer of the Royal Stables had taken pity on him. Amid wailing and groaning, the man had pulled and pulled, ending Jahan's suffering. Even so, Jahan could not think of a single soul in Istanbul brave enough to remove an elephant's molar.

'What's the matter?' Taras asked as soon as he entered the stable and saw his face. 'A head on a pike looks happier than you.'

'It's Chota. His tooth is killing him.'

'If we were only in the Taiga,' said Taras with a sigh. 'I know of a shrub that can mend him in an instant. Grandma is fond of it.'

Jahan gaped at him in astonishment. 'Is your granny still alive?'

'Aye, she's one of the damned,' said Taras. Seeing Jahan's surprise he added drily, 'No worse curse than to bury all your loved ones and still keep breathing.'

Years later Jahan would remember this moment but now the words whizzed by him like a current of air.

'Get garlic, lots, fennel, oil of clove . . . a tad of anise, no more . . . Mix them.'

Jahan obtained the ingredients from the kitchen and pounded them in a mortar until they turned into a gooey, green paste. When he showed him the concoction, Taras was pleased. 'Now rub it on the beast's gums. This will give him comfort – for now. The tooth needs to be pulled out.'

Jahan rushed back to the barn. The elephant resisted his attempts with such fierceness he could apply only half the paste, and he wasn't sure he had swabbed the right molar anyway. Chota's mouth reeked of an unpleasant odour. He had not been able to eat anything and hunger, as always, made his blood boil. Stitching together two mufflers, Jahan placed the remaining ointment inside and tied it around the animal's head, against the inflamed skin. Chota looked so funny he would have laughed had the poor thing not been in such agony.

Out on the streets, Jahan searched for an itinerant tooth-drawer or barber. The first man he asked burst out laughing upon learning the identity of the patient. The next was a fellow with such a menacing aspect that Jahan did not dare to take him to the menagerie. He was about to give up when he recalled the one soul in this city who knew everything about everything – Simeon the bookseller.

The quarter around the Galata Tower was swarming with people. Merchants walked in tandem with pedlars; emissaries and dragomen moved aside to let ox-carts pass; an ambassador in a *tahtirevan* breezed along, carried by black slaves; dogs roamed in packs. He saw men going to classes at the yeshiva, the elderly chatting in corners, a woman pulling her son by the hand. Words in Spanish, French and Arabic swirled in the wind.

Rounding a corner, thinking of Chota, he was rushing when he stopped in his tracks. Ahead of him, merely a few steps away from Simeon's house, was the traveller he had drunk with at the roadside inn. Next to him was Yusuf, the mute apprentice, his eyes on the ground. The man said something, after which Yusuf nodded and walked away.

In a burst of memory, Jahan remembered how they had been robbed on the way back from Rome. Suddenly, he suspected that the man in front of his eyes had had something to do with it. 'Hey, Tommaso!'

The Italian turned round. His eyes grew small as he caught sight of Jahan. Sprinting fast as an arrow, he disappeared into the crowd. Jahan gave chase for a while, though it was clear he would not be able to catch him. Dispirited, he strode back, knocked on Simeon's door.

'You all right?' the bookseller asked.

'Was Yusuf here a moment ago? With a blond man?'

'What blond man? I haven't seen Yusuf in weeks.'

'Never mind,' Jahan said with a sigh. 'I need your help.'

'Good timing, a ship's arrived. There're new books from Spain.'

'I'll look at them later. I need to help the elephant first.'

When Jahan told him his problem, Simeon's mouth twisted into a grimace. 'I'm a man of ideas; never operated on an animal.'

'Do you know of anyone?'

'None better than you. Tell you what, I'll see if there's anything in one of the books. Then you can do it yourself.'

'Fine,' said Jahan weakly.

'You'll need to sedate him. Get lots of *boza*. Better yet, sleeping draught.'

Simeon said that, in the past, physicians had used hemlock, which had killed many a mortal and saved a few. Nowadays they preferred nightshade and mandragora, the latter a plant that unleashed an awful shriek when torn out of the soil. But the best was opium. Galen recommended it for jaundice, dropsy, leprosy, headache, coughs and melancholy. For a man Jahan's age and size, two spoonfuls was the right amount. Since an elephant weighed as much as a mountain and was as tall as a tree . . . Simeon's eyebrows arched as he made a calculation. 'You are going to need a cask!'

'Where am I going to find that?'

Simeon said, 'The Chief White Eunuch. There's no miracle he cannot perform.'

Jahan returned to the palace with a book under his arm and misgivings in his head. Nobody messed with Carnation Kamil Agha. He hadn't forgotten the scolding he had received from him when he had first arrived. Even so, mustering courage, Jahan went to see him. To his surprise, the man was agreeable, kind even.

A cask of opium was provided at a stroke. Jahan did not inquire how it was acquired. Years in the palace had instilled in him the code of silence. Two tamers hoisted up Chota's upper jaw; two others held down his lower one. The elephant, in pain and tired, did not put up much of a fight. For good measure, with the help of a funnel, they poured a jug of mulled red wine into his listless mouth.

Little by little, Chota's breathing slackened off; his face melted like wax, his eyes glazed over. His legs gave way under his enormous weight and he tumbled down. They tied him with hawsers and chains and ropes, in case he woke up and attacked them in a fit of delirium. In this state Jahan started to operate on him.

He began with a chisel, quickly moved to a hammer. Dara the giraffe-tamer, Kato the crocodile-tamer and Olev the lion-tamer took turns pounding, thumping, clouting. Then pulling, yanking, wrenching. After what felt like an eternity, Jahan rooted out a tooth – like the fang of a giant snake from a tale a *meddah* would tell in a coffee-house somewhere.

'Give it to me,' ordered the Chief White Eunuch, his eyes glinting.

Jahan now grasped why the man had been so nice to him from the start. Having appropriated the cabinet of curiosities that had once belonged to Hurrem Sultana, he wanted to add Chota's tooth to it. Jahan felt a shudder as he wondered where he kept this cabinet and what else it might contain.

Upon learning that Rustem Pasha had passed away, Jahan felt many things at once, but sorrow wasn't among them. Princess Mihrimah's husband . . . the father of her three children . . . the royal favourite who had touched her every night . . . the *devshirme* who had risen too fast . . . the great Grand Vizier, much respected and much feared . . . The man who had sent Jahan to the dungeon and expected him to kiss his hand upon release . . . had gone the way of all flesh. He had been suffering from dropsy for a while, that much Jahan knew. For no matter how he had tried to keep the man away from his thoughts, every passing day Jahan had heard something new about him and hated him more.

A month later Mihrimah summoned Sinan – sending word that he should bring along his Indian apprentice.

'Chief Royal Architect, I want you to build an exquisite mosque for my late-lamented spouse, may heaven be his abode.' She was wearing sombre colours befitting a widow.

Jahan waited behind his master, his hands clasped, his gaze fixed on the carpet, and he thought to himself he would be in charge of this mosque and put a sign in it, somewhere, subtle but obvious to the knowing eye. He would etch his dislike of Rustem Pasha into the very monument dedicated to him. If it were a sin to think such things, he was sinful, for sure.

Unaware of his thoughts, Mihrimah kept talking. There was no need to fret about the sums, as she would cover all the costs. She demanded a spacious courtyard and a row of vaulted shops to provide revenue for the mosque. She was keen to make generous use of the best Iznik tiles: sage-green, sapphire-blue and a red as dark as yesterday's blood.

'It shall be as you wish, your Highness,' said Sinan.

'I want it to be glorious,' said Mihrimah. 'Worthy of my late husband's noble name.'

Jahan sighed inwardly. Resentment coiled inside him like a serpent. He lamented, almost against his will, having accompanied his master into this house of riches. But then, as if she had noticed his discomfort, Mihrimah turned to him.

'I haven't seen the elephant in a while. How is the beast doing?'

'Chota missed you, your Highness,' said Jahan quietly.

She inspected him, taking in the marks of time. 'How can you tell?'

'Many a day I found him waiting with his eyes fixed on the path your Highness had graced.'

Mihrimah raised her hand, as if to touch the air between them. 'Well, tell Chota that I was away, trapped in another life, but I shall come back and visit him, for I have never known a white elephant like him.'

'He will be happy to hear this, your Highness.'

'Tell him that none of this was in my hands.'

Jahan's eyes slid to the sky. A kite hovered above, soaring on an up-draught, beautiful and free. He said, 'I am sure he understands, your Highness. And I am sure he still awaits your return. Elephants never forget.'

She nodded slowly. 'You may go now. May God guide you.'

As the master and the apprentice were taking their leave, Mihrimah murmured, 'You said elephants never forget. What about elephant-tamers?'

Jahan paled. He felt the gaze of his master, who was startled by the informality of the conversation he had just heard. But for once he didn't want to hide. He didn't want to pretend. Bowing his head, he said, 'Neither do they, your Highness. Neither do they.'

Istanbul, the seat of the throne, weary of fires and earthquakes though it was, bulged at the seams. A honeysuckle of a city, it drew from near and far people of every kind – bustling, seeking, yearning. There were far too many souls under the same sky, outnumbering the stars at which they gazed – Muslims, Christians, Jews, believers and heretics of each faith, talking to God all at once, their pleas and prayers for succour and good fortune carried on the wind, mingling with the cries of seagulls. Jahan wondered how the Almighty could hear any of them over the commotion.

Towards the end of the summer, the Shayh al-Islam, Ebussuud Efendi, railed against Sinan. He declared that the marble plaques the architect had moved from the Hagia Sophia during a reconstruction were damned, and had brought one calamity after another upon the Istanbulites. In the end, not knowing where to place the cursed stones of the old church, Sinan and the apprentices used them in the tomb of Hurrem Sultana, trusting she wouldn't mind.

In 1566, the first day of May it was, war was waged to conquer the fortress of Szigetvar, and the elephant's services were required. Miserable as he was to hear this, Jahan complied. He might have been training as Sinan's apprentice, but he was, and would remain so long as Chota was alive, the Sultan's mahout.

They reached Belgrade in June; the Danube River ran as far as the eye could see – rowdy, alluring, grand. Sultan Suleiman, who up to then had been riding in front of them, slowed down his horse, a sorrel mare, to a trot. Little did Jahan know that this was because the Sultan's gout had become so painful that he had difficulty keeping his seat on the mount. His Grand Vizier, Sokollu – an astute man with a measured voice and an earnest expression, a *devshirme* from a Bosnian village called Hawk's Nest – had considered having him carried in a litter but ultimately rejected the idea. Such a move would only dishearten the troops, who would rather see tadpoles raining from the sky than their commander frail and fading. That was when a solution was found: Chota.

Jahan was instructed to ready the elephant for carrying the Lord of East and West. 'Make sure your animal knows who's riding him,' he had been forewarned.

The next morning Jahan saw the Sultan up close for the first time in several years. His skin, drained of colour, reminded him of the cold ashes that gathered in a fireplace, the flames long gone. His high forehead, which he had passed on to Mihrimah, was lined with wrinkles, an obscure calligraphy inked by time. Bowing low, Jahan kissed the hem of his kaftan – a robe of no fine cloth, since Suleiman still shunned opulence. His guards helped him up into the howdah. Once he was settled, Jahan took his seat on Chota's neck. In this manner, they carried on.

They arrived at Szigetvar on the fifth day of August. It was a sweltering afternoon, the fields flecked with dandelions. They set up camp and brought over the siege cannons, pulled by dozens of oxen. Then they erected the Sultan's tent, with its seven white horsetails, atop a hill from where the sovereign could gaze at the fortress they had sworn to capture. Inside the castle, the count Nikola Subic Zrinski was in command. His people had hung enormous cloths, the colour of blood, from the ramparts.

'What does that mean?' Jahan asked a foot-soldier.

'It means they'll not come out of that damn castle. They'd rather die.'

Stubborn and staunch, the count and his soldiers defended their citadel. Days turned into weeks. A month passed. The heat became unbearable. For food, they had roasted millet, nuts, dried meat and a piece of hard mare's-milk cheese each. The flocks of sheep and goats that they had brought from Istanbul were waiting, ready to be slaughtered. How the enemy withstood the hunger and their diminishing numbers, Jahan could not say. The Sultan's army would charge; the fortress would hold out. Many fell on both sides, more from the Ottoman than from the enemy lines. But where the defenders had hundreds, the Ottomans had thousands. They buried their dead in pits deeper than the deepest wells and prepared themselves for another charge. Time and again they sent emissaries asking the count to surrender, promising safety should he do so. Sultan Suleiman offered to let him become the ruler of Croatia under Ottoman direction. Every messenger returned with the same answer: they would fight.

The sounds of the Ottoman cannonades echoed through the rolling hills. The enemy's resistance was unshakable. The holes in the defences opened during the day were repaired at night by men, women and children. They used everything they had to fortify the walls – timber, fabric, carpets. Nothing was spared. Not even an exquisite silk tapestry that must have belonged to a wealthy family. Water nymphs danced on its surface, holding lyres, their hair shimmering like moonlight on dark waves. Jahan could not take his eyes off it. Nor could the Janissaries. There was something enchanting in the image of this lustrous paradise, its brightness and softness so alluring that the commanders, suspecting sorcery, ordered the tapestry to be bombarded. They attacked that part of the wall ceaselessly, until all the lustrous colours disappeared into a dull rag of soot and slag.

One clear afternoon in September, Jahan was riding Chota, bringing the Sultan back to his tent, when they heard a blast that would ring in their ears for days on end. The ground shook; billows of smoke rose above the clouds. The elephant jerked, almost throwing them down.

Jahan yelled orders at Chota, trying to soothe him while he gaped at the pitch-dark sky.

'Mahout – what's going on?' the Sultan demanded from where he lay on cushions inside the howdah.

'My Lord, they have blown up their arsenal . . . and themselves.'

'What did you say?' The Sultan sat up, leaning forward for a better look. 'So they have,' he murmured. 'So they have.'

For a long, horrified moment the sovereign and the mahout watched the blaze. Chota swung his trunk and flapped his ears in a frenzy. Oblivious to the animal's unease, the Sultan ordered, 'Go near. I want to see.'

Jahan obeyed, hoping that, midway, the elephant would not become overwrought. But when they reached the scene it would be he who would be shaken. The ground was strewn with shattered weapons and severed limbs; it was impossible to say which were the enemy's and which were theirs. Jahan's breath came in gasps as his gorge rose. Bile filled his mouth and nearly caused him to vomit. He hid his face with his hands.

'Don't cry,' the Sultan said. 'Pray.'

Ashamed of his weakness, Jahan straightened his shoulders. 'I shall pray for our soldiers, my Lord.'

'No,' he said. 'Pray for them all. There's no difference any more.'

This man who had, throughout the forty-six years of his rule, relentlessly fought one war after another; who had ordered his brightest Grand Vizier and perhaps his only friend to be killed; who had watched his eldest son being strangled, caused another son to die of sorrow and arranged for a third to be murdered far away in Iran; who had made himself the strongest of all the Ottoman sultans – this man had just said, in a field of dandelions and death, that in the end there was no difference between the soldier inside and the soldier outside the enemy stronghold, the Christian and the Muslim, leaving Jahan with a riddle that he would not solve for many years to come.

The next morning, the smell of burning flesh still canopied the battlefield, a stench so thick no wind could carry it away. Jahan felt as if the smell had lodged in the back of his throat, making it hard to breathe, let alone swallow.

Still, like any other day, he made Chota ready for the sovereign, and they waited in front of his tent. Yet it was Sokollu who walked out after a while, saying, in a whisper, that he wished to have a word with the mahout. By now Jahan had lived in the seraglio for long enough to know that if a Grand Vizier wished to speak with a common servant, something terrible must have happened or was about to. Jahan followed him, his heart in his mouth.

Inside the Sultan's tent, though there was plenty of daylight, a lamp glowed dimly in one corner. Across from it, on a velvet sofa, was the Sultan, lying perfectly still.

'Listen, son,' said the Vizier. 'What you see, no one knows. D'you understand?'

'Is he –' Jahan faltered.

'That's right, sadly. Our Sultan has passed away, may he dwell in Paradise. We will mourn later. You and I have an important duty.'

Not knowing where to look, Jahan stared, wide-eyed with woe, at his feet. Sultan Suleiman, aged seventy-two, had not lived long enough to glory in their triumph.

'It's essential that we hide the truth from the army.' Sokollu spoke carefully, haltingly; a man who believed that words, like money, should be used sparingly. 'Our Sultan will sit on the elephant as if it were any other day. You shall take him around.'

Jahan winced as it dawned on him that he would have to place a corpse on Chota. He asked, 'What if somebody wants to speak to the Sultan?'

'Make sure the elephant does not go near anyone. If the Janissaries see the Sultan from afar, that'll be enough. They don't need to hear his voice. All they need to know is that he's alive.'

Suddenly they heard footsteps. The guards were bringing someone in. Sokollu, having ensured only the most trustworthy could pass through the threshold, craned his head to check who was entering. It was a short, bull-necked Tatar.

'Oh, it's you. Come forward.'

The Grand Vizier took out a scroll from his robe, kissed it and put it on his forehead. 'Take this to Prince Selim.'

The man bowed low.

'Be fast as the wind. Do not stop anywhere on the way. Eat mounted. Don't sleep. Don't waste time. The fate of the empire depends upon you.'

Jahan wondered how long it would take to gallop from Szigetvar to Kutahya, where the Prince was serving as Governor. It was not enough that the news of his father's death should reach him without delay; he, too, had to arrive at Istanbul in time. An empty throne was an ominous sign; anything could happen in the gap between the father's death and the son's ascension to the throne.

Sokollu brought out a Qur'an from a mother-of-pearl box. 'I need you to swear on the holy book. Both of you.'

They did as told. Nevertheless the Grand Vizier didn't seem satisfied. He inquired where they were from.

'Hindustan,' Jahan said.

'Kazan,' the messenger replied.

Sokollu took out a dagger, gilded and bejewelled. 'Give me your hands.'

He made a cut on the messenger's forefinger, then on Jahan's. Blood trickled from their hands on to the sheath of the dagger. 'If one of you gives the secret away, I shall kill you both.'

Jahan did not understand why his life should depend on a stranger, and the messenger must have felt the same way, for he turned to him with a frown. Still, neither dared to protest. Sokollu gave them two silk handkerchiefs to wrap around their fingers.

'Now go, my son,' he said to the messenger; 'may Allah guide you.'

Jahan took a last look at the man whose loyalty he now counted on. They nodded at one another in silent farewell. Jahan would not know that years later it was this same messenger who would bring Master Sinan to the palace on the night when Sultan Suleiman's grandson killed his five brothers to secure the throne.

No sooner had the messenger left than the physician came in. An ex-*converso* from Salamanca who had fully returned to his religion. He spoke Ottoman with a lilting accent. He, too, was sworn to secrecy, though without a holy script, since the five books of Moses were not present – and, for some reason, his finger was spared.

'Can he help me?' the physician asked, nodding towards Jahan.

Sokollu, his back now turned to them, was absorbed in forging the Sultan's signature, sending out letters and orders in the sovereign's name. He waved dismissively, saying over his shoulder, 'Go help.'

The physician opened a jar that filled the tent with a pungent smell. A mixture of myrrh, cassia and other spices. They undressed the Sultan and anointed his entire body. What Jahan saw next he would not be able to tell anyone, no matter how badly he might want to. It would penetrate his dreams, time and again. The Chief Physician cut open the left side of the Sultan's chest and pulled out the heart. It resembled a red bird in his palms, and, even though it lay motionless, for a second Jahan feared it was still beating. Holding it with both hands the physician placed it on a silver basin. Then he sewed the wound with twelve perfect stitches. Jahan glanced up at the man in horror. '*Effendi*, why did we do this?'

'The heart is the centre of our very being. It was our Sultan's last wish. Should he die here, he wanted his heart to be buried on the battleground.'

Choosing the best kaftan they could find in the trunks, they dressed the corpse. Finally, they combed his beard, lined his eyes with soot and coloured his cheeks with a rosy powder. When they were done, Sultan Suleiman looked healthier than he had while he was alive.

'Take off that robe,' Sokollu remarked as soon as he saw what they had done. 'Too glamorous. He wouldn't wear that.'

They settled on a plain robe and readied the corpse. At dusk, three elite guards, having finished inspecting the camp, arrived to report that all was quiet. With their help the elephant was brought to the entrance. Chota was anxious, sensing something was wrong.

'What's the matter?' Sokollu asked, irritated.

'My Lord, give me time with the beast, I beg.'

Jahan spoke sweetly to Chota, telling him that he would be carrying a dead man. Just for a few days, he assured him. After much cajoling and many apples, the animal calmed down, allowing them to place the Sultan into the howdah. Jahan took his usual place on the elephant's neck and rode on, his eyes fixed on the circling vultures in the distance. When he saw a few of them descend upon the bodies strewn about far down below, he had to turn away. Twenty thousand men were lost during the siege of Szigetvar.

On the way back, they learned that Prince Selim had made it to the city. The messenger had succeeded. Sokollu was immensely relieved. There being no more need to pretend, he ordered his guards to reveal the truth. The Sultan's body was brought down from the howdah and placed in a litter, which was then pulled by two white stallions. In this way they reached the capital. The people of Istanbul were waiting for them. Thousands had gathered on both sides of the road, tearing their hair and their garments, beating their chests. Jahan saw fearless warriors break into tears, men sob like boys.

On the heels of the father's burial came the son's enthronement. Selim wanted the people to celebrate as they had never done before. Earthquakes, diseases, death . . . calamities had fallen so thick and fast that there had not been any joy left, much less hope. They had had enough of mourning. Now it was time to rejoice.

The *ulema* were appalled. Even Sokollu was frightened of their reaction. It was his adviser Feridun Beg who convinced him that it was fine to let the multitude have a bit of fun. He said, 'Can a body be constipated all the time? The world needs to empty its bowels. Let them make merry, my Vizier.'

On the day Selim ascended the throne, Chota was arrayed in a magnificent headdress and a silver mantle decorated with gems. The elephant led the royal procession through the streets of Istanbul. People waved, cheered, sang loudly. And, once again, Jahan could not believe how suddenly the public mood changed from sorrow to rejoicing, how quickly their river of tears ran dry. If they moved between gloom and glee with such ease, did this mean they could pass from love to hatred just as effortlessly?

Once the new Sultan had been enthroned, Chota and Jahan went back to work on the construction sites. In the mornings they would leave the menagerie, always through the same path; in the evenings they would return, tired and thirsty, smelling of dust and mud. At or about this time Master Sinan started to build a bridge over the bar that connected the Buyukcekmece Lake to the sea – long, arched and graceful.

On a night in December, having finished the bulk of the construction, they were returning to the city – the master and the three apprentices in a carriage, Jahan ahead of them, riding Chota. As soon as they turned round a bend they heard a noise, far off from the city, and somewhere in the midst of it a scream, sharp and bloodcurdling. When Jahan lifted his head skywards he saw a cascade of orange, yellow and red – the colours so bright they hurt his eyes. He shouted, 'Fire!'

The carriage came to a stop and they got out. Sinan looked devastated. He said, 'We ought to go to help.'

'Why don't we go with Chota?' Jahan said. 'It'll be faster.' They all climbed up into the howdah while Jahan planted himself on the elephant's neck.

They trudged along the streets, following the shouts that pierced the air like splintered glass. As they went, the wind blew stronger, hotter, scattering the firestorm from one wooden house to the next. Jahan blinked repeatedly, dazzled as much by the glow as by the commotion. The flames licked the night sky in swirls of colour so vivid that it felt almost solid. Every now and then a blaze went up, trees glaring like Murano chandeliers.

Each corner they turned displayed a sight more harrowing than the previous one. Animals trotted around, lost, dazed. Families tried to save what little they had, men lugging baskets and barrels, women pale with fright, babies crying their hearts out. Children, only they, remained dauntless, scampering about as if in the midst of a game the grown-ups had invented for them to play.

In front of their eyes entire neighbourhoods went up in smoke.

Rooms in which mothers had given birth, where circumcisions were celebrated, life was conceived and the sickly drew their last breaths – these places with the memories they held turned to cinders. Nothing remained except a lingering warmth and, strewn about on the ground, clothes, shoes, trifles, a piece of a brick that was once a wall. They came to a halt at a thoroughfare where the fire had hit the worst. Sinan, taken aback, asked to be brought down. As the Chief Royal Architect he had worked hard to prevent this calamity, having the streets paved, checking the buildings. All for naught.

There were Janissaries idling, humping cases, talking to people, but with leaden steps, almost reluctant. Sinan marched up to one of them – a man sitting on a piece of timber, gazing around dully.

'Why aren't you doing something?'

The Janissary, not expecting to be questioned and not recognizing the architect, snapped out of his reverie. 'What?'

'Why are you not helping the people?'

'I am,' said the man morosely.

Another Janissary edged nearer. He said they had not been quenching the flames because they were waiting to hear from their agha, who was sick in bed.

At this Sinan's face darkened. 'What orders do you need to hear? How can you hold off when the city is in flames?'

While Sinan was talking with the Janissaries, the mahout and the elephant, distracted by a sound, veered into a side street. Further down the road Jahan saw two women screaming at each other, beside themselves. From neighbours he learned they were the wives of a merchant who was away travelling. When the fire broke out, the women had run out of the house, grabbing their children, each assuming that the other had snatched the newborn baby.

Jahan looked at the burning building and at the crying women.

'You wait for me here. I'm going in,' he said to Chota. He wouldn't dream of taking the elephant with him, knowing how scared he was of the flames.

Slowly, Jahan made his way towards the smouldering house. He took every step with the utmost care, listening out for the slightest sound. Once he crossed the threshold, the flames assaulted him from all sides. The upper storey above the front rooms had collapsed, but the building was still intact at the back. Jahan saw a brass candleholder and snatched it out of habit, even though it was of little worth. A few steps ahead he got luckier: an empty inkpot of gold and emerald. Coughing and rasping, Jahan fumbled through curtains of smoke, his eyes watering so much he could barely see where he was going. He dodged a burning timber that fell right down in front of him. The wood hit his shoulder, knocking him down. There was no way he could go any further.

Suddenly, a soft coil of flesh grabbed him by the waist and lifted him up.

'Chota! How did you get here?' Jahan exclaimed.

In lieu of a response the elephant led him towards the depths of the house – or what was left of it. Chota moved his ears as though catching an imperceptible sound. The animal's sensitive feet must have been burning, but the mahout would not think of that until later.

Jahan could not open his mouth for fear of swallowing more smoke. Every breath hurt. Taking off his jacket, he wrapped it around his face. Chota shoved him from behind, gently but firmly. Hedged in by flames, Jahan lurched forward into the second room, then steadied himself. The elephant waited behind him.

There it was – the cradle. Its gauzy tulle covering must have helped the baby to breathe. Jahan grabbed the bundle, without checking whether the child was alive. With one hand the baby, clinging to life, clutched at Jahan. It had cried so much its voice was gone; its rosebud mouth was closed. Yet its strength was surprising, and it must have been contagious, too, for both Chota and Jahan were calmer now.

By the time Chota and Jahan emerged, the number of people watching on the street had tripled. Sinan and the apprentices, too, were there, having heard the story of the beast that had plodded into a burning house. The mother of the baby dashed towards them and plucked the baby away from Jahan. Then she began praying, laughing, thanking, crying, trying to kiss Jahan's hand, Chota's skin, all at once, with no fear of being trampled by the elephant.

Jahan tottered towards Sinan, who was greeting him with open arms. 'I am furious at you . . .' he said, 'but proud, son, so proud.'

The apprentices embraced him. Even so, Jahan could feel a coldness exuding from them. He had outshone them, and this they hadn't liked.

It turned out the Chief Janissary Agha had really been ill. Yet that was not the reason why he had delayed sending instructions to the soldiers. The army, demanding an increase in their pay, had seen the fire as an opportunity to prove how essential they were. As the Grand Vizier had been slow in granting the rise, the agha had been slow in giving the command to his Janissaries to put out the flames.

The mahout and the elephant headed to the master's home, smothered in soot and reeking of cinders. Jahan wrapped Chota's feet. Two of his nails were broken, bleeding. He had patches of burned skin all over. The scars from that night would remain and never heal.

Later on, from Sinan's garden, Jahan stood gazing at the city below, wraiths of smoke whirling here and there. At dawn there were no birds chirping, no hearths crackling, no seagulls swooping; everything had plunged into silence. It had become nippy; the cold felt strange following the heat of the night.

After the fire died out, the extent of the devastation was clear. With the exception of the Jewish quarter, which was built of stone, street after street had been razed.

'The fire was our teacher,' Sinan said when they all gathered again. 'He taught us a lesson.'

That same week Sinan went to the palace and obtained the permissions that he needed. Sleeping little, he drew plans. Streets would be enlarged by half a cubit on each side. There would be no house taller than two storeys. More brick and stone, instead of wood, would be used, he decided.

No sooner were the new rules introduced, however, than people began to defy them. The fire had been a teacher, true. But Istanbul, where forgetting was easier than remembering, never learned its lesson.

One evening Sangram came to see Jahan with a bowl of *sutlach*, just as he had done so many moons ago. He was very old and frail, and every now and then he shook his head uncontrollably, as if arguing with some invisible companion. Jahan took the treat, thanking him. As he watched him eat, Sangram asked, 'Did you hear what Captain Crazy-head has done this time?'

Jahan almost dropped his spoon. 'What?'

Captain Gareth's fleet had run into an armada. In the ensuing combat the seaman bit the hand that had fed him all these years and turned traitor. Starting on the side of the Ottomans, he had ended toasting the Pope. Knowing he would be gutted alive if caught, he had fled the Ottoman territory. He could not return to Istanbul. Not that he minded. Having been given sanctuary by the papacy, he was quite content with his new banner, hunting for Ottoman sailors.

When Jahan heard this he was dumbstruck, flooded with disturbing memories. Captain Gareth was the sole reason he had ended up in the royal menagerie. It had been the man's plan to disguise him as an animal-tamer and place him a stone's-throw away from the riches in the seraglio. A plan that had worked seamlessly once the sailors in his command had got rid of the real mahout – hurled into cold waters, just like that. 'Never liked the chap's wits,' the Captain had said by way of explanation, though Jahan never understood how he could have disliked this man, who spoke not a word of Turkish or English and stared at the waves all day long. Inside the hold they carried merchandise from Hindustan and a white elephant on the brink of death. Jahan was only a cabin boy, escaping his stepfather. He was a mere youngster from a town in Anatolia. What did he know about elephants? As he stood there, remembering all of this, another thought occurred to Jahan. Why was Sangram suddenly telling him about Captain Gareth?

'So you knew . . .' Jahan whispered.

'How could I not?' Sangram said. 'You told me you were from Hindustan. You spoke not a word of any of our languages and the stories you told made no sense.'

'Why didn't you inform on me? You could have told everyone, "This boy is an impostor, he is lying."'

Sangram smiled. 'I was going to . . . but then I changed my mind. I didn't want you to suffer. You seemed like you'd had your share of hardships – why bring more pain?'

Jahan stood up, kissed the man's bony hand.

'You were only a lad; now look at you,' Sangram said, overwhelmed with tenderness.

Jahan bit his lip. How bizarre it was. While he had been running after things that were never going to happen and resenting life for the gifts it had denied him, there had been people supporting him without drawing attention to themselves. They had given and expected nothing in return.

Sultan Selim was determined to enjoy, revive and expand the menagerie. Unlike his father, who had barely acknowledged the existence of his animal subjects, the new sovereign took an interest in their lives. He often visited the wild beasts, sometimes on his own, mostly in the company of his courtiers. In particular, he was enthralled by the big cats – tigers, cheetahs and lions – and, for a reason unbeknown to anyone, had taken a shine to the ostrich. The apes aroused his curiosity with their arcane sounds and gestures. Yet it was Chota he loved best. He was fond of rides atop the elephant. To this end he had ordered a larger howdah with a foldable ladder to be supplied. Chota had been presented with a new headdress: bright turquoise, lined with golden tassels and adorned with peacock feathers. To Jahan's dismay there was an equally and ridiculously showy outfit for him – a shimmering silvery jerkin with embroidered blue tulips and a white turban. The Sultan had a penchant for ornateness – both in himself and in those around him. He liked spending time with dwarves, mutes, buffoons, preferring their company to that of his viziers and advisers with their dreary talk.

A poet and an archer, Selim was a sad, troubled man, with a neck so short as to be almost non-existent, a florid complexion and shoulders rounded as though crushed under an invisible weight. He became Sultan at the age of forty-two, no longer in his springtime. All his life he had been waiting, praying and plotting for the Ottoman throne; yet when the moment came, he was not ready. Jahan thought of him as a flickering candlelight – nervous, erratic, awaiting the wind that would one day put him out.

His brother Bayezid – his biggest rival – had been executed in Iran, leaving Selim the sole heir. That must have gratified him, one would expect. Instead, it had turned him fretful. If princes could be killed so easily, and without any remorse or recriminations, whom could he trust in this world? He drank amply. He ate voraciously. He slept with the prettiest women. He went hunting – deer, duck, partridge, wild boar. Nothing quenched his thirst. One glance at his dress was enough to see the difference between him and his father. In his passion for opulence he adorned himself with rare gems, wore refined brocade, heady perfumes. He lined his eyes with kohl, which gave his gaze a hardness that didn't quite match his personality. That his turbans, decorated with plumes in garish colours, were taller than Sultan Suleiman's did not escape anyone's notice.

His many women had many children. But there was one concubine who surpassed all others and became his wife – Nurbanu the Venetian, the enchantress. The name her mother had given her was Cecilia. She said she came from a family of high standing and would have lived as a noblewoman had she not been taken as a slave by the corsairs at the age of twelve. Unfriendly mouths completed the parts of the story she left out – that though fathered by a patrician, she was born out of wedlock. Nurbanu never gave up sending letters to her relatives in Corfu and Venice. She also wrote to the Bailo, the Doge, the Senate.

In response she not only received a round of correspondence but also gifts. Like Selim himself, Nurbanu cherished splendour. Recently, upon her request, she had been sent a pair of lap-dogs from Venice, with clipped, creamy coats, that never left her side. Funny creatures they were, barking at every moving thing, unmindful of their size. Before each meal their food was tried by a taster in case some wicked soul attempted to poison them. There were quite a few who would have liked to do so.

At nights, around the fireplace, the tamers talked about her, exchanging rumours and tall tales. The code that required everyone to be silent was still observed, but not as strictly as before. Though they were careful with their choice of words and used a secret tongue, they gossiped to their heart's content. Other things changed, too. From the courtyard of the eunuchs to the tower of the Chief Physician, from the chambers of the princes to the dormitories of the Zuluflu Baltacılar, the Halberdiers of the Tresses, the seraglio rang with sound. Every noise that had been suppressed during the reign of Suleiman was now set free, eddying round the corridors.

On days when the weather was balmy the Sultan delighted in boating with his companions, eating and drinking as they glided round the Golden Horn, sucking on musk lozenges to sweeten their breath. Selim believed that as long as his Grand Vizier Sokollu held the reins the empire would run just fine. Although he was not capable of absorbing the intricacies of the state, there was a part of him that would rather have remained a poet, or an itinerant bard, had he not been confined to the throne.

The *ulema* hated his ways and accused him of being a sinner. The Janissaries berated him for not leading the army from battlefield to battlefield. The people compared him with his father, finding him weak and cursing the ghost of Hurrem – which still roamed the marble halls – for giving birth to no better. Selim placated them, making endowments, distributing riches, just so they would leave him alone. Thanks to his generosity, the nasty things that were said about him were washed away like writing on wet sand – only to be written all over again a short time afterwards.

Among Selim's closest courtiers were poets, elegists and musicians. There was a poetess called Hubbi Hatun. She could recite for hours, her eyes closed, her voice rising and falling like a seagull in the gust. There were balladeers who knew songs from all corners of the empire and could sing in a dozen languages, sending their audience from bliss to despair, from despair to bliss. There was a painter who, when he got a bit tipsy, said some day he would use his own blood for the colour red.

Jahan knew them all. They strolled through the rose gardens in their easy-going fashion, after which they would stop by the menagerie, watching and feeding the animals. They were a raucous bunch that loved to feast and roister as much as their patron did. Their visits were sudden, random. It could be at any hour of the afternoon or the evening.

One Thursday, in the dead of night, the tamers woke up to the sound of music and laughter. They blinked at each other through sleepy eyes, struggling to fathom what was going on.

'Where are the damn servants?' a voice boomed in the dark.

Donning their garments, they rushed out, lined up. The Sultan and three guests were there – sprightly and, by the look of things, heavily drunk.

Selim bellowed, 'Where's the mahout?'

Jahan took a step forward, bowed low.

'We've been looking for you. We wish to ride the elephant.'

'Now, my Sultan?'

The question was met with bursts of tittering while the Sultan glowered. Jahan mumbled his apologies and hurried to the barn. Chota grumbled, not willing to abandon the land of dreams where he was stomping merrily. Half pleading half threatening, Jahan was able to bring him out and put on the howdah.

The Sultan, the musician, the poet and the minstrel climbed up. Jahan noticed the Sultan had gained weight; he puffed as he made his way. The servants who had come with them were carrying baskets loaded with food and drink. With ropes each basket was hoisted into the howdah. Chota lifted Jahan with his trunk and placed him on his neck. In this state they began their night-time promenade.

Jahan thought they would stay inside the imperial gardens, but, as they reached the outer gate, he heard Selim say, 'Keep going, mahout.'

'Where, my Lord?'

'Go, don't stop until I tell you.'

The guards, their eyes wide with astonishment, moved aside to let them pass. Chota, still sleepy and in an ill mood, plodded at a snail's pace, refusing to speed up despite Jahan's prodding. Inside the howdah, they didn't seem to mind. They were singing. The sound of a lute filled the air. They passed through the winding streets where nothing, not even a leaf or a shadow, stirred.

'Mahout, stop!' ordered the Sultan.

Jahan did as told.

'Jump down!'

This, too, Jahan did.

'Now catch!'

Giggling like children, they lowered a basket. Inside there was a wine bottle and a cup. The Sultan said, 'Drink!'

'My Lord –'

'Come on. Do you have any idea how annoying the sober are to the merry?'

Jahan filled the cup and downed it. A peal of laughter followed. The Sultan, clearly amused, said, 'Drink another.'

So it went. Before he knew it he had consumed the whole bottle. He asked Chota to pull him up, and, as the animal did so, Jahan's head spun like a cartwheel. He sat there, his face blotchy, his anguish hidden, until he heard the Sultan say, 'Tell me, mahout, have you ever been in love?'

Jahan said, a little uncertainly, 'All I know about love is that it brings heartache, your Highness.'

From the howdah came the saddest melody, fluttering in the breeze like a feather from a bird long gone. The poet recited: *Behold the beauty that expands the heart within the mirror of the rose* —

In that moment Jahan thought that God, who must be watching them, would understand the pain and the fear that they felt for being so small, so perishable. He clapped heartily. His forwardness, which any other time would have brought trouble, was met with laughter and joy.

All at once a howling voice pierced the air. 'What the hell is goin' on?'

In front of their eyes was a man, tottering. He had the raw look of someone who had just woken up. The doorway where they had stopped was his bed, apparently. Too drunk to find his way home, he had dozed off there.

Jahan tried to warn the poor fellow. He leaned over and whispered, 'It's the Sultan sitting here!'

'Aye,' the man barked. He pointed at Selim. 'That's the Sultan!' He pointed at the courtiers. 'These are the archangels . . .' He pointed at Chota. 'This beast is the *zebani* in hell. And I am dead.'

The Sultan broke in, 'What are you doing on the streets at this hour?'

'Nothing,' said the man.

'You can barely stand but you are searching for more drink, right? Don't lie! Have you no shame?'

Dazed, lost, the man leaned forward as if he wanted to kiss Chota's trunk. 'Searching, yes. But not wine.' He patted his chest. 'I am looking for love!'

The courtiers chortled and so did the Sultan, despite his irritation. 'At this hour, on empty streets. You're hopeless.'

The drunk lifted his head, his arms folded over his chest. 'Maybe I am. But how about you?'

Jahan was worried sick. He dared not glance at the Sultan, fearing the punishment he would now inflict on this insolent subject. Yet when Selim spoke again he sounded calm, almost compassionate. 'Catch!' Something rattled on the cobblestones. The man picked it up and stared quizzically at the ring in his hand.

The Sultan said, 'If you find what you're looking for, come to the palace and show my seal. Tell them you have a message for the Lord of the Empire.'

The drunk, only now realizing this really was the Sultan, lurched forward to kiss his hand or his hem or his feet, but, being unable to reach any of those, hugged Chota's leg instead.

'Stay away,' Jahan said. 'You're going to get trampled.'

The man took a step back, lost for words, shaking, sweating, mumbling his gratitude, flummoxed and glad to be alive.

Selim ordered, 'Let's go, mahout.'

On the way back they were silent and suddenly sombre.

Since they had arrived in the Ottoman palace, there were times when Chota had been neglected, even mistreated, but he had always been the one and only. There was no other elephant in the menagerie. No other royal elephant in the empire. Everything changed the day a carrack moored in the port of Galata.

The month of April it was. The Judas trees were in full bloom, the city wrapped in perfume, when the ship dropped anchor. Among its cargo were three animals: a zebra, a giraffe and an African bush elephant. They were brought to the palace on carts, wretched and ailing, after a harrowing voyage. The giraffe, with its black tongue and peaceful eyes, sadly did not survive for long. The zebra was sent off to the Lion House. As for the elephant – a twenty-year-old male that was named Mahmood – he recovered and stayed. Along with him came an unfriendly face – Buziba.

By this time Chota had reached thirty years of age. Though not at all doddering in elephant years, he no longer had the agility of his heyday. Nonetheless, with each passing summer he had become smarter, sharper. Jahan now understood why battle-scarred warriors preferred aged elephants to young ones. Sound in body and limb as they might be, the youths tended to be foolhardy – like human beings.

Mahmood was placed in the same barn as Chota while Buziba joined the other tamers in the shed. Initially, Jahan tried to give him a wide berth but it was impossible. Every evening they supped together, every afternoon they attended to their elephants side by side. Had Buziba heard what a *hamam* was, he gave no indication of it. He seldom bathed, if at all, and never cleaned his surroundings. Contrary to the custom in the palace, he ate noisily. At meal times Jahan avoided the seat beside him to avoid the crumbs he spewed left and right.

Jahan wasn't the only one who was vexed by the newcomers. Chota, too, was perturbed. Incensed. He resented Mahmood munching his hay, drinking his water, getting his treats. On occasion he would knock over the other's bucket or filch his food. An angry elephant was a dedicated avenger.

One morning, when Jahan entered the barn, he found Chota stamping on the mantle that Buziba would throw upon Mahmood whenever they went out for a walk.

'Shame on you!' Jahan hissed, keeping his voice level so as not to be heard by anyone else. 'Get off that thing.'

Too late. The mantle was ground with grime.

'What's the matter?' came Buziba's voice from behind.

There was no point in denying Chota's misbehaviour and Jahan didn't try. 'I shall clean it, I swear.'

Buziba picked up the cloth but not before muttering under his breath something that Jahan took to be a curse. 'You think I'm stupid? I know what's happening,' he said, his voice not so much upset as satisfied. 'You and your beast are jealous.'

'That's not true.'

'It is, for a reason. Soon you're going to be shown the door, the two of you. Anyone can see which elephant's better.'

Jahan opened and closed his mouth, unable to object. Someone had seen his innermost fear and said it out loud and the universe had heard it.

The next day the Sultan appeared accompanied by his courtiers. Just as Jahan moved to get Chota ready for a ride, Selim said, 'Let's try the new elephant.'

Buziba threw himself to the ground, declaring that he and the animal would happily serve the Sovereign of the House of Osman, the Commander of the Faithful and the Successor of the Prophet, the Shadow of God on Earth, the most generous and the most virtuous and the most righteous of all rulers who had come to the throne and were yet to come.

Jahan had never heard so many honeyed words, dripping with thick, sticky syrup. Even so, the Sultan seemed pleased. Like lightning, Chota's howdah was placed on Mahmood, Jahan's jacket was handed to Buziba – that awful jacket that Jahan had hated with his entire being but now thought the world of. While Jahan gnawed his lips and Chota swung his trunk back and forth, Mahmood and his mahout replaced them, just like that.

252

Off they went. Even after they vanished from sight, the wind carried their sounds – or so Jahan thought in his misery. He caressed Chota, who coiled his trunk around Jahan's waist. They stayed like that for a good while, seeking refuge in each other's company.

The next morning all hell broke loose. There was a pond behind the barn, surrounded by moss like a green, furry carpet. The water was no more than a puddle with fish but Chota loved to spend time there. Jahan had obtained permission for him to take a dip, every now and then, since Selim found the sight of an elephant splashing water rather endearing.

When Chota and Jahan reached the pond they found Mahmood settled in Chota's usual place. Next to him was Buziba, dangling his bare feet into the water, basking in the sunshine with his eyes closed, his mouth half open.

Jahan considered his options. There was no point in starting a fight, which would reach the ears of the Chief White Eunuch and get him in trouble. Yet he could not let this pass. Chota stood beside him, quiet as a mouse, as though he, too, was considering his options.

Gingerly, Jahan walked towards Buziba and tapped him on the shoulder. Yanked out of his reverie, he flinched. 'What do you want?'

'This spot belongs to Chota.'

Not a single emotion on his wooden face. Closing his eyes again, Buziba yawned and went back to swinging his feet lazily, as if Jahan and Chota weren't standing there waiting for a response.

Jahan said grudgingly, 'Let's go, Chota. We'll come back some other time.'

Jahan had barely taken a step when he heard a splash. Chota, that blessed soul, had done what he hadn't dared to do. Buziba, now in the pond, unleashed a curse, coughing, waving his hands. He clearly didn't know how to swim, and Jahan ran to him.

'Take my hand, I'll pull you out.'

Buziba stopped, having just realized how shallow the pond was. Standing up, dripping water, he got out by himself and marched past them in a ball of fury.

So it began. Their war. Every day they found a new excuse to be at each other's throats. Jahan could barely focus on work for Sinan, for fear that while he was away Buziba might harm Chota. He lost sleep, ate little. He recalled what Sinan, with a touch of compassion in his voice, had once said: 'Balance is what keeps us upright. Same with buildings. Same with people.' Jahan had lost his balance. Chota, too. The elephant spent the days staring ahead with fixed eyes, as though he wished, with all his being, to be beyond the walls of the barn he shared with his enemy. Two weeks into this torment Jahan came up with a plan. By then the weather had become colder, and the summer was drifting away. Balaban's Gypsies, recently back from Thrace, would soon be heading southwards. Jahan decided to visit them before they left.

They welcomed him like a long-lost brother. Tamarind sherbets were served, mouth-watering aromas surrounded them – sour-grape molasses, goat's cheese, spinach *pide*, roasted meat. Children ran about, women smoked, grannies laughed toothless laughs. As they stuffed themselves, they inquired about the Sultan, eager to hear the latest palace gossip. Jahan explained how he'd had to give the guards a backhander in order to sneak out and that he had to return before the evening patrol.

'So what brings you here?' Balaban wanted to know.

'I need help,' Jahan said. 'Can we talk alone?'

'No need. This is family,' Balaban said, opening both hands.

Leaning closer, Jahan dropped his voice to a whisper. 'Is there something that would make a male burn for a female?'

Balaban grinned. 'Aye, it's called love.'

'Not like that. For . . . mating. A powder or a drink that makes one desire.'

Balaban stopped chewing and regarded Jahan. 'You sick?'

'Not for me. For an elephant.'

'That beast needs no boost. What do you have against poor Gulbahar?'

'Oh, it's not for Chota!'

Jahan told him everything – how he had lost his peace of mind because of another elephant and another mahout. He expected Balaban to make a wisecrack at his expense, but when he finished the Gypsy nodded solemnly and said, 'Don't sorrow. We'll help.'

Jahan took out the pouch he had brought and put it on the table.

'Is that from the Sultan or from you?' Balaban inquired.

'The Sultan knows nothing about this. He shouldn't.'

'Then keep it,' Balaban said in his crisp, jovial way. 'Now go. We'll find you.'

Jahan returned to the menagerie. In his head a witch's brew fermented – shame, hope, guilt. Two days later a boy came looking for him, carrying a jar. 'Somebody sent you this.'

Jahan studied him – the bright black eyes, the dimpled smile, the olive skin. No doubt he was related to Balaban. Inside the jar there was a powder the colour of turmeric. He dipped in the tip of his finger and tasted it. It had a mild flavour, a bit salty. It could blend into anything.

Smuggling pomegranate sherbet from the kitchen, he mixed it with a spoonful of powder. The moment Buziba left he gave the drink to his elephant, who guzzled it happily. Not a thing happened. Next day he tried again, increasing the dose. Again, naught. He poured the entire powder into Mahmood's rice gruel and watched the elephant cram it all down.

As luck would have it, that night Sultan Selim appeared with his companions, eager for another session of merrymaking.

'Mahout!' the Sultan exclaimed.

Jahan bowed. 'Yes, my Sultan.'

'Where is the other mahout?'

Buziba came running, his face drenched in sweat. 'Your Majesty, the elephant is unwell. I beg you to forgive us for tonight.'

'What's wrong with the beast?' the Sultan demanded.

As though in response a terrible sound came from the barn, followed by a crash. The Sultan headed towards the noise, the others following.

It was the strangest sight. Mahmood, in his frenzy, had rammed into the wooden panel on the side of his stall and one of his tusks had got jammed in the plank. He could move neither forward nor backward. His male organ was swollen, dripping. He bellowed – more with rage than with exasperation. No one dared to go near, including Buziba.

That was the end of Mahmood. Though he was released from the wooden plank, his fury and frustration did not subside. Eventually he had to be fettered. He broke his chains, knocked down the walls, charged into trees. Worse were the sounds he made – trumpeting, wailing, bawling. Before the month was over, Mahmood and Buziba were sent to the old church near the Hagia Sophia.

No one suspected anything – save Olev. 'It was you, right?' he asked, his eyebrows moving together.

When Jahan, already filled with remorse, did not respond, Olev went on, 'I remember the day you arrived. Your elephant was an infant; so were you. I remember watching you and thinking to myself, how will he survive in the palace, a lad so good-hearted and gullible. Whereas now, look at you! You've become one of us, more's the pity.'

Jahan glanced up. 'What does that mean?'

'It means you fight battles that aren't needed,' said Olev. 'You are stronger. Beware, though. If you carry a sword, you obey the sword, not the other way round. Nobody can hold a weapon and keep their hands clear of blood at the same time.'

'I can – don't you worry for me,' said Jahan. But as soon as he said this, he felt a sharp pang of regret, fearing that he may have tempted fate.

Since the day Selim had ascended the throne, whenever Istanbul crushed his spirits, which happened often, he took off for Adrianople – the city where he had spent part of his youth. There he could hunt, loaf and drink to his heart's content, away from judging eyes and wagging tongues. Like every man who was aware of being widely disliked, the Sultan felt beholden to those who supported him – and the people of Adrianople always had. So several years into his reign Selim decided to reward this loyalty by commissioning a mosque, not in the capital, as expected, but in his sanctuary town.

The moment it was announced that the sovereign would pay for a splendid mosque, the backbiting began. They said there was a reason why Istanbul had not been chosen. Having never commanded the army on a battlefield, the Sultan lacked the face to order so grand a monument in the seat of the throne. How could Selim's mosque be within close proximity to Suleiman's mosque, when the son could not hold a candle to the father? That is why, they said, the new construction could only have been in Adrianople.

Words like black bile. Regardless, Sinan – and the four apprentices – laid the foundations for the Selimiye in April. The Sultan awarded his architect a robe of gold and silver, showing how much he trusted him. Everyone on the site – from woodworkers to the galley slaves – watched in anticipation, neither sanguine nor gloomy. Somehow they seemed to sense they were bringing into existence something unique. They laboured with this knowledge – and this fear. It was a sin to create anything this lofty, as though to rival the Creator. The imams and the priests and the rabbis might not like to hear it, but deep inside they suspected that, sometimes, even God got jealous.

The idea for a mosque had come to the Sultan in a dream. He beheld the Prophet Mohammed – recognizing him not from his face, since no earthling could see that, but from his aura. Selim promised him that should he conquer the island of Cyprus, he would build a fabulous Friday mosque with its spoils. The Prophet gestured to the angels waiting by his side. Gliding in the air, glowing like fireflies, they disappeared and returned with a scroll. On it was the design of the Selimiye.

Enchanted and excited, the next morning the Sultan did not want to wake up. When he ultimately did, he told what he had seen to his Grand Vizier. Sokollu, shrewd and sharp as he was, believed that a ruler's dreams could be of two sorts: those he should not share with anyone, not even with his Grand Vizier, and those he should ensure were made known to everyone. This, he deduced, was of the second kind.

By midday, Sokollu broached the subject with the *Nishanci*, the Head of the Chancery. A man with a sweet tooth, he mentioned it to the Head Halvah Chef, who, in turn, related it to the merchant responsible for the nuts used in the royal kitchens. In the afternoon, the story left the palace in a pistachio cart, reaching the outskirts of Istanbul. From there it reached the streets of wool-dyers and leather-tanners. By the time the evening prayer was filling the air, hundreds had heard about it. Before the week was over, the whole city, including the Venetian Bailo, had come to know that the Prophet had demanded that the Sultan save Cyprus from the Christian infidels.

Selim visited the tombs of his ancestors and the grave of Ayyub the Martyr. The spirits gave him their blessing to wage a war. Yet, when the time came to embark, he did not go with the navy. The conquest would be made not by the Sultan's sword but by the Sultan's dream. The rewards would be huge. Nicosia was conquered and sacked until little remained of the town it once was. Famagusta, after being pummelled for months, was taken next – along with hundreds of captives.

In the meantime, back in Adrianople, the Chief Royal Architect and his apprentices were working their fingers to the bone. Sinan regarded each task as a cocoon in which to take shelter from storms of all kinds: once he was within, he shunned the outside world. He had no interest in wars, much less in triumphs. Nevertheless, it was only after the capture of the island that the works gathered momentum. Tribute money poured in, bringing more workers, more materials.

Oddly, as the mosque built in his name rose higher and higher, the Sultan descended lower and lower. The two of them, the man and the building, were inextricably linked in a profound yet inverted way – like night and day. For one to exist the other had to perish. With every nail hammered, with each stone added on to the edifice, something was taken away from Selim – health, happiness, power and, ultimately, *kismet*.

While working on one of the eight massive piers of the Selimiye Mosque, one autumn afternoon, the master sent word to his apprentices that he wished to see them. Upon arriving at his tent, Jahan saw the others lingering by the entrance. He perched on a bench beside them, waiting for Sinan to end his meeting with some glass-makers.

Davud looked dour and distrustful, as was his wont. He whispered, 'Master would never tear the four of us away from work. There must be something gravely wrong.'

Thankfully, the glass-makers soon left, saving them from making foolish guesses. They found the master sitting on a carpet decorated with blossoming trees in the middle and a procession of deer, gazelles, tigers and lions along the borders – woven in the city of Herat in Khorasan and presented to Sinan by a Kurdish beg for whom he had built an alms house. In his right hand, propped up against cushions, Sinan held a rosary, which he thumbed slowly. Jahan knew that he carried a different one for each of his moods: the azure opal when he was immersed in thoughts, the yellow amber when blithe, the black onyx when eager to start a new project. Today it was the pale green beryl, which he took when preoccupied. On the low table in front of him was a cup of coffee and a glass of water. Next to them lay a sketch Jahan recognized: the Hagia Sophia.

One by one they sat down on the carpet, facing the master. He was silent until they had settled; the sound of the beads, now moving faster, filled the air. Then he told them what had been preying on his mind.

The area around the Hagia Sophia, over the years, had been packed with hovels, every one of which had been built unlawfully. Several complaints had been made to the Chief Kadi of Istanbul, to no avail. At long last, seeing how desperate things were becoming, Sinan had sent a petition to the Sultan. In his letter he had criticized the ignorant men who, taking the cubit-rule in their hands, had raised structures without any knowledge of the craft or care for the environs.

'Our Sultan considered his humble servant's request,' Sinan said.

A committee had been formed. The Chief Kadi, the mosque's imam, religious scholars and the doyens of draughtsmen and masons would get together to inspect the damage and report their findings. After that, provided the Sultan agreed to it, Sinan would repair the Hagia Sophia.

'For this I need to go back to Istanbul, and I'd like you to accompany me.'

Jahan bowed his head, glowing with excitement. What an honour it would be to renovate this pearl of architecture – once a beloved basilica, now a grand mosque. The building that had goaded Justinian to exclaim with pride, 'Solomon, I have surpassed thee!' Yet, at the same time, Jahan had the distinct sensation that there was more to it than they had been told. He said, 'Should our Sultan give permission for the mosque to be restored, what will happen to the surrounding houses?'

A shadow crossed Sinan's face. 'They will be demolished.'

Jahan took a breath, understanding Sinan's conundrum. His master had to make a choice between the people and the building, and he had clearly chosen the latter.

Back in Istanbul, on the day of the meeting, much to their astonishment, they were joined by the sovereign and his entourage. Eager to see the situation with his own eyes, Sultan Selim had decided to come, attended by his grandees and viziers. Thus they walked around the Hagia Sophia. What they beheld was distressing beyond words. Gutters ran alongside the mosque's outer walls, leaking a murky water that left those who came into contact with it dirtier than before. On its edges frogs croaked, rats scampered, and faeces piled up – of animals and humans alike. Around a bend they saw the carcass of a dog, its jaw missing, its eyes open wide as though still in horror.

All the people living around the mosque had recently moved to Istanbul. Leaving their villages behind, they had migrated to the *seat of the throne* without a shelter awaiting them, kinsfolk to trust or land to till. Having heard from others that the area around the Hagia Sophia was unoccupied and within easy reach, they had put down roots there. It wasn't only sheds of all sizes that encroached on the ancient building. There were ateliers, stables, sheep pens, milking parlours, chicken coops, latrines. Together, they leaned against the mosque, pushing into it from four sides. Such had been the pressure that the western walls of the Hagia Sophia, where the settlement was the most dense, had begun to tilt inwards.

The entourage entered a cobbler's workshop. The artisan, wild-eyed with fear and dumbfounded at the sight of the Sultan, trembled and stuttered, unable to answer a single question. Mercifully, he did not faint. Down the street, in a lean-to, they saw huge cauldrons in which the intestines of animals were boiled to make candles. So horrible was the stench that the Sultan, holding a silk handkerchief to his nose, bolted out. The rest followed in haste.

One of the residents of this motley neighbourhood had built a cattle-shed and a three-storey house, renting the spare rooms to students and pilgrims. Another, in an attempt to open up a well in his back garden, had excavated deep into the ground, damaging the foundations of the Hagia Sophia. A third had raised a house that collapsed, miraculously without hurting anyone; after this he put up a second, this time succeeding in keeping it upright. Now a pile of rubble lay in his garden, where children played and dogs roamed.

When the tour was over, the Sultan called from atop his stallion: 'Chief Royal Architect, step forward.'

Sinan did so, bowing low.

'This is outrageous. It's my wish to have the mosque restored.'

Sinan bowed again, closing his eyes in gratitude.

'I give you my blessing. Start the restoration without delay. Set up buttresses where needed. Demolish the sheds. None of them were built with my permission.'

The Sultan waved a ring-bedecked hand, at which two servants came forward – one leading the way, the other carrying a kaftan of pure silk trimmed with ermine. The Grand Vizier took this and turned to Sinan, who was still kneeling, and asked him, in a gentle voice, to stand up. In this way, the architect was presented with the robe of honour.

Davud, Yusuf, Nikola and Jahan cast furtive glances at one another, unable to suppress their smiles.

'Well, then. You may begin the work,' the Sultan declared, pulling the reins of his horse, ready to leave.

'Your Majesty, one of the unlawful buildings is a storehouse that belongs to the palace,' said Sinan. 'Are we permitted to knock it down along with everything else?'

Sultan Selim hesitated, though briefly. 'Do what you need to do.'

The next day, they inspected the neighbourhoods of Zeyrek and Kalenderhane. Here, too, they found unlicensed constructions aplenty. Sinan decided to carve a space thirty-five cubits wide around the holy mosque and level everything within that area. He made his apprentices write down the plan for the work in detail. Not once, but twice. One copy for the approval of the Sultan, one for the archives of the architects in Vefa. They put on record their pledge to: fix up the parts of the Hagia Sophia, inside and outside, that had fallen into disrepair; bring fresh water to the mosque by means of new canals; cover the leaking roofs with lead; replace the wooden base of the minaret, dilapidated and crumbling, with a strong, brick one; open up a three-cubit-wide strip around the madrasa by dismantling the sheds; leave a clear space thirty-five cubits wide both left and right of the Hagia Sophia and knock down every unlawful structure; use the stones, bricks and planks obtained from the demolitions in the repair of the Hagia Sophia.

Shortly after he had received the list, the Sultan not only sent his approval but also issued a decree:

To the Chief Kadi of the city of Istanbul and the head of the endowment of the Hagia Sophia Mosque

This is my order to you and it ought to be followed at once and in its entirety. When it was reported to me that the Great Mosque suffered from the wear of time and the tear of people, and begged to be mended, I personally inspected the area in the company of the Master of Royal Architects and other experts, may God increase their wisdom, and have come to the conclusion that the restoration is essential and, as such, ought to be executed, since the repair of revered sanctuaries is the behest of God the Almighty and a noble responsibility for the Sultan.

Therefore, I command you to help the Chief Royal Architect and his draughtsmen, and to make sure that whatever they need is provided so that they can excel in their task.

Buoyed by the decree, Sinan and the apprentices embarked on the work. With them were eighty-five labourers equipped with mallets and sledgehammers, as well as a great quantity of gunpowder. Animals, too: oxen, camels, mules and Chota.

When they reached the Hagia Sophia, they found a throng of people waiting. They stood in the way, a wall of flesh and bone, not letting the labourers pass. Dark, hollow eyes squinted with exasperation, mouths drawn tight. The anger in the air was palpable. Unused to hatred of this kind, the apprentices were taken aback. So was their master, his face drained of blood, and suddenly looking very old.

'What's going on?' asked Sinan.

'We are destroying their homes,' said Nikola.

'Master, allow me to talk to them.' It was Davud who said this. 'They come from where I come. I know my people. We don't want to turn them into enemies.'

'He's right,' Jahan said. 'We ought to persuade them before we start.'

Pulling his cloak around him, as though exposed to a draught, Sinan conceded. 'Davud, go, speak with them. Make sure you tell them we shall compensate them for their losses. Our Sultan gave his word.' Then he turned to the labourers. 'We shan't do anything today.'

The next morning when they arrived the street was empty and things seemed calm. That is until the foreman came running, his face flushed crimson, and said, without offering so much as a greeting, '*Effendi*, pray.'

'What is it?' Sinan asked.

'They have stolen our tools, broken our carts. They are not letting us work, wicked people!' A crowd – larger and angrier than the one from the day before – had gathered on the other side of the mosque, he explained.

'What do they want?'

'They say this is an infidel's temple,' explained Snowy Gabriel. 'The nerve of them! They spread mean rumours about you, forgive me for saying so, master.'

'What do they say?' asked Sinan.

Snowy Gabriel lowered his gaze. 'They say since you are a Christian convert, you want to destroy the homes of good Muslims for the sake of a church.'

Sinan said, his brow puckered in concern, 'Mosques, churches, synagogues are built to honour God. How can they be disrespected?'

The mob heard none of this. In the ensuing days, the apprentices dealt with one trouble after another. The labourers were intimidated. Two animals were found dead, poisoned. Fearing something might happen to Chota, Jahan stopped bringing him to the site. Not a nail could be hammered, not a stone removed.

A week later Sinan sent his apprentices to the Chief Kadi to get help. He was a grey-bearded man with sunken eyes and a cautious mien. Jahan had expected him to be angry at the squatters. Instead, he was furious at Sinan.

'Your master wrote to the Sultan, and our Sultan, benevolent as he is, took his plea seriously. Look where it has brought us now.'

'*Effendi*, aren't these people to blame?' Jahan asked. 'They have unlawfully built around the Hagia Sophia and —'

'Right,' the Chief Kadi cut him off. 'I'll see what I can do. Don't expect miracles.'

The apprentices left the kadi's place demoralized. Jahan understood that the people who could help them would refrain from doing so, out of bitterness or laziness or jealousy of Sinan's success.

Things might never have improved had it not been for the fatwa that was issued soon after. The Grand Mufti's words rained on the city like hailstones, quenching all fires, small and large.

Question: There are those who say, on the subject of the repair of a holy mosque that was formerly a church, we are not leaving because an infidel's building is bound to collapse, and it is not important if it collapses, and there are those who support them, saying that anyone who renovates an infidel's temple is an infidel. What shall be done about such people and those who follow them?

Answer: Anyone who says such erroneous things is an infidel himself and shall be executed. Those who prevent the work will be punished. The restoration of the mosque shall proceed steadily, as befits the righteous sharia.

From then on, things simmered down. There were no more mobs on the streets, though minor incidents occurred here and there — pilfering of equipment, mostly. Sinan returned to Adrianople with Yusuf to complete the Selimiye Mosque. Jahan didn't like this. He would rather keep an eye on Yusuf. He still had not been able to question him about his secret meetings with Tommaso, and seeing him alone with the master made him uneasy.

Davud, Nikola and Jahan were left in charge of the work around the Hagia Sophia. Every few days they were to send their master a letter to keep him apprised of what they had accomplished. Gradually the letters dwindled away, a guilty silence filling the distance between the master and the apprentices.

This they never confessed to Sinan, but the apprentices who stayed in Istanbul were ill at ease. Every day they tried to forewarn the inhabitants of the hovels they were going to demolish, tried to give them enough time to remove their belongings. But the people were either too slow or reluctant, so time and again the same sorrowful scene erupted: entire families, amid tears and curses, dragging away what little they had – kitchen utensils, lamps, mats, toys, a cradle, a kilim, a bird in its cage.

Jahan began to wander around the quarter to clear his head, sometimes with another apprentice, more often alone. One such day, he and Nikola were passing through a grimy alley cramped with half-emptied ateliers when they saw two children coming towards them. A girl and a boy – sister and brother, given the resemblance – with sage-green eyes glittering over dark freckles, which gave them a look of mischief. They had close-cut hair, a precaution against lice. Both were barefoot.

Bending his knees, Jahan said, 'Hey, little ones. You should not be here on your own. Where do you live?'

The girl pointed to a shed at the end of the alley. Nikola and Jahan exchanged a guilty glance. It was one of the places they would raze the next morning.

The boy grabbed his hand and began to pull with all his might. From under his large, frayed shirtsleeves, his wrists showed, two white sticks. Jahan understood, with terror, that the child wanted them to follow him to his house. He said, louder than he intended, 'No, I can't come with you.'

The children were adamant. While the boy beseeched with his large, liquid eyes, the girl tugged at Nikola. In the end the apprentices could not resist them.

A fusty odour of mildew and decay hit Jahan and Nikola as they stepped into the hovel the children called home. Inside the first room, a sick man lay on the floor. He was attended by a woman covered from head to toe. When she saw them she left the room in a hurry.

'My father,' said the girl.

At the sound of her voice, the patient, who until then had been list-less, turned his head. The stare he gave Jahan was one of pain. When he opened his mouth only a sibilant whisper came out. The girl, un-shaken, leaned towards him, listened, nodded and said, 'He asks if your name is Azrael.'

Jahan shuddered. The man was clearly having hallucinations, confus-ing him with the Angel of Death. A voice inside his head told him to leave. Instead he wished the man good health and followed quietly be-hind the children into the bowels of the house. Nikola limped alongside him. In the second room they saw twin babies sleeping in the same cradle, their mouths open, a sliver of sunlight over them. One of the babies had a malformed lip. Identical twins who would never look alike.

The children urged them to keep walking. Passing through a low-ceilinged, dim corridor they stepped into the backyard; the two apprentices were surprised to see how close they were to the Hagia Sophia. There was an empty chicken coop on one side. A rickety wooden door opened on to a patch of soil used as a toilet, its stench sharp. Beside that door was a brindled mother cat, her teats swollen, sprawled in a basket with five kittens of the same colour.

The girl took one of the kittens by the neck and pressed its nose against her skinny chest. The animal made no noise, smothered by love. Then, brusquely, she held the delicate creature up, and said, 'Take it.'

'Oh, no. I can't do that.'

'Yours,' she repeated.

Jahan was equally stern. 'I don't want a kitten.'

Her face collapsed. 'They will die here.'

Seeing his sister's distress, the boy snatched the kitten and shoved it towards Jahan. The kitten, now panicking, scratched Jahan's thumb. Jahan flinched, but suppressed a yelp, and said, 'I'm sorry. It's not in my hands to save your kitten.'

Shaken, the apprentices retraced their steps through the house and into the street, where a number of neighbours had gathered, having heard of their presence. Someone threw a stone, striking Nikola on his shoulder.

The apprentices started to run. In their confusion they took a wrong turn, dashing into a field, brambles tearing at their ankles. Their chests were heaving, their senses on the alert, waiting for someone to leap at them from behind the bushes. When they slowed down, Nikola gasped, 'I don't want to do this.'

'Nor I,' Jahan said.

Back on the construction site they found Davud working. When he saw them, a look of concern came over his face. 'You well?'

Jahan told him what had happened. The sick man, the children, the babies . . .

'Don't let it affect you,' said Davud. 'They had no right to build that shed.'

'But they had nowhere else to go.'

'They'll be compensated. Our Sultan said so.'

Jahan said, 'You know as well as I do that it won't be enough.'

'What can we do?' Davud murmured, running his fingers down his beard. 'Our master entrusted us with the task.'

'Yes, and where is he now? Building the Sultan's mosque while we have to deal with this mess.' No sooner had the words left him than Jahan halted, shaken by his own anger. 'Forgive me.'

'I already have,' said Davud with a brotherly smile.

That week they delayed writing to Sinan, none of them feeling up to the task. They avoided one another, as if the more time they spent together the more they were reminded of their guilt. Then came a letter from the master.

My diligent apprentices,

I would have been with you had I not been given the task of finishing our Sultan's mosque without delay. The urgency of the Selimiye Mosque compelled me to leave you on your own. I did so knowing you were more than capable of taking care of the Grand Mosque of Hagia Sophia. Nonetheless, I'm aware that this is our hardest task. In our craft we seldom see people. We befriend stone quarries, converse with tiles, listen to marble.

This time, however, you are face to face with the people whose homes you must demolish. This is onerous. If I could, I would have moved each of those families to a safer home with plenty of land and trees. But this is beyond me. And it is beyond you.

Only remember that cities, too, are like human beings. They are not made of stones and wood, solely. They are of flesh and bone. They bleed when they are hurt. Every unlawful construction is a nail hammered into the heart of Istanbul. Remember to pity a wounded city the way you pity a wounded person.

    May God grant you according to your desire and keep you balanced,
    Sinan, the humble and lowly pupil of Seth and Abraham, the Patron Saints of Stonemasons and Architects

That autumn the apprentices razed the countless hovels to the ground. Fast as they worked, the newcomers were faster. Even as they pulled down structures and moved away the rubble, in other parts of the city new buildings were set up, equally unlawful, equally unsafe and ugly. The regulations that Sinan developed regarding the width of the streets and the height of the houses were once again disregarded. Jahan was dismayed. Never before had he thought that among an architect's tasks would be the protection of the city from its inhabitants and the protection of the past from the future.

The dome – that was what everyone raved about. In his letters to his Chief Royal Architect, the Sultan demanded a dome bigger than that of the Hagia Sophia. His mosque would proclaim the triumph of Islam over Christianity and show the entire world who were the favourites in the eyes of God. All this talk made Jahan nervous. Much like their ruler, the people goaded the architects into a contest, pitting Sinan against Anthemius the mathematician and Isidorus the physicist, who had designed the infidel church in days of yore.

'Is there something bothering you?' asked Sinan. 'You seem withdrawn.'

A fine film of sawdust covered their shoes and a thin veil of sweat shone on their foreheads. Although they were exhausted they kept working as if each day were their last. Jahan said, 'I can't wait to finish and go.'

'We'll be done in four weeks, Allah willing,' Sinan said, his voice trailing off.

Even that was too long, yet Jahan did not object. He was ashamed of complaining when the master, over eighty years old, toiled from dawn to dusk. Despite their pleas he would not rest. Similar to a moth drawn to the fire, Sinan was attracted to the dust, dirt and drudgery of construction sites. His hands rough, his fingernails split, underneath the silk kaftans he wore for ceremonies he was a labourer to his core. It had an undeniable effect on his apprentices. The sight of him in the field, not unlike the sight of a commander at the battlefront, prompted everyone to keep working ever harder.

'This mosque is wearing us out,' Jahan said.

Sinan grew pensive. 'You've noticed it.'

Not expecting his master to affirm his fears, Jahan stammered, 'You know it.'

'Think of a baby in the womb. She lives off her mother and tires her. While we deliver a building, we are like the mother. Once the baby is born, we shall be the happiest souls.'

The comparison between building and giving birth made Jahan

smile. Yet instantly he had another thought. 'But I don't understand. The Sultan doesn't work with us. Why does it sap his strength?'

'He is still attached to his mosque,' said Sinan.

'We've worked on other buildings. Bridges, mosques, madrasas, aqueducts . . . Why have I never felt this way before?'

'You did, you just don't remember. That, too, is in the nature of things. We forget how we felt the last time. Again, like a mother.' Sinan paused, as though unsure whether to say the next thing. 'But then some births are harder than others.'

'Master . . . are you telling me that what we create can kill us?'

'What we create can weaken us,' said Sinan. 'Rarely does it kill us.'

Three weeks later, the Sultan sent a letter informing them that he wished to come and personally supervise the final touches to his mosque. He would travel to Adrianople leading a royal cavalcade. For this he needed an elephant. Since Mahmood had fallen out of favour and not yet clambered his way back up, Chota was, once again, in demand.

With his master's blessing, Jahan took Chota and returned to the palace. He enjoyed seeing his old friends at the menagerie while the elephant rested in the barn. The next morning they were ready to join the procession.

It was spectacular. The Janissaries, the elite guards and the archers – all were rigged out in bright colours. Several concubines accompanied the Sultan, seated inside heavily curtained carriages. There was excitement and pride in the wind. Underneath, however, there loomed disquiet, like dark clouds gathering in the distance on an otherwise bright and sunny day. The Christians, appalled by the loss of Cyprus and by their cathedrals being turned into mosques, had assembled a Holy League. They sought revenge. The forces of the Pope, the Spanish and the Venetians, overcoming ancient feuds, had united. As they were making ready to journey to Adrianople, a naval battle between the Ottoman and Christian forces was under way in the Gulf of Corinth near Lepanto.

In an hour Sultan Selim strutted out, his face round and red. After saluting the soldiers he motioned towards his horse – a pure-bred black stallion. That was when the strangest thing happened. The horse, for no reason at all, lurched forward and tripped. A gasp rose from the audience. It could only be a sign – an ill omen.

Selim, visibly upset, ordered the horse to be taken back to the stable. He was not going to ride a jinxed animal. Swiftly, a substitute was found: Chota. Since the Sultan was bent on leaving the capital with grandeur and reaching Adrianople in much the same way, what better than an elephant to carry him? Jahan was ordered to prepare the howdah and the shiny, jingling headdress, which Chota disliked immensely.

The Sultan held on to the dangling ladder and, with difficulty, managed to ascend. He was about to sit inside the howdah when Chota, either because the headdress had made him itchy or some demon had poked him in the eye, swayed his body with such force that the sovereign lost his balance. His turban, that huge mound with plumes, slipped off and plummeted, landing right in front of Jahan down below. Grabbing it, the mahout scrambled up the ladder.

For the first time they were eye to eye: Jahan on the ladder, the Sultan inside the howdah. Jahan lowered his head. Still, for one fleeting instant, their gazes crossed.

'My Lord,' Jahan said, as he held on to the rope with one hand and offered the turban with the other.

'Give it here,' Selim said, his voice tinged with irritation.

The turban slipped from the Sultan's hand, toppling over yet again. Below on the ground the servants scurried to pick it up. They handed it to Jahan and he to the Sultan. This time Selim took it carefully, wordlessly, his face as pale as a cadaver's. He said, 'You may go, mahout.'

Jahan hurried down the ladder, tapped Chota's trunk. The animal hoisted him to his usual place on his neck. With prayers and praises they set forward. The people lined up on either side of the road and stared with admiration. Still, despite the splendour, discomfort had descended upon everyone. Other than the beat of hooves, the rattle of cartwheels and the jingle of the bells on Chota's headdress, there were no sounds. Jahan had never seen so many people making so little noise.

Their spirits lifted as they left Istanbul behind. But dark news welcomed them at the city gates of Adrianople. The entire Ottoman fleet had been lost in a humiliating, harrowing defeat. If *kiyamet* had another name it would have been Lepanto. Hundreds were drowned, killed, enslaved. People were shocked but that didn't last. After perplexity came discontent, and after discontent, rage. Suddenly everyone was seething at the Sultan.

For the first time in years Jahan was afraid to walk on the streets. Once when Chota and he were out walking, someone threw a stone at them. Whizzing past Chota's head it crashed into a tree trunk. Jahan looked around, searching for the culprit. He saw a few boys playing knuckle-bones, a hawker selling offal and pedestrians strolling along. It could have been any of them. In that moment he could not help thinking they were being held in contempt, for they were the Sultan's elephant and the Sultan's mahout.

The mood on the construction site, too, was sombre. What had started with hope had turned into gloom. Zeal and despair. Might and loss. Cyprus and Lepanto. The Selimiye, as though built upon an invisible pendulum, swung between opposites. And in the midst of everything was Master Sinan, unaffected, untouched, working.

They carried on. The minarets were slender, graceful and taller than any other they had seen or heard of. Four tiers of windows on three galleries brought in ample light, reflecting off the tile panels, rendering the mosque bright and cheerful despite the workers' disposition. The sandstone facades were the colour of honey, warm and inviting. The space inside was massive, uninterrupted. Wherever one knelt one could see the *mihrab*, where the imam sat and led the prayer. Everyone was equally close to God.

Greek painters were brought from the island of Chios to help with the decoration. There was a Mohammedan artist, too, a dreamy man by the name of Nakkash Ahmed Chelebi. Such was his regard for the mosque that he would come at different times of the day just to see, to admire. While out in the open sea, islands were captured, fleets were sunk, Muslims killed Christians and Christians killed Muslims, in Sinan's cocoon-like universe they worked side by side.

Supported by eight piers of marble and granite, displaying eight sides, the dome rested atop a square with semi-domes on each corner. As enchanting as it was, inside and outside, it was its size that everyone was curious about. Masters in the science of geometry joined forces with Takiyuddin, the Chief Royal Astronomer, and meticulously took measurements. They all wanted to know the answer: had their deep blue dome of heaven surpassed that of the Hagia Sophia?

It had. If one were to measure from the level of the dome's base to the top, it was higher. The Selimiye Mosque's round dome, with its higher apex, had outdone the flat dome of Justinian's church. Yet it hadn't. If one were to calculate the distance from floor level to the top, theirs was lower and the Hagia Sophia's higher.

Higher and lower simultaneously. And Jahan wondered, though he never could bring himself to ask, if, amid the flurry of excitement and anticipation, that was exactly what Master Sinan had intended.

Marcantonio, the time-serving Bailo, was leaving Istanbul. He had spent six years under the Ottoman skies, and, unlike many a traveller into this land, had become, if only in a small way, an Istanbulite. Being a cordial person he had friends galore, two of whom he held in high esteem: the Grand Vizier Sokollu and Sinan.

For he was a man-of-letters, familiar with sculpture and architecture, this zesty emissary from Venice. Time and again he went to see Sinan, whose work he declared, with a snap of his fingers and a hearty laugh, *fabuloso*. Sinan, too, visited him, despite those who frowned upon him for befriending an infidel.

There was one more soul in this city of whom the ambassador had grown fond: Chota. Every time Marcantonio ran into Jahan he asked about the animal's health, bringing treats. Imbued with a spirit of inquiry, he interrogated Jahan about elephants – not as to what they ate nor how much they weighed nor how long they lived. Jahan was used to being asked such things. Marcantonio's questions were different. Was it true that elephants, like women, were prone to weeping when heartbroken? When the beast went to sleep, what, in Jahan's humble opinion, did he dream? Did he have a notion of an Elephant-Self or did he only grasp the world external to him? Unable to answer these questions, several times Jahan had let Marcantonio feed and ride Chota in the hopes that he might find the answers himself.

On a fine day in spring Marcantonio appeared in the menagerie with two servants walking behind him and carrying a huge frame.

'A farewell gift for the Grand Vizier,' the Bailo said with a roguish smile.

'May I take a peek?' Jahan asked.

When they pulled down the cloth Jahan was surprised to see it was a painting of the Italian envoy clad in a turban and a kaftan. He sat on a sofa – not crossing one leg over the other like the Franks but one leg folded backward and the other bent at the knee like the Ottomans. Through the open window in the background one could view Istanbul – lush green hills, fluffy clouds, the bluest sea dotted with caïques.

At first sight the portrait did not resemble the Bailo. Marcantonio had sallow, porous skin, whereas his painted image glowed with youth and health. The crook in his nose, the hair in his nostrils, the mole on his cheek that he powdered every day with care, had all been erased. It was as if by wearing the Ottoman garb and agreeing to pose for the painter he had slipped into another realm where everything was softer, brighter. At the bottom of the frame there was a dedication: *Domino Mahomet Pacha Musulmanorum Visiario amico optimo*.

The longer Jahan stared at the portrait the more he felt it was alive. Slowly, the caïques began to glide into the sea, their oars splashing water, the clouds on the horizon turning a fiery red. Then, gingerly, the man in the portrait rolled his eyes towards the Bailo, as if to assess how much they were alike. With a shudder Jahan pulled down the cover. He was certain there was a spirit hiding in the frame, though he couldn't tell whether it was good or evil.

On Wednesday, while the apprentices were busy working on a sketch, another gift arrived from Marcantonio, this one for Master Sinan. A box of carved rosewood encrusted with the golden initials MB. Inside was a leather-bound tome, *Ten Books on Architecture*, by Vitruvius. It was translated, with a commentary added, by none other than Marcantonio's brother.

Even though he had studied the treatise before, Sinan was delighted to get this new edition in Italian. Clasping the box to his chest, he retreated to the library. But first he called for Jahan. 'Come help me to read this.'

That, however, was not easy. Written in a refined, courtly Italian, Jahan found the text hard to interpret. Every sentence was a strain. Bit by bit, he was able to wade through the pages. Sinan listened carefully, his eyes narrowed in contemplation.

Architecture was a science, the book said. It was based on three qualities: *forza*, strength; *utilità*, which Jahan translated as use; and *bellezza*, beauty.

'Tell me, which of these three would you sacrifice if you had to sacrifice one?'

'*Bellezza*,' Jahan replied assuredly. 'We can't compromise on strength or purpose. We could do without beauty, if need be.'

Sinan's face said otherwise. 'We can't give up beauty.'

'Then which one should we sacrifice?'

'None,' Sinan said with a tender smile. 'If you give up one, you will end up losing all three.'

Just then the *kahya*'s son rushed in, carrying a letter, which he said had been sent from the palace. Sinan broke the seal and read it, his eyes glittering with amber flecks. He said Sultan Selim was throwing a banquet for Marcantonio. A huge honour, no doubt, and one that showed the sovereign had been fond of the Bailo.

'How generous of our Sultan,' Jahan commented.

'Well, it looks like you'll be there, too.'

'Me?' Jahan could not believe that his name was in a royal letter.

Not quite, as it turned out. First, the letter was from Grand Vizier Sokollu. Second, it was not the mahout's name but the elephant's that was mentioned. Knowing how fond the Bailo was of the creature, Sokollu required Chota to entertain the audience on that evening. Jahan's heart sank.

'You're upset,' said Sinan.

'I'm the apprentice to the Chief Royal Architect, but the Vizier sees me as a mahout.'

'Cheer up,' Sinan said. 'I'd like you to accompany me to the banquet. Once you've eaten, you can perform.'

Jahan gaped at him, barely containing his excitement. This meant he was to sup not with the tamers in the menagerie, waiting for his turn, but in the grand hall with the guests. Yet, instead of thanking him, he heard himself say, 'Chota doesn't know any stunts.'

'He doesn't need to. Parade the animal. A simple trick will be enough. They want to see what God has created more than what you can make the elephant do.'

Even so, Jahan was distressed. Despite the passage of time, the catastrophe in the days of Hurrem Sultana was still fresh in his memory. Resentful though he was, he began to practise tricks with Chota. For the occasion the elephant had been given a new yellow mantle, and when he donned it, from a distance, he looked like a globe of fire. On his feet he wore anklets – silver circlets with a hundred tiny bells. As soon as Jahan put them on Chota, the animal was perplexed. Taking a few awkward steps, he halted, walked again, stopped again, unable to fathom where the noise was coming from.

The afternoon of the big day, Jahan washed, brushed and oiled Chota tusk to tail. Then he put the mantle and the anklets on him.

'So handsome,' Jahan cooed. 'If I were a lady elephant I'd fall for you.'

For a split second Chota's eyes, too small for his head, crinkled with mirth. In this state they passed through the gates into the inner courtyards.

The evening started with a gift-giving ceremony. The Bailo was given shawls, shoes, bejewelled belts, nightingales in gilded cages and a fat pouch, which contained ten thousand akces. A murmur of appreciation rose as everyone commended Sultan Selim's generosity, even though he was yet to appear. The ambassador was ushered to the dining place. Inside a high-ceilinged chamber, four tables had been prepared for the most notable guests. Marcantonio and the Grand Vizier and Master Sinan would be at the same table.

The Sultan would be eating alone, as was the palace custom. Jahan thought about the Frankish kings and queens who always dined amid their retinue. He wondered which was better, their way or the Ottomans'? Who would want to watch the monarch chewing on a chicken leg or chomping and belching like a mere mortal? Not seeing the Sultan at table only added to his respectability. Yet, at the same time, it made him more unreachable and, eventually, harder to understand. It was easier to love someone you shared bread with.

Meanwhile the rest of the guests, including Jahan, were led into smaller rooms. About fifty boys, of similar height and size, dressed in green *shalwar*, began to serve. Deft and fast, they brought large, round trays and set them on wooden legs. Upon these they placed spoons and olives, pickles and spices in bowls so small no one would dare dip in a finger for fear of breaking them. Next they carried basins and silver pitchers for everyone to wash their hands. Finally they distributed towels and *peskirs* for the guests to put on their laps and use to wipe their fingers.

Knowing how important manners were, Jahan glanced left and right, observing what the others did. The worst sin you could commit at a banquet was gluttony. Even if it were your favourite dish, you had to eat slowly, showing no sign of greed. Jahan was careful to use the three fingers of his right hand, without dripping oil. Mercifully there were others like him checking out what everyone else was doing. A few times their stares crossed and they nodded politely.

They were served wheat soup with a hunk of dark bread, which was so filling Jahan could have stopped eating there and then. But as soon as the crocks were taken away they were brought vine leaves stuffed with meat, rice with pine nuts, chicken kebab, chicken with mushrooms, buttered lamb, fried pigeons, roasted partridges, lamb's feet, goose stuffed with apples, brined anchovies, a huge red fish from icy waters up north, *borek* with shredded meat, egg with onions. They were served *hoshaf* in bowls and lemonade in pitchers. His appetite now piqued by the delicious smells, Jahan tasted every dish. As they kept eating, the *cesnici* and *kilerci* walked around, making sure everything ran in perfect order. Then came the desserts: almond baklava, pear baked with ambergris, cherry pudding, ice-crushed sweetened wild strawberries and heaps of honeyed figs.

After dinner the guests collapsed outside on to the seats prepared for them. Fire-eaters pranced around in their shiny jerkins, tumblers turned backwards somersaults, sword-swallowers bolted down the sharpest blades. Three brothers appeared: a *cemberbaz*, who played with hoops; a *shishebaz*, who played with bottles; and a *canbaz*, who played with his life, doing a little caper on a cord stretched high above. When it was their turn, Chota and Jahan marched with feigned confidence. They performed, luckily without an incident, what few stunts they knew. Chota plucked the flower in Jahan's belt and gave it to the Bailo, who accepted it with a happy laugh.

Afterwards, the three of them – the master, the apprentice and the animal – departed from the palace, each drawing into his thoughts. There was a sense of finality in the air. The Bailo was going away, the summer was coming to an end. Sultan Selim had not emerged all evening, and there were rumours his health was deteriorating. It seemed to Jahan that, in truth, this world, too, was a spectacle. One way or another, everyone was parading. They performed their tricks, each of them, some staying longer, others shorter, but in the end they all left through the back door, similarly unfulfilled, similarly in need of applause.

Shortly after the inauguration of the Selimiye Mosque, the Sultan was laid low by melancholia. Such was his gloom that he could not even delight in the great monument to his name. Jahan found it odd that the ordinary folks who prayed in the mosque revelled in its architecture and splendour more than the sovereign who had paid for it. It was the humours in his body that were causing him misery. He had too much black bile in his blood and, as a result, could not help feeling sad day and night. He had been duly cupped and bled, and made to take helle-bore and vomit, but the sadness had not oozed away.

In the company of his master, fellow apprentices and Chota, Jahan returned to Istanbul. With the white elephant he settled back in the menagerie. It was there, one afternoon in December, that the Sultan showed up. He brought with him a Sufi.*

Jahan was in the barn, checking the elephant's fodder. Lately a series of younger tamers had been appointed to take care of Chota, one after the other, but Jahan still saw to the animal's needs, making sure he was looked after. So it was there, as he was checking the standards of care, that he heard the Sultan and the Sufi wending their way through the rose gardens. He climbed up to the hayloft. Through a crack in the wooden planks he spied on them. Selim's withered face had a sickly yellow hue, his beard was ragged, and he had put on more weight. His eyes were swollen. He must have been drinking again. Or else, Jahan realized with horror, crying.

The Sultan and the Sufi sat on a stone bench near the cages of the wild cats. Jahan could not believe that the Commander of the Faithful and the Successor of the Prophet of the Lord of the Universe had dropped himself down on that cold, grubby seat. Their voices were like the susurration of a river, and most of what they said he could not catch. Then he heard, spilling from the lips of Selim, 'Is it true that Allah loveth the purifiers?'

It was the Surah of Repentance, Jahan knew. The Sultan was so

*Halveti Shaykh Suleiman Effendi.

fond of the prayer that he had had it written in *thuluth* on the wall of a mosque he had commissioned in Konya. Jahan felt an immense sadness, which made him bolder than he normally would have dared. Leaving his hiding place, he went outside to welcome them.

'How is the beast doing?' Selim asked, having never learned Jahan's name.

'He is fine, my Lord. Would your Highness like to ride his elephant?'

'Another day, mahout,' said Selim distractedly.

There would be no other day. The same week, Selim fell down in the *hamam* and hit his head. They said he was drunk when he died. Others argued he was sober but so absent he hadn't seen where he was going. The son of a man too dominant, the ruler of an empire too vast, the bearer of a soul too tender, the dreamer of poems too delicate, Selim the Sot, Selim the Blond, Selim the Forlorn, left this world when he was fifty years of age. Nurbanu packed his body in ice, keeping his death a secret until her favourite son, Murad, arrived from his post in Anatolia.

Sultan Murad ascended to the throne. He first had his brothers executed and then buried his father. Even though he loved an imposing mosque as much as every other ruler, he valued neither majesty like his grandfather Suleiman nor beauty like his father Selim. Neither *forza* nor *bellezza*. What mattered now was *utilità*. Function over grandiosity. Function over beauty. From this day forth, nothing would be the same for Sinan and his four apprentices.

One night in the menagerie they awoke to an awful din. A jumble of neighing, barking, grunting, bellowing and groaning rent the air. Throwing his blanket aside, Jahan sprang to his feet. The other tamers were also stirring. Taras the Siberian, at ease in every calamity, was the first to walk out while the rest fumbled for their garments and boots. Groping like a blind man in the dark, Jahan stepped into the garden, where a wedge of moonlight glimmered shyly. There was a torrent of light pouring from above – a cascade in every shade of red. It took him a heartbeat to recognize what it was.

'Fire!' someone shouted.

Jahan was witnessing yet another blaze in the heart of the palace. The gardens, pavilions and passages, always so quiet you could hear the swish of your hair as you strode along, now pulsed with cries of help. The silence code dating back to the days of Sultan Suleiman had gone up in smoke.

The calamity had broken out on the other side of the inner walls, along the eastern edge of the second courtyard. Jahan knew what was located there: the royal kitchens. The pantry, larder, butlery and cook-house were smouldering. Just recently the master and the apprentices had repaired those buildings. Now they were burning. The flames had jumped westward, slowly but steadily engulfing the aviary. Jahan wondered if anyone had set the birds free. The thought of hundreds of pairs of wings flapping in horror, unable to take flight, pierced him to the quick.

The first courtyard where they currently were was still untouched by the fire. Even so, the wind was strong, fickle. It blew in their direction every so often, bringing thick, grey ashes like dead butterflies. The smoke pricked their eyes, filled their lungs. The monkeys, seized by a fright larger than their reason – teeth bared, eyes glazed – were banging on the iron bars. The tamers had to move the menagerie to a place of safety.

That, however, was no small feat. Under duress animals were capable of the strangest behaviour. The royal gardens, though not their native domain, was nevertheless home. Nobody could say how they would react when forced out of their cages into wooden crates. Having only a few carts at their disposal, the tamers could only proceed piecemeal, relocating a few animals at a time. Unprepared and baffled, they debated among themselves what to do. The Circassian grooms wanted to wait until they had received orders from the Chief White Eunuch. Another wave of fumes and cinders blowing in their direction was enough to silence them. There was no time to lose.

First they moved the apes. Not because they were more valuable but because no one could stand their ruckus. Next Jahan led Chota out of the barn. Wise soul that he was, Chota did not cause any problem. If anything, he was helpful, complacent. He didn't mind pulling the carriage on which they placed the monkeys and gorillas, many of them shrieking and jumping up and down, tottering like unruly drunkards.

The creatures that could trot out were allowed to do so – horses, camels, zebras, giraffes, gazelles and reindeer. Fearing that a sudden noise could startle them into a stampede, the tamers were careful, alert. They tied the animals to one another by the neck, making a caravan of unlikely companions. Some mounted on horses, others on carts, the trainers followed their animals. Despite their care, no sooner were they beyond the palace walls than the zebras, as though jinxed, bolted down the hills, dragging the rest of the caravan with them. The tamers shot after them like demons. Drenched in sweat and dust and curses, they managed to rein in the zebras before they caused the entire herd to tumble over, one on top of another.

With the help of sticks and nets, treats and threats, they loaded the royal animals on to carts. Off went the snakes, chameleons, ostriches, turtles, raccoons, weasels, peacocks and the terrified llamas. Next came the foxes, hyenas, panthers and leopards. They transported them outside the palace gates and down the slopes towards an opening by the quay, unsure how far the flames were capable of reaching.

The elephant and the mahout made several round-trips, bringing fodder and water for the animals. When they were done, Jahan placed a basket of leaves in front of Chota, leaving him in the care of the Chinese twins, and returned to the menagerie for a last inspection. This was partly because of an old habit. True, since Captain Gareth had disappeared he had stopped stealing, but, like every thief, he knew that a fire was an unmissable opportunity to chance on unexpected riches. But this was not the only reason for his return. He was thinking about Mihrimah. For a while after the demise of her brother Selim she had not visited the palace. But tonight she, too, was in the harem. Was she frightened, Jahan wondered. He thought about her nursemaid, who must be having a terrible time breathing with her asthma. In a couple of hours, for all he knew, the flames could reach their chamber. He wanted to be sure they were fine and safe.

The guards at the gate were too distracted to pay him any attention. By now the blaze had drawn closer, lapping over the walls towards the rose gardens, embers leaping in a sprinkle of gold. When he reached the enclosure of the wild cats, Jahan was surprised to see the lions were still locked up – two females and one male. The mighty beasts, restless and tense, paced up and down, growling at something in the distance as though faced with an enemy only they could detect.

Outside the cage stood Olev. Perky as usual he yelled, 'Hey, Indian. Why did you come back?'

'Just wanted to see if everything was all right. You need a hand?'

'My girls are scared; my boy doesn't want to come out. I'll have to drag them. Don't want the poor things burned to a crisp.'

Smiling at his own joke and without a weapon to protect him, Olev opened the iron door and entered the cage. Jahan watched him approach one of the females, talking in a calm, steady tone. The cat stood motionless, her gaze fixed on the tamer's every gesture. Gingerly, Olev placed a hoop around her neck and carefully led her out. He ushered her up a plank and into a wooden crate placed on a cart. Next he moved the second lioness in the same way. As she walked out, the male stared from a corner, his eyes two slivers of dark citrine.

The back of Jahan's neck felt hot. Apprehension began to creep over him. Dawn was breaking in the distance. There was something on Olev's face that hadn't been there before. The slightest quiver in his nostrils, a twitch of his mouth. It was the two of them in the cage – the tamer and the lion. In his hand Olev held a rope, limp and listless, as if he didn't know what to do with it. For the first time Jahan saw him hesitate. The lion snarled, no more than an inaudible growl, as if he, too, were caught between opposing urges. Heart racing, Jahan grabbed a club and put one foot into the cage.

'Step back,' Olev said. 'Go away!'

Drawing a breath, Jahan did as he was told.

'Close the door!'

This, too, Jahan did. He felt numb, unable to think properly. Olev's flame-coloured pony-tail came loose, spreading out on his collar. He wiped the sweat off his brow, momentarily distracted. In that instant the lion turned to him with another snarl, as though he had just noticed him, as though this wasn't the man who had taken care of him for years, feeding him every day before he fed himself. The beast lifted his paw, his claws stretched open; he sprang on the man.

Olev fell down. There was not a trace of pain on his face, only astonishment. The look of a father disappointed in his son. Outside the cage Jahan dashed about like a madman, waving his arms, shouting. The club still in one hand, he hit the bars of the cage in the hope of distracting the lion. It worked. Pulling back, the animal took a few steps towards Jahan.

In the meantime, Olev stood up, unsteady. Instead of walking towards the door, he edged nearer to the cat, calling him. It happened so fast. Like a dream Jahan watched it occur, in front of his eyes. The lion, now taking his gaze off Jahan, turned back and pounced at his tamer, fastening his jaws on Olev's neck.

Jahan screamed, his voice that of a stranger. He smashed the club, kicked the bars, shouted at the cat. Finding a cudgel nearby, he ran back, too terrified to remember to pray. He went into the cage. There was a pool of blood where Olev lay. The lion, having lost interest in him, had returned to his corner. Slowly, not moving his gaze from the cat, though unsure what he would do should he spring, Jahan hauled the wounded man outside. Olev's eyes were open, flicking about, his throat spurting blood. His neck had been torn open, his jugular vein ripped. As soon as he dragged him out, Jahan closed the door. He didn't care if the flames reached the lion. He wanted him to burn.

They buried Olev in a graveyard not that far from the seraglio. The male lion, despite Jahan's wish, had survived. As it turned out, the flames never reached the menagerie and all their efforts had been for naught.

The royal kitchens were reduced to ashes together with parts of the harem and the Privy Chamber. Sinan and the apprentices would have to rebuild them all over again.

After Olev's funeral – attended only by the animal-tamers and equerries – something came over Jahan. He was seized by a presentiment, as if, in one death, he had seen the deaths of them all. He raged deep inside, not at the lion that had killed a friend but at everyone else; at himself, for leaving Olev on his own in that cage and acting too late; at the new Sultan, for not giving a tinker's curse about his servants perishing while serving him; at Master Sinan, who, unaffected by disasters, kept making building after building; at God, for allowing them to err and suffer so yet still expecting them to pray in gratitude. Yes, the world was beautiful – a beauty that irritated him. What difference did it make whether they were hurt or happy, right or wrong, when the sun rose and the moon waned just the same, with or without them? The one creature he did not take umbrage at was Chota, and he spent as much time as possible beside him, soothed by his calmness.

The anger was not all. Something else accompanied it – an ambition he had never known before. There was a part of him that wished to defy not only the master who had made him his apprentice, the Sultan who had made him his mahout, and the God who had made him weak, but most of all Mihrimah, who, during all these years, had made him a silent sufferer. He worked hard, spoke little. This, more or less, was his mood when Sinan and the three other apprentices arrived at the palace to, once again, repair the damage.

'We'll add new baths and pavilions by the shore,' Sinan said. 'The harem and the Privy Chamber need to be repaired. We shall enlarge them again. Everything we build ought to match the spirit of the building.' He paused for a moment. 'I want you to draw a plan. Whoever brings me the best, shall be my Chief Assistant.'

Jahan was surprised to hear this. Until this day they had been treated as equals, even when they knew they were not. Now their master was making them compete against one another. He knew he should have been thrilled. Except his heart was not in it. Still, he worked – though not beside the other apprentices in the shade of the gardens. He went to the barn, sat next to Chota and finished his sketches there.

A few days later Sinan wanted to talk to him – urgently. Jahan saw that he had placed the designs side by side, all four of them.

'Come,' he said. 'I want you to look at these and tell me what you see.'

Not knowing which scroll belonged to whom, Jahan inspected the three drawings. He compared each with his own. It seemed as if he alone had proposed knocking down the baths and building them anew at the back of the harem. Even though Mihrimah no longer lived there, he had made his design with her comfort in mind. As he studied the sketches, he began to recognize the purposeful strokes of Davud, the meticulous tracing of Nikola and the light flowing hand of Yusuf.

'What do you think?' Sinan asked.

Uneasily, Jahan pointed out the best in each drawing. Sinan said, 'I know what their strengths are. Tell me their weaknesses.'

'This one was hastily done,' Jahan said. The other, he explained, in his desire to copy his master, had not contributed from his soul.

'How about this?' Sinan asked, showing Jahan his own scroll. 'I like that it cares about the harem population and makes it easier for them.'

Jahan felt his face burn.

'But it takes no notice of the surroundings. There's no harmony between the new additions and the old structure.'

Sinan's eyes glimmered. He took out the last design. 'And this?'

'Careful, balanced. He's respected the building and expanded it in proportion.'

'That's right. What I'd like to know is why your design, which is the better one, pays no attention to the palace.'

Jahan's face clouded over. 'I cannot say, master.'

'Yours was the best but it had one flaw. We do not raise buildings that float in empty space. We reflect the harmony of nature and the spirit of the place.'

Thus the mute apprentice became the Chief Assistant. Blushing up to his ears, a shy smile hovering on his lips, Yusuf kept his gaze on the ground, as if he wanted to disappear therein. As for Jahan, he had learned something about himself: that he had reached a point in his craft where he could either improve or destroy his talent. Davud, Yusuf, Nikola – these were not his rivals. His most fearsome rival was none other than himself.

They spent the summer expanding the palace and repairing the areas where the fire had wreaked havoc. Accustomed as they were to toiling on all sorts of sites, this one felt different and oddly quiet. For once there was no idle talk among the labourers, no jokes or quips as they carried the planks, hoisted the pulleys or ate their soup. When they erected an uncut marble column, dozens of men pulling at once, the hawsers slashing their palms, there were no shouts of *Allah, Allah*. Just as there were no words of praise from the foremen when one of them did a fine job, intent less on commending than on prodding everyone else to toil harder. Even the sounds of the mallets, saws and axes were less ear-splitting than usual. An awkward silence descended on everything, leaving them dazed, as if they had just woken up from a slumber. Such was the impact of being close to Sultan Murad.

During those weeks Jahan met servants he had never come across before and learned about halls he had not known existed. The palace was a maze of rooms within rooms and paths that drew circles, a serpent swallowing its tail. It was lonely enough to make you love your own shadow and crowded enough to leave you gasping for air.

There were far more people under its roof than at the time of Sultan Suleiman – more women in the harem, more guards at the gates, more pages serving more dishes. Like a fish that couldn't sense when it was full, the palace kept absorbing more and more.

Once the apprentices finished rebuilding the kitchens, they started the additions to the outer part of the harem. The concubines, having retreated into the inner chambers, were out of sight. Jahan hoped to see, if not Mihrimah, then something that belonged to her – a handkerchief with her initials, a velvet slipper, an ivory comb. None of these he found. A few days later Mihrimah sent him word. She and *dada* were going back to her mansion. *At midday we shall be passing by the First Gate.*

Seated on one of the higher branches of an apple tree, Jahan waited, elated and terrified. In the drowsy heat the sun glowed through the ripe fruits, which nobody dared pick because they belonged to the Sultan – who had no time for such trifles. Jahan flinched at a distant rattle. A carriage appeared, moving slowly. It seemed to Jahan that he and only he had reached a standstill while the world had moved on. Everything was familiar in a strange way. Next to the vastness of the universe his heartbeat was inaudible. He was an observer. No more. The leaves rustled, the slugs inched forward, a moth's wings beat in the breeze. Jahan savoured every detail, sensing he would never have this moment again. Time became a river. He stood by the grassy bank and stared at the water flowing by, alone and forsaken. The carriage came to a stop. A hand, as graceful as a bird, fluttered out of the window and pulled the curtain aside. Mihrimah looked up to where Jahan was perched, her face softening as she took in his adoring gaze. She saw one more time that, despite the decades and the distances and the wrinkles and the greying hair, nothing between them had changed. Jahan took a long look at her, without averting his eyes or bowing his head; he stared straight into her eyes. Her lips curled into a tender smile and she blushed a little. She pulled out a handkerchief from her bosom, smelled its perfume, glanced up at him and then dropped it for him to come and fetch afterwards.

It was a sweltering afternoon during Ramadan – fasting had slowed them down. Jahan didn't mind the hunger that much, but the thirst was killing him. No matter how many cups of water he drank at *sahur*,★ as soon as he came to the site the next morning his mouth felt dry as dust. Hours later, unable to bear it any more, he would steer towards the back of the kitchens, where there was a fountain. He would rinse his mouth to get rid of the rusty taste. If he swallowed a few drops at the same time, so be it. It was a sin, cheating like this. Yet he was hoping God wouldn't mind if he consumed a few droplets of His endless water.

As he headed towards the fountain, Jahan noticed a figure ahead of him. Fast and furtive, it disappeared amid the bushes. He recognized the mute apprentice and began to follow his steps. He decided now was the time to talk to him to find out if he was the traitor.

Yusuf went straight to the pond where Chota would refresh himself now and then; he sat there, his face impossible to read. At first, Jahan thought he, too, had come here to quench his thirst. But all he seemed to be doing was staring at his reflection in the water, sad and subdued, as though he had just departed from someone he dearly loved. Jahan watched him for a while. So quiet and distracted was Yusuf that, save for the movement of his hands and the occasional glance he threw in the direction of the construction site, he might have been inanimate, another queer creature in the Chief White Eunuch's collection.

Then, as though in a dream, he took off his gloves. His hands were slender and white, without a trace of burns. Why had he lied to everyone, Jahan wondered. What happened next was more baffling. Yusuf began to hum a song. His voice, the voice no one had ever heard, was lilting, dulcet. Realizing he had stumbled on something dark, something he would not know what to do with, Jahan held his breath, studying the apprentice who, all this time, he had taken for dumb.

Yusuf fell quiet again; the moment disappeared. Jahan tried to

---

★ The meal eaten the night before a fast.

retreat discreetly but in his haste he stepped on a twig. With a flinch Yusuf turned and saw him. His face fell, his lip jutted out like a child. So deep was his panic that Jahan almost ran to him to say not to worry; he would not reveal his secret. Instead he went back to work and tried to put the whole thing out of his mind. Still, he could not help glancing at Yusuf, who kept his head bowed low, his eyes fixed on the ground.

That evening after supper Jahan allowed himself to mull over the mystery. The hairless face, the long, curved eyelashes, the way he sat demurely with his gloved hands resting upon his lap. It was all beginning to make sense. The next morning he found Yusuf covered in soot and powder, drawing. Upon seeing Jahan, he darkened, his back stiffening.

'I'd like to talk,' Jahan said. 'Come with me, I beg.'

Yusuf followed him. They walked silently until they found a shady spot under a tree. They sat on the ground, cross-legged.

Jahan cleared his throat. 'I always envied you. You have a gift. No wonder master picked you as his Chief Apprentice.'

They were distracted by a passing porter carrying a basket of stones on his back. Once his footsteps faded away, Jahan went on. 'But you were acting strangely . . . I suspected you'd had a hand in the accidents.'

Yusuf's face crumpled in surprise.

'Now I understand there was a reason why you were secretive. You are not mute. You have been hiding your voice because . . . you are a woman.'

His – her – eyes clutched at his, wide and frightened, as though Jahan were an apparition. Her lips moved, empty of sound at first – a voice that had not been used for so long it faltered like a chick learning to fly. 'Will you tell anyone?'

'Well, I'm not trying –'

Her hands trembling, she cut in, 'If you tell, it'll be the end of me.'

Jahan looked at her in awe and nodded slowly. 'I give you my word.'

Discovering the mute apprentice's secret had made Jahan curious not only about her but also about Sinan. He was certain his master knew.

What's more, he suspected it had been his idea all along. Sinan wanted, allowed and encouraged her to work with them, a woman among hundreds of labourers, year after year, building after building. The whole week he pondered this dilemma. In the end he went to see him.

'Indian apprentice,' Sinan said brightly. 'You have something to ask, I can tell.'

'I'd like to know, if I may, how you choose your apprentices.'

'I pick them from among the skilful.'

'There are many such in the palace school. They'd make better draughtsmen.'

'Some might –' Sinan left the sentence hanging.

'I used to think we were the best students you had come across. My vanity! Now I understand we have talent but we are not the finest. You do not choose the finest. You go for the ones who are good but are . . .' He halted, searching for the word. 'Lost . . . abandoned . . . forsaken.'

It was a moment before Sinan spoke. 'You're right. I choose my apprentices with care. Those with aptitude but also with nowhere to go.'

'Why?'

Sinan drew in a slow breath. 'You have been to the sea, the big sea.'

Though not a question, Jahan nodded.

'Have you ever seen sea turtles washed ashore? They keep walking, with all their might, but the route is a wrong one. They need a hand to turn them back, towards the sea, where they belong.'

Sinan pulled at his beard, which had whitened a great deal in the past months. 'When I saw you, I thought you had a great head on your shoulders, and would learn fast, if only I could turn you away from wrong habits, from the past, and direct you towards your future.'

As Jahan listened to his master, he found the word he was looking for: *broken*. He was beginning to understand what Sinan was doing, what he had been doing all along. Jahan, Davud, Nikola and Yusuf. The four of them, utterly different yet similarly broken. Master Sinan was not only teaching them, he was also, gently but firmly, fixing them.

Jahan kept his word. He did not share Yusuf's secret with anyone, not even Chota, seized by a superstition that it would pass on from the animal to the howdah, from the howdah to the people he carried. Gradually, during breaks, Yusuf told him her story – or what remained of it – and her name of many summers ago, Sancha.

There was a big, milky-white house covered in wisteria, she said, in a town called Salamanca. Her father was a renowned man of medicine. Tender with his patients, strict with his wife and children, he wished nothing more than to see his three sons continue his noble profession. He insisted that his daughter, too, should be educated. As a result every tutor who came to the house taught all four children. The summer she turned eight, the plague entered through the city gates. Death claimed the boys one after the other. Only Sancha was left, burdened with the guilt of being alive when those who were more beloved had gone. Her mother, numb with grief, sought refuge in a convent in Valladolid. Only Sancha and her father were left. She took care of him, though he clearly despised her efforts. Even so, little by little, he began to teach her. Not medicine, since he believed that women were by nature incapable of this, but other disciplines – arithmetic, algebra, philosophy. He taught her everything he knew. Being a good student, she learned fast, at first less out of her thirst for knowledge than in the hope of earning her father's love. In time, she had better tutors. There was one architect, old and in penury, who spent a great deal of time instructing her, and in between lessons tried to steal kisses from her.

Her father had friends like himself, men who cherished wisdom. *Conversos* and Catholics, and an Arab among them. Still, there was plenty of fear and suspicion. Heretics were burned at the stake, the stench of smouldering flesh polluting the wind. Her father, whose health had begun to deteriorate, declared that in a year she would be married to a distant cousin. A wealthy merchant she had never met before and already hated. Pleading, crying, she tried to convince him not to send her off, but to no avail.

The ship she took to meet her fiancé was raided by corsairs. After weeks of suffering, none of which she wished to remember, she found herself in Istanbul, enslaved. She was sold to a court musician who happened to be an acquaintance of Sinan. The man was a gentle soul and treated her well, allowing her, upon her request, to have pen and paper. His two wives, however, tormented her every day. Jealous of her youth and beauty, they bitterly complained that she did not help them the way a concubine should. They had checked her head to toe and could verify that she had no parts missing, but still they doubted she was a woman. Even though she had been converted to Islam and renamed Nergiz, she was secretly drawing Christian churches with crosses and bells. The musician listened to their carping, but not even once did he ask to see the sketches to which they referred.

One day, while the musician was away on a journey, his wives ripped Sancha's drawings to pieces and beat her so badly that her clothes were torn to tatters. The same evening he returned. Her fate might have been different had he been back a few days later, when her bruises had healed. As it was, he saw her marred face, swollen eyes. He also found the shredded sketches. One of them had escaped intact. Taking this, he showed it to Sinan. To his surprise the Chief Royal Architect was impressed and keen to meet the owner of the drawing. The musician explained to Sinan that it belonged to a concubine of his, a young damsel, though no longer a virgin, pretty as sunshine, whom he was happy to give to Sinan as a gift. He could do with her what he pleased. If the girl remained in his house, his wives would trample on her like a shoddy rug.

That was how Sancha ended up in the Chief Royal Architect's house. She was allowed to use the library and make her sketches so long as she helped Kayra, the master's wife, with the housework from morning till noon. A year into this life, Sinan began to tutor her. He was pleased with this unlikely pupil, yet never considered taking her to construction sites.

The week Sinan laid the foundation stone for the Shehzade Mosque, Sancha begged to be allowed to work with him. Refused repeatedly, she took hold of a pair of scissors and cut her long hair, the colour of burnt umber, which she left in a pile at the master's door. When Sinan came out the next morning, he stepped on a silky turf of hair. He understood. He provided her with boy's clothes. When she put them on he was half amused and half astounded. She could easily pass as a lad. The only obstacle was her voice. And her hands. It could be solved by silence and a pair of gloves. Sinan decided she would be his mute apprentice.

Sancha told Jahan all of this one afternoon while they were working on the Molla Celebi Mosque. A hexagonal domed baldachin, four turrets with domical caps. The two of them sat outside on a bench facing the half-dome over the *mihrab*.

'No one knows?' Jahan asked.

'The master's wife, Kayra. She does.'

'Who else?'

'Only one,' said Sancha. 'This Italian architect, Tommaso. He is always following our master. He heard me speak once, I'm afraid.'

Jahan was about to reply when he caught a sound like that of a nocturnal animal rustling off to the side. He turned back with fright. There was an eerie quiet, and he sensed, with all his being, that they had not been alone. His heart thudding against his chest, he stood up, glanced around. He saw a few men in the distance, prowling around. One of them he recognized. It was Salahaddin's brother. Jahan remembered their bitter exchange at the cemetery. He knew the young man hated Sinan, holding him responsible for his brother's death. Jahan feared he might have come here to harm the master. Then again, they could be thieves. There were always a few around construction sites, looking for materials to loot. Not wanting to alarm Sancha and add to her distress, he watched the intruders a bit longer and kept his suspicions to himself.

'I saw you with Tommaso,' Jahan said after a pause. A shadow crossed his face as a new thought occurred to him. 'He is blackmailing you.'

Sancha lowered her eyes.

'But you are not rich. What does he want from you?'

'He is not after riches,' Sancha said, twisting the end of her shirt between her fingers. 'He wants the master's designs.'

Jahan looked at her in horror. 'Did you give them to him?'

'All he's got is a few mediocre designs. He thinks they belong to Master Sinan. I drew them for him.'

A smile passed between them. A sense of fellowship, which, had Jahan not known the truth about her, he would have called brotherhood. What Sancha didn't say, then or later, and it would take Jahan a while to discover, was that there was a secret buried in her heart. It had kept her strong. And loyal to the core. On the loneliest nights when she cried herself to sleep, the thought of him being under the same roof, even if a life away, the thought of him caring for her, even if in a fatherly way, had warmed her soul.

She was his apprentice. She was his concubine. She was his slave. And she was no older than his daughter. Yet Yusuf Nergiz Sancha Garcia de Herrera, a soul who carried too many names in her slender body, was in love with Master Sinan.

They never found another chance for a talk as intimate and honest as this one. The same day a new accident occurred. A stone block slipped off the pier abutting the prayer hall and fell to the ground, wounding two galley slaves and killing Sinan's dedicated foreman, Snowy Gabriel.

The accidents were sporadic enough to be attributed to fate, but they were also strangely similar, strangely persistent.

If not put to use, iron rusts, woodwork crumbles, man errs, Sinan said. *Work we must.*

Following in his footsteps, the four apprentices toiled as though tomorrow were the Day of Judgement and they must finish before everything turned to dust. They constructed Friday mosques, *masjids*, madrasas, Qur'an schools, bridges, baths, hospitals, lazarettos, alms houses, granaries and caravanserais for travellers from far and wide. Most of these were ordered by the Sultan; others, by his mother, wives, daughters and succeeding viziers.

Not everything Sinan built was commissioned by the wealthy and the mighty, however. The shrines, to begin with. These, too, the apprentices put up in earnest. Many a time their master paid for these himself. And the sole reason they kept erecting them year in, year out, was because someone somewhere had seen them in a dream. Sinan, in his capacity as the Master of the Royal Architects, not only felt responsible for raising structures and surveying towns; he also oversaw holy dreams.

Anybody could come with such a demand – a soldier, an innkeeper, a scullion, even a mendicant. They knocked on Sinan's door, respectful but resolute, and secretly proud, as though they had been entrusted with an important letter from the skies. Then they related their dreams. More often than not, these were about saints and sages who were terribly upset that their graves had gone to rack and ruin. Or martyrs who, showing where their remains lay, asked for a proper funeral. Or mystics executed for heresy and buried furtively, if at all.

The dead in the visions were impatient, their behests urgent. So were the dream-petitioners – as Jahan called them. They expected the architect and the apprentices to stop doing whatever they were doing – such as building a Friday mosque – and follow them. Some even made threats. 'It's a powerful saint, this one. If you don't do as he says, he'll put a curse on you.'

Every week one of the apprentices was put in charge of the dream-suitors. His impossible task was to listen to every one and weed out those who were honest from the crooks. This is how many a Thursday afternoon Jahan found himself perched on a stool facing strangers. There would be a scribe by his side, bent over the table, scratching his pen without a break. No matter how full of gibberish or trivia, every appeal had to be written down. Sinan would greet the petitioners cordially. He would announce that his wise apprentice was here to hear what they had to share. Flicking a sideways glance in Jahan's direction, he would leave with an impish smile at the edge of his lips. Under the scrutiny of dozens of eyes, studying his every move, Jahan often broke into a sweat. The room felt small, stuffy. Suddenly there was not enough space for these people and their vast expectations.

They came from everywhere. Bustling ports and forsaken hamlets. And they implored the apprentices to go and build everywhere – a town, a farmstead or a property home only to snakes. Most of the dream-petitioners were men of varying ages. There were schoolboys accompanied by their fathers. Occasionally, there would be a woman. She would wait outside while her husband or brother passed on her dreams.

Once some peasants requested that a Byzantine fountain, which supplied water to a village, be restored. Although they had applied to the kadi, their efforts had so far been in vain. Then a tinker had a holy dream. A forceful and furious saint confided in him that beneath the fountain lay the remnants of a Sufi *dergah*. As long as the water kept flowing the souls of the dervishes rested in peace. Now that the water had run dry, they were disturbed. Therefore the fountain had to be repaired – without delay.

When Jahan offered his master an account of his interviews, Sinan singled out this story as one to which they should give serious attention.

'But, master, do you believe they are telling the truth?' Jahan objected.

'They need water; it doesn't matter what I believe.'

They rebuilt the fountain, cleaning the ditches that brought water from the mountains. The villagers were pleased; so was Sinan.

It was around this time that a miller arrived. He said that while grinding grain he had heard a woman singing – sweet and captivating. Fearing it must be a *djinn*, he had headed for the hills. The next day the voice awaited him, although he had thrown salt over his left shoulder and spat three times on fire. The village elder advised him to read the Qur'an before going to sleep. This he did. That same night a woman appeared in his dream. Her face shone as if there were a lantern under her skin. Her lustrous, blonde hair spilled on to her shoulders. She explained that she had been strangled upon the orders of the Mother Sultana, though she did not give her name. Since then her soul had been roaming the earth, searching for her body, which was deep under the sea. Recently a fisherman had pulled up the tortoiseshell comb that had been on her head and come loose when she was thrust into the sea with a rock tied to her feet. Not knowing what to do with it, the fisherman had put it in a box. She wanted the miller to find the comb and bury it as though it were her flesh and bone. In this way, she would have a tomb and find some peace.

'Why didn't she reveal herself to the fisherman?' Jahan asked incredulously.

'He's trouble,' the miller said. 'He lives a stone's throw away from Rumelian Castle. There's a cottage, blue like a robin's egg.'

'Have you been there?'

'Of course not, *effendi*. She told me all that. I'm a poor man, my wife's ailing, I've got no sons to lend me a hand. I can't ride that far.'

Jahan understood what was being asked of him. 'I can't go either. I'm needed here.'

The disappointment in the man's eyes went through Jahan like a flamed arrow. Still, his biggest surprise came when Sinan, once he told him the story, urged Jahan to go to nose around. So, the next day, the elephant and the mahout were on their way.

Finding the fisherman was easy; speaking to him, impossible. With eyes dark with bitterness and a mouth that clearly hadn't smiled in ages, he was a callous soul. One look at him and Jahan knew there was no way he would let him rummage through his belongings. Jahan made another plan. As soon as they were behind the hills, he halted the elephant and jumped down. After tying Chota to a willow, which the animal could have pulled up without much effort, he said, 'I'll be back in a moment.'

Quiet as an owl, Jahan retraced his path. He tiptoed around the garth and into the shed, which stank of fish. He found a few boxes but none of them had a comb inside. He was about to leave when he caught sight of a basket on the floor. His hands shaking, he peered into it. The comb was there. Mottled brown and amber, cracked at the edges. He pocketed it and took to his heels.

Thankfully Sinan didn't inquire how the article had been acquired. Instead he said, 'We need to lay her to rest. She needs a tombstone.'

'But . . . can we bury a comb in place of a body?' asked Jahan.

'If it's the only thing left from a person, I don't see why not.'

By a mulberry tree, Sinan and the apprentices dug deep. They placed the comb inside. As they threw earth on the grave, they prayed. In the end, the woman in the miller's dream, whether real or not, had a headstone. One that said:

Pray for the soul of one whose name was not discovered
Loved by the Almighty, He hath known her always.

In the spring of 1575 the astronomer Takiyuddin began to visit Sinan more often. The two of them would retreat to the library, talking for hours. There was something new and big in the air; Jahan could sniff it out like freshly baked bread – something that excited these elderly men as though they were boys again.

The Chief Royal Astronomer and the Chief Royal Architect had always respected each other. Time and again, Takiyuddin had been present at the inauguration ceremony of a mosque, helping with the measurements. Likewise, he consulted Sinan about the laws of arithmetic, on which both were experts. The two men read effortlessly in several languages – Turkish, Arabic, Persian, Latin and a bit of Italian. Over the years they had exchanged a multitude of books and ideas and, Jahan suspected, quite a few secrets. If their fondness for numbers was one thing they had in common, another was their diligence. Both believed that the only way to thank Allah for the skills He had given them was to labour hard.

Despite everything they shared, they could not have been more different. Takiyuddin was a man of passion. His face was an open book that revealed every emotion crossing his heart. When joyful, his eyes lit up; when thoughtful, he fingered his rosary so hard that the string would almost snap. In his obsession with learning he was rumoured to have hired grave-robbers to bring him corpses to study. Should anyone ask why a stargazer might show interest in the human body, he would say God had designed the small cosmos and the big cosmos in parallel. He often complained about the arrogance of the *ulema* and the ignorance of the people. With so much fire in his spirit it caused his friends no small amount of worry that he might burn himself. Fervent and animated, he stood in contrast with Sinan, who rarely showed his fervour and had, overall, a placid demeanour.

Except now Sinan, too, seemed excited, if not apprehensive. He spent his days reading and drawing, which was normal, but he also looked out of the window in a distant and distracted way, which was not. A couple of times Jahan heard him ask the servants whether anyone had brought him a message.

One Wednesday, as the apprentices were working in the master's house, the awaited courier arrived with a scroll. Under prying eyes, Sinan broke the seal, read the letter. His face, stiff with suspended eagerness, softened into a smile of relief.

'We are building an observatory!' he announced.

A house to study the dark expanse above their heads. It would be bigger than any that had been erected before, East and West. Astronomers from all over the world would come here to hone their skills. Sultan Murad had promised to support Takiyuddin in his wish to discover the invisible dome.

'This will alter our grasp of the universe,' Sinan remarked.

'Why would it concern us?' asked Davud.

In response Sinan said that knowledge, *ilm*, was a carriage pulled by many horses. If one of the steeds began to gallop faster, the other horses, too, would speed up and the traveller in the carriage, the *alim*, would benefit from it. Improvement in one field backed improvements in other fields. Architecture had to be friends with astronomy; astronomy with arithmetic; arithmetic with philosophy; and so on.

'One more thing,' Sinan said. 'You are going to build the observatory. I shall look after you but it will be your achievement.'

The apprentices gaped at him in disbelief. They had worked upon many buildings but had never created one on their own.

Nikola said, 'Master, we are indebted. You have honoured us.'

'May God light your path,' said Sinan.

In the weeks ahead the apprentices presented their designs to the master. Having been given a site on a hill in Tophane, they checked the soil, measured the moisture. Even though still vying with one another to be the master's favourite, they joined forces. The excitement of building together outweighed any jealousies.

Takiyuddin, in the meantime, was the happiest soul in the empire and the most restless. Hovering about the site, asking questions that made no sense to anyone, he could barely wait to see the completion of his beloved observatory. Weeks into the construction, he was seized by a fear of death. Morbidly fascinated with accidents and diseases, he was afraid of departing this life before the edifice was finished. Never before had Jahan seen an intelligent man drive himself so mad with worry.

Instruments were brought from near and far. Books and celestial maps were gathered for the collection to be housed inside the observatory. Round and spacious, flooded with light pouring through high windows, with a staircase that spiralled down into a basement chamber, the library was a place Jahan was fond of and he was proud of having contributed to its design.

As the construction progressed, Jahan was able to learn more about Takiyuddin. Born in Damascus, schooled in Nablus and Cairo, he had then settled in Istanbul, trusting it to be the right city for his skills. Here he had thrived, climbing all the way up to the rank of Chief Royal Astronomer. Jahan would later learn that it was he who had instigated this whole venture, convincing the Sultan of the necessity for a royal observatory. That, however, did not mean he had persuaded everyone in the court. Hugely respected by some, loathed by others, of friends and foes Takiyuddin had plenty.

Benefiting from the findings of the mathematician Jamshid al-Kashi and the tools perfected by Nasir al-Din al-Tusi, Takiyuddin was keen on furthering the achievements of the Samarkand Observatory, built by Ulugh Bey – an astronomer, a mathematician and a Sultan. Almost two hundred years ago, he said, the finest scholars had unravelled many secrets of the universe. Their accomplishments, rather than being refined, had been forsaken and forgotten. Precious knowledge had been lost for future generations. There were gems of wisdom, far and wide, waiting to be found, like caskets of treasure deep under the ground. Learning, therefore, was a matter less of discovering than of remembering.

Takiyuddin often alluded to Tycho Brahe – a star-gazer in Frangistan. By coincidence, at the time the apprentices were laying the foundation stone of their observatory, Brahe's was being erected in far-off Uraniborg. The two men, instead of locking horns with each other, had been exchanging letters of mutual esteem and admiration.

'We love the same woman,' Takiyuddin said.

'What d'you mean?' Jahan faltered.

'The sky, we are both besotted with her. Sadly, we are mortal. After we are gone, others will love her.'

Once the celestial instruments had been placed in their respective spots, on heavy cast-iron stands, Takiyuddin showed Sinan's apprentices around. Everywhere he turned Jahan saw astronomical clocks with three dials, exquisitely crafted and precise. In a chamber towards the back they noticed water pumps of different sizes, which Takiyuddin said had nothing to do with the azure but were simply another passion of his. Upstairs there was a massive astrolabe with six rings – *dhat al-halaq*. This was used to assess the latitudes and longitudes, so they were told. Another device, *libna*, mounted on the wall, consisted of two large brass quadrants and helped to calculate the declinations of the stars and the sun. Lengthy pieces of wood, which by their humble appearance seemed meaningless, turned out to measure the parallax of the moon. An implement with a copper ring assessed the azimuths of the stars; the one next to that determined the equinoxes. Jahan's favourite was a sextant that measured the distances between the celestial bodies.

In each room they entered they found a device that unravelled yet another secret of the blue firmament. The court astronomer explained that with heavenly bodies, as with so many things in life, one had to find the right guide. Rather than taking the moon as his reference point, he studied two wandering stars: one was called Venus, the other Aldebaran – a name Jahan liked so much he kept repeating it to himself, as though it were poetry.

Unlike the instruments, which were new, the books and manuscripts in the library were ages old. It was here that Takiyuddin kept his treatises on geometry, algebra and the forces of motion. He was particularly pleased that in a recent decree, addressed to the kadis of Istanbul, the Sultan had ordered the people who possessed valuable collections to hand these over to the royal observatory. *When you receive this order, find those books based on astronomy and geometry, and give them to my honourable astronomer, Takiyuddin, so that he may continue his excellent work, under my protection.*

With an endorsement so strong they thought nothing could go wrong. Immaculate inside, immaculate outside, the observatory, *their* observatory, with its windows iridescent in the evening sun, shone atop a hill in Tophane.

The opening ceremony was glorious. Above their heads the sun hovered bright and generous, the sky a seamless blue. Regardless, the air felt crisp and chilly, as though both the winter and the summer had wanted to be present on such a day. Seagulls swooped far ahead, not shrieking for once; swallows dipped and drank water from the marble fountain in the courtyard. The smell of myrrh on their robes and beards mingled with the sweet fragrance of the halvah Takiyuddin had ordered to be doled out to the workers, who had toiled hard to finish on time.

Sinan was present, clad in a cinnamon kaftan and a bulbous turban, the fingers of his right hand moving around an imaginary rosary. The apprentices stood some steps behind him, trying hard to conceal their pride. For, although it was Sultan Murad's health and triumph and the Chief Royal Astronomer's success that they were here to pray for, the students of Sinan had contributed much to this observatory. They could not help but be pleased with the two buildings they had designed, constructed and made ready for use – under the auspices of the master but still theirs alone. This was their creation, may the Creator forgive the word, which belonged only to Him.

Beyond the observatory grounds was an expanse of onlookers and well-wishers, their voices carrying in the wind. Foreign envoys observing the happenings, merchants calculating what this could bring to them, pilgrims murmuring prayers, beggars seeking alms, thieves searching for prey, and children perching on their fathers' shoulders to get a glimpse of the place where you could watch the sun and the moon, and even learn where the shooting stars went when they tumbled down.

Takiyuddin, tall and erect, stood at the centre, wearing a flowing garb white as alabaster. Forty sheep and forty cows had been sacrificed early on, their meat distributed to the poorest of the poor. Now a drop of their blood shone on his forehead, between his eyes. To his left and to his right twenty-four astronomers had lined up, their faces shining with delight.

Abruptly, all sound subsided. A ripple of excitement went through the audience. Sultan Murad was coming. Like water, his presence flowed into the courtyard, filling each empty space, long before his cavalcade was spotted in the distance. The Shadow of God on Earth was going to open the biggest observatory in the seven climes. Once the Sultan and his guards had arrived and settled, a Sufi sheikh began to pray, his voice at once loud and mellow.

'May Allah afford His protection to our magnanimous Sultan!'

They echoed in unison, savouring the word as if it were a tasty morsel. *'Amin!'*

'May Allah have mercy on our glorious empire and guide us in all our deeds and help us to join those who have been through this world before and have not erred! May Allah look after this house and reveal the secrets of the heavens to those and only those who can bear them.'

'Amin!'

As Jahan listened to the Sufi's words, his gaze strayed towards the *ulema*, the religious seniors, who were watching the ceremony. There had been rumours that the Shayh al-Islam, when asked to lead the communal prayer, had refused. Jahan observed the man's face. He looked composed, his expression tranquil as a pond. Just then he pursed his lips, his mouth twisting into a scowl, as if he had tasted something bitter. Jahan didn't think anyone had noticed, enraptured, as they were, by prayer. But he had seen it, that tiny gesture, and his chest tightened.

For a moment that was as brief as the ascent of a soaring condor, Jahan knew in his gut, even though there was nothing obviously out of the way, that something was wrong. He had the intense feeling that Sinan was also aware of this – hence the nervous motion of his fingers. In the meantime Takiyuddin, in his exhilaration, had not suspected a thing.

Later on Jahan would contemplate this moment at length. Sinan had not had much experience with the *ulema* but he could nonetheless sense their profound dislike. Takiyuddin, on the other hand, knew them far better than anyone. After all, he had served as a judge, a theologian, a *muwakkit*, the keeper of time, and a teacher at a madrasa. Yet he did not share the unease that the master and the apprentice had felt that day. Perhaps, Jahan would conclude, with closeness came blindness and with a certain distance, awareness.

Takiyuddin was writing a treatise on heavenly beings, a book he called a *zij*. Therein he registered the positions and distances and motions of the sun and the moon and the stars and the celestial bodies. This would take him years, he explained, but when finished it would be a guide in perpetuity.

'A *zij* is a map,' he explained. 'A map of the divine creation.'

Long ago an infidel sage by the name of Aristo – a man who had taught the great Askander everything he knew – held that the earth was at the centre of the universe and that it was peacefully at rest, unlike other celestial bodies. He left it to astronomers to find the sum of the spheres that rotated around it, the cumulative number of the many domes that moved above their heads.

'Have you been able to count them?' Jahan asked when, following the inauguration, he and Davud paid him a visit.

'Eight,' Takiyuddin said decidedly.

It was an impeccable number and for a good reason – the shape of the earth, the arrangement of the heavenly bodies, the layers of the universe, everything was put in order by God for human beings to see, study and contemplate. The more Takiyuddin talked, the more garrulous he became. He said as brilliant as Aristo had been, he had got things wrong. It was the sun that was at the heart of the universe, not the earth. The other bodies revolved round this ball of fire in perfect circles. He showed Jahan a book that, he said, proved this beyond doubt. Jahan read aloud its title, the words in Latin gliding on his tongue, smooth and round, something to do with the revolution of spheres. *Koppernigk.* What a strange name, he thought, yet the Chief Royal Astronomer had pronounced it with such veneration that from his mouth it sounded like an incantation.

'He had a sweetheart but never married,' said Takiyuddin, pointing at the leather-bound tome as if it were alive. 'He raised his sister's children and had none of his own.'

Davud asked, 'Why didn't he become espoused?'

'God knows. But probably for the woman's sake. What wife can bear a husband who sees only the skies?'

Davud and Jahan eyed each other, thinking the same thing. Although Takiyuddin was married, he slept in the observatory most nights. They did not dare to ask if, when talking about Koppernigk, he had been alluding to himself as well.

Thanking the architect and his acolytes, Davud and Jahan bade them farewell. Scarcely had they stepped outside when they were engulfed by a wave of fog, penetrating and sinister. Fumbling like two blind men, they found Chota, climbed up to their places and slowly, very slowly, trotted towards the city.

A few steps into this walk Jahan felt an urge to turn back and look. Something strange happened then. Of the two tall buildings that formed the observatory, not a single thing could be seen – not even a flickering candle from the windows or a glow from the instruments on the upper terrace. So fully had its contours sunk into the sea of grey that in that moment it felt like the observatory had never existed and that everything said and done under its roof had been nothing more than prints in the sand.

One gusty day, upon returning from work – Jahan on Chota's neck, the master and the apprentices inside the howdah – they found Taki-yuddin waiting in the courtyard, a troubled look on his face. Having not visited him in a while, Jahan was astonished to see how much he had changed. The excitement that had glossed his features in the early months of the observatory had worn off, leaving an older and gaunter face beset by tension. After a brief interchange of greetings, the two elderly men retreated into the pavilion in the garden, under a canopy of vines, their voices subdued, strained.

Unable to get near, unwilling to stay away, the apprentices strode to the kitchen, where, despite the grumbling of the cook, they perched beside the window – the one spot in the house where they could spy on their masters. From this distance it was not possible to hear what they were saying. Even so, nothing could hold them back from making guesses of their own.

'Something's wrong,' murmured Davud. 'I feel it in my bones.'

'Maybe they are only having a discussion,' said Nikola, not ready to abandon his customary sanguineness.

Takiyuddin had brought along one of his acolytes – a young star-gazer with a pockmarked face and the thinnest beard the colour of sunset. When he joined them, the apprentices began to badger him, asking what was happening. Though he tried to evade their questions, he soon laid everything bare. 'My master observed a comet in Sagittarius.'

Jahan cast a glance at the others. Nikola seemed confused; Davud suspicious; there was no way to tell what was on Sancha's mind, since her eyes were fixed on the floor. Assuming he was not the only ignorant one around, he asked, 'What's that?'

The star-gazer sighed. 'Long-haired star. Huge. It's coming our way.'

'What will it do?' Davud inquired.

'My master will say.'

'Surely you must know something about this,' Davud insisted.

'Some comets have caused floods. In one kingdom all the women with child miscarried. Another time three-legged frogs rained from the sky.'

The apprentices listened aghast. Spurred on by his own voice, the man recounted one calamity after another. 'Another comet brought a dry spell that lasted for seven years. Winds so strong that all the saplings were uprooted. Locusts devoured any plant that was left.'

'Sssh, they're coming,' Nikola said, even though there was no way they could be heard from the outside.

Embarrassed, not unlike badly behaved children, they went into the garden to welcome the two masters. Whatever it was that troubled Takiyuddin seemed to have blighted Sinan's mood, like a canker that passes from one tree to the next.

'Look at them,' Takiyuddin said, pointing at the apprentices.

'Gossip flies faster than a comet,' said Sinan in the waggish voice he reserved for fatherly reproach.

'Particularly if someone can't hold their tongue,' Takiyuddin chided, his stare resting on his own acolyte, who instantly lowered his head, colour rising to his cheeks. Quietly the astronomer added, 'It's fine. The entire city will learn about it anyhow.'

Encouraged by this, Jahan demanded, 'What does it all mean?'

'Allah is great and so are His omens,' Takiyuddin said. 'We mortals might not see it that way, but in the end it always is.'

Jahan stared at the court astronomer, tongue-tied. His answer, which offered scant comfort, had weighed him down. He wasn't the only one. Until that moment the apprentices had been more preoccupied with inventing menaces where they saw none. Now they felt threatened by a force they had neither the wisdom to grasp nor the might to defeat.

Sinan was correct about the speed of gossip. In the ensuing days Istanbulites talked about nothing else. Fearful whispers and dark foreboding seeped into the cracks in the walls, filled in the gaps in the cobbles, passed through the holes in the locks, flew down the sewers, sullied the very air. Soon after, the Sultan declared he would hold a conclave of notables, viziers and members of the *ulema*. An impromptu council where Takiyuddin would give an account of things. Jahan's excitement soared when he heard that Sinan, too, had been asked to come and offer his opinion.

'Please take me with you,' Jahan pleaded.

Sinan threw him a burning look. 'Why, just because you are curious?'

'If not me, take another one of us. We built this observatory —'

He didn't need to go on. Sinan yielded. 'Go, get ready.'

After the midday prayer the master and the mahout reached the palace. Like the others they were ushered into the Audience Chamber. There were about forty dignitaries, some of them with their attendants, lined up on both sides of the vast room. Sitting on a golden throne in the heart of everything was Sultan Murad.

Takiyuddin was brought in. Jahan watched him kneel and kiss the Sultan's hem, bow again, salute the members of the *diwan* and wait demurely, his hands clasped, his gaze on his feet. In that moment no one wanted to be in his place.

'Chief Royal Astronomer, you are here to tell our benevolent Sultan what the comet promises to bring,' said the Grand Vizier Sokollu.

'If your Highness permits,' Takiyuddin said and took out a scroll from the inside of his robe. He began to read it aloud: 'I, Takiyuddin ibn Ma'ruf, in my capacity as the Chief Royal Astronomer, have seen a comet in Sagittarius. After consulting my *zij* and making use of my turquet, as the great Nasir al-Din al-Tusi had once done, I found its longitude to be at 26 Sagittarius and its latitude at 22 degrees north. In my measurements I have taken three major stars as my reference points: Aldebaran, the bull's eye; Algorab, the raven; and Altayr, the flying vulture. For days on end I have observed the motion of the comet to understand its temperament. The details of its progression I have written down at length for young astronomers to study after my soul departs this world of shadows.'

Here Takiyuddin paused. Not a single sound could be heard in the chamber.

'I slept little for the next seven nights. My apprentices and I took turns, studying —'

'Spare us what *you* have done,' said Sokollu. 'Tell us what the star will do.'

Takiyuddin drew breath, as if imbibing this moment, this room; he took it in, the faces of friends and foes watching his every move, and perhaps he felt as lonely as the comet he had been tracking. Placing his finger on the scroll, he skipped to the end: 'I've found that the comet is attracted by Venus, its tail stretches eastwards, its motion is from north to south. By studying the constitution of the comet and the temperament of the planet it is drawn to, I have come to the conclusion that, unlike the comets that have visited our skies in days of old, this one has a benevolent nature. It does not wish us harm.'

A quiet rumble of relief rose. Into this the Sultan, speaking for the first time, said with a bob of his head, 'That's good. Tell us more.'

'It shall bring rainclouds aplenty; the harvest will overflow,' said Takiyuddin.

'What about on the battlefield?' asked the Shadow of God on Earth.

'Our troops shall gain a major victory, your Majesty.'

Another wave of excitement rippled through the room. Eyes grew wide, glittering with delight. With that, the meeting was concluded.

None of it came to pass, however. The war with Iran did not go as expected. Even though the Ottoman Army was triumphant, the losses were too enormous to fool anyone. A drought followed. For months on end pantries remained empty, children went to bed hungry. Worse was the earthquake that left entire neighbourhoods in ruins. Afterwards the plague hit again. People died en masse and were buried en masse. Wherever one turned there was poverty and grief.

The comet had brought misery. But to none more than to Takiyuddin. The *ulema* started to scheme about him. Having waited for an opportune moment to strike at the court astronomer, the new Shayh al-Islam, Ahmed Shamseddin Effendi, attacked with all his might. *It is because of the observatory that this calamity has fallen on the city.* Who were they to watch God? It had to be the other way round: God should watch them. Human beings ought to have their eyes on the ground, not pointed towards the vault of heaven.

The Sultan ordered the observatory to be demolished.

The morning they heard the news the apprentices ran to the master's house. Hardly able to speak, they looked past one another as though they were walking in a dream.

Meanwhile Sinan spent the rest of the day sitting in the pavilion alone, perhaps remembering another time when he and Takiyuddin had been there, hopeful and faithful. After the evening prayer he came out and said in a voice so soft and mellow it belied the hardness underneath, 'You made it; you should raze it.'

'But master –' Nikola tried to protest.

Jahan's self-control broke. Since Olev's death there had been much anger in his heart and now it exploded. He said, 'Is this why you let us build it? You didn't do it yourself because you knew this was bound to happen.'

The others gaped at him. It was the kind of thing they had all thought on the quiet, but they were astonished that he had had the discourtesy to say it out loud. Sinan said, 'I wasn't aware. If I had known I'd not have asked you to do it.'

But once he began Jahan couldn't stop. He insisted, 'Then why don't you defend our observatory? How can you let this happen?'

Sinan smiled sadly, the lines around his eyes deepening. 'There are things that are in my hands and things that are not. I cannot prevent people from destroying. All I can do is keep building.'

The evening before the demolition, they retreated to their own corners, avoiding conversation. The master was upstairs in the *haremlik* with his family; Nikola in the workshop; Davud nowhere to be seen; Sancha in her room at the back of Sinan's house; and Jahan cloistered in the barn. The poor *kahya*, unable to convince them to sup together, had to send everyone their food on separate trays.

Jahan missed spending time alone with the elephant and attending to his every need, so tonight he chased away the young helper. In his heart of hearts, he believed that no one could look after the animal the way he did. Just as in the olden days, he washed the urine off the floor, shovelled the dung, topped up the water in the barrel, renewed the leaves in the trough. He scoured Chota's feet – the big, round front and the smaller, oval hind – careful not to hurt the doughy footpads underneath. He pored over his toenails, all eighteen of them, which he then trimmed, cleaned and rubbed with balm one by one. Drudging at construction sites and trudging up steep hills, year after year, had eventually taken its toll. Four of his toenails had split and one was about to fall off.

Jahan inspected the animal's trunk for warts, pleased to find none, and his tail for fleas and mites. He examined the soft tissue behind his ears for elephant lice, which were the worst. It was odd to see a beast this huge utterly helpless in the face of the most infinitesimal creature. But the truth was one louse could ruin an elephant's temper. Though he found a few tiny brown lumps, thankfully there was nothing alarming. After washing him Jahan checked his back for wounds and abscesses. Where his skin was dry he applied ointment. While he did this, Chota waited patiently, basking in the attention. Jahan, too, enjoyed the effort. It helped him to forget his despair, even though he knew it wouldn't be long before he remembered it again. When he was done, Chota swung his trunk as if to ask him how he looked.

'There, handsome as gold,' Jahan said.

It was then that he heard footsteps behind the slightly open gate.

'Down here,' he yelled, expecting to see a houseboy with his meal. To his astonishment, it was Sinan. Wiping his hands on a greasy rag, Jahan scurried over to him. 'Master, welcome.' It didn't sound right to invite him into a barn, so he added hastily, 'You want me to come out?'

'Let's talk here. Better.'

Jahan spread Chota's mantle on a mound of hay, making an odd chair, half velvet, half straw.

'I never thought there'd come a day when I'd ask you what I'm about to ask now,' Sinan said after settling down.

'What is it?' Jahan said, though he was not sure he wanted to hear the answer.

'I need your skills. Not as a draughtsman. Your earlier skills, if one may call them such.'

Seeing Jahan draw a blank, he explained, slowly, 'Back when you used to help yourself to other people's belongings, I mean. I know you don't do it any more.'

Shame. Horror. So the master knew all about his pilfering. A rush of guilt ran down to his fingertips. Still, he did not deny it. 'Yes, right . . . but . . . I don't understand.'

'I need you to steal a few things for me, son.'

Jahan stared at him.

'Tomorrow, as you know, the buildings shall be razed. The instruments. The books. It happened so fast Takiyuddin did not have time to save much. The doors are locked and no one can get in.'

Jahan nodded, finally beginning to see what he was suggesting.

'If we could get at least a few books, it'd be some consolation to our friend.'

'It would indeed, master.'

'You don't have to accept, of course,' Sinan said, dropping his voice to a whisper. 'It could be a bad idea.'

'I think it's an excellent idea.'

'It could be dangerous, son.'

'Stealing always is, master, if you pardon my saying so.'

Sinan regarded his apprentice with a wistful smile, his head cocked to one side, as if the very sight of him both hurt and restored his spirit.

'This has to remain a secret between us,' Sinan said after a pause.

'And Chota,' Jahan said. 'He can walk more quietly than a horse. And he can carry more things.'

'All right. We'll take him with us.'

'We? You mean you're coming with me?'

'Certainly. I cannot send you on your own.'

Jahan thought about this for a moment. If he were caught, he would be taken for an ordinary thief. If Sinan were caught, he would lose his reputation, even his position in the court. His workers, his family, his students, each of whom looked up to him as a father figure, would be devastated. He said, 'I cannot work with someone else beside me. It's against my nature.'

The master objected. The apprentice resisted. Sinan said he was calling the whole thing off. Jahan said it was too late, now that he had heard about it he would do it anyway. It was a bizarre war of words. They quarrelled without quarrelling.

'Fine,' said Sinan, conceding in the end with a perfunctory wave of his hand, which Jahan took as less a gesture of defeat than a sign of trust.

Afterwards the master handed Jahan a pouch of coins. If he were to run into the night watchman, he should try to bribe him. It might work. It might fail. It depended on the man's disposition and what Providence had in store for Jahan.

At the sound of an approaching footfall they both flinched. A boy appeared, carrying a tray with a bowl of steaming soup, bread, water and baklava. They waited until he had served the food and left.

'Eat,' the master said. 'It'll be a long night.'

Jahan tore a piece of bread, dumped it into the soup and swallowed it down, scalding his tongue, as a thought occurred to him. He said, 'Is there anything in particular you want me to carry off?'

'Well,' Sinan replied, raising an eyebrow, expecting to be asked this. 'Not the instruments; they are too big. The books should be saved, as many as possible. If you can, find his *zij*; you know how he exerted himself on it.'

The map of the moon, the sun, the stars and the celestial bodies. Years and years of work. Why hadn't the Chief Royal Astronomer taken it away with him?

As if reading his mind, Sinan said, 'Takiyuddin kept his valuable things in the observatory. That was his home.'

Jahan had a few spoonfuls of soup; then he popped another piece of bread into his mouth and put the rest into his sash. 'I'm ready to go.'

There was a full moon glowing over the city, a bonfire from a bygone age. Amid shadows, Jahan rode Chota towards Tophane.

Against the leaden sky the buildings resembled two sorrowful giants hugging each other. A stab of pain went through Jahan as he realized that by this time tomorrow they would be gone. He jumped down and listened to the night to make sure there was no one around. Quietly, he told Chota to wait for him there, rewarding him with pears and nuts, which the beast instantly gobbled up. Jahan had brought large sacks to carry the books. After grabbing them and kissing Chota's trunk three times for good luck, he made straight for the observatory.

First he tried the main entrance. There was a rusty padlock dangling from it. He fiddled a bit, making use of the blade and the spike he had brought with him in his sash. It would not be too hard to prise it open, he judged; yet he would be unable to put the thing back together in one piece. Tomorrow morning everyone would know someone had broken in.

He crept behind the walls and checked the back doors on both sides. Since there was a passage between the buildings, it made no difference which door he went through so long as he found a way. Then he saw what he needed: a round window on the ground floor. He recalled that this winter it had come loose and never been fully repaired. Takiyuddin had complained, saying the labourer had done a mediocre job. Then he had forgotten all about it. So had everyone else.

The next moment Jahan was there, prodding. In a little while, the hinge gave way with a click. Pushing the window open, he slipped in. It was so dark inside, and he was so unprepared for this, that his knees buckled under him. He waited till his eyes had adjusted to the gloom, after which he began to identify things. He climbed up the spiral stairs and reached the library; a powerful smell of paper, vellum, ink and leather hit him in the face. Each shelf was an open wound bleeding into the night. Staggering, he glanced left and right. There were thousands of books, maps and manuscripts. How was he to know which ones were more precious than others? How could he judge? By their age? By their author? By their theme?

Jahan scampered from row to row, picking up the books at random, sniffed and touched them, then brought them near the window, where a wedge of moonlight shimmered. Words in Latin, Arabic, Ottoman, Hebrew, Greek, Armenian, Persian rained on him. He gasped. Suddenly, he was furious at himself. He was losing precious time with his doubts. Panicking, he took out the sacks he had brought and began to fill them with whichever books he could lay his hands on. Since he could not choose, he would not. He would save them all.

In went the first shelf, then the second and the third. One sack was full already. The second sack swallowed the next three shelves. That was it. He took a step forward, doddering like a drunken man. It was too heavy. He had to remove some of the tomes, his hands trembling, his teeth chattering as though he had been left in a cold shaft of air.

'I'll be back,' he whispered.

He went out, found Chota, unloaded the books up into his howdah and returned, running, panting. He cursed himself for not having thought of bringing a wheelbarrow. That would have been smarter. Again he filled the sacks, five more shelves, and again he dashed out. He could not count how many times he was able to make this return trip. He was puffing so hard he feared someone would hear him and it all would come to naught.

Swallowing with a dry mouth, he tried to recover his composure. Outside the window the dawn was breaking. He told himself this had to be the final trip. This was it. Whatever he could save, he saved; whatever he could not, he let go. That was when something happened, something he would never reveal to anyone even years later as an old man. The books and manuscripts and maps and charts started to call his name: first in muted, then in increasingly shrill tones, begging him to take them with him. Jahan could see their mouths of ripped paper, their tears of ink. They threw themselves off the shelves, stepped on each other, blocked his way, their eyes wide with horror. Jahan felt like a man in a boat searching for a dozen to save in a storm while hundreds were drowning around him.

His eyes watered. He filled three more sacks and left quickly, as though being chased by an invisible force. How he mounted Chota, how he reached Sinan's home, he would not remember afterwards. He gave all the books to his master and refused to get anywhere near them for fear they would talk to him again.

'Indian apprentice, you've saved so many,' Sinan said.

'I abandoned many more,' Jahan said dourly.

A line of worry furrowing his forehead, Sinan emptied the sacks, wiped the books and hid them in his library. Later on he would inform Jahan that he had rescued 489 books.

Only when Jahan returned to his room and put his head on his mattress and managed to calm his breathing did he realize that he had not, in his haste, remembered to look for Takiyuddin's *zij*. In the end the court astronomer had not been able to stave off what he most despised. Knowledge and wisdom had to be cumulative, an uninterrupted flow from one generation to the next; and yet the young astronomers who would come after him would have to start from the beginning all over again.

The next day, shortly after dawn, the sky bleeding into the city, there they stood, the six of them – Sinan, the apprentices and the elephant, ready to destroy what they had erected. Not a pigeon ruffled its wings in the eaves, not a breeze stirred. Jahan noticed tears in Sancha's eyes. No one uttered a word.

All day long, in charge of the teams of labourers who arrived with their sledgehammers and mallets and powder, they smashed up the doors and windows, caved in the walls. Chota pulled with all his might at the ropes tied to the wooden posts. People came to watch. Some of them cheered and clapped; most stood in stunned silence. Five days later, as the last stone was hauled away, there were prayers, just as there had been three summers ago when Sinan's apprentices had laid the foundation stone. Only this time the spectators were thanking God for knocking down an edifice of sin.

Something inside Jahan shattered along with the observatory. If it weren't for his love of Mihrimah and his loyalty to Sinan, he would have abandoned this city of broken bricks and burned wood. Go away, whispered a voice within – but where? He was too old to undertake adventures new. Go, implored the voice – but how? Much as he took umbrage at her ways, Istanbul had seized hold of his soul. Even his dreams did not happen elsewhere. Go, warned the voice – but why? The world was a boiling cauldron, the same stew of hopes and sorrows near and far.

For years on end he had devoted his life to a city where he had been – and still was – a stranger; his love to an unattainable woman; and his youth and strength to a craft that, though valued, was dismissed at the slightest change of events. What they raised in years, stone upon stone, could be destroyed in one afternoon. That which was treasured today was treated with contempt tomorrow. Everything remained subject to the whims of fate, and by now he had no doubt that fate was whimsical.

The ensuing weeks were his most sombre days in Istanbul. He could not help asking himself why they worked so hard at small details when no one – not the Sultan, not the people, and surely not God – minded how much effort they expended. They seemed to care for nothing but the size and the stateliness of the buildings and not offending the Almighty. Why did Sinan pay this much attention to the finest details when only a few noticed, and fewer appreciated them?

Nothing ruins the human soul more than hidden resentment. Outwardly, Jahan kept doing the things he always did – toiling alongside his master and feeding Chota, even if he did not attend to his every need any longer. Inwardly, however, numbness seized his heart, wiping away signs of joy, like melting snow erasing the footprints of life. He was losing his faith in his workmanship. Little did he know, back then, that the worth of one's faith depended not on how solid and strong it was, but on how many times one would lose it and still be able to get it back.

The coldest day in forty years, they called it – the day Mihrimah died. Street cats in Scutari froze while jumping from one roof to the next, hanging in the air like crystal lamps. The mendicants, the pilgrims, the roaming dervishes and those of no fixed abode had to seek refuge in alms houses for fear of turning into ice. Why she chose such a day to leave this world, Jahan would never know. She was born in spring and loved flowers in bloom.

She had been ill for months, her health declining despite the number of physicians around her increasing every day. Jahan had seen her six times during those dire months. On each occasion she was a bit thinner. More often he had seen Hesna Khatun, the reluctant courier. The old woman would come to the menagerie bringing messages from the Princess and wait to one side while Jahan composed his answer. Jahan would take his time, choosing his words carefully, despite the nursemaid huffing and puffing beside him. Finally, with a glare she would take his sealed letter and vanish.

Thus it was a letter Jahan was expecting that January morning in 1578 when the nursemaid appeared in the menagerie, wrapped in a fur cloak. Instead she said, 'Your Highness would like to see you.'

Closed gates opened wide before him; hidden halls were illuminated. The guards who saw him coming turned their heads, pretending not to notice. Everything had been arranged. When Jahan reached her chamber he fought hard to keep his smile intact. Her face was inflamed, her body swollen. Her legs, her arms, her neck, even her fingers were bloated, as though she had been stung by the wasp she had been running from as a girl.

'Jahan, beloved . . .' she said.

Jahan stopped feigning equanimity and buried his nose into the trimming of her bedspread. That was where he had been all this time – somewhere on the edge of her existence. Seeing him crying, she lifted her hand and said softly, 'Don't.'

Immediately Jahan apologized. Again, she said, 'Don't.'

The air in the chamber felt stale, because of the closed windows and the heavy curtains. Jahan had a sudden urge to open them but he stayed put, motionless.

She ordered him to come close, closer, despite the burning gaze of Hesna Khatun. She placed her hand upon his hand and, though they had touched before, always on the sly, this was the first time he felt her body open up to his. Jahan kissed her on the lips. He tasted the earth.

'You and your white elephant . . . have brought joy into my life,' she said.

Jahan tried to utter something to raise her spirits, but he could find no words that she would allow. A while later a servant brought her a bowl of custard, flavoured with rosewater. The sweet scent that any other day would have whetted her appetite now made her retch. Jahan gave her water instead, which she drank thirstily.

'When I am not around you may hear things about me that you might not like.'

'No one may dare to say such things about your Highness.'

She gave a tired smile. 'Whatever happens after I am gone, I want you to think of me with warmth in your heart. Will you promise to take no notice of gossip-mongers and slanderers?'

'I shall never believe them.'

She seemed relieved but instantly frowned as a new thought crossed her mind. 'What if you doubt me?'

'Excellency, I'll never –'

She didn't let him continue. 'If you ever have suspicions about me, remember, behind everything there is a reason.'

Jahan would have asked her what she meant had he not just then heard a shuffle of approaching feet. Her three children were brought in, walking in single file. Jahan was surprised to see how tall Aisha had become since the day he had last seen her. One by one they kissed their mother's hand. A deferential silence hung in the air, the youngest boy pretending to be composed, though the tremble of his lower lip betrayed him.

Once they had left, Jahan gave Hesna Khatun a painful look. He could see from her constant fidgeting that the nursemaid wished him to leave. He didn't want to go. It was a small relief when Mihrimah, sensing his discomfort, said, 'Stay.'

As darkness descended, her breathing turned shallow. Jahan and

Hesna Khatun waited on each side of her, she praying, he remembering. Hours passed in a haze. Well past midnight Jahan fought to keep his eyes open, seized by an irrational conviction that so long as he watched over her she would be fine.

The call to prayer woke Jahan up. There was no movement in the room, not a sound. Seized by a cold panic, he staggered to his feet. He stared at the old woman, who looked like she had not slept a wink.

'Gone,' Hesna Khatun said acidly. 'My gazelle has gone.'

Ten months later Sinan and the apprentices put the finishing touches on Sokollu's mosque. A central dome, eight arches, eight piers and a two-storey courtyard. An enclosed portico bathed with sunlight from copious windows adjoined the nigh-on square prayer hall. The *minbar* was of pure white marble framed with turquoise tiles. Around the interior of the mosque ran a balcony, dainty and elegant. Though not as majestic as a Sultan's mosque, it had a strong character, like the man himself.

The Grand Vizier Sokollu arrived to view the construction, escorted by advisers, sentinels, lackeys and flatterers. He inspected the building that would make him immortal, asking endless questions, impatient for the labourers to finish. He carried himself with dignity, the most far-sighted man in the empire, always astute. By now he had served under three Sultans: Suleiman, Selim and Murad. How he had survived for so long, when many a statesman had lost his head for the slightest failing, was a question many asked. He was rumoured to be assisted by a female *djinn* who was besotted with him and whose name no earthling could pronounce. Whenever Sokollu was in danger, this *djinn* warned him.

Jahan watched the fuss from a distance. He had not forgotten that faraway day in Szigetvar, when they had placed into Chota's howdah the body of the deceased Sultan Suleiman, all the while pretending that he was alive. Since then, like a dedicated carver, time had chiselled Sokollu's features, giving his face a stern look. It was in that moment, as Jahan was thinking how much the man had aged, that the Grand Vizier stopped and turned back. His eyes gleamed when he saw the mahout.

'The elephant-tamer,' the Grand Vizier exclaimed with a contemptuous snap of his fingers. 'Why, you have white in your hair. You have aged!'

Jahan bowed respectfully and said nothing. Since Mihrimah had gone, he felt his years more heavily than ever.

Sinan joined in. 'Jahan is one of my best apprentices, my Lord.'

Sokollu asked Jahan how he was doing and where the elephant was, though he did not pay attention to the answer to either question. In an hour the Grand Vizier galloped away. Jahan did not take his eyes off him until he became no more distinct than the shadows along the road and was, eventually, swallowed by the dusk. That same night a storm blew down the staves, bent over the trees and flooded the pits, leaving everything in disarray.

Next morning Jahan found the site covered in mire. Dirty rivulets ran on all sides. Ahead of him a dozen labourers were pushing to dislodge a cart stuck in sludge. Another team was erecting a massive timber with the help of steel pulleys, shouting in unison *Allah, Allah*, as though the construction was a holy war to be won. On the sloped roof there were workmen mending the damaged parts. Wherever he looked he saw people working away to fix things. The only one not working was Chota, wallowing in a brown pool, delighted.

There was a makeshift shed outside the mosque, opposite the narthex, where the master retreated whenever he needed to rest. On that day, suffering from back pain, he spent the afternoon there, lying on a flat surface, wrapped in warm towels. A Jewish physician arrived and drew two bowls of blood from him to release the malignant humours. He then applied poultices to his aching joints.

After the evening prayer the door was opened and the master walked out, pale and drowsy but otherwise fine. He waved at Jahan, and was about to mouth a salute when something strange happened. One of the workmen on the roof who was pulling up the lead sheets lost control of his load. The rope he was holding snapped, sending the entire load plummeting just as Sinan was passing by.

A cry pierced the air. Loud, sharp and distinctively female. It was Sancha. Three words spilled from her lips, 'Master, watch out!'

The lead sheets came down with a horrible crash. Sinan, having miraculously veered aside, was spared. Had he not moved, they would have sliced him in two like the Sword of Damocles.

'I'm fine,' Sinan said when they ran to him.

That was when, one by one, all heads turned to Sancha. She blushed up to her ears under their prying stares, her lip sagging.

Into an awkward silence Sinan said, 'How blessed we are to hear Yusuf's voice. Fear loosens tied tongues, they say.'

Sancha, trembling, lowered her head, her body that of a rag doll.

During the remaining hours of work she avoided everyone. Jahan dared not go near her. The workers were suspicious. *There is a* hunsa *among us*, they whispered with sidelong glances. Someone who was half woman, half man, forever stuck in limbo. The possibility that Yusuf was a woman had not occurred to anyone.

The next day Sinan's Chief Apprentice was absent from the site. And the day after that. It was explained that, feeling unwell, Yusuf had to go away for a few weeks. Where or how, no one inquired. Somehow all and sundry, having stumbled upon a secret, had sensed that it was better, safer, to know nothing. Only Jahan understood that this was the end – Sancha would not be working with them again. She would be putting herself and the master in peril if she were to return. She had gone back to the life she abhorred: the life of a concubine.

The same week Jahan was wending his way through the site, lost in thought, when he glimpsed a rope that Chota had trampled in the mud. Unthinking, he picked it up. As he inspected it, his face sank. The two strings on the sides had snapped, leaving the fibre splintered, while the strings in the middle were shorter and straight, as if slashed by a blade. Someone had thinned the rope by cutting its core. Outside it looked like an ordinary rope; inside it was weak as an eggshell.

Straight away Jahan went to see his master. 'Someone laid a trap.'

Wordlessly, Sinan squinted at the rope. 'Are you saying this was no accident?'

'I don't believe so,' Jahan said. 'Why did you come out of the shed, master?'

'I heard someone call for me,' said Sinan.

'Must be the same person who planned this. He knew the rope would break because he cut it. Poor San . . . Yusuf tried to save you. And now he is doomed!'

'Since you know so much already . . .' Sinan said, his eyes infinitely sad, 'you should know she is at home with my family.'

'Master, working with you is her only joy. You ought to bring her back.'

Sinan shook his head. 'I cannot have her here any more. It isn't safe.'

Jahan pursed his lips, trying to bite back words that he might regret afterwards. 'Are we not going to investigate who did this?'

'What can be done? I cannot interrogate every man on the site. If the workers suspect I don't trust them, they'll lose their will to work.'

Uneasiness came over Jahan. He, on the contrary, believed that Sinan should question everyone until the culprit was found. He said, in a voice he didn't know he was capable of, 'Michelangelo mourned his assistant like his son. Whereas you . . . don't even care for us. Glass, wood, marble, metal . . . Are we not like these in your eyes, mere instruments in your constructions?'

Into the ensuing silence Sinan said, slowly, 'That's not true.'

But Jahan was no longer listening.

Even with one apprentice missing the master finished Sokollu's mosque on time. Prayers were chanted; hennaed sheep and rams were sacrificed. Sokollu, glowing with pride and joy, gave *baksheesh* to the labourers and freed a hundred of his slaves. Shortly afterwards, at a meeting of the *diwan*, a man dressed up as a dervish asked to see the Grand Vizier. Like Sokollu, he, too, came from Bosnia. For a reason nobody could fathom, then or afterwards, Sokollu gave him permission to come in, to come close.

He was stabbed by the stranger, who was caught and killed before anyone could discover the reason behind the bloodshed. Sokollu, Sokolovic, the Grand Vizier and one of the last patrons of architecture, was gone. The female *djinn*, if there was one, had failed to warn him this time.

After Sokollu's assassination the Sultan would appoint a succession of viziers, one after the other, none coming close to their predecessor. All at once, it was as though a lid had been lifted and the boiling cauldron underneath exposed. The imperial treasury was empty, the coins not worth their value. The Janissaries were furious, the peasants upset, the *ulema* dissatisfied, Master Sinan too old and too frail, and his mute apprentice no longer by his side.

In his dream Jahan was in his village. He trudged through the path leading to their house, the sun hot on his neck. Finding the gate open, he strode in. There was no one in the courtyard. Then he noticed a faint movement under a tree – a tiger. Not far from it a peacock strutted, a deer grazed on a scrubby tuft of grass. He plodded with the utmost slowness so as not to draw attention to himself. A vain attempt since the cat had already noticed him. Its eyes flicked to his, uninterested. At each step he came across other animals – a rhino, a bear, a giraffe. In his absence his family had built a menagerie.

Their house had been enlarged with more rooms, additional floors. Desperately, he searched for his mother and sisters, trotting along the marble corridors. Upstairs, in a room that resembled the Sultan's palace, he stumbled upon his stepfather, sitting by himself. The man pointed towards the back garden – only there was no back garden any more. In its stead ran a rowdy river. Far ahead in a boat being dragged by the current was Sinan.

Jahan shouted. At his voice Sinan stood up and lost his balance, fluttering his arms like a bird about to take flight. The boat capsized, sending him into the water. Someone was shouting next to Jahan's ear, poking him on the shoulder.

'Wake up, Indian!'

Jahan did, his heart beating fast. Staring at him was the last person he expected to see: Mirka the bear-tamer. Jahan scowled at him, the memory of that night years ago returning as fast as a sword pulled out of its sheath.

Mirka took a step back, his hands raised in a gesture of defence. 'Something happened. We had to tell you.'

Only then did Jahan notice the boy standing beside him. It was Abe, Chota's new tamer – a young, slender, black African, no older than sixteen. A kind soul but so inexperienced Jahan wouldn't trust him with a rabbit, let alone an elephant.

'What happened?' asked Jahan.

Mirka averted his gaze. 'The beast's gone. He ran away.'

Kicking off the blanket, Jahan leaped to his feet and seized Abe by the arm. 'Where were you? Why didn't you keep an eye on him?'

The boy went limp, an empty sack in his hands. Mirka pulled Jahan away from him. 'It's not his fault. The beast went on a rampage, snapped his chains. Never seen him this mad.'

'Something must have irritated him,' Jahan said. 'What did you do to him?'

'Nothing,' Abe answered, his voice dripping with fear. 'He was possessed.'

Jahan changed into his *shalwar* and splashed water on his face. They tiptoed past the dormitories. Upon reaching the menagerie, they stopped at the entrance of the empty barn, looking for clues that weren't there.

'Which way did he go?' Jahan asked.

A glance passed between Mirka and Abe. 'He went out the main gate. The guards could not stop him.'

Jahan's heart sank. In a city so vast how could he find Chota before he got himself into trouble?

'I need a horse and a letter of permission,' Jahan said to Mirka.

'We'll ask the Chief White Eunuch. He'll be furious when he hears. But we've got to find the beast.'

In a little while Jahan was outside the palace gates, riding with no idea about which way to go. The streets sprawled in front of him, opening like fans. His horse – an aged, pale brown steed – was reluctant to gallop, though it soon gained pace. They passed through squares and bazaars.

Rounding a corner, Jahan came across a watchman with two Janissaries on his heels. The watchman lifted a cudgel, yelling, 'You, stop!'

Jahan did.

'Are you a *djinn*?'

'No, *effendi*, I'm a human like you,' Jahan said.

'Then get off your horse! What are you doing outside at this hour, defying the Sultan's rules? Come with us.'

'*Effendi*, I'm from the palace,' Jahan said, as he held on to the pommel of the saddle with one hand and gave him the letter of permission with the other. 'An animal escaped. I have been sent to fetch it.'

Reading the letter, the man mumbled, 'What sort of an animal?'

'An elephant,' Jahan said. When there followed no response, he added, 'The biggest creature on land.'

'How are you going to catch it?'

'I'm his tamer,' Jahan said, his voice breaking. 'He'll do as I say.'

Jahan wasn't sure about this but luckily they did not press him further. He felt their eyes on his back even after he had left the street.

It was only when he saw a *muezzin* on his way to a mosque for the morning prayer that he realized how long he had been out searching. He remembered the ancient graveyard overlooking the Golden Horn and the talk that had passed between him and Sangram a lifetime ago. *I heard a strange thing about these beasts. They say they choose where they'd like to die. This one seems like he has found his place.*

When Jahan reached the site he was looking for, a wisp of cloud was hiding the moon, and a tang of salt was in the wind. He caught sight of a large shadow ahead, perhaps a boulder. Jumping off his horse, he approached. 'Chota?'

The boulder shifted.

'Why did you come here?'

Chota lifted his head and let it drop immediately. His mouth, most of his teeth gone, opened and closed.

'Naughty boy! Don't do this again.' Jahan hugged his trunk, weeping.

Together they witnessed the break of day. The sky showed them its brightest hues, like a cloth merchant hawking his precious silks. Jahan watched Istanbul with its seagulls, steep slopes and cypress trees, seized by a dawning comprehension that their time in this city was coming to an end. Strangely, it didn't make him feel sad. That would come later, he knew. Sadness was always belated.

After much begging Jahan managed to convince Chota to follow him to the palace. They put him in his barn, chained him with stronger fetters, filled his buckets with new fodder and hoped his escape would soon be forgotten. Yet the mahout finally had to face what he had refused to see before. The elephant was dying. And the great beast wanted to be alone when the end arrived.

After the Master

There was a tree in Paradise unlike any on earth. Its branches were translucent, its roots absorbed milk instead of water, and its trunk glittered as if ice-bound, though when one got close to it, it was not cold, not cold at all. Every leaf of this tree was marked with the name of a human being. Once a year, during the month of Shaban, on the night between the fourteenth and the fifteenth day, all the angels gathered around it, forming a circle. In unison, they flapped their wings. Thus they raised a powerful wind that shook the branches. Gradually, some of the leaves fell off. Sometimes it took a leaf quite a while to drop down. At other times, the descent was as quick as the blink of an eye. The moment a leaf reached the ground the person whose name was written on it breathed his last. This was why the wise and the learned would never step on a dry leaf, lest it bore the soul of someone somewhere.

In 1588, a rainy day it was, Master Sinan's leaf touched the soil. He had worked until the final moments, his health and his mind always strong. It was only in the last weeks that he was bedridden. The three apprentices clustered around him, together with the head foremen who had worked with Sinan for so long. The women, clad in their veils, lined up by the door, and even though Jahan dared not glance in their direction, he knew one of them was Sancha, Sinan's loving concubine.

His voice merely a whisper, the Chief Royal Architect told them, in the faint light that seeped through the blinds, that he had written, signed and sealed his will. He said, 'You shall read it when I am gone.'

'You are not going anywhere, master. May God always keep you with us,' Nikola said, furtively wiping a tear.

The master lifted his hand, as if to wave away such pleasantries. 'There is something important you should know. The accidents . . . the delays . . . I have found out how they happened. It was in front of my eyes . . . all this time, I never saw.'

Suddenly the air in the room changed. Everyone held his breath, waiting to hear more. A tense anticipation gushed into the space where there had only been sorrow a while ago.

'Wait for forty days after my death,' Sinan said, stumbling over his words. 'Open my will and see which one of you I'd like to become my successor, God willing. You ought to carry on building. You ought to surpass what I've done.'

'Master . . . about the accidents, you were saying. Aren't you going to tell us who's behind them?' Jahan asked.

'Jahan . . . fiery spirit . . . you were always the most curious one,' Sinan said with difficulty. 'It all must have happened for a reason. One must think of the reason, not hate the person.'

Remembering Mihrimah's final words, Jahan felt an ache so powerful he couldn't talk. She, too, had mentioned that everything had a reason. He waited for an explanation, but it didn't come. In a little while the apprentices were ushered out, as they had tired the master enough. It was the last time Jahan saw him. The next night, earlier than usual, Sinan went to sleep. He did not wake up.

And this is how after almost fifty years as the Chief Royal Architect and 400 exquisite buildings, not counting his many shrines and fountains, Sinan departed this world. He had always left a flaw in his works to acknowledge he wasn't perfect or complete, as such qualities belonged solely to God. In much the same way he died, at the glorious but imperfect age of ninety-nine and a half.

On the seventh day following Sinan's death his family summoned a prayer meeting for his soul. Relatives, neighbours, pashas, artisans, students, labourers and passers-by . . . came from far and wide to attend the rite. There were so many guests that they spilled into the courtyard and from there on to the street, all the way down to the next neighbourhood. Even those who had never met him mourned his loss as if he were one of their own. Hard-boiled candies and sherbets were offered, meat and rice distributed to the rich and the poor. Olive branches were burned while the Qur'an was recited from beginning to end. *Yusuf Sinanettin bin Abdullah.* His name was uttered in unison, over and again, an incantation that opened closed hearts. Halfway through, Jahan caught the whiff of a fragrance he knew well: the blend of ambergris and jasmine with which his master perfumed his kaftans. He glanced around, wondering if he were here, watching them from an alcove or a niche, listening to what was said in his absence, smiling that smile of his.

Jahan reflected on Sancha, knowing she was somewhere in the house, behind these walls, her forehead pressed against the glazed window, her short hair adorned with a gauzy scarf. It pained him so much, the knowledge that she could no longer work with them, that he had to chase away his thoughts, like a flock of black crows.

After the prayer, the apprentices walked together for a while – Nikola, Davud and Jahan. The sky was murky and overcast, as though to reflect their mood. Dry leaves hovered in the breeze; seagulls plunged for a morsel. They kept running out of conversation. It wasn't only grief. There was something else, something that hadn't been there before. Jahan understood that throughout all these years Sinan had been the invisible thread holding them together. True, in the past, they had displayed petty jealousies, but Jahan had always attributed these to a shared love of the master and a wish to excel in his eyes. Now he saw that, in truth, they had been more different than alike, the three of them, three passing winds, each headed in a different direction. He wasn't the only one who sensed this. All at once, they were weighing their words like polite strangers.

As they made their way across a bazaar, they stopped to get some flatbread with *pekmez*.* None of them had eaten at the house of mourning and the walk had made them hungry. Jahan was haggling with a vendor when, right behind him, he heard a sneeze. Glancing sideways, it was not from a stranger, as he had expected. Instead, it was from Nikola, now half covering his face, as though in shame. When he pulled his hand away, there was a drop of blood on his palm.

'You all right?' Jahan asked.

Silently, Nikola nodded. His eyes were two shooting stars in the serene firmament of his face. Davud, engrossed in the turtles that a peasant was selling, seemed not to have noticed anything. Turtles were sought after these days, as their shells, when crushed into a powder and eaten with yoghurt soup, were said to cure many an illness.

Under the swooping boughs of a willow tree they tucked into their food, gossiped about the people who had attended the ceremony and those who had not shown up. But there was one question nobody dared to broach: who among them would replace their master? They would have to wait for the will to be opened. Until then, it was futile to speculate. How could they know what was cast in the runes, written in the stars, when even Takiyuddin had not? So they spoke about this and that, curt words that did not add up to anything, and soon afterwards each went his own way.

The next day, Jahan was summoned to the Chief White Eunuch's quarters and informed that he was to start teaching at the palace school – a reputable job that filled him with apprehension and pride in equal measure.

Later on, when he met his students, he found in their young faces innocence and curiosity, pretension and ignorance, dexterity and laziness. Which of these qualities would take precedence over the rest, he wondered; would schooling make any difference or had their paths already been drawn? Had his master been alive, he would say, 'Every man is given his own *kismet*, for God never repeats the same fate twice.'

Immersed in his own concerns, weeks passed by. It was only then that it occurred to him he had not heard from either Davud or Nikola. He sent both a message. When no answer came from either, he was

---

* A sweet syrup made from grapes.

338

worried, particularly for Nikola. Davud had a wife and children; Sancha still lived in Master Sinan's house; Jahan had Chota and a bed in the menagerie and now another one in the palace school. But Nikola had only his aged parents, both of whom had recently passed away. He realized how little he knew him. All these years they had toiled side by side, summer and winter, and yet they still remained a mystery to each other.

On Tuesday morning, Jahan decided to visit Nikola. Fog had settled into the city; the sun was a blurry halo behind billows of grey. At first glance, the settlement of Galata on the far side of the Golden Horn was the same as always. Houses – half stone, half wood – were arranged in rows like decayed teeth; there were churches with no bells; the scents of candles and incense wafted from the chapels; and a medley of people – Florentines, Venetians, Greeks, Armenians, Jews and Franciscan monks – milled about.

Jahan rode his horse at a trot, observing his surroundings. As he went deep into the back alleys, the crowd thinned. It became quiet. Too quiet. Something was not right. Closed shutters, bolted doors, packs of ravenous dogs, dead cats on the pavement and a foul smell that enveloped everything. Upon entering Nikola's street, he shuddered, as though a nippy breeze had passed through him. There were crosses painted on some of the houses, and prayers in Latin and Greek, unfinished and unintelligible, scribbled in haste.

Jumping off his horse, he went near another sign, only this one was on Nikola's door. He didn't know how long he stood there staring, unable to leave, unwilling to go inside. A neighbour, a man with a back so hunched that he seemed bent, approached. 'What do you want?'

'My friend lives here. Kiriz Nikola – you know him?'

'I know everyone. Don't go in there. Stay away.'

'What is it?'

'The curse, it's back.'

'You mean . . .' Jahan halted, detecting the man's contempt for his ignorance. It was the plague again. 'How have we not heard about it?'

'Dolt! You only hear what you are allowed to hear,' the man said before he strode away. He didn't go too far. From the threshold of the house across the street he kept watch, his eyes like narrow slits.

Jahan took his sash off and wrapped it around his mouth and nose. He pushed Nikola's door. Had it been locked, he would have given up. But it was ajar, propped open with a wedge to make sure it wouldn't close. Whoever had placed this here intended to return and knew there was no one inside to open the door.

Upon entering the house, a heavy stench hit him like an unexpected blow. He found himself in a corridor, narrow, musty and dim. He had to wait for his eyes to adjust to the gloom. The first room was empty. In the next one, by the pale light of a candle, a man was lying on a mat. His dark hair lacked lustre, his skin was drained of colour, his high domed forehead was covered in sweat – it was and it was not Nikola, this man with a few days' stubble on his always carefully shaved face. Beside him was a small wooden figure of a man with a chestnut beard and long hair.

There were two clay bowls by his side: one with water, one with vinegar. His clothes were damp with sweat, his lips chapped. Jahan put his hand on his forehead. It was burning. At Jahan's touch he flinched. With a great effort he turned his head towards him, unseeing.

'It's me, Jahan.'

Nikola's breath came out in sputters, like the crackle of a smouldering log before it burns out. 'Water,' Nikola rasped.

He drank greedily. Through his open shirt Jahan saw spots on his chest, a purple that verged on black, and a nasty swelling in his armpit. He had a pressing urge to run away from this place of suffering, but, while his mind whispered cowardice, his body stayed anchored. Soon there was a rattle at the door. Two nuns appeared. Long dark cloaks, white muslin masks on their mouths.

'Who are you?' the elder one demanded. 'What do you want?'

'I'm his friend,' Jahan said. 'We worked together under the late Chief Royal Architect.'

A startled silence hung in the space between them. 'I'm sorry if I spoke harshly,' she said. 'I took you for a thief.'

Jahan felt a rush of dismay, dreading that this woman with eyes old and calm as stones had seen through him. Unaware of his thoughts, the nun went on. 'Nobody comes to these houses. Only robbers.'

'Robbers?'

'Yes, they come to steal from –'

She did not finish her sentence. Instead she moved towards Nikola. She made him drink out of the flask she had brought and wiped his forehead with a flannel dipped in vinegar, touching him without any sign of the repugnance that Jahan had felt. Meanwhile the other nun was busy wiping excrement off the sheets.

Jahan wanted to ask them if they were not afraid of death but he kept his thoughts to himself. He whispered, 'Are there many others?'

'No, but there will be.'

Nikola started to cough. Blood spilled from his mouth and nose. The elder nun, seeing Jahan's horror, said, 'You should go. There is nothing you can do here.'

Saddened but somehow relieved to hear this, Jahan asked, 'How can I help?'

'Pray,' was all she said.

Jahan inched towards the door, then stopped. 'That figure over there, who is he?'

'Saint Thomas,' said the nun with a tired smile. 'The patron saint of carpenters, builders, architects and construction workers. He was also known as a doubter. He doubted everything, could not help it. But God loved him just the same.'

Two days later Jahan heard that Nikola had died. In a world where everything was in flux, he, the most stable and reliable soul he had known after Master Sinan, was gone. Then followed the others. Hundreds of them. From Galata the disease travelled to Uskudar, leaped to Istanbul and, as if thrust by an angry hand, bounced back to Galata. Once again, mobs took to the streets, looking for someone to blame. Nor was the palace immune. The Chinese twins who took care of the apes went the way of all flesh. The monkeys turned aggressive, unhappy in the royal cages where their forefathers had once been such privileged guests. Taras the Siberian hid in his shed, ashamed to be alive at his age.

Then Sangram died. This kind-hearted, loyal servant of the seraglio, who had always wished to return to Hindustan some day, breathed his last miles away from his homeland. The next victim was Simeon the bookseller of Pera. His wife, duped by some tinkers and vendors, agreed to sell his books for a handful of aspers. Piled on rickety carts, those precious books from all the world over left Pera and travelled to their new destinations. Many got lost on the way. Simeon, who had always desired to be in charge of a magnificent library, had not even been able to bequeath his own collections to someone who would appreciate them.

Jahan, who learned about all this much later, waited in suspense, wondering who would be the next. But for a reason he could not comprehend the disease spared him and continued on its pilgrimage south like a predatory bird, casting a dark shadow over the villages and towns it passed through. In the Christian cemetery, not far from the Virgin of the Spring, where Emperor Justinian's church was no more but the holy spring remained, Nikola's headstone read:

Architect Nikola ascended to the skies like the towers he built
May his soul rest in the vault of heaven
And Saint Thomas be his companion

Upon returning to the palace, Jahan found Chota alone. When he saw his old tamer, the animal trumpeted and stomped his feet. Jahan patted his trunk, offered him the pears and nuts he had brought along. In the past Chota would have smelled them long before Jahan arrived. But lately he had lost his ability to smell, along with his strength.

Perching on a barrel, Jahan told him about Nikola's funeral. The animal listened to his every word, squinting in his usual way. When Jahan wept, Chota's trunk slid around his chest, hugging him. Once again, Jahan had the impression that the white elephant understood everything he said.

In a little while they heard footsteps. Two shadows appeared at the door. Sangram's lad, who had taken over, so resembled his father in looks and demeanour that they all called him Sangram, as though the same soul had been resurrected and death was merely a game. Abe, Chota's keeper, was with him.

'Jahan is here!' said Sangram the son, happy to see the man he had known and loved as an uncle.

'I'm here but where was *he*?' Jahan rasped, pointing at Abe. 'Why do you leave the elephant unattended? He's got a broken toenail. Do you have any idea how that must hurt? It needs to be trimmed and washed. It's a mess around this place. When was the last time you cleaned?'

Mumbling his regrets, Abe grabbed a brush and started to sweep every which way. In the sunrays falling through the wooden cracks, dust was swirling. Sangram the son approached with a troubled stare. 'You heard the news?'

'What news?'

'Davud. He has been raised.'

'What did you say?'

'Everyone's talking about it. Your friend is the new Chief Royal Architect.'

'Our Davud?' Jahan stammered.

'Well, not *ours* any more. He is way up there!' said Sangram the son, pointing at the ceiling, where a spider had woven a cobweb and a horsefly, long dead, dangled.

'You mean they . . . opened the will?'

Sangram the son looked at Jahan with unmistakable pity. 'They did. Your master wished him to be his successor, it appears.'

'Well . . . that's good,' stuttered Jahan, feeling dizzy, as though a precipice had opened up under his feet and he was falling, falling fast.

A few days later Sinan's wife Kayra, according to the custom, freed several of the household slaves. The first one to be granted *berat** was Sancha.

Jahan had always suspected that Kayra had mixed feelings about this unusual concubine under her roof – a woman who had shared things with her husband that she never could. If she had been averse to Sancha's dressing up as a man and working on construction sites, she must have kept her feelings to herself. Even so, Jahan had little doubt that Kayra was aware of Sancha's love for the master and didn't like it at all. Between them the two women had dug a silent abyss that no one, not even Sinan, could bridge. And now that he was gone, Sancha's was the last face Kayra wished to see. Still, she did not ill-treat her slave. Buying satins, taffetas and perfumes, she gave Sancha her blessing before she let her go. This is how, after decades as a captive in Istanbul, Sancha de Herrera, the daughter of a renowned Spanish physician, was freed.

She sent Jahan a letter. Her words burst with excitement and apprehension. Timidly, she asked if he would help her with the arrangements for leaving, because she did not know the first thing about what to do, where to begin. She said she would have loved to get Davud's help as well, but that he was unaware of the truth. At times, she wasn't even sure who she was any longer: Yusuf the builder or Nergiz the concubine. Jahan answered without delay:

Esteemed Sancha,

Your letter has brought me happiness and despair. Happiness because finally you are free to go. Despair because you are leaving. I shall come and help you next Thursday. Do not worry about being ready. You have been ready for this for a long, long time.

On the chosen day, Jahan visited her in Sinan's house. For the first time since they had met, he saw her wearing a dress – an emerald-green gown with a cone-shaped skirt that brought out the colour

---

* Document given to a freed slave.

of her eyes. On her still-short hair was a matching headdress of the sort ladies wore in the land of Frangistan.

'Don't stare at me like that,' she said, blushing under his gaze. 'I feel ugly.'

'How can you say that?' protested Jahan.

'It's the truth. I'm too old for pretty clothes.'

Watching her cheeks turn a darker shade of pink, Jahan said quickly, teasingly: 'Imagine, if all these years the masons had known there was a beauty among them, they'd have stopped work to write you poems. We couldn't have built a thing.'

She chuckled and cast her eyes down; her fingers ran along the pleats of her gown, under which was a farthingale of whalebone. 'It's so tight I can hardly breathe. How do women manage this?'

'You'll get used to it in no time.'

'Nay, it's going to take me years. I'll be dead by then,' she said, smiling – a smile that instantly disappeared. 'I wish he had seen me like this.'

Above them the sky was blue and bright, as still as a looking glass. Outside, a cart rattled by. Peeping out of the window, Jahan saw it was loaded with cages of falcons, their eyes hooded. Distracted by the birds, he had not realized that Sancha, beside him, was weeping. A lad who was a girl, a mute with the gift of speech, a concubine yet an architect, she had lived a life of lies and layers – no less than Jahan.

'What is upsetting you?' Jahan asked. 'I thought you'd be overjoyed now that you're free.'

'I'm glad,' she said, unconvincingly. 'Only . . . His grave is here. Everything we did together. He has more marks on this city than any Sultan.'

'Master's gone,' Jahan said. 'You are not leaving him.'

She tried, for a brief moment, not to talk about him, struggling with herself, losing. 'Do you think he loved me?'

Jahan hesitated. 'I believe he did. Otherwise why would he have allowed you to join us? He'd have been in trouble if anyone found out.'

'He put himself in danger for me,' Sancha said with a speck of pride. 'But he never loved me. Not the way I loved him.'

This time Jahan did not respond. Nor did Sancha seem to be waiting for an answer. She said, 'I heard there is a Venetian ship setting sail in two weeks' time.'

Jahan nodded. Several times in the past days, he had observed its topmast looming over the roofs and trees. 'I'll make arrangements.'

'I'd be grateful,' Sancha said. Trepidation flickered in her eyes. 'Come with me. There is nothing that binds you here.'

Jahan was surprised to hear her speak like this. All the same, he decided to take it lightly. 'Ah, we'd build mansions for Spanish grandees.'

She held his hand, her touch soft and cold. 'We might find a patron. I have made inquiries. We could take care of each other.'

Watching her familiar gestures, Jahan felt a stir in his heart. He saw what she saw. United by the memory of the master, their hearts numb to all but their craft, they could work together. Love was not needed. Better without it. Love only brought pain.

'If I'd been younger, we could have had children,' she said slowly, as though weighing each word.

Despite himself, Jahan beamed. 'Girls with your eyes and your bravery.'

'Boys with your curiosity and kindness.'

'What about Chota?' Jahan murmured.

'Chota is old. He has been happy in the palace. He'll be fine. But you and I need to go on building –'

'*Wisdom does not rain from the sky, it springs from the earth, from hard work*,' said Jahan, remembering the words of their master.

'The dome,' Sancha went on. 'We should raise domes that remind people there is a God and that He is not a God of revenge and hell but of mercy and love.'

Jahan rested his head in his hands and closed his eyes.

'I'm frightened,' she said. 'It's been such a long time since I was torn from my father's land that I'm a stranger to their ways now.'

'You'll be fine,' Jahan said, trying to reassure her.

'I will, if you come with me. What do you say?'

In that moment Jahan understood that life was the sum of the choices one did not make; the paths yearned for but not taken. He had never felt as much compassion for Sancha as he did now – the moment when he understood that he would refuse her. She saw it in his face, his

resistance. A flash of hurt flickered in her eyes, but she did not cry. Her
tears she kept for the master, her one and only love.

'Pray remember me,' Jahan said.

Only the slightest break in her voice betrayed her disappointment
when she said, 'I shan't ever forget.'

About a week later, the Venetian ship, a three-masted carrack with a
rounded stern, was ready to return home. The Venetian traders had
been losing their privileges to French, Dutch and English merchants.
The Captain wore his unhappiness like the jacket that wrapped him
tight. Even so there was enough of a bustle to distract him from his
worries. The toing and froing of sailors loading the barrels and sellers
hawking their merchandise. A small gathering of passengers waited off
to one side: Jesuit priests, Catholic nuns, travellers, a British well-born
fanned by his servants. Other than these the rest were rough seamen.

Shielding his eyes from the sun, Jahan looked around, unable to see
Sancha anywhere. It occurred to him that she might have changed her
mind. Perhaps when she woke she realized that the land of her childhood was far and elusive, a dream impossible to reclaim. But then, as
he zigzagged his way through the barrels waiting to be loaded, he saw
her before him, her shadow extending away from her, as though it and
only it had decided to stay.

To his surprise, she had gone back to her apprenticeship clothes and
stood beside him as a man. 'I like it better like this.'

Jahan looked over her shoulder for porters. There were none.
'Where are your things?'

She pointed at a rucksack on the ground.

'Your robes? Kayra's gifts?'

'Don't tell her. I gave them to the poor.' She opened her bag, showed
him the carved box Sinan had made for her. Next to it were a dozen
scrolls and a necklace of some worth. 'I'm taking these. Master bequeathed them to me.'

They walked silently until they reached the ramp that connected
the ship to the land.

'I did not get a chance to wish Davud farewell,' she said. 'Give him

348

my regards and good wishes. I can't believe he is the Chief Royal Architect now.'

'I shall tell him,' Jahan said pensively. The truth was he had not been able to congratulate Davud himself. He hadn't felt like it. He inhaled a lungful of air. 'Make sure nobody finds out you're a woman. If you sense any —'

'I can take care of myself.' She held herself ramrod straight.

'I know you can.'

She lifted her eyes to his. 'I . . . had a nasty dream last night. You were trapped. You called for me but I couldn't find you. Be careful, will you?'

Someone shouted an order from the stern of the ship. Jahan felt his throat closing. Everything was changing, flowing, like sand between his fingers. Mihrimah had crossed the great divide and he couldn't wait to join her when his time came; the master and Nikola were gone; he and Davud rarely saw each other; Chota was not long for this world; and now Sancha was leaving. He had been wrong to pity Nikola for being alone. He was just as lonely. For a moment the desire to accompany Sancha, the one person who cared for him, was almost too strong to endure. He would have gone had it not been for the elephant.

That afternoon, under shrieking seagulls and a wash of sunlight as gauzy as muslin, he watched the prow of the ship slice with ease through the water, at every heartbeat taking the mute apprentice, and her story, further and further away.

Unable to put his thoughts on paper, Jahan found a scribe to help him write to Davud. After listening, the man set off and scribbled without a pause, save to dip the pen into the ink. When he was done, Jahan was holding a letter dripping with salutations and felicitations. It cost six aspers.

Jahan wasn't expecting an immediate answer – not from a man who had risen so high. Yet Davud wrote back: the scroll was sealed in red, the handwriting – by a scribe of an upper rank – elegant. Everything had happened swiftly, he explained. *Our gracious Sultan, may he live a hundred years, upon opening the will of Master Sinan and learning about his last wish, bestowed a distinguished honour on me, his humble subject. He threw the precious robe of our master on my insignificant shoulders.* How could he have rejected it, Davud asked, as though he needed affirmation. He told Jahan to come to see him. They would share memories and talk about forthcoming works, just like in the old days.

Much as Jahan wanted to pay him a visit, he could not. His heart was not pure. It worried him that Davud would see it in his eyes, the jealousy oozing out of his pores. Until recently they had been equals. Now his friend was a man favoured by fate. Jahan understood that between people with a similar standing the hardest thing to accept was when one moved up and the other did not. In those rare moments when he managed not to feel envy, he was ridden with guilt. Instead of being happy for Davud and praying for his success, he begrudged him his good fortune. If Sinan were alive, Jahan thought, he would have been ashamed of him.

So he waited. Days passed by. Whether he wanted to or not, he heard constantly about Davud – how, in a ceremony in his honour, he had been given a golden chisel, pouches of coins and Master Sinan's seal – a carved jade ring. Snippets of information rained down from everywhere – how he was seen in a kaftan so precious that no one could wear it unless allowed by the Sultan; how he was fond of Circassian concubines and filled his harem with them; how he had married second and third wives, each as winsome as a fairy; how he had peacocks strutting in his courtyard and a falcon brought from Samarkand. Half of these tales Jahan suspected were false. The remaining half were enough to fill his heart with bitterness.

Jahan kept teaching at the palace school, finding consolation in the innocence of his students. At night, alone in his bed, he designed buildings that would never be built. One of these was a garden where wild animals roamed free and people walked through a maze of tunnels with large panes of glass that enabled them to watch the beasts without putting themselves in danger. Chota lost three more toenails. A mysterious disease, Jahan suspected, and stopped accusing Abe of neglect. The elephant had got old. So had Jahan, though he was unwilling to accept this.

A month later he received a message informing him that a building was to be raised on the fourth hill – a new mosque – and he had been appointed as head foreman. He would be paid a generous sum. It showed how much Davud trusted him. While he was burning with envy, his friend had decided to honour him. Jahan could not avoid seeing him any longer. Composing a letter – writing it himself this time – he thanked him for the privilege and asked permission to visit. Davud sent a reply, inviting him to his new house in Eyup, by the Golden Horn.

It wasn't a hard place to find; the locals raved about it. A mansion with a sweet-smelling garden that extended as far as the eye could see. There was no need to knock on the door; he was expected. A manservant welcomed Jahan at the iron gates; ushered him across a pathway into the house and then into a wide, bright room facing south. Left on his own, Jahan glanced around. There wasn't much furniture – yet what little there was, was exquisite. A cabinet inlaid with mother-of-pearl and matching low tables; a sofa topped with embroidered cushions; gilded sconces on the walls; a silken Persian carpet so pretty one dared not tread on it; and, in the middle, a brass brazier, now asleep. Somewhere a chime, caught in a breeze, tinkled dreamily. There was an intense silence throughout the house. Neither the voices of women from the harem side nor the clatter of a coach from the street. Even the cries of the seagulls did not seem to reach this roof. He wondered how Davud's wife had responded to the change – and to the new wives. It was one of those things in life he would marvel about but never discover. In a while, another manservant arrived announcing that his master was ready to see him. Jahan followed him upstairs, one hand on the balustrade as if to draw strength from it.

Davud had gained weight. Clad in an azure kaftan and a high turban, his beard trimmed round and short, he looked different. Sitting behind a walnut table, he was holding a plume, having just signed a document. Four apprentices attended him: two on each side, their hands clasped, their heads bowed. They were similarly attired.

When he saw Jahan enter the room on the heels of his servant, Davud stood up and broke into a smile. 'At last!'

An uneasy instant passed between them as Jahan puzzled over how to greet this man who until yesterday had been his friend but who was now his master. He was about to bow when Davud, having walked towards him, laid a hand on his shoulder.

'Outside this room I might be senior. Inside, we are friends.'

Relieved though Jahan was to hear this, his voice, when it came out, sounded hoarse, guilt-ridden. He offered his well-wishes, apologizing for not having visited earlier.

'You are here now,' Davud said.

Jahan told him Yusuf had left the city, though he provided no details. If Davud suspected the truth about Sancha, he didn't give anything away. Instead he murmured, 'Only two left.'

'What do you mean?'

'Out of four, it's just you and me now. We are Sinan's heirs. We ought to support each other.'

A black servant walked in carrying a tray laden with drinks that he placed, quiet as a whisper, on a low table. The apprentices on the other side of the room stood utterly still. Like a row of saplings, Jahan thought, their roots boring holes in the carpet down to the ground floor.

The rose sherbet was heavenly, served with cloves and chilled with crushed ice from the mountains of Bursa – a privilege exclusive to the wealthy. Next to it was a plate piled with three different kinds of baklava and a bowl of thick cream.

No sooner had they downed their drinks than Davud said, 'There's so much work, I can barely keep up. My wives complain. You are the Chief Royal Architect, yet you don't even repair the fence around the house, they say.'

Jahan smiled.

'I need an honest man like you by my side. Be my right hand. We'll do everything together. You'll be my head foreman.'

Beholden, Jahan expressed his gratitude. Simultaneously, he thought about his students at the palace school, realizing unhappily that he would have to stop teaching.

His confusion must have been obvious, for Davud asked, 'What is it? Do you find it difficult to receive orders from me?'

'That's not true,' Jahan said, although they both knew it was.

'In that case there's nothing to discuss.' Davud clapped his hands. 'Now, eat!'

While they ate their baklava, Davud told Jahan about the changes he wished to introduce. With a series of rebellions and skirmishes racking the Anatolian plains, it was harder than ever to bring construction materials from the interior. Massive Friday mosques were not commissioned any more. There was not enough in the coffers. Those days were over. Without the spoils of holy war no sovereign could spend so much on constructions. For architecture in the capital to continue to prosper, wars had to be won near and far.

'You see, our master died at the right time,' Davud said wistfully. 'He'd have been heartbroken if he were alive today.'

Outside the window, the sun was setting, painting the room a silken orange. They prattled on about which craftsmen they preferred to work with and which ones they would rather shun, banter that swirled with no immediacy and no weight, like wispy balls of dust.

Soon a courier brought a letter – important, by the look of it. Davud sat at his desk, his apprentices on either side. Seeing how busy he was, Jahan rose to his feet.

'Stay,' Davud said into his inkpot. 'Let's sup together.'

'I wouldn't want to take your time.'

'I insist,' said Davud.

Having nothing to do, Jahan stood by the window for a while, watching a fishing boat glide with the pull of the current, further and further away from the line where the sea lapped the shore. Slowly, he walked towards the bookshelves in the corner. Inhaling the fragrance of ink, vellum, paper and time, he ran his fingers along the spines. He saw *On War against the Turk* by this strange monk named Luther and *The*

Book of the Governor that an Englishman called Elyot had dedicated to his king. He found treatises from the library of King Matthias of Hungary. And there, among the leather tomes, some thick, some thin, was Dante's *La Divina Commedia*. The gift he had received from Simeon the bookseller and, after reading it again and again, he had given to his master. His hands trembling, he pulled it out, feeling the familiar heft of it, and he glanced through the pages. There was no doubt: it was his copy. Clearly, Davud had taken possession of Master Sinan's collection.

A servant approached, lighting the candle in the sconce nearby. Jahan's shadow grew on the wall, tall and restless. He spotted *De Architectura* by Vitruvius, which he removed and held for a while, the book that had travelled from Buda to Istanbul. It was while he was returning it that he caught sight of a scroll at the back of the shelf, half squashed. He opened it, recognizing instantly the design of the Selimiye Mosque. He admired its magnificence now more than before. Jahan noticed marks made by another pen in lighter ink – as if someone had worked on it after the design had been completed, changing various sections of the construction. It must have been the master, he deduced. Probably Sinan had been studying why and where things had gone wrong. Jahan's eyes searched the border of the paper for a date. *18 April 1573*. He tried to remember what they were doing on that day. Nothing came to mind. The murmurs in the background escalated as Davud, having finished his work, rained instructions on the servants about to prepare the dinner. Quickly, Jahan put the scroll back and joined him.

They were served cold yoghurt soup, followed by rice with lamb, capons stewed in sorrel sauce, pheasants cooked in beef broth, *borek* with mutton and a huge, oval platter of steaming meat, which he could not identify.

'This one was sent from heaven,' Davud said, although it was improper for a host to boast about food.

'What is it?' Jahan said, although it was improper for a guest to ask about food.

'Venison! Hunted yesterday.'

Jahan's stomach clenched as he recalled the stag he had seen in the forest while he was waiting for Sultan Suleiman. So as not to be rude he forced himself to take a bite.

'It melts like sugar. I have observed that the quicker the animal dies the better the taste. Fear spoils the flavour.'

Jahan chewed, the deer a lump in his mouth. 'I didn't know you went hunting.'

Davud, having noticed Jahan's discomfort, moved the bowl away. 'Not I. I don't have the time for that. Don't think I have the heart either.'

As they were parting, Davud saw his guest to the door. Up this close, Jahan caught a scent on his friend's clothes – raw and leafy and strangely familiar – one that dissolved so fast in the night breeze that he didn't have time to remember when or where he might have smelled it before.

Whenever Jahan could get away from his remaining classes at the palace school and his new construction work with Davud, he ran to Chota's side. Taking his designs with him, he drew in the barn, sitting on a pile of hay that the other tamers called, teasingly, 'the throne.' Chota watched him, rapt, though Jahan wasn't sure whether he *saw* him. His eyesight, which had never been good, had deteriorated.

Poor Abe was doing his best, and not because he feared Jahan's wrath but because he liked the white elephant. Despite his efforts, Chota had lost another tooth, one of his last three. He could neither chew nor bite any more. Jahan did not need to put him on those mammoth scales used by the sailors in the port of Karakoy to know that he had lost a lot of weight. Of late, Chota drowsed on his feet in fits and starts and lost his balance, jerking to and fro. While drinking water, taking a bath or plodding around the garden, his movements would slow down, his head would droop and before he knew it he would be fast asleep, roaming the kingdom of dreams. It pained Jahan to see the elephant helpless and confused. A few times he caught him staring longingly at the linden tree, which he so loved to nibble.

They mashed his food – leaves, nuts and apples – into pulp, mixed it with water and poured this concoction, with the help of a funnel, into his mouth. Though he spilled most, some of it reached his stomach. Chota did not attempt another escape, becoming more and more sedentary, refusing even the briefest excursion to the pond. Abe shovelled up his excrement, cleaned his trough, fed him milk and sherbets, but everyone was aware that the creature was melting like a lump of wax over a fire.

Back in the dormitory, Jahan found it hard to sleep. He tossed and turned, fretting over how Chota was doing. It was on one such sleepless night, surrounded as he was by the customary silence, that he began to think about his master's will. He could not believe that Sinan had not mentioned him or Chota in his last wishes. The master he had known and loved would have bequeathed something, however little or large, to the two beings who had worked with him so closely for so long. Sancha had taken away with her a box, a necklace and several designs, saying the master had given them to her. Wouldn't Sinan have left something to them too? Perhaps Sinan had, but no one had cared to tell Jahan about a matter this trivial. If the master had a final gift for Chota, Jahan wanted to learn about it without delay, for he had no doubt that the elephant was dying. Thus motivated, he went to see the Chief White Eunuch.

'I wanted to ask you about Master Sinan's will. Have you seen it?'

The man squinted his blue eyes lined with kohl. 'Why do you ask me?'

'Because you are the highest palace official I can talk to.'

'Well . . . I have seen the will.'

Jahan's face brightened. 'Was there any mention of Chota?'

'Now that you ask, I remember him leaving a pretty mantle for the elephant. I'll make sure the beast receives it.'

'Much obliged,' said Jahan, frowning at his feet as if they annoyed him. 'How about . . . me?'

'For you, your master left his books.'

'Then why didn't Master Davud tell me? I have seen Master Sinan's books in his house. Do you mean those books are mine?'

'Those must be different ones . . .' said Kamil Agha impatiently. 'Too many questions you ask, Indian. I'll see to it that they send you the mantle and whichever books are yours. Now go back. And stop spending so much time with that beast. You are an architect. Behave like one.'

Jahan nodded but something was not quite right.

The following afternoon, three weeks after Chota had escaped, Jahan came back from class to find Abe sitting on a rock, crying.

'The beast,' Abe said, his sentence hanging in the air.

Quietly, Jahan entered the barn. Chota was alone, inhaling with difficulty. Jahan rubbed his trunk with his palms, offered him water, which he declined. The elephant fixed his reddish-brown eyes on his tamer, and in those eyes Jahan saw traces of every road, long or short, that they had walked together. He remembered how Chota had disembarked from the ship fifty years ago, covered in dirt and faeces, on the brink of collapse.

'I'm sorry,' Jahan said, tears running down his face. 'I should have taken better care of you.'

He did not leave Chota's side that day and fell asleep beside him that night, listening to the animal's steady breathing. If he had any dreams, he did not recall them. In the morning he opened his eyes to the clack of a woodpecker on a nearby tree, like a message in cipher. Inside the barn it was silent. Jahan did not want to look at Chota, yet he did. The elephant was lying down, unmoving. His body was bloated, as if while he was asleep the wind had rushed through his trunk and blown him up.

'He should have a proper funeral,' Jahan said to no one in particular, after he had washed, embalmed and perfumed the animal, which tired him so much he had to rest for a while. Remembering how Nurbanu had preserved the body of Sultan Selim until his son reached the throne, he then found blocks of ice. Not that it helped. The elephant was too big, the ice too little. Still, he was adamant that the body should be preserved until a ceremony, befitting Chota's grandeur, was arranged.

Within the hour his words had reached the ears of Carnation Kamil Agha. The man turned up in the menagerie; overseer of everything he was, including grief and madness.

'I hear now you have been asking for a rite.'

'Chota was sent by a great Shah to a great Sultan,' said Jahan.

'He's a beast,' said the Chief White Eunuch.

'A regal beast.'

More astonished than annoyed at this breach of manners, the Chief White Eunuch said, 'Enough folly. Make your farewells. The French emissary is going to dissect him.'

Jahan let out a gasp of pain, as if punched in the gut. 'You mean cut him open? I'll never let him do that!'

'It's the Sultan's wish.'

'But does the –' Jahan could not finish. *Does the Sultan know this is no ordinary animal?* The question echoed in the deepest corners of his soul. He wished Master Sinan were alive; he would know what to do, how to speak.

That same day Chota's body was bedecked with wreaths and garlands of flowers and loaded on to a carriage pulled by five oxen. In this
state the elephant was paraded, one last time, through the streets of
Istanbul. People craned their necks, awed and delighted. They clapped,
cheered and shouted. Leaving their tasks they followed the cart, often
less out of pity than curiosity. Jahan rode ahead, staring straight into
the horizon, over and beyond the sea of spectators, not wishing to see
anyone. Miserable, mournful, he reached the residence and there he
delivered the elephant's body to the ambassador like a sacrificial lamb
to the butcher.

The next day Jahan was summoned to the chamber of the Chief White Eunuch. His first thought was the man was going to reprimand him for staying in the menagerie the night Chota died. In the end, Jahan had defied his orders and refused to give the carcass to the French emissary, not that it had changed anything. The cutting had gone ahead. But it was enough to infuriate the Chief White Eunuch for years to come. Strangely, Jahan didn't care. A boldness that he had never known before had taken hold of him.

Upon being ushered into his room, Jahan bowed, slowly and reluctantly, and waited, his eyes fixed on the marble floor.

'Lift your head!' The order cracked like a whip.

Jahan complied. And for the first time since he had arrived at the palace and was given an unforgettable slap by him, he stared straight into the Chief White Eunuch's eyes – the colour of dark blue thistle.

'I've been watching you all these years. You have ascended fast. No other tamer has come close to what you have achieved. But that's not the reason why I am fond of you. Shall I tell you why?'

Jahan remained silent. He'd had no idea Kamil Agha was fond of him.

'Every *devshirme* is made of melted steel. Remoulded. You are one of us, Indian. Strange thing is, no one converted you. You did it on your own. But you know where you made a mistake?'

'I cannot say, *effendi*.'

'Love!' The corners of his mouth turned down as if the word had left a sour taste on his tongue. 'There are plenty of apprentices in our city. Hundreds of them. They respect their masters. You *loved* yours. Same with the elephant. Your job was to look after him; make sure his belly was full. You *loved* the beast.'

'It's not something I do consciously. It just happens.'

'Don't love anyone too much.' The eunuch's lips parted in a sigh. 'Since your master has gone, I shall take over as your guardian. Be faithful to me, and you won't suffer defeat.'

'I am not in a war, *effendi*.'

The man pretended not to hear this. 'I shall help you. There's a house where they wash off despair. They call it the *hamam* of sorrows.'

Jahan blinked, remembering the name from a moment in time so distant it might have been from a life not his own.

'We go there and we forget. Everything. Do you understand?'

Perplexed as he was, Jahan said he did.

'Good, get ready. I'll take you there tonight.'

After dark, a servant came to collect Jahan. A hulking, broad-shouldered man, deaf and mute like the rest. Jahan followed his torch across the courtyard, through a half-concealed back door. Nobody gave them so much as a glance. Had it not been for the flies circling their heads, charging blindly into their nostrils and mouths, and the sound their feet made as they scrunched along the gravel paths, he could have believed they were invisible.

Above the city the sky was a mantle of velvet – a black so intense as to be blue. A carriage, pulled by four stallions, was waiting. Even in the dim light Jahan could admire its gilded buckles, carved ivory panels, curtained windows that no eye could pierce. Inside sat the Chief White Eunuch, clad in a cape trimmed with ermine. As soon as Jahan settled in, the eunuch rapped the ceiling with his cane. Off they cantered.

The carriage travelled with such speed and noise that Jahan was certain there were people watching them – bakers on their way to knead bread, mothers nursing sleepless babies, thieves running off with their haul, drunks downing their next bottle or the pious up and about for an extra prayer. How many were aware of the Chief White Eunuch's nocturnal excursions and kept quiet about them? There were secrets a whole town might know about that still remained secrets.

They got out near a back alley so narrow and dusky that Jahan hesitated to enter it. The coachman led the way with a lamp barely emitting any light. Dilapidated wooden houses, hunched up like old crones, loomed to their left and right. After what felt like eternity, they reached an ornamented gate. The Chief White Eunuch knocked three times with his ring, waited, then tapped twice with bare hands.

'Hyacinth?' said a voice from behind the door.

'Hyacinth!' repeated the Chief White Eunuch.

For one stunned moment Jahan couldn't breathe. He had an awful suspicion the eunuch knew the nickname his mother had given him as a boy. Unnerved, he had no desire to go inside with this man, but the gate had already opened.

They were greeted inside by the shortest woman Jahan had ever come across. Barring her bosom, everything about her was tiny – her hands, her arms, her feet.

She laughed. 'Never seen a dwarf? Or never seen a woman?'

Jahan blushed, which made her laugh louder. She turned to Kamil Agha, asking, 'Where did you find him?'

'Name is Jahan. He's an architect. Talented but soft.'

'Well, we've got the cure,' she said. 'Welcome to our *hamam* of sorrows!'

The Chief White Eunuch, familiar with his surroundings, plumped himself down on to large, bright cushions and ordered Jahan to follow suit. Before long, five concubines appeared, carrying musical instruments – lute, tambourines, lyre and a reed pipe. His gaze slid from one face to the next, until it came to rest on the last woman. With her wide forehead, chiselled nose, sharp chin and large hazel eyes, she bore a striking resemblance to Mihrimah. Jahan felt dizzy. As if she was aware of the effect she was having on him, she tilted her head in his direction and gave a smile, full of mischief. They began to sing a cheerful melody.

On a silver tray the guests were served balls of paste, the colour of saffron, the size of a walnut. Choosing one, Jahan held it carefully between his fingers. Kamil Agha took three, which he swallowed one after another, and then reclined, eyes closed. Emboldened, Jahan popped his into his mouth. It tasted funny. Pungent and sweet at first, then spicy, like crushed seeds and wild marjoram. Next came the wine – carafes of red. He drank with caution at first, not trusting anyone.

The dwarf lady sat beside him. 'I heard you lost a loved one.'

'My elephant.'

Jahan waited for the chuckle that didn't follow. Instead she said, after she had filled his cup, 'I know how it feels. I had a dog myself. When he died I was devastated. Nobody understood. *It's just a hound, Zainab.* What do they know! Better to make friends with animals than humans.'

'You're right,' Jahan said as he took another sip. 'Animals are more truthful.'

The music went on, accelerating. The tray with paste balls was brought back. This time Jahan took a larger one and washed it down with more wine. Hard as he tried not to glance at the woman who so resembled Mihrimah, he could not help it. Even her seraphic smile, the slightest curl of her bottom lip, was exactly like hers. The billowing folds of her veil framed her face, translucent and light like the morning mist. She seemed more at ease and confident than the other women; perhaps she had less to worry about.

It was Zainab's voice that brought Jahan back to his senses. 'You want me to show you his garments?'

'What?'

'My dog's clothes? You want to see them?'

'I'd like to.'

The Chief White Eunuch, by now quite tipsy, frowned at them but said nothing. Glad to get out of his sight, Jahan followed Zainab into the recesses of the house. She led him into a vast room where everything was small: the bed, the low tables, the carpet. In one corner of the room there was a minuscule rosewood cabinet with dozens of drawers. It contained the smallest leather vests, furs, shawls. There was even a waistcoat of sorts. He must have been a boxy creature, for the articles were compact. Sniffing slightly, Zainab said he was only a puppy when she found him. She had looked for his mother everywhere, eventually convinced that, just like her, the dog had no one to rely on. From then on they had been inseparable.

Jahan handed her his handkerchief, which she took gratefully, and blew her nose. She stared at him as if seeing him anew. 'Put me up on this chair.'

She was light as a child. Her eyes fastened on him, she said, 'I have been in this trade for thirty years. Seen hell, seen heaven. Met angels, met demons. I survived because my lips are sealed. Never meddled in others' affairs. But I took a shine to you. You seem like a fine man.'

A rattle was heard from the next room. Perhaps a mouse was stuck between the floorboards. She dropped her voice to a whisper. 'The eunuch. Be careful with him.'

'Why do you say that?'

'Just beware,' she said, jumping down from the chair.

When they returned to the room the singing was still going on, though the tone had altered from gleeful to melancholy. Zainab sat beside the Chief White Eunuch and began to lavish praise, food and wine on him.

Jahan's eyes dropped as he slouched back. He could have fallen asleep if it hadn't been for a voice that hovered over the music. 'May I?'

It was her – Mihrimah's replica. Jahan's heart skipped a beat.

She knelt in front of him, the sleeves of her dress sweeping his knees, and poured him a glass of wine. When he finished it, she took his shoes off, pressed his feet against her bosom and began, very gently, to rub. Panic rose inside Jahan like black bile. He was afraid of desiring her. He held her hands, whether to stop her from touching him or him from touching her, he couldn't tell.

'You like my hands?' she asked.

'You remind me of someone.'

'Really? Was it someone you loved?'

Jahan downed his next cup, and watched her instantly replenish it.

'Where is she now?'

'Dead,' he said.

'Poor darling.' She kissed him. Her lips tasted like icy sherbet. Her tongue reached for his tongue and retreated. Despite himself Jahan was aroused. She held him tightly, pressing her palms on the nape of his neck. Suddenly Jahan realized everyone had vanished – the musicians, Zainab, the Chief White Eunuch.

'Where are they?' Jahan asked, his voice full of unease.

'Calm down, everyone is in their room. We are good here.'

They kissed again. She guided his hands up and down her body, encouraging him to fondle her breasts, her hips, wide and round. He pulled up her skirts; layers of taffeta ruffled under his weight. His fingers travelled between her legs, caressing her wet, dark cave. Panting, he was on top of her, undressing himself, undressing her, unable to stop.

'My lion,' she whispered in his ear.

He bit her neck, first gently, then harder.

'Call me Mihrimah,' she said, breathing heavily.

A voice screamed inside Jahan's head. He shoved her away, unsteady as he tried to stand up. 'How do you know her name?'

She flinched. 'You told me.'

'I did not.'

'You did. Just now, remember.'

Had he told her? He could not be sure. Seeing his bewilderment, she said, 'The wine confused your mind. You told me, I swear.'

He held his head between his hands, overtaken by a wave of nausea. Perhaps she was telling the truth. He would have believed her were it not for the slightest twitch of her jaw – a simple reflex or a sign of nervousness.

'Go away, I beg,' he said.

'Don't be a child,' she said with a scathing smile and pushed herself against him.

Sucked into the softness of her bosom he felt trapped. Seizing both her wrists so tightly that his knuckles turned white, he seemed, for a moment, about to surrender to her charms. Instead he pushed her, too fast, too hard. She fell down heavily. A gasp rose from her lips, unfinished. Then silence. Jahan staggered, seeing, for the first time, the iron grate of the fireplace that she had fallen against, knocking her head. Before he could collect his thoughts, the door opened and Zainab entered the room, running, shouting. Bending over the woman, she listened for breath. Her face collapsed.

'She's dead,' Zainab cried. She turned to Jahan, her eyes wide with horror. 'You've killed the eunuch's mistress.'

Jahan ran out of the room as fast as his legs could carry him, into the garden and through the dark alleyway, fearing that a shadow might pounce on him at any moment. By the time he reached the street his forehead was beaded with sweat and his chest was heaving so hard he was sure they could hear it back in the *hamam* of sorrows. No sooner had he taken a step than a wave of despondency hit him. He had nowhere to go. He could not return to the palace dormitory. That would be the first place the Chief White Eunuch would search. He could ask for help from the tamers in the menagerie but he did not trust them all, and one betrayer was enough.

Just as he was panicking an idea surfaced in his head: Davud. His *konak* was large enough to hide in for a few days, if not weeks. Eminent and celebrated, Davud could even find a way to shield him from the wrath of the Chief White Eunuch. But he could not walk to Eyup in the middle of the night. He needed a horse. The carriage that had brought them was waiting in a stable nearby. He headed in that direction, praying the coachman would be asleep.

He was not. Truthfully, he was wide awake and in merry company. The man was following his master's example. While the Chief White Eunuch was roistering with hashish and wine, his servant was enjoying a frolic of his own. Jahan tiptoed quietly, although needlessly; the coachman and the whore were too lost in each other to notice him. The horses, though skittish, stood still and attentive, their ears pricked, their eyes alert, sensing what was taking place.

Jahan approached one of the four mounts still fastened to the coach – a stallion greyer than the cobblestones outside. Slowly, very slowly, he held its straps and escorted it towards the gate. In that instant, the coachman emitted a yelp of pleasure; his thrusts became urgent. Jahan pulled the animal by the reins, harsher than he intended. The horse swung its head. Mercifully, it did not whinny. Jahan uttered a prayer; he must have chosen the most docile one of the pack. Still, he could not help but suspect a spirit was guiding him – Mihrimah's or Nikola's or

Master Sinan's. It could even be Chota's, for all he knew. He had many ghosts on every side.

Before long he was riding at full speed, the wind thrashing his hair. He was no longer afraid of the *djinn* that dwelled in dusky corners, having accepted that they were less frightening than humans. Careful to stay in the dark, avoiding the watchmen, he arrived at Davud's mansion. The servants, perplexed as they were to see a guest at this ungodly hour, took him upstairs to their master, who had already gone to bed.

Davud shuffled his feet with a puzzled look. 'Is everything all right?'

'I beg your pardon, I had nowhere to go,' Jahan said.

Jahan accepted the musk sherbet a servant brought. His hands were trembling so badly that he spilled some of it on the carpet. He tried to wipe the stain off with his sleeve, which only made it worse. Unable to think straight any more, he stared at the floor, seeing what he had failed to see the first time he had visited. Queer, the trivial details that caught one's attention when dreadful things were happening. He now saw that it was Master Sinan's carpet.

'I've . . . killed someone.'

Davud turned ashen. 'Who? How?'

'The Chief White Eunuch's mistress . . .' Jahan said, unsure how to continue.

He gave an account of the night – the dwarf lady, the musicians, the concubine who had tried to seduce him, and God knew had succeeded, though he did not mention her disturbing resemblance to Mihrimah.

'I don't know –' Jahan gulped for air. 'Lately, things have been strange. I have the feeling it has something to do with Master Sinan.'

At this Davud raised an eyebrow. 'The master, may Paradise be his abode, is beyond the trifles of this world.'

'Right, bless his soul. But I uphold his legacy. You said so the other day. There are only two of us now.' Jahan paused, staring at his friend with a fixed intensity. 'You might be in danger, too.'

Davud dismissed the idea with a sweeping motion of his hand. 'Don't worry. Nothing can happen to me.'

'I killed her . . .' Jahan said once more in a daze, rocking his body like a child in need of consolation.

'I shall make inquiries tomorrow morning. You need to get some rest.'

Upon Davud's orders a bed was provided with bowls of sweetened figs and dates and a jug of *boza*. Jahan drank and ate little, after which he tumbled into a dark, disturbed slumber.

He slept despite the demons preying on his soul. When he woke, it was high noon and there were brand-new garments on the sofa. Donning them with gratitude, he went to see Davud, who was waiting for him downstairs with his three children – the youngest a girl not yet four. The boys were the doubles of their father and clearly adored him. Jahan felt a pang of sorrow. He had neither a wife nor offspring. He had arrived in this city of shadows and echoes by himself and, after so many years, here he was once again, alone.

'I have bad news,' whispered Davud, so as not to be heard by the children. 'You were right: she died, it seems.'

Jahan gasped, struggling for air. Until then he had secretly hoped that it was a minor injury.

'What are you going to do now?' Davud asked tenderly.

'I can't stay in Istanbul. I'll have to go.'

'You can stay with us as long as you wish.'

Jahan's face broke into a smile. He was touched by Davud's generosity. Any other notable in his position would have shunned a man in trouble. True, he had come here intending to spend some time. Yet now, after seeing Davud with his young ones, he realized he could not put them in danger.

'I'm in your debt, but I should go. Better that way.'

Davud gave this some thought. 'There's an orchard near Thrace, belongs to my father-in-law. You'll be out of harm's way there while things simmer down. I'll give you a horse. Go and wait to hear from me.'

They decided it would be safer to set out in the dark. Jahan passed the day playing with the children, flinching at the slightest sound from outside. After supper, Davud gave him the steed, a cape to keep him warm and a pouch of coins. He said, 'Keep your heart pure. You'll be back in no time.'

'How will I ever repay you?'

'We grew up together,' Davud said. 'Remember what the master said? Not just brothers. You are the witnesses to each other's journeys.'

Jahan nodded, his throat tight. He remembered the rest too. *You are the witnesses to each other's journeys. You will know, therefore, if one of you goes astray. Follow the path of the wise, the awakened, the loving, the hard working.*

They embraced, and for a moment it was as if in their clasp there was an indistinct thump, a third heart beating next to theirs; it was as if Sinan, too, were there, watching, listening, praying.

Jahan walked, slowly and steadily, among the shadows. He picked his way through the dark streets. This he had not told Davud, but he had decided not to leave Istanbul without paying a last tribute to Chota. He reached the French ambassador's residence. Improper as it was to visit an emissary – or anyone – uninvited, he hoped to be forgiven.

The servant who answered the door thought differently. His master liked his sleep and could not possibly be disturbed. But Jahan was persistent. Between the two of them they raised such a racket that soon a sleepy voice rose from inside the house. 'Who is it, Ahmad?'

'Some insolent pauper, master.'

'Give him bread and send him away!'

'He doesn't want bread. He says he needs to talk to you about the elephant.'

'Oh!' There followed a brief silence. 'Let him in, Ahmad.'

Without a wig and powder, wearing a nightgown that reached his knees and revealed the enormity of his belly, the figure Jahan found in the hall didn't quite resemble the ambassador he knew.

'I beg your pardon for intruding on you,' Jahan said, bowing low.

'Who are you?' the ambassador asked.

'I'm the mahout of the elephant you have cut, your Excellency.'

'I see,' Monsieur Brèves said, remembering the brazen tamer who had reluctantly handed him the corpse.

Jahan blurted out the lie he had prepared on the way. 'Last night I had a horrible dream. The poor elephant was in pain and begged me to lay him to rest.'

'But that has been done,' Monsieur Brèves said. 'The corpse had started to stink, I'm afraid. We buried the beast.'

A stab of sorrow entered Jahan's chest. 'Where is his grave?'

The man didn't know. He had asked his servants to get rid of the carcass and so they had. When he noticed Jahan's sadness, he said, 'Cheer up, my friend. Come, there's something I'd like to show you.'

Together they entered a room overflowing with books, notes and mementoes. Monsieur Brèves, unlike other envoys, who were mostly interested in power struggles, had a great knowledge of the Ottoman Empire and spoke impeccable Turkish, Arabic and Persian. Having studied the written works, he was keen to establish an Arabic printing press in Paris to help books to travel as freely as ambassadors did.

Jahan now understood why his appearance at his door unbidden hadn't angered Monsieur Brèves. In truth, he was glad to have found someone with whom he could talk about the dissection he had conducted. Burning to relate his achievements, he handed Jahan the sketches he had drawn. While not a fine artist, he had nonetheless set down in great detail the anatomy of an elephant.

'One day, I shall write a treatise,' he said. 'People ought to know. It's not every day that they get to see the inside of such a magnificent creature!'

Involuntarily, Jahan's eyes slid to a shelf where a tusk shone, bright and polished. The ambassador, following his gaze, said, 'A keepsake from Constantiniye.'

'May I hold it?' Jahan asked, and when he was given the nod he took it with care. A wave of gloom swept through him. His eyes brimmed with tears.

Monsieur Brèves regarded him silently, his face twisting as he quarrelled with himself. In the end he sighed and said, 'I think you should take the tusk.'

'Really?'

'Clearly you loved the beast more than anyone,' the ambassador said, waving his hand in a gesture of nonchalance or commiseration or both. 'I have my drawings. That'll be enough to impress everyone in Paris.'

'I am grateful,' Jahan said, his voice breaking.

Jahan set off with the tusk in his hand. In comparison with the night before, he was more hopeful. The tusk radiated a glow that warmed his soul. It was as if Chota were with him. On his shoulder he carried a rucksack with a few items that Monsieur Brèves had allowed him to take – a shovel, a candle, a red scarf and a string. Jahan had a plan.

Back on his horse he rode with purpose. When he reached the Mihrimah Mosque, he jumped off and walked along the outside walls. He spotted a Judas tree flushed with rosy blossoms. By that patch he dug a deep, rectangular pit. He could have kept the tusk with him but that would have been selfish. Chota deserved to have a headstone. It was always the sultans and the viziers and the opulent who had lofty monuments to their names. The poor and the destitute would have had nothing, once they were gone, were it not for the prayers of their kith and kin. Every mortal being left behind a mark, no matter how small or ephemeral, except animals. They served, they fought, they put their lives in danger for their masters and when they died it was almost as if they had never existed. Jahan didn't want Chota to meet the same end. He wanted him to be remembered with appreciation and love. Perhaps it was blasphemy, but he didn't care. It pained him to think that Chota could not go to heaven. If people prayed for him, he thought, the elephant had a better chance of ascension.

He carefully laid the tusk inside the hole. 'Farewell. I'll see you in Paradise. I hear they have nice trees to eat.'

In that moment a strange calmness came over him. He was, for the first time, at peace with himself. He was part of everything and everything was part of him. So this was it, he thought. Centre of the universe was neither in the East nor in the West. It was where one surrendered to love. Sometimes it was where one buried a loved one. Shovel by shovel, he covered the hole until it was smooth. Then, using the strings, he hemmed in the pit. Where he imagined Chota's head would have been he stuck in a dry branch and tied it with the scarf. Next to it he placed the candle. He sat by it, cross-legged, bolt upright. Now all he needed to do was to wait for someone, anyone, to walk by.

It did not take long. A young, willowy goatherd approached. He stared at the grave, then at Jahan, then back at the grave again. 'What is this, *effendi*?'

'It's a tomb.'

The youngster's lips moved in a quick invocation. When he finished, he asked, 'Who died? Anyone familiar?'

'Hush. Be respectful.'

The goatherd's dark eyes widened. 'Who was it?'

'A saint. A powerful one.'

'Never heard of a saint in this area.'

'He did not want to be known for a hundred years.'

'Then how is it that you know?'

'He revealed his tomb to me in a holy dream.'

Kneeling beside Jahan, the goatherd tilted his head to the side, as if hoping to get a glimpse of the corpse under the earth. 'Does he cure any diseases?'

'He cures everything.'

'My sister's barren. Been married for three summers, still waiting.'

'Bring her here. The saint might help. Bring her husband, too, in case it is him.'

'What's he called?'

'Chota Baba.'

'Chota Baba,' the goatherd repeated deferentially.

Slowly, Jahan stood up. 'I must go. Keep an eye on this grave. Make sure no one disrespects him. You are the guardian of the shrine of Chota Baba. Can I trust you?'

The goatherd nodded solemnly. 'Don't be worrying yourself, *effendi*. I shall keep my word.'

This is how the city of seven hills and a hundred shrines, old and very old, Muslim, Christian, Jewish and pagan, gained yet another saint to visit at times of desperation, at times of joy.

After riding the entire afternoon Jahan arrived at a crossing where the road forked – the path to his right led northwards over dried-up river-beds to Thrace. This was the route Davud had counselled him to take. The path to his left meandered westwards through flatlands and rolling hills; it was more splendid – greener, prettier, yet less preferable, since it was not only circuitous and rugged but also dangerous, with bandits roaming its woods. Jahan was about to turn right as planned when a thought occurred to him. If Chota were alive, he would have plumped for the other path, he knew. And without premeditation and for no particular reason, so did he.

For a while he rode at a canter, drinking in the landscape. The air smelled of pine, mud and dampness. Guided by a strange instinct, he roamed about, deviating from the agreed course. Soon the sun went down and the moon – a thin, pale crescent – rose in the east. That was when Jahan recalled the inn that he and Davud had dined in as young, excited apprentices, on their way back from Rome. If memory served him correctly, it was in this area.

By the time he found the inn, darkness had descended. A groom took his horse to the stable while he made his way inside. Everything was exactly the same: the stuffy rooms upstairs, the vast, noisy dining hall downstairs, the strong odour of roasted meat. The unchanging nature of the place should have come as a comfort, a sweet reassurance in a world where everything was disappearing, but it didn't. Instead it filled him with an immense despair. His mind was awash with images of the *hamam* of sorrows. The face of the concubine, as she leaned over him in a kiss, transformed into the face of Mihrimah. Even though he knew this was impossible, there was a part of him that felt he had killed his beloved and that, secretly, he had wanted this.

He sat at a rough-hewn table near the stone fireplace, full of feverish thought, listening to the crackle of the logs over the din of laughter and gossip. Houseboys scurried left and right, brothers by the looks of them. In a little while, a young lad came to take his order. Having a cheerful, chirpy mien, he asked Jahan who he was and where he was going. In his eyes Jahan saw the sparkle he'd had when he was the boy's age – a reckless curiosity for the world and a hidden wish to leave one's place of birth in the belief that real life was elsewhere.

When the lad brought him his stew – a steaming pot of beef and vegetables in a thick, spicy broth – Jahan said, 'Last time I came here you were not yet born.'

'Really?' the lad said, intrigued. 'My pa must have taken care of you.'

'Where is he?' Jahan asked between mouthfuls.

'Oh, he's around. A bit hard of hearing in his right ear. The left is fine. I'll tell him about you. These days all he does is talk about the past.'

Nodding, Jahan went back to his stew. As he was wiping the bowl clean with a hunk of bread, the innkeeper appeared. He had gained weight and had a belly the size and shape of a barrel. Jahan watched the lad point in his direction, saying something in his father's ear. In a second the man was by Jahan's side.

'My boy tells me you're an architect and that you were here way back.'

'That's right: I was here with my friend,' Jahan said, raising his voice.

The man squinted and stood ramrod straight for a moment too long. Then he said slowly, 'I remember.'

Jahan didn't believe him. How could he have any recollection of them, when he had seen hundreds of customers come and go? As if he had read this disbelief, the innkeeper sat opposite him and said, 'I did not forget you two because of that companion of yours. Strange fella, that one. I thought to myself: are these friends or foes?'

Perplexed, Jahan stared at him. 'What do you mean?'

'He asked for a cleaver. I said what are you going to do with it? We get all sorts of rogues here, don't want trouble. How was I to know he wouldn't sink it into someone? He promised to return it. And he did, in truth.'

Jahan pushed aside his empty plate, suddenly nauseated. But the expression on the man's face said he hadn't finished.

'I was suspicious. I peeked from the door. You were downstairs. Everyone was.'

'What did you see?' Jahan asked.

'Your *friend*,' he said, pronouncing the last word mockingly, 'was cutting up a book. Leather cover it had. He chopped at it like it was some tree.'

'We were robbed,' Jahan said. 'My drawings . . . my journal. All were gone.'

'No, *effendi*. Nothing's stolen in my inn. We run a decent place. Your "friend" destroyed your things. God knows what he did with the pieces.'

'But . . . why would he do that?'

'Hah! If you find out, come tell me, 'cause I have been wondering that myself.'

After the man left, Jahan ordered some ale, which they brewed in this region. He shuddered, as if the wind outside were blowing through his bones. When he finished his drink, he left a generous tip and went back to the stable.

'Has my horse been fed and watered?'

'Yes, *effendi*.'

'Saddle it up.'

'You leaving? There's a storm coming. The forest is dangerous at night.'

'Not going into the woods,' Jahan said. 'I'm returning to the city.'

Through rows of elms and over bubbling brooks, he rode back to Istanbul, the storm chasing him like a hound nipping at his heels. His horse started at each crack of thunder; the storm grew closer and louder at every turn. Somehow he managed not to get caught in the rain, fleeing the leaden clouds following behind. He charged into fields of black – a black so complete and absolute as to suck up all other shades – one after another. He wondered if this was what death would be like. If so, it didn't feel frightening, only profound.

Jahan raced across a valley strewn with huge boulders that resembled, from a distance, old men huddling for warmth. As he passed by, he had the odd feeling that they were watching him with the dull stare of those who, having seen too many excitements that ended in disaster, had none left of their own.

Near Istanbul, the storm skewed right, cutting off his path and reaching the city ahead of him. A lightning bolt struck far off, washing the domes and hills with a bright blue lustre. In that blaze of light, descending almost vertically, it felt like the skies had opened up to reveal the vault of heaven, if only for the briefest moment. Once again Jahan thought to himself what a beautiful city this was, however stony-hearted. Soon the sodden ground under his horse's hooves turned into cobbled roads. He headed to the Belgrade Gate – the one entrance that he guessed would not be closed at this hour.

He was right. A company of Janissaries stood sentinel with their shields and swords and high headwear; one of them was dozing on his feet. Jahan told them he was a teacher at the palace school and showed them his seal. They questioned him suspiciously but not altogether disrespectfully, in case he might have connections high up in the seraglio. Finally, bored, they let him go.

For a while Jahan rode watching the sea, now the colour of ink, in the distance. The gale, fast and furious, blew down the gables, snapped the saplings, churned the waves. All at once, it started to pelt down. *The Little Day of Judgement*, the locals called such squalls of lashing rain, the world rehearsing for the final deluge. Hard as Jahan tried to keep to under the eaves as he rode, by the time he reached Davud's mansion he was soaked to the bone. A dog barked somewhere, a man yelled in an unfamiliar language. Then came silence, enhanced rather than disturbed by the constant noise.

When he had visited this place earlier, he had not paid attention to how well it was protected – lofty walls, iron gates, a hedge of shrubs. He recalled Davud's words: *My wives complain. You are the Chief Royal Architect, yet you don't even repair the fence around the house, they say.* Tethering the horse to a post, he walked towards the fence around the back garden, searching for the section in need of repair. He found a place where a few of the pales had buckled and crumbled. After prodding a bit, two of them gave way, making a hole big enough to pass through. The garden welcomed him with its heady fragrances. He paced back and forth, deciding how best to break into the house.

It was easier than he had thought. Jahan knew that a well-fortified house had in general but one flaw: an owner's hubris. Confident that no thief would ever breach its defences, such a place was not checked

377

regularly. In time, even the highest wall crumbled, the sharpest spike lost its edge. Through a wooden hatch that turned out to be fortuitously loose on its hinges, he crept in and found himself in what seemed to be – or what smelled like – the pantry. As his eyes got used to the gloom, he was able to move about in slow, steady strides. Surrounded by crocks of honey and molasses, kegs of goat's cheese and butter, strings of dried vegetables and fruit, pots of grain and nuts, he could not help but smile at what Chota might have done with such food. He remembered the night when he had sneaked into the royal observatory, his heart thumping. Everything was different back then. His master was alive and thriving; Chota was alive; and he was a man in love.

Down the corridor, ensconced in a niche, a lamp glowed faintly. Jahan took it and made his way upstairs. The room he and Davud had dined in the other day looked larger, as if it expanded after dusk. He approached the bookshelves, not knowing what he was searching for but trusting that he would recognize it once he found it. He hadn't had a chance to inspect the scrolls, and this was what he set about doing now. Unrolling one of them, he studied it. Nothing unusual. He spent less time with the next two drawings: one of a bazaar; the other of a lazaretto. Deep from the bowels of the house came a rustle as light as the wing beat of a moth. His back stiffened. He grew still, listening. Not a sound. Only the dark and its numbing calmness.

He opened a roll of paper, recognizing his master's handwriting.

My faithful apprentice Jahan,

I came to see you today, was not allowed. It is the second time they have blocked my way. The Grand Vizier's orders, so I am told. I shall try to reach our Sultan and get special permission. Until then I shall send you this letter so that you know I pray for your well-being, my son, and that while you spend your days inside those walls, I have no joy outside.

Jahan gasped. He had come, after all. His master had visited him in the dungeon. He had tried to reach him and failed. Instantly another thought followed. Why had he not received this letter? What – or who – had kept the letter away from him all this time?

His hands trembled as he inspected the next scroll – the design of the Kırkcesme aqueducts. The site of their third major accident: the one that had killed eight workers, among them Salahaddin. Once again he saw his master's handwriting, the gentle strokes of his gold-nibbed pen. Upon his penmanship, in a slightly different shade, was a second imprint. Similar to the lines he had found on the scroll of the Suleimaniye Mosque. He examined the scratch marks, all of which happened to be the spots where the injuries had occurred.

In the third design – that of Molla Celebi Mosque – Jahan caught a detail that almost choked him. Till then he had focused on the areas around the scaffolding. Yet here there were markings on the half-dome over the *mihrab*. A memory floated into his head. He remembered how Sancha, her face ashen, her accent lilting and her shadow long in the grass, had told him the story of her capture as they sat in that location. He recalled the men – one of them Salahaddin's brother – prowling about while she was talking and his feeling that something about them was not quite right. At the time he and Sancha had taken them for petty thieves stealing materials from construction sites. It happened often. There was no end to the things people ran off with, mostly out of poverty, sometimes for the sheer pleasure of it.

Now he understood those men had been there to sabotage the building as part of another plot; they had been waiting for him and Sancha to leave. But since they stayed, they had unknowingly prevented them from doing what they had been ordered to do. Instead the accident had occurred on the other side of the prayer hall. Somebody had been taking notes on Master Sinan's designs not *after* the incidents, in order to study where things had gone wrong, but *before*. In his dismay, Jahan dropped the scroll, cursing his clumsiness. He got on his knees to pick it up and was still hunched over when three pairs of feet entered the room.

Davud, wearing a nightgown, a servant on each side, stood opposite him. 'Look what the night has brought us! Thought it was a burglar, but it's a friend!'

Slowly, Jahan stood up. He would make no attempts at denial.

'What were you looking at?'

'Molla Celebi Mosque,' Jahan said, his forehead breaking out in a sweat.

'Not one of our best, but surely the prettiest we made,' Davud said with a smile that quickly vanished. When he spoke again his voice sounded husky and hard. 'I should have destroyed those drawings long ago, but I couldn't bring myself to do it. They reminded me of our old days, our golden times. It was a mistake, I now see. Look what my softness cost me.'

Involuntarily, Jahan glanced at the men behind him, their eyes gleaming in the light of the candles they carried. A barb of fear entered his stomach as he recognized one of them: the deaf-mute who had ushered him into the Chief White Eunuch's carriage only a few days before. It now felt like another life.

'Why did you come back? Have I not provided you with a fast horse and a safe place?' Davud asked.

Jahan responded tartly, 'You did. To get me out of your way, I suppose.'

'Be grateful. Only Sheitan lacks gratitude.'

'What I don't understand is why you said you wanted me to be your foreman. Why the charade?'

'Because I did, Allah is my witness. At first I thought we could work together. You ruined everything; you were asking too many questions about the master's will. Why don't you ever accept things as they are?' Davud stared past Jahan, towards the window; rain was beating against it relentlessly. 'You were always like this,' he muttered, sounding weary, disappointed almost. 'Too curious for your own good.'

'The Chief White Eunuch and you are accomplices.'

'*Accomplices*,' Davud echoed. 'Such a harsh thing to say.'

'What would you call it?'

Ignoring the question, Davud went on, 'I told him it was not a good idea to take you to that house of sin. He didn't listen. He thought he could buy you off with harlots and hashish.' He stared at Jahan as if for solace. 'If he had let me handle it, none of this would have happened.'

'Master was always worried he was losing his designs. But he wasn't. You were stealing them,' Jahan said. 'And the accidents . . . You planned them. Salahaddin's brother. That lad worked for you. He never understood it was you who had killed his brother. How many others have you deceived? How could you?'

There was a brief silence until Davud turned towards his servants and said, 'Go, wait outside.'

If both men were deaf and mute, which Jahan knew they were, they must have been trained to read lips, for they left immediately. It was just the two of them now. The room felt colder and darker, too, as the servants had taken their candles with them. The shy, small lamp Jahan had brought from downstairs was their only light.

'It was you, all along,' Jahan said, his mouth parched. 'When we were repairing the Hagia Sophia, you talked with the locals and things got worse. What did you tell them?'

'The truth,' Davud said, spitting the words from his lips like a fire spitting embers. 'Told them they were being kicked out of their houses so that the Sultan and his puppets could enjoy the sight of an infidel shrine.' Davud paused, as if washed by memories. 'You and Nikola were so gullible. I bribed those children. Told them they should drag you two into their shed, show you their sick father, the kittens . . . I knew you would be touched.'

'You knew we would be angry at the master,' Jahan said. 'You betrayed him.'

Davud gave a look that was nigh on painful. 'I did no such thing.'

'You have done everything you could to harm him – is this not treachery?'

'No,' Davud said calmly. 'It is not.'

Trying to suppress the quiver in his voice, Jahan said, 'When we were in Rome, we saw a painting. A disciple who had turned traitor. Didn't you find yourself in him?'

'I remember the painting. But I was no disciple and our master was no Jesus.'

'That man, Tommaso . . . The Italians . . . Were they after master's designs or was it just a ruse of yours?'

'Tommaso, yes. Greedy man, but too small, insignificant. I used him for a while. Afterwards there was no need.'

Until that moment Jahan had seen a mix of emotions on Davud's face – rage, sorrow, resentment. The one thing he had not observed was regret. 'Do you feel any remorse at all?'

'Remorse, for what? You want to believe I'm dishonourable. Sheitan's henchman . . .' Davud's voice waned, then rose again. 'True, I lied to our master. I pretended I had a family back in the village. I wrote them letters, sent them gifts. It was a sham.'

'I don't understand.'

Davud laughed an unhappy laugh. 'I have no kin back in the village. All slaughtered. By your great Sultan.'

'Which one?'

'Does it matter?' Davud said with an impatient gesture. 'Are they not the same? Suleiman? Selim? Murad? The father, the son, the grandson. Don't they keep repeating what their ancestors did?'

'I feel sad about what happened to your family,' Jahan said.

'It was Sultan Suleiman. We'd had a poor harvest, another one, could not pay the levy. We were not Shias, but many said that come the winter we should pack up and go to the Shah of Iran. Better over there than here. Our poets recited, our women sang. Your Sultan wanted to teach us a lesson. He did. I was ten years old.'

Outside the rain slackened to a drizzle. Jahan could hear a fishing boat splashing nearby.

'They beheaded a few. Left them on pikes for three days. More people rebelled. Their bodies dangled in the wind for a week. Still see them in my dreams. Everyone rebelled. They came back. This time they razed the village.'

'How did you survive?'

'My mother pushed me into the larder, closed the door on me. I waited. I was more hungry than afraid. Stupid boy. When I walked out it was night-time. I saw the moon shine on corpses. My brothers, my uncles, my mother . . .'

It was a while before Jahan spoke again. 'Why didn't you tell Master Sinan? He would have helped you.'

'Really?' Davud gave him a disdainful look. 'Did master resurrect the dead? Is he like Jesus in that way?'

'Master loved you like a son.'

'I loved him like a father. A father in the wrong. A great architect. But a coward. Never uttered a word against cruelty. Or injustice. Even when you were rotting in the dungeon he did not move a finger!'

'Have mercy. What could he have done? It was not in his power.'

'He could have said to the Sultan, let go of my apprentice, my Lord, or else I'm not building for you.'

'Have you lost your mind? He'd have been put to death.'

'It'd have been a decent end,' Davud countered. 'Instead he wrote you miserable letters.'

'You knew about it?' Jahan's face fell as he took this in. 'He trusted you with the letters. You told him you had found a way to send them to me in the dungeon, but you never did. You wanted me to be cross with my master.'

Davud shrugged as if the remark had no relevance. 'All he wanted to do was build. One project after another. But who will pray in those mosques? Will they be unwell or hungry? Didn't matter. Every year, work, work. Where do the resources come from? Another war. Another slaughter. Did he mind? He didn't care for anything else.'

'That's not true!'

'Every colossal mosque we built was raised thanks to the revenues from another conquest. On their way to the battleground the army would raze villages to the ground, kill more of my people. Our master never cared for these sorrows. He refused to see that, without bloodshed elsewhere, there would be no money, and without money there would be no building in the capital.'

'Enough!'

Davud dropped his voice, speaking gingerly, as if addressing a petulant boy. 'You come from another land. You can't understand this.'

Jahan's shoulders slumped. 'You were not the only one making up stories. I'm an orphan. I've never seen Hindustan. Never kissed a Shah's hand. It was a lie.'

Davud studied him. 'The master knew it?'

'I believe so. He protected me.'

'The elephant?'

'Destiny,' Jahan said. 'God brought us together.'

'So we had one thing in common. Still, you are not me.' Davud broke off. 'There are two kinds of men, this I have learned. Those who covet happiness. Those who seek justice. You long for a happy life, whereas I long for *adalet*. We shan't agree.'

Jahan strode to the door. Davud shouted, 'Where do you think you're going?'

'Don't want to be near you.'

'Fool! I cannot let you go.'

Until then, it had not occurred to Jahan that Davud could harm him. As if to help him comprehend this, Davud said, 'You know too much now.'

Jahan opened the door. The two servants were there, blocking his way. They pushed him back into the room.

'Tell your dogs to leave me alone,' Jahan yelled.

'Pity it had to be this way,' said Davud as he left the room. 'Farewell, *Indian*.'

Jahan was so perplexed it took him a moment to act. He began to shout at the top of his voice. Surely there were people in the house who would hear and come to see what was happening. His children, his wives, his concubines.

'Help! Somebody help!'

One of the men shoved him with such force that he fell down. Jahan tried to pray, but the words would not come. He took deep breaths, ready for the strangling that was sure to follow. It did not. Outside a bird warbled a song. The dawn was breaking.

They hit him on the back of his head with something hard, heavy. The floor tilted beneath his feet. The bird's chirping was the last sound he heard before everything went dark.

There was a mantle — stiff and heavy as brocade — wrapped around his head, choking his breath, blocking his view. He wanted to take it off but his hands were tied, as were his feet. Through a slit in the fabric he glimpsed his surroundings, blurred as they were, slowly realizing there was nothing on his face. It was his eyes that were not seeing. The right one was swollen, unblinking, shut. The left one, half open, fluttered in a lonely panic to make sense of where he was.

Jahan tasted blood in his mouth. He must have bitten his tongue during the fight. For there was a fight, he remembered. His body remembered — the soreness in his limbs, the ache in his knuckles, the throb that still drilled a hole in his skull and, worst of all, the pain that shot through his right foot. His cheek stung, though he would not discover the reason until later. He recalled how Davud had walked out of the room, leaving him at the mercy of his guards, and how everything had stopped. The next thing he knew he was in a carriage that was riding hell for leather. The deaf-mutes, one on each side, had not expected him to recover consciousness so soon. They began to hit him again. Jahan fought back. In a frenzy, he opened the door and jumped out of the carriage with its horses still galloping at full speed. He tumbled into a ditch, twisting his foot. Such was the state the deaf-mutes found him in. Then it went pitch-black again.

His chest hurt now as he drew in a gulp of stale, sour air. His fingertips touched the hard surface, confirming what he suspected: he was lying on an earthen floor, bundled up in a hut somewhere. There was a persistent susurration in the distance, which he found oddly calming. He must have passed out; he couldn't tell for how long. When he came around it was so cold his teeth were chattering. Either his other eye had also closed or the night had descended.

The first time he soiled his *shalwar* the shame was worse than the stench. None of that mattered afterwards. The hunger he could deal with for a while. The thirst was dreadful. Thirst hewed his flesh, bit by bit, the way an axe would eat into a log, hacking its way into his veins. He kept smacking his lips as if he had been served a delicacy. That made him laugh. He feared he was losing his mind.

The incessant swish in the background he later recognized to be the sea – a discovery that was soothing and frightening in equal measure. Soothing, for he had always loved the ocean. Besides, he was probably not far from Istanbul. Frightening, because it brought to mind stories of concubines being fed to the fish. He shouted for help, over and over again. No one came. If Chota were here, he would tell him how peculiar it was to die alone and unheard in a city this crammed and clamorous.

As he drifted in and out of a stupor, time dragged on. In between bouts of pain, he nodded off, waking with a start, as though his soul refused to admit defeat. An anger he knew not from whence got hold of his soul. He, the apprentice to the great Sinan, had not climbed all that way to end so low. Sundered as they were, he could not for a moment believe Davud would abandon him to death. And yet Davud did not arrive. Nor did his underlings. Jahan could not guess whether it was dawn or dusk. Or how much time had gone by since he had been dragged here. How many days could a human being survive without water, he wondered. Elephants could make it up to four, he had read. He had no clue whether he would fare better.

He dreamed of Mihrimah, laughing under a honeysuckle vine, thirteen years old again. Her body untouched by hands other than her own, her face unmarred by spleen, her soul unspoiled by ambition. The way she had been when they first met, a happy, happy girl.

'Come,' she whispered, extending her hand.

Jahan attempted to move towards the garden where she waited. But halfway through something distracted him. A noise coming from the other side. Footsteps. Not by the door, though. Somebody was trying to break in. There was a loud, sharp clank – the sound of a boring tool on wood. The window must have been opened, since a cool, crisp draught swirled in.

'Clear,' a voice said. 'Go!'

Something heavy landed on the floor with a thud. A man. Another followed suit. The two intruders tiptoed around, unaware of Jahan's presence. The lamp they carried illuminated a tiny patch.

'Find that trunk. It must be here.'

'Ogh, what's this smell?'

'A dead rat, I'd say.'

'You sure there's treasure in this hollow?'

'How many times have I told you? Those two oafs were carrying something big. Seen it with me own eyes.'

'Sober eyes or drunk eyes?'

'I know what I'm sayin', dolt. There's a secret here.'

Thieves! Jahan shuddered. They could cut him to pieces. Still, he had nothing to lose. He was dying anyhow. A dry croak rose from his lips.

'What was that?'

'What was what?'

Jahan's breath rasped in his throat.

'Who's there?' one of them yelled, his voice dripping with fear. If Jahan didn't say a word, they would beat a hasty retreat, taking him for a *gulyabani*.★

'Help,' Jahan pleaded.

It didn't take them long to find him amid the boxes and crates. Surrendering to his fate, Jahan slipped into blankness but came to, trembling. One of the men was holding him by the shoulders and shaking him like the branches of some mulberry tree.

'What are you doing? Poor fella's been clobbered enough.'

'Trying to wake him up.'

'Yeah, well done. Now he's totally smacked!'

'You wake him, then.'

'Go get some water.'

They poured a bucket of seawater on Jahan's head, the salt burning the cuts and grazes on his skin, drilling down to his bones. He moaned in pain.

Just then another voice was heard – gruff and strangely familiar. 'Hey, what's goin' on?'

'We found this one here. Looks like someone roughed him up, chief.'

Footsteps drew closer. 'The man is dying of thirst, muttonheads! They've pummelled him like a dirty old rug and what do you do? Pour seawater on his wounds! Step back! Stay away, butchers!'

★ Evil spirit.

Jahan heard the thump of a flask being opened. Wetting his hand-kerchief with sweet water, the man pressed it to his lips. 'More,' Jahan begged as he strove to suck the cloth.

'Brother, take it easy. Not so fast.'

They began to wipe his face, curious to see the star-crossed soul underneath the blood and the mud and the grime. Jahan wanted to say something, but it was too exhausting, every word, every gasp. His head drooped.

'God Almighty. Bring that lamp closer,' the same voice bellowed. 'May the sky fall on our heads, it's Jahan! He's got no wits, this man! A snail knows better! I find him freezing in water, I meet him in the dungeon, now he's in with the rubbish! Always in trouble!'

Jahan stammered, 'Ba . . . laban?'

'Indeed, brother.'

Jahan burst out laughing – the cackle of a mad man.

'He's lost his little mind, chief,' said one of the Gypsies.

'Poor chap,' said the other.

To both of which Balaban shook his head and said tenderly, 'Nay, he's got an elephant's strength, our brother. He'll be fine.'

Freeing him from his ropes, they helped Jahan to stand up, though he could not walk. His right foot was a mess of empurpled flesh, swol-len to twice its size. They grabbed him, a man under each arm. As soon as they stepped outside, the wind pricked his skin like splintered glass. He didn't mind. It was over. Once again in his life, just as he was going down fast, ready to cross to the other side, a Gypsy's hand had pulled him back, pulled him up.

Balaban's wife, taking Jahan into her care, applied a poultice to his wounds and pigeon dung to his cuts. Morning and evening she forced down his throat a brew that was the colour of rust and tasted no better. The cut on his cheek, which bled whenever he moved a muscle, had to be sewn, she declared. So she did, her fingers not trembling once, even when he screamed and kicked in agony. When done, she assured him that from now on he would have lovers galore, since women were fond of men scarred on the battlefield.

'I was in no battle,' Jahan protested weakly.

'Who's goin' to know that? They'll drop in your path like ripe plums. Mark my words,' she said, spitting in her palm and stamping it on the wall. 'But your foot looks bad. We've summoned the Mender.'

'Who's that?'

'You'll see,' she said mysteriously. 'When he's done, you'll be as good as the Almighty first made you.'

Stubby and scraggy as a reed, dressed in tatters and with a wooden spoon dangling from his neck, the man who showed up the same afternoon didn't seem at all remarkable to Jahan. How wrong he was. With a quick glance at Jahan's foot, the healer declared it was not broken but badly dislocated. Before Jahan could ask what that meant, he had shoved the spoon in Jahan's mouth, taken his foot in the hollow of his hand and twisted it. Jahan's scream was loud enough to frighten the pigeons in the courtyard of the Suleimaniye Mosque. Later the Mender would show him the teeth marks on the spoon. Apparently, his weren't the only ones.

'All broken bones?' Jahan asked when he could speak again.

'Those and women giving birth. They bite harder.'

'Keep an eye on your piss,' continued the Mender. He explained there were six shades of yellow, four of red, three of green and two of black. A healer would not waste time looking at the patient; he would inspect his urine and see what was wrong. At his behest Jahan peed in a pot and watched the man swirl, sniff and swallow the liquid.

'No hidden bleeding in the organs,' said the Mender. 'Advent of dropsy. Prone to melancholy. Otherwise, fine inside.'

Thus sewn, fixed, washed, fed and tucked up in bed, Jahan slept uninterrupted for two days. On the third afternoon, when he opened his eyes, he found Balaban by his bed, weaving a basket while waiting for him to come round.

'Welcome to the land of the livin'. Wonder where I'll save your skin next time.'

Jahan chuckled, although it hurt because of the stitches in his face.

'How is the elephant?'

'Chota is dead.'

'Sorry, brother. How sad.'

They were pensive for a moment. Jahan was the first to break the silence. 'Do animals go to heaven, you think? Imams say they won't.'

'What do they know about animals? Farmers do. Gypsies do. But imams, nay.' Balaban paused. 'Don't brood. When I go to heaven, I'll have a word with God. If He says there's no room for creatures, I'll beg Him to spare Chota.'

Jahan's eyes lit up with amusement. 'You steal. You drink. You gamble. You bribe. You still think you're going to Paradise?'

'Well, brother . . . I look at the holier-than-thou. I say to myself, if these chaps are goin', I sure am goin', 'cause they are no better than me. That's how I measure my sins.' Balaban poured himself some wine. 'Pity he won't see his father.'

'Who?'

'Your elephant's son.'

'Chota has a son?'

'*Tatcho!*★ You thought all that effort brought no result! Poor Gulbahar was pregnant forever. Did you know?'

'Yes,' Jahan said, nodding. 'They have long pregnancies.'

'Long? Seemed like an eternity!'

'What did you name him?'

'Remember, you told me four elephants held the universe. If one moved, there were earthquakes, you said.' Balaban took a sip. 'I named him Panj. It means five. Just in case, you know, someone should stand in the centre.'

Jahan's throat constricted.

★ True.

390

'Do you want to see him? Your grandson?'

'Indeed!'

Placing Jahan on a horse-drawn litter, they took him to the barn. There he was, Chota's son, swinging his trunk, grey as a storm cloud. Jahan told the driver to take the litter closer so that he could touch the beast. Under the watchful gaze of the mother elephant, he patted the son's trunk and offered him a nut, which the animal accepted with delight. Sniffing, Panj searched for more; smart, suspicious, spry. Jahan's eyes brimmed with tears. For an instant he had the feeling that he was staring at Chota. Something from him continued in this creature, who had never seen his father and yet was, except for his colour, already so like him.

They left the barn, the horse pulling lazily. As they were crossing the courtyard, Jahan caught a fragrance in the breeze that sent a signal to an obscure part of his brain. He shouted, 'Stop!'

They ran to his side, fearing he had been hurt.

'Where does this smell come from?' Jahan asked.

'Nothing stinks around here. Lie down,' snapped Balaban.

One of the lads broke into a grin. 'I know what he's talking about. *Daki dey* was burning herbs.'

Balaban said, 'Go get her.'

In a little while they brought in a woman with an upright gait and a dark moustache. She said, 'Chief says you wanted to see me.'

'This thing you were burning,' said Jahan. 'What is it?'

A look of annoyance crossed her face. 'It's called mullein. We throw it in the fire every Monday morning. And at full moon. The smoke keeps the evil spirits away. If you have enemies, you'd better boil it and take a bath in it. You want some?'

'Tell me . . . Who else would use it? Other than the Romany, I mean?'

She gave this some thought. 'Those who have trouble in breathing. They carry it everywhere.'

'People with asthma . . .' Jahan mumbled, dismayed. He closed his eyes, the floor shifting beneath his feet.

That night, as they sat around a peat fire, Balaban's wife threw salt in the flames. Embers burst like sparkles of gold. His eyes transfixed by the display, Jahan said, 'I should be on my way soon.'

Balaban nodded, expecting to hear this. 'When?'

'There is one last person I need to visit. Then I am done with this city.'

Davud was right when he said Jahan was not a man of revenge. But he was also partly wrong. Jahan understood it wasn't only happiness that he sought in life. He also yearned for the truth.

She peered down at the water in the silver bowl. Its surface had formed ripples and its bottom had turned black. She frowned, not liking what she spotted. A sound like a whistle pierced the air every time she inhaled. Her condition had worsened over the years. She placed her hand, shrivelled and lined with veins, upon the cat's head.

'Do you see what he's up to? Maybe he's no fool after all.'

She glanced at the window, which was letting in a draught. How many times she had ordered the maidservant to keep it closed. But the silly girl threw it wide whenever she found the chance, claiming it was hot and stuffy. She did it to chase away the smell, of course. It wasn't only her farting and her perspiration that soured the air, she knew. Underneath she gave off an odour like an ancient book that smelled of dust no matter how often it was wiped. The maidservant was scared of her, scared of the *witch*. For that's what everyone called her behind her back.

She wore a silken garment, too bright and too ornamented for her age, some might have said. She didn't care. The sleek fabric did not lessen the ache in her joints or her hunched shoulders. Her body was a graveyard of memories. And each passing day as blurry as a shadow dancing on a wall. She had stopped quarrelling with God. She no longer asked Him why He had let her live when He had taken everyone else too early, too fast. She carried her age as a curse she was proud to be afflicted with. A hundred and twenty-one years old. That's how old she was. Her hair was no longer red and wavy, but it was still thicker than many a maiden's plait. Her voice was strong, unwavering. The voice of the younger woman who still resided inside her.

She pulled away from the bowl as if she feared the man down there was watching her, just as she had been watching him all these years. She reached for the pouch on the table, opened it and scattered the herbs on to her palm and sniffed. When the rattle in her chest calmed somewhat, she murmured, 'He's discovered us, that Indian. He's coming to find us.'

The Abode of the Disfavoured, they called it. A giant of a mansion half hidden by tall pine trees and high walls. This was where the concubines who were no longer in the Sultan's eye or had never been or never would be were sent in due course. Those who were jealous or ambitious in the extreme and had become entangled in the darkest intrigues might also find themselves under this roof, having lost their chance to ascend at the palace. Harem servants and odalisques too old or too sick to work would end up here as well. As a result, its inhabitants were a mixed bunch of young and aged, pretty and ordinary, hardy and ailing.

A mirthless place it was – the ceilings seldom echoed with laughter; the carpets only occasionally, if ever, were trodden by dancing feet. Bitterness exuded from the chimneys like steam from a sizzling dish. What little singing was done was mostly so sad there would not be a single dry handkerchief left. The residents did not ponder the future, for there was no future to ponder. Nor present. There was only the past. They looked back to the old days, resenting the mistakes made, the opportunities squandered, the paths untaken, the youths misspent. And on winter nights, when it was so cold their prayers froze in the air, never reaching the ears of God, many felt their hearts freeze alongside the solid earth outside, no matter how many stones they boiled and put in their beds.

A few had resigned themselves to the women they had become, though more had turned spiteful. A great many were pious, having dedicated the rest of their lives to the Almighty. Being pious did not mean being at peace, however, and they rarely were. Although each and every one, when asked, would say they believed that everything, good and bad, was in His hands, they still preened themselves on their achievements and accused others of their misfortunes. The contrast between the royal harem and its bleak counterpart was stark. Strict and stable in its rules and codes, the harem was nevertheless a versatile world, fluid and fickle. Its inhabitants had wishes and aspirations to spare. At night they had dreams aplenty. Whereas in the Abode of the

Disfavoured it was the dreams that withered first, then, gradually, the dreamers.

This is where Hesna Khatun had been living for the last fifteen years, though she had so frightened the other women she had been banished to a three-room cottage at the far end of the second garden. She didn't mind. Should she wish it, she could still go to the mansion Princess Mihrimah had endowed for her, but she found its vastness and emptiness suffocating. It was better here, however modest. Besides she did not have to see, day in day out, the courtyard with its roses and flowers, whose heady scents crushed her chest, making her wheeze and cough. Her asthma had worsened. Even so, she never asked for help. They could hate, fear or shun her, if they wished, but she would never allow anyone to pity her.

'They may all go to hell,' she drawled, before she realized she had said it out loud. It happened often lately. She found herself saying things that were in her head and would have been better off staying there.

Walking with leaden steps, she extended her hands towards the fireplace. She was always cold. Spring or winter made no difference; she kept the fire burning. When she had warmed up a bit she took her brush and turned towards the cat on the windowsill. 'Let's make you pretty, shall we?'

She held the cat and sat down on the sofa to comb its hair. The animal stood still, a bored look in its eyes.

There was a knock on the door. A slave boy appeared, no older than seven, his voice breaking. 'There's a messenger, *nine*.* He has brought you an urgent letter.'

'Tell that liar, whoever he is, there's nothing urgent for me any more. Send him away.'

The boy gaped at his feet, too frightened to meet her gaze.

'Why are you lingering, ignorant boy?'

'The man said, if she refuses to see me, tell her I have brought a message from Princess Mihrimah.'

At the mention of the name, Hesna Khatun flinched, blood draining from her cheeks. Never a woman who bowed to threats, she composed herself. 'How much did he pay you for this? Have you no shame?'

* Old woman, granny.

The boy's bottom lip sagged; he let out a whimper ready to break into a cry should she scold him again.

'What's the use of shouting at you?' she said. 'Go fetch the rascal. I'll give him a roasting myself.'

No males – unless they were eunuchs or boys – were allowed in the Abode of the Disfavoured. Certainly no strangers. Still, the nursemaid had her own rules. There were some benefits, after all, to being feared as the *zhadi*.

In a moment, Jahan appeared, followed by the boy who, not daring to enter, closed the door and waited outside.

'So it is you,' Hesna Khatun said, her voice a dry, throaty grumble.

They regarded each other with a dislike neither of them cared to conceal. He saw how impossibly old and thin she had become. Every inch of her face was furrowed; her back was crooked; her ears had enlarged. From under her scarf a streak of silver hair showed, reddened with henna on the ends. As unrecognizable as she was, she had the same calculating, hard stare as always.

'How dare you utter her name?' she rasped. 'I should have you lashed.'

'I had no choice,' Jahan said. 'Otherwise you wouldn't have seen me, *dada*.'

She recoiled upon hearing the name that Mihrimah, and only Mihrimah, had called her. Her mouth opened and closed in an angry silence.

Knowing the effect the word would have on her, Jahan was observing her every move. He stood tall and erect, neither bowing low nor kissing her hand. His insolence had not escaped her. She said, 'To what do I owe your visit – and lack of manners?'

He took a step towards her, only now noticing the snow-white cat curled on her lap. Carefully, he took out the hairpin he had stolen years ago and placed it on a table for her to see. 'I want to return this. It is yours.'

'How generous. At my age one needs a hairpin,' she said scathingly. 'Is that why you are here?'

'I came to tell you I'm going away for good.'

'So long, then,' Hesna Khatun said with a condescending smile.

'And before I leave there is a score between us that needs to be settled.'

'You and me? Don't think so.'

Stung by her mockery, Jahan closed his eyes for an instant and addressed the darkness inside his eyelids. 'You were more than a nursemaid. You cared for Mihrimah from the time she was a baby. She adored you, told you her secrets.'

'I raised her. Sultana Hurrem, may God forgive her rotten soul, had no time for her children. Surely not for her daughter. Not until she reached the age of marriage. Then she wanted to make her an innocent dupe in her games.' Hesna Khatun paused, short of breath. 'Do you know I was her wet nurse too? Mihrimah grew up on my milk,' she said, touching her flat chest with pride.

Jahan said nothing, feeling the encroachment of a sorrow he knew only too well.

'When Mihrimah burned with fever I, not her mother, waited by her bedside. When she fell down, I swathed her knees. I wiped her tears. When she had her first blood, she ran to me. She thought she was dying, poor thing. We slap a girl in this state. You can't do that to a Princess. So I held her in my arms. I said, "You are not going to die, your Highness. You are a woman now."'

Reaching out her fleshless hand she caressed the cat on her lap. 'What did the Sultana do? Aside from using her children to write letters to the Sultan? *Come back from war, my lion, return to my arms. Your absence kindled in my heart a fire that does not abate. Your infants are desolate. Your daughter Mihrimah is in tears.* Always scribbling rubbish.'

'How do you know what she wrote in her letters?'

A hoot of laughter rose, high-pitched and full-throated. 'In the harem there are no secrets,' Hesna Khatun intoned. 'The Sultana was a cunning wife but a careless mother. She doted on her sons. She forgot her daughter.'

Ambushed by the memory of an afternoon, Jahan puckered his lips. He recalled Mihrimah confiding in him how lonely she was and his own surprise that a woman who had everything could ever feel this way. 'When she was a child the Princess had the best tutors. Her father wanted her to be well read. You used to attend classes with her. Mihrimah was so fond of you; if you weren't around, she wouldn't listen. Everything that was taught to her, you also learned.'

'So, is that a sin?'

'Not at all,' Jahan said. 'Hurrem didn't notice how devoted Mihrimah was to you. She was too preoccupied with the Sultan – and her plots. She let you take control of her daughter. Then something happened. Hurrem didn't want you around any more.'

'How do you know all this?'

'Mihrimah told me but I never put the pieces together. Till now. Why was the Sultana upset with you?'

'The Sultana . . .' She began to cough, as if her name was a poison she had to purge from her body. When she spoke again, her voice sounded strained. 'Once Hurrem wanted to go to Bursa with her children. My Mihrimah didn't want to travel. She was only nine. She said to her mother, if *dada* comes, I'll go. That was when Hurrem understood her daughter loved me more than she loved her.'

'And she sent you away.'

'Allah knows she did. She tried to get rid of me. Twice.'

'What happened then? How did you come back?'

'Mihrimah stopped eating. She got so ill they feared she would die. They had to bring me back. As soon as I reached the palace I asked for a bowl of soup, fed her myself.'

'Is that when people started to gossip?' Jahan asked. 'They called you witch. They accused you of casting a spell on the Princess.'

'The biggest *zhadi* was the Sultana! Everyone knew that. She's the one who spread rumours about me. Oh, the evil in her!'

'A war of two witches,' Jahan said, transfixed.

Hesna Khatun gave him a disdainful look. 'Well, she's dead, and I'm still in the land of the living.'

A shudder ran through Jahan. 'How about the second time? You said the Sultana sent you away twice.'

'That was . . . when Mihrimah was betrothed to Rustem Pasha. Hurrem didn't want me around. Can you believe? She sent me on a pilgrimage when my daughter needed me most. They put me on a ship. How I cried, Allah is my witness.'

'On the way back your ship was attacked by corsairs, we heard.'

'Oh, it was a sham.' She broke off, seized by another fit, her body convulsing. 'The Sultana wanted to finish me off. She arranged the attack to get me killed or incarcerated. One way or another. Wouldn't have made a difference to her.'

'How did you escape?'

She glanced up, her eyes brimming. 'My daughter saved me. She stopped eating again. She cried so much that Sultan Suleiman sent an Ottoman fleet to save me – me, a nursemaid! Who has heard of such a thing?'

'Where did your power come from, *dada*?'

'Sorcery, you think? It came from love! My daughter loved me.'

Jahan leaned forward, his gaze fixed on the cat. 'You loved Mihrimah, too. But it wasn't only her you doted on . . . I have been thinking about this. You were besotted with the Sultan – how could I have missed this before.'

Her expression darkened.

'You burned for him,' said Jahan.

'He burned for me,' she said with pride. 'It was me he wanted, not Hurrem. That vixen was in our way.'

'Do you really believe that? You are not in your right mind,' Jahan said so softly that it was almost a whisper. 'You live in your dreams. And wishes.'

She wasn't listening. 'If it had not been for that she-devil, Mihrimah would have been my daughter. But she was, I always knew she was. Our child. Mine and Sultan Suleiman's.'

For a moment they were quiet – she sourly, he disconcertedly. It was he who spoke first. 'When the Sultana passed away, Mihrimah became the most powerful woman in the empire. You were in the background. In the shadows. Unseen. Unsuspected.' Suddenly Jahan broke off. 'Why is that cat not moving?'

'She's sleeping. Don't bother her,' Hesna Khatun said. 'Why are you here?'

'To find the truth –'

'Truth is a butterfly: it lands on this flower and that. You run after it with a net. If you capture it, you are happy. But it won't live long. Truth is a delicate thing.'

Her breath was laboured, her body ached down to the bone. She was tired, he saw, but he was not ready to let her go. 'Where does Davud fit into all this?'

A shadow crossed her face.

'He was your puppet for years. It was you who sabotaged my master's buildings. People died. Why?'

Hesna Khatun caressed the cat harder. Not a purr. Not a swing of its tail.

'I never suspected you, *dada*. No one did. Who would have suspicions about a nursemaid? You were clever, left no trace.'

'There must have been one. Otherwise you wouldn't be here,' she said bitterly.

'The herbs you burned for your asthma. Mihrimah's hair and clothes always smelled like that. The other day Davud had the same smell. I remembered afterwards.'

'You have a strong sense of smell, Indian,' she said, propping herself up.

'My elephant taught me.' Jahan paused, stroking his beard. 'You used Davud, but he got out of control. He would not listen to you any more.'

Pulling her cat closer, she sat still as a stone.

'Why did you do it? For riches? For mightiness? Who bribed you? Was it the Italians? Did they want to stop my master?'

'Oh, shut up . . . What nonsense,' Hesna Khatun said. 'You want to know the truth? Hear me out. You think I could have done it without the consent of your Princess?'

'You are lying. Mihrimah is dead. She can't defend herself,' Jahan said. 'How can you blame her? I thought you loved her.'

'I loved her more than anyone. More than anything. That's why I did as she told me and never asked why.'

'Liar!'

'We believe in what we choose to believe,' she rasped.

Anxiety gathered on Jahan's face like a brewing storm. 'Why would Mihrimah wish to weaken my master?'

'She had nothing against your master. Lots against her own father.'

'Sultan Suleiman?'

'He was the greatest of sultans and the greatest of sinners, may God forgive him. I never begrudged him, for I knew he was misled by that hellcat Hurrem. But Mihrimah didn't see it that way. She could not blame her mother. So she blamed the person she loved the most – her father.'

'I don't understand.'

'Sultan Suleiman and Mihrimah were very close. She was his only daughter, his jewel. When she was a child he used to take her

400

everywhere with him. But then everything changed. He became strict, fearful. He saw enemies everywhere and began to neglect his daughter. Mihrimah was hurt, though she never complained. Then the Sultan executed his Grand Vizier. The man whom Mihrimah had called uncle and loved so much. He killed another Vizier. Your master made a mosque for him. And then he put to death his own sons – Mihrimah's brothers.

'She was devastated. Torn between her love for her father and her hatred of him. How many times my beautiful daughter moved her quarters into the harem, just to get away from the Sultan. Then she moved back . . . She loathed him. She adored him. My confused child.

'Mihrimah was richer than the treasury. None stronger than her. But her heart was broken. It didn't help that they married her off to that Rustem. What an awful marriage that was, God knows. Unhappy till the end. She never wanted him. Never.'

Feeling dizzy, Jahan walked towards the chest in a corner and sat on it. From here he could see the cat on the old woman's lap. It had strange eyes – one eye jade-green, one blue and glazed over.

'The accidents began with the Suleimaniye Mosque,' Jahan muttered. 'You tried to disrupt our work.'

'Mihrimah knew she could never triumph over her father, and she had no intention of doing so. All she wanted was to make things more difficult for him. The mosque your master was building was going to immortalize Sultan Suleiman and show his grandeur to posterity. We decided to slow you down. It was a little revenge.'

'And you needed an apprentice to be your pawn,' said Jahan.

'We considered each of you. Nikola was timid. Yusuf we couldn't approach; like a clam, he wouldn't open up. You, we kept aside. Davud was the best. Angry, ambitious.'

'But Davud wouldn't obey you forever!'

'At the beginning he did. Then he got greedy. We didn't touch him. We could have. It was a mistake, now I know. After Sultan Suleiman's death, Mihrimah called him and said it was over. He swore he would stop but he didn't. Secretly he defied her orders. He had an issue with your master, I believe.'

A feeling of nausea took hold of Jahan. 'I smelled your herbs on Davud *after* my master's death. Why were you still seeing him?'

It was a moment before she responded. 'Davud wanted me to help him become the Chief Royal Architect. He said if I didn't help him he would tell everyone what we had been doing for all these years.'

'He blackmailed you!'

Her jaw went slack.

'What happened to my master's will? Did he want Davud as his successor?'

'No,' she said calmly. 'He had you in mind.'

Jahan regarded her, at a loss.

'Your master had written it down. He wanted you. That was his wish. He kept one copy in his house. One in the archives of architects in Vefa.'

'Is that why Davud took the entire library? He destroyed the wills.'

'He wanted to make sure there were no other copies anywhere else,' she said. 'Now you know everything. Leave, I am tired.'

She turned towards the window, no longer interested in him. In the light of the setting sun her face was carved stone. Her ways pierced Jahan to the quick, not so much her coldness as her air of nonchalance. She did not regret anything, not even when she was, at her age, so close to death.

Jahan said, 'Did she ever love me?'

'Why do you ask such a stupid thing?'

'I need to know if that, too, was a lie. For years I felt guilty if I desired another woman.'

She regarded him with a mixture of contempt and disgust. 'Who the hell were you? An animal-tamer? A mouse reaching for a mountain! A servant of the Sultan in love with the Sultan's only daughter! And you have the nerve to ask me whether she loved you? What a simpleton.'

As she moved her arm, Jahan had a full view of the cat. It was Cardamom, the same grimalkin from years ago. Stuffed. In place of its eyes were two gems – one sapphire, one emerald.

'She *liked* you, like a pet, like a gown. Like the *lokum* she tasted. But you'd get bored if you ate it every day. Nay, she never loved you.'

Jahan pursed his lips, wordlessly.

'Fool,' she whispered. '*My beautiful fool*. That's what she called you. That's why she adored you so. But would you call that love?'

Rising to his feet, Jahan staggered. He could bring this to an end. He could kill her there and then. Strangle her with her scarf. The door was closed. No one would know. Even if they did, no one would lament her passing. He took a few steps towards her, saw the fear in her gaze.

'How old are you, *dada*? You must be way over a hundred. Is it true you were damned with eternal life?'

Hesna Khatun was about to laugh when a dry cough stopped her midway. 'I . . . wasn't the only one.'

'What do you mean?' Jahan asked in panic. But even as the words left him he knew the answer.

'Think, which artisan, which artist, which man of great ambitions wouldn't want to live for as long as I have?'

Jahan shook his head. 'If you are referring to my master, he was an exemplary man. Nothing to do with a witch like you.'

'At what age did he die?' Her cackle turned into a cough.

Before she could catch her breath, Jahan snatched the stuffed animal from her hands and hurled it into the fire. Cardamom's fur was set ablaze, the gems glowing amid the flames.

'Don't,' she screamed too late, her voice splintered.

'Let the dead rest in peace, *dada*.'

As she watched the burning cat, Hesna Khatun's chin quivered with fury. She said, 'May you suffer from my scourge, Architect.'

Jahan headed towards the door as fast as he could. He opened it, but not before he had heard her last words.

'May you beg God the Almighty, down on your knees, to be taken, for it is enough . . . it is too much. May He hear you pleading . . . may He see your agony and pity you, oh, poor apprentice of Sinan, but still . . . still may He not let you die.'

Every morning Balaban sent one of his men down to the harbour: 'See if the storm's passed and the clouds've left.'

Each time the beagle came back with the same news: 'The clouds are there, chief. Not goin' anywhere.'

Davud's henchmen were prowling around, inspecting the passengers, checking the freight being loaded. Having learned this, Jahan knew it would have made more sense to give up travelling by sea. He should have slipped into a cart heading out of the city gates. Once out of danger he could try his luck at another port – perhaps Smyrna or Salonika. Yet, dangerous as it was, he was bent on departing from Istanbul the way he had arrived. And somehow Davud, knowing him well, understood this.

Together Balaban and Jahan hatched a plan, deciding it would be safer to arrive at the port in disguise.

'I could pass as a Roma,' Jahan suggested. If they went around in similar attire and banded together, they might pull it off.

Balaban wasn't convinced. This could make things harder – on land and in the water. 'You don't want to be treated like us, brother. It's no paradise being a Roma.'

Next they considered dressing him up as a merchant. If he gave the impression of being wealthy and important, he might have less trouble while boarding. But as soon as the ship was riding the waves, the sailors would rob him blind. Jahan had to look respectable without looking rich. In the end, it was decided he would pose as an Italian artist – a dreamer of sorts, who had been roaming the Orient selling his talents and was now returning home, older and wiser. Should anyone inquire about his paintings, he would say they had been shipped earlier. If things went as expected, he should reach Florence in ten days.

Finding him the right costume was no problem for Balaban and his men, though getting the correct size proved tricky. They handed Jahan a sack of clothes – a shirt of linen, a doublet with odd sleeves, a leather jerkin and breeches that could be tied above the knee. Each of fine fabric and each too big.

Balaban grinned when he saw Jahan. 'Signori Jahanioni, you've shrunk!'

They laughed like the boys they were deep inside. Balaban's men had robbed the Venetian Doge's clerk in plain daylight – a man clearly sturdier than Jahan. Yet, after a few alterations by Balaban's wife, everything fit perfectly. She insisted on dyeing Jahan's hair and beard with henna. When she had finished, Sinan's apprentice could barely recognize himself in the mirror. His outfit was crowned with a velvet hat – purple on black. By now his bruises had healed. Only the scar on his cheek remained, a reminder of a night he would rather forget.

On the day of Jahan's departure, Balaban and his men climbed on a carriage pulled by a donkey. In his honour it was garlanded with flowers and ribbons. So many had huddled into the wagon that the poor donkey could barely move, let alone trot. Cursing the law that forbade Gypsies from riding horses, then quarrelling among themselves, they tried to persuade one another to stay behind – to no avail. Everyone wanted to escort Jahan. In the end, they arranged three carriages. Up and down the streets they proceeded in a gaudy convoy, ignoring the stares of the townspeople, who gaped at them, half in amazement, half in disdain, as if they had descended from a different Adam and a different Eve.

Midway through, Balaban's uncle began to sing; his voice – rough and hoarse but mellow – carried in the breeze. One of the boys produced a reed pipe from his sash and picked out the melody.

When Jahan asked what the song was about, Balaban said in a whisper so quiet that Jahan had to crane forward to hear him, 'This man goes to a wedding. Everyone is happy, dancin', drinkin'. So he dances, too. He cries.'

'Why does he cry?'

''Cause he loves the girl, dolt. And she loves him. They are marrying her to another fella.'

Jahan's chest felt heavy as the music subsided – first the lyrics, then the tune. The gloom must have been contagious. An awkward silence fell. Close to the port, on a lush hill, the carriages came to a halt.

'We'll drop you here; better this way,' said Balaban.

One by one, they hopped down. Jahan took off the cloak he had been wearing to hide the Italian garments underneath. He hugged each of them, kissing the hands of the elderly and the cheeks of the children. Balaban, meanwhile, didn't budge, leaning against the cart, chewing a straw. When Jahan had said farewell to all, he strode towards Balaban; then he noticed the Gypsy had something in his hand, round and blue as a robin's egg.

'What's this?'

'An amulet. *Daki dey* made it for you – to protect you from the evil eye. Wear it upside down on the sea; and the right way up when you reach the shore.'

Jahan bit his lip to choke back the sob rising in his throat. 'I'm grateful.'

'Listen, about the harlot . . . We made inquiries. Seems there were eight women in that *hamam* of sorrows.'

'Right?'

'Well, there're still eight, I hear. No one left, no one came.'

'What are you saying?'

'I'm sayin', there was no funeral. Something's queer. I don't want you to suffer all your life. Maybe you didn't kill anyone, brother. It was a fraud.'

'But the dwarf lady . . .' said Jahan. 'She was on my side.'

Balaban sighed. 'Sad you're goin'. Glad you're goin'. You are too trusting to survive in Istanbul, brother.'

Clumsily, the Gypsy chief pulled Jahan close and punched him teasingly on his stomach, brother to brother. Balaban said, 'Who am I goin' to save from trouble now?'

'You can save Chota's son. Will you take care of him?'

'Oh, don't you fret. We'll tell him what a great pa he had.'

While Jahan fumbled for words that didn't come, Balaban jumped on the carriage, grabbed the reins, his eyes cast down. His men followed suit, patting Jahan on the shoulder. Once they had settled, the carriages sallied forth. Everybody waved – but Balaban. Jahan waited for him to turn and glance back one last time. He didn't. His long, dark hair flapping in the wind, the Gypsy chief stared ahead. As they were about to round a bend, the carriage stopped and Balaban peered back. Although it was too far away for Jahan to be able to tell, he thought he saw the trace of a smile on the Gypsy chief's face. He raised his hand in valediction. Balaban did the same. Then they were gone.

Pain surged inside Jahan, sharp as a knife thrust into his flesh. He sat on a tree stump, thinking. He did not know what Providence had in store for him, and once again he was diving into it with the recklessness of the ignorant. Even so, there was no going back. As the sun made its way up, he, too, set forward on his way.

As always, the harbour was teeming with voyagers, seafarers and slaves. No sooner had he stepped on to the wharf than its vibrancy and vastness swallowed him. It was one of the best ports, they said. Ships could get in without having to use their oars or pray for the winds to fill their sails. Captains could trust the current to bring them in. The two opposite tides of the Bosphorus, unlike the city itself, were predictable, dependable. On this day, there were plenty of vessels about, though only a few kept their sails ready-rigged. There was a three-masted carrack, sleek and majestic, that was destined for Venice. That was the one Jahan was aiming for.

Now that he was an Italian artist, he stared with fascination at each curiosity and doffed his hat at every woman – nun or damsel. He saw pilgrims, Jesuit priests with hair shirts and cowls, and dignitaries with the permanent stain of ink on their fingers. There was a scribe sitting behind a makeshift desk. People had gathered around him, watching his plume compose magic. Jahan struck up a conversation with an Albanian vendor, from whom he bought honey sherbet. A man was trying to lead a hooded horse – a thoroughbred black stallion – up the ramp from shore to ship. Where were they taking the animal, Jahan wondered, and would the beautiful creature survive the voyage.

It was as he was standing there watching the scene that Jahan noticed, at the periphery of his vision, Davud's two deaf-mutes. They were wending their way through the crowd, coming in his direction. Jahan held his breath, sipping his drink. They passed by, paying him no attention.

A moment later the shrillest scream pierced the air. 'Stop, you bastard!'

That magnificent horse had risen up on its hind legs and knocked the page straight into the water. Laughter rippled through the port, quickly muffled by yells and cries as the horse, still hooded, cantered down the ramp, running headlong into the spectators. Blocked by bodies and boxes on every side, he was not able to bolt as freely as he could have wished. Still, unwilling to stop, he trampled whatever was in his way.

The page, saved from the water and dripping with fury, was shouting orders and curses. Jahan caught up with him. 'What's the horse's name?'

'What the hell you askin'?'

'Tell me its name!' Jahan said, losing patience.

The man raised his eyebrows. 'Ebony.'

Jahan scurried after the horse. The hood had slipped off but seeing its surroundings had only increased its panic. 'Ebony,' Jahan called, over and again, keeping his voice as level as he could manage. Horses did not exactly recognize their names. Yet they could catch a familiar tone when they heard one, just as they could perceive the intention behind it.

Hemmed in, the stallion was revolving, neighing and tossing its head nervously. Jahan stood in front of it, showing his empty hands. He approached step by step, one soothing word after another. Had it not been tired, the horse would not have allowed him to get near. But it was. Grabbing it by the reins, Jahan caressed its neck tenderly.

On an impulse, Jahan turned back. There, only a few yards away, stood the deaf-mutes, staring at him without so much as blinking, their expressions impossible to read. Were they suspicious or simply intrigued? Having glanced once, Jahan dared not do so again. A knot gripped his chest. A trickle of sweat rolled down the nape of his neck. His clothes felt ridiculously heavy as it occurred to him what a nuisance they would become should he need to make off quickly. He had two pouches, one inside his robe, the other sewn into the hem of his shirt – courtesy of Balaban's wife. If he were to run now, the coins would jingle, adding to his discomfort.

It was as he was contemplating his options that the crowd, as if slit from side to side by an invisible knife, parted. The French ambassador was coming. The man who had dissected Chota's body with a dispassionate curiosity. Beside him was his wife, attired in an embroidered jacket-bodice and the greenest velvet gown, holding a handkerchief to her nose against the stench, her eyebrows puckered. They sauntered by without recognizing him, heading for the ship he had set his sights on. A flock of servants were at their heels, carrying boxes and cages in which hissed, cooed and squawked creatures of all kinds. Monsieur and Madame Brèves were returning to France, taking their private menagerie with them.

There were peacocks, nightingales and parrots, their feathers bright as springtime. There was a falcon, a hawk and an exotic bird with an enormous beak – a gift from the Sultan. But it was the monkeys that everyone was jostling one another in order to see – a female and a male, dressed as a miniature noblewoman and nobleman. Clad in silk and velvet, the two monkeys were watching the crowd with partly frightened, partly mirthful eyes. The female monkey bared her teeth from time to time, as if she were laughing at the humans the way they were laughing at her.

Taking advantage of the commotion, Jahan slipped away, setting a steady, swift pace. Not once did he glance back. He steered a zigzag path through crates, ropes and planks, amid sailors, porters and beggars. There was another carrack far ahead. He had no idea where it was bound, but he felt pulled towards it. It occurred to him that Davud might have guessed his intention to go back to Rome, and advised his guards to keep a close eye on all vessels to Italian ports. It would probably be wiser to take a ship in a different direction. He could then disembark at the first port and make his way to Michelangelo's land. With this conviction he reached the carrack and climbed up the plank.

'We don't take on strangers,' said the Captain after listening to him. 'How do I know you're no criminal?'

'I'm an artist,' Jahan said and, fearing he might ask him to paint his portrait as proof, he added, 'I draw landscapes.'

'Funny trade you've got. You get paid for that?'

'If I find a generous patron –'

'Fancy that!' the man remarked dourly. 'Some of us break our backs. You live a dainty life. Nay, you can't come. You'll bring us bad luck.'

'I bring good luck, I can assure you,' Jahan said. 'To prove my trust-worthiness, allow me to offer this.'

Taking out his pouch, he emptied it on the table. The Captain's eyes glinted; he reached out for a coin and bit its edge. 'Fine, get a move on. Stay in the hold. You may eat with the men. Make sure I don't see you around.'

Jahan gave a tight nod. 'I promise you won't.'

They were not raising anchor for another day. Jahan spent this time waiting below in an airless cabin. Only when they set sail did he muster the courage to go upstairs. The city glimmered in the distance – the bazaars, the coffee-houses and the graveyards with cypress trees and upright stones with *turbehs*. The place where he had learned to love and learned never to trust love. He saw the minarets of the Suleimaniye and the Shehzade mosques, the father and the son. He saw the dome of the Hagia Sophia, a glint on the horizon. And he saw Mihrimah's Mosque, as secretive as the woman it was named after.

Putting his right hand on his heart, Jahan saluted them, acknowledging the sweat and the prayers and the hopes that had gone into building them. He hailed not only the people but also the stone, the wood, the marble and the glass, the way his master had taught him. The seagulls followed them for a while, shrieking their goodbyes. When the gusts blew more strongly, they returned to the city. Strangely, their leave-taking felt as gloomy as his own.

The curse . . . How could she call it such when it was a gift, Jahan thought at the beginning. Gradually he would recognize how life had outwitted him. What he had taken to be a gift he would learn, later on, was a scourge; what he had received as a bane he would come to see as a blessing. But back then, following *dada*'s advice, he was thinking, who among all the artists and architects in the world would not wish to live a hundred years or more, never fearing that time would come to an end in the midst of a new work, which could, for all one knew, turn out to be the best he had ever done. Without fear of death, Jahan was spared fear of failure. Exempt from such apprehension, Jahan could design more, design better, perhaps even surpass his master. Determined, excited, he travelled to one port after another. He went to Rome, France, England and Salamanca, where he expected to find Sancha, but there was no trace of her.

That he worked hard and asked for little money, together with his knowledge, kept him in demand. Although he was no member of any guild and could not be employed, he was able to ply his trade indirectly, sketching for other architects, always underpaid. It troubled him slightly that the spell, though it gave him strength and additional years, had not made him look a day younger. While he showed no sign either of debility or of senility, he visibly carried his age. People, sensing something unusual, something dark, asked him how old he was. When Jahan said he was ninety-six, ninety-seven, ninety-eight . . . they stared at him wide-eyed. A glint of suspicion flickered in their eyes, as they wondered whether he had made a pact with the devil – albeit only once had he heard anyone voice this aloud. Whichever way he travelled, south or north, it was the same: human beings sharing a lack of trust, if not a lack of sympathy, for anyone who lived beyond the allotted number of years.

That was when Jahan began to think maybe the witch was right. Maybe his master had made a pledge with her. Sinan had lived longer than every major craftsman in the empire. He had raised more buildings than any mortal could ever have dreamed of raising. At some point, he must have smelled like Hesna Khatun's herbs, though, no matter how hard Jahan racked his brains, he could not recall this. Then, having tired of everything, he must have asked for it to be brought to an end. Shortly before his death, he must have visited the witch. For the last time. If so, there must have been a way to break the spell, and by leaving Istanbul Jahan had lost this chance.

Years passed by. Almost a hundred, he took a ship to Portugal, from where, he had heard, one could sail to the New World. One sunny afternoon, on the front deck, he noticed a man – willowy and slender. His heart leaped. It was Balaban, sitting between a coiled rope and a cleat. Unthinking, he lunged forward, chuckling, until he noticed, too late, that it wasn't him.

'I'm sorry, I thought you were someone else.'

'A friend, I hope,' the stranger said. 'Come, sit, enjoy the sun while it lasts.'

He rambled on about his troubles, his voice rising and falling. He claimed to have had too many sins from which to flee. He was going back to his family a wiser man. Tired of talking, he asked, 'What is your skill?'

'I build. I am an architect.'

'You should go to Agra, then. Shah Jahan, your namesake, is building a palace in memory of his wife.'

Although he shrugged, Jahan was intrigued. 'What happened to her?'

'She died in childbirth,' the stranger said sadly. 'He was quite devoted to her.'

'It's not exactly my route.'

'Change your route,' he said. Just like that.

In the year 1632 Jahan arrived in Hindustan, in order to see what the plans for this palace, which everyone was raving about, were actually like.

Some cities you go to because you want to; some cities you go to because *they* want you to. The moment he set foot there, Jahan had the feeling that Agra had been pulling him, leading him all along. On the way there he had heard so much about the Shah and the city he wished to glorify that when he reached Agra it was almost as if he were returning to a place where he had been before. He wandered around, inhaling the smells, which were bountiful and pungent, the sunlight stroking his skin, the faintest ache on his scar.

Jahan went to see the construction on the bank of the Yamuna. There, with the help of a traveller who spoke a bit of Turkish, he was introduced to one of the draughtsmen. After hearing his credentials and seeing the seal of Sinan, the labourer took Jahan to their overseer. A strapping man with a protruding nose, bushy eyebrows and a bashful smile, Jahan instantly liked him. His name was Mir Abdul Karim.

'Your master was a great man,' he said in a voice strengthened from explaining things to people, inferiors and superiors alike.

He pored over the few designs Jahan had brought along, inspecting them with meticulous care. Placing a cup of honeyed milk and a set of quill pens on the table, Mir Abdul Karim showed him several drawings of the construction project, asking his opinion of each, which Jahan gave in earnest. The overseer said nothing, though a mirthful glitter in his eyes suggested his satisfaction at the answers. Next Karim asked Jahan to draw a floor plan based on the measurements he provided there and then. When Jahan had finished, the overseer seemed content. Taking a quiet breath, he remarked, 'You cannot go anywhere before you meet the Grand Vizier.'

In this way, after another round of introductions, Jahan found himself summoned by the Shah. Seated high on his Peacock Throne, his heavy-lidded eyes gleaming with loss and pride, his beard and moustache white with grief, and his attire devoid of jewellery and ornaments, he reminded Jahan, in more than one way, of Sultan Suleiman. The Shah sorrowed over the death of his beloved wife, Mumtaz Mahal – the Paragon of the Palace – the woman who had borne him fourteen children in eighteen years. Her body had been buried on the banks of the River Tapti. Now they were bringing her to Agra to be reburied for eternity.

He had loved her more than any woman and at the expense of his other wives. They said such was his devotion to, and confidence in, her that she would read all his *firmans* and, should she approve, put the regal seal on them. She was not only his consort, but also his companion, confidante and counsellor. In her absence he was inconsolable. He still visited her private apartments at nights, as though chasing her fragrance – or apparition – and when confronted with the emptiness of the chambers, he burst into tears.

A younger Jahan would have been nervous to meet the bereaved Shah whose name he shared. His face would burn, his palms would feel clammy and his voice would quiver for fear of saying something wrong. Not any longer. Having neither secrets nor expectations, he could stop railing at himself and be simply an observer, calm and unruffled – and free. Wherever this new temperament had come from, he wished, belatedly, he had attained it before, while standing in front of every Sultan, Sultana and Vizier who had appeared in his life. The placid humour of his master that he once so disparaged he now held dear.

The Shah inquired about Sinan's works, of which, surprisingly, he was well aware. Each question Jahan answered briefly but candidly. Unlike the ruler's ancestor, Babur – whose mother tongue was the same as Jahan's – the Shah spoke no Turkish. They communicated with the help of a dragoman, who translated from Persian to Turkish, Turkish to Persian; words in common were captured and held, like butterflies caught in a net between them.

The meeting having reached an end, Jahan was being ushered out, walking backwards, when the Shah said, 'You never married, I heard. Why is that?'

Jahan stopped, his eyes cast down. Silence thicker than honey covered the hall. It was as though the entire court was waiting to hear what he had to say.

'I had pledged my heart to someone, your Highness –'

'What happened?'

'Nothing,' Jahan said. Those who grew up with stories of love that inevitably ended in rapture, revelry, chivalry or calamity could not fathom why for many people love amounted to naught, eventually. 'She was beyond my reach and did not love me. It was not meant to be.'

'There're plenty of women,' the Shah said.

Jahan would have liked to say the same thing to him. Why did he still mourn his wife? What he could not put into words, the Shah understood. A thin smile etched on his lips as he said, 'Maybe not.'

The next afternoon, Jahan received a letter from the palace nominating him as one of the two Chief Royal Architects for the Illuminated Tomb – the *rauza-i-munavvara*. He would be paid generously in rupees and ashrafis, and every six months rewarded accordingly. But it was one line, in particular, that stayed with him: *I hereby ask you, Jahan Khan Rumi, the builder of memories, the descendant of the respectable Master Sinan, who was second to none, and was followed worldwide, to contribute to the raising of this most glorious tomb, which will invoke the admiration of generations after generations, until the Day of Judgement, when no stone will stand upon another under the vault of heaven.*

Jahan accepted, despite himself. He joined the team of builders and, even though he was in a foreign land where he knew not a single soul and had no past to recall should the present prove too gruelling, he felt strangely at home.

The project was massive. Expensive. Fraught with difficulties. Thousands of labourers, masons, stone-cutters, quarries, bricklayers, tile-setters and carpenters were toiling at full tilt. It was possible to hear a babel of languages moving from one place to another. There were sculptors from Bukhara, quarrymen from Isfahan, carvers from Tabriz, calligraphers from Kashmir, painters from Samarkand, decorators from Florence and jewellers from Venice. It was almost as if the Shah, in his determination to see the building completed as quickly as possible, had called on every craftsman on earth who might be of use to him. Implacable, stubborn, he held sway over everyone to the point just short of drawing the designs himself. That he had some knowledge in the craft made life harder for his architects. Jahan had never met a monarch so involved in a construction. Every two days the Shah would hold a conference with them, asking questions, stating opinions and coming up with new impossible demands, as crowned heads often tended to do.

Shah Jahan was a man who pledged his wrath in steel, his love in diamonds and his grief in white marble. Under his auspices Jahan wrote to a number of masons in Istanbul, inviting them over. He was delighted when Isa, his favourite student, agreed to come. He felt compassion and admiration for him and for all that he could achieve with his talents and his youth. He wondered if Master Sinan had regarded them with similar feelings. If so, it was a pity that Jahan had not understood.

There were elephants on the site. Restlessly, they carried the heaviest marbles and planks. Sometimes in the afternoons, under the setting sun, Jahan would watch them wallow in puddles, a thrill of affection running through him. He could not help but think if human beings could only live more like animals, without a thought to the past or the future, and without rounds of lies and deceit, this world would be a more peaceful place, and perhaps a happier one.

I got married. The Shah, having remembered our exchange, had given orders to find me a good-hearted bride. They did. My wife, sixty-six years younger than me, was a woman of a kind disposition and wise words. When she was two months with child, she had lost all her family in a flood. As Mirabai the poetess had once done, she declined to join her husband on his funeral pyre. Her eyes were darker than all my secrets, her smile was always ready to blossom; her black, lustrous hair flew between my fingers like perfumed waters. Many a night, admiring her profile in the candlelight, I told her what she already knew: 'I'm too old for you, Amina. When I die, you must marry a young man.'

'Don't put a curse on us, husband,' she would say each time. 'Hush, now.'

The next autumn Amina's baby was born, a boy with dimpled cheeks. I loved him as if he were my own. I named him Sinan; and, remembering my master's first appellation, I added Joseph; and, out of respect for my wife's family, I named him Mutamid, after my father-in-law. Here he was, our son, Sinan Joseph Mutamid; no other like him in this vast expanse of countless souls and even more gods, thriving under the Agra sky, each day growing taller, stronger; an Ottoman lad in India, although I had been a fake Indian in the Ottoman lands.

He has his mother's radiant complexion and hazel eyes. The occasional frowns on the broad sweep of his forehead hint at his impatience and curiosity about the inner workings of each thing he observes. When he began cutting teeth, his mother and his many aunts placed several objects in front of him to divine the path he would follow in life — a silvered mirror, a plume, a golden bracelet and sealing wax. If he chose the mirror, he would be keen on beauty, a painter or a poet. The plume: he would be a scribe. The bracelet: a merchant. The wax: a high official.

Sinan Joseph Mutamid was still for a moment, scowling at the items scattered at his feet, as if they contained a riddle to solve. The women, in the meantime, kept cooing and calling him, so that he would pick what they had in mind for him. He ignored them. Then, with a flick of his wrist, he reached out and grabbed the amulet on my neck, Daki dey's protection against the evil eye.

'What does that mean?' Amina said, looking worried.

I chuckled, pulling her close to me, regardless of what her sisters might think. I said, 'Nothing bad, trust me.' It just meant that he would make his own decisions, no matter what they laid out in front of him.

When we go out, the three of us, the whole town gawks at us. At times I come across men who, with their lewd jokes and jarring laughs, insinuate what a lucky rotter I am for having such a wife; or they ask how I manage to satisfy her at my age. So we find another way of walking on the streets. My wife, with the child in her arms, saunters ahead of me. I fall behind, trudging slowly, contemplating them — her tenderness as she caresses the boy's head; his trusting, winsome smile; their murmurs like the distant soughing of waves from a city now far away. I take it all in, conjuring another moment in time, knowing that after I am gone they will still be strolling; nothing will change. And the knowledge of this, instead of filling me with sorrow, fills me with hope, yes, tremendous hope.

There is nothing about my wife that reminds me of Mihrimah. Neither her voice, nor her mien, nor her temperament. On starry nights when she lies on top of me, her warmth covering my skin like a mantle, when I am ashamed of my age and aroused by her softness, she slides on to me like a sheath on to a sword, her beauty swallowing my ugliness, whispering into my ear, 'God sent you to me.' I know that I would have never heard such words from Mihrimah, even if we had been destined to be together. No, my wife could not have been more different from her. And I could not have been more content. Yet . . . not a single day has passed since I left Istanbul without Mihrimah crossing my mind. I still remember her. I still ache. A travelling pain that moves so fast from one limb to another that I cannot say whether it exists. She is the shadow that follows me everywhere, towering above me when I feel low, draining the light from my soul.

A year after I started working for the great Shah, I was asked to design the dome of the Illuminated Tomb, which they now name the Taj Mahal. I, too, have had a change of name. Though they still call me Jahan Khan Rumi, everyone, even little children, knows me as the Dome Maker.

I inspect the site every morning. It is a long walk and takes me a while. The other day, a novice turned up with an elephant by his side. 'Why don't you let the beast carry you, master?'

They helped me to climb up. I sat inside the howdah and looked at the workers toiling endlessly, building for God, building for the sovereign, building for their ancestors, building for a noble cause, building without knowing why, and I was so glad I was up there alone and not down there with them, because I could not stop the tears from streaming down my face and I sobbed like the frail old man I have become.

I am aware that I won't be around to see the completion of the Taj Mahal. If I don't die soon, it could only mean dada's curse still holds. Then I should abandon this land on my own. I have left instructions for Isa and my pupils, should they wish to follow my advice — after all, with apprentices you never know who will continue your legacy, and who will let you down. It doesn't matter. With or without me, the building will be raised. What my master did inside the dome of the Shehzade Mosque, our first major construction — where there were no accidents, no betrayals, and we were as one — I shall do inside the dome of the Taj Mahal. I will hide somewhere a detail for Mihrimah, which only the knowing eye will recognize. A moon and a sun, locked together in a fatal embrace — such is the meaning of her name.

We have been told to inscribe on pure marble: In this world this edifice has been made/To display thereby the glory of the Creator. I would have liked to add underneath: And the love of another human being . . .

The four borders of the Taj Mahal are designed to be identical, as if there were a mirror situated on one side, though one can never tell on which one. Stone reflected in the water. God reflected in human beings. Love reflected in heartbreak. Truth reflected in stories. We live, toil and die under the same invisible dome. Rich and poor, Mohammedan and baptized, free and slave, man and woman, Sultan and mahout, master and apprentice . . . I have come to believe that if there is one shape that reaches out to all of us, it is the dome. That is where all the distinctions disappear and every single sound, whether of joy or sorrow, merges into one huge silence of all-encompassing love. When I think of this world in such a way, I feel dazed and disoriented, and cannot tell any longer where the future begins and the past ends; where the West falls and the East rises.

Author's Note

I am not sure whether writers choose their subjects or whether their subjects somehow come to find them. For me, at least, it felt like the latter with *The Architect's Apprentice*. The idea for this novel emerged for the first time on one sunny afternoon in Istanbul, while I was inside a cab that was stuck in traffic. I was looking out of the window and frowning, already late for an appointment, when my eyes moved across the road to a mosque by the seaside. It was Molla Celebi, one of Sinan's lesser known beauties. A Gypsy boy was sitting on the wall next to it, pounding on a tin box that was turned upside down. I thought to myself that if the traffic did not clear any time soon, I might as well begin to imagine a story with the architect Sinan and Gypsies in it. Then the car moved on and I totally forgot the idea, until a week later a book arrived by post. It was Gülru Necipoğlu's *The Age of Sinan: Architectural Culture in the Ottoman Empire*, sent by a dear friend. Inside the book, one particular drawing caught my eye: it was a painting of Sultan Suleiman, tall and sleek in his kaftan. But it was the figures in the background that intrigued me. There was an elephant and a mahout in front of the Suleimaniye Mosque; they were hovering on the edge of the picture, as if ready to run away, unsure as to what they were doing in the same frame as the Sultan and the monument dedicated to him. I could not take my eyes off this image. The story had found me.

While writing this book I wanted to understand not only Sinan's world but also those of the chief apprentices, workers, slaves and animals who were there alongside him. However, when one is writing about an artist who has lived as long ago, and produced as much, as Sinan, the biggest challenge is the reconstruction of time. It took from seven to nine years to finish a mosque, and Sinan constructed more than 365 buildings of various sizes. So, in the interests of narrative pace, I decided to jettison a strict chronological order and to create my own timeframe, with actual historical events absorbed into the new time-line. For instance, in reality, Mihrimah got married at the age of seven-teen, but I wanted her to marry later, to give her and Jahan more time together. Her husband, Rustem Pasha, died in 1561; yet, for the sake of the story, I wanted him around a bit longer. Captain Gareth is an en-tirely fictional character, but he is based both on European sailors who had joined the Ottoman navy, and on Ottoman sailors who had switched sides. Their stories have not yet been told.

It was a conscious decision to bring Takiyuddin into the story at an earlier point in history. In fact, he became the Chief Royal Astrono-mer at the time of Sultan Murad. But the trajectory of the observatory was important to me, so I shifted the date of Grand Vizier Sokollu's death. The painter Melchior and the ambassador Busbecq were histor-ical characters who arrived in Istanbul around 1555, but I have fiction-alized the moments of their arrival and departure. In several books I have come across allusions to a group of Ottoman architects in Rome, but what exactly they were doing there remains obscure. I imagined them as Sinan's apprentices, Jahan and Davud. And there really was an elephant named Suleiman in Vienna, whose story has been beautifully narrated by José Saramago in *The Elephant's Journey*.

Finally, this novel is a product of the imagination. Yet historical events and real people have guided and inspired me. I benefited enor-mously from a great many sources in English and Turkish, from Ogier Ghiselin de Busbecq's *Turkish Letters* to Metin And's *Istanbul in the Six-teenth Century: The City, the Palace, Daily Life*.

'May the world flow like water,' Sinan used to say. I can only hope that this story, too, will flow like water in the hearts of its readers.

Elif Shafak
www.elifshafak.com
twitter.com/Elif_Safak

Acknowledgements

My heartfelt thanks to the following beautiful people: Lorna Owen for reading an earlier version of this novel and her wonderful comments; Donna Poppy for her clear-sighted suggestions and unique contribution; Keith Taylor for his wisdom and patience; Anna Ridley for her support and her smile; Hermione Thompson for her generosity; and the wonderful team at Penguin UK.

I am particularly obliged to my two main editors on both sides of the Atlantic: Venetia Butterfield and Paul Slovak. Working with you, feeling connected in mind and spirit, sharing the same passion for stories and storytelling, have all been a pleasure, privilege and enrichment for me. A good editor is a true blessing for a novelist and I am blessed with two great editors.

My principal agent, Jonny Geller, is surely every author's dream. He listens, he understands, he encourages, he knows. Daisy Meyrick, Kirsten Geller and the World Rights team at the Curtis Brown Agency have been amazing. I also wish to thank Pankaj Mishra and Tim Stanley for their comments and conversations during the earlier phases of the novel, and Kamila Shamsie for helping me find the name of the white elephant. My gratitude to Gulru Necipoglu, who has been of tremendous assistance both with her personal views on history and with her magnificent opus on Sinan's architecture. My special thanks to Ugur Canbilen (aka Igor) and Meric Mekik, who is like no other!

It is hard for me to express my gratitude to Eyup, who knows what a terrible wife I am and most probably harbours no hopes for any improvement, and for reasons I can never comprehend is still by my side. Biggest thanks, of course, to Zelda and Zahir.

This novel was first published in Turkey, though it was written in English first. I owe a huge thank-you to readers from all walks of life who have commented on the story and the characters and, to my surprise, have embraced Chota like a long-lost face from the past.

Elif Shafak
November 2014

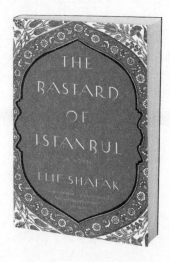

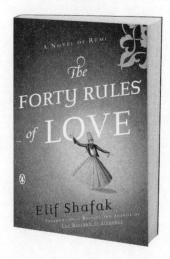
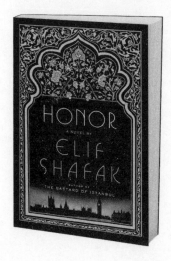